COLLEGE CLASSICS IN ENGLISH

General Editor

NORTHROP FRYE

EDMUND SPENSER

A SELECTION OF HIS WORKS

Edited by

IAN C. SOWTON

York University

MACMILLAN OF CANADA – TORONTO

MACMILLAN & CO LTD – LONDON

ST. MARTIN'S PRESS – NEW YORK

Library of Congress Catalogue Card No. 66-13409

Printed in Canada by Universal Printers Limited

Contents

Introduction

I

While she did not always think so, Queen Elizabeth I was fortunate in her public servants and advisers. She was especially fortunate in her poets. Marlowe, Sidney, Spenser, Donne, Shakespeare, and Ben Jonson would be bright stars enough for any monarch's crown even though two or three of them, at one time or another, had to shine a bit obscurely within prison walls. Marlowe, Sidney, and Spenser all flourished during the Queen's reign and were outlived by her; Donne, Shakespeare, and Jonson began their careers during her reign and all three survived her by a good few years. During their own lifetimes all six were well known and had achieved brilliant and fixed places in English literature. Of them all Spenser perhaps stood highest in contemporary opinion. Thomas Nashe (1567–1601), who had one of the most devastating pens in all of English prose and who was not given to praising fellow authors, called Spenser "the Virgil of England".[1] Given the tastes and literary values of his time, Nashe could not have offered higher praise. Since then the fashion in literary star-gazing has often changed, as any fashion will. Shakespeare alone has always been in vogue; each of the others has had to suffer periodic eclipses of fashion. But these days Spenser's star, especially, has emerged again as bright as ever.

Like most of the great English poets Spenser served the commonwealth in other ways besides his writing. Following an education at the Merchant Taylors School in London and at Pembroke Hall, Cambridge, Spenser in his mid-twenties became secretary to John Young, Bishop of Rochester. After a year as

[1]Virgil (70-19 B.C.), one of the greatest Roman poets, chiefly famous for his epic, the *Aeneid*. During the Renaissance the epic was commonly held to be the highest form of poetry. Spenser, too, is chiefly famous for his epic poem *The Faerie Queene*.

secretary to the bishop, he returned to London in 1579 as a member of the household of the Earl of Leicester (1532–88). Perhaps he was actually employed by Leicester. To be in the service of such a great lord was one of the surest ways to begin and advance a career in public life; but if Spenser was in the Earl's service, it did not in this particular case bring him any notable preferment. Nevertheless, his brief association with Leicester was very important to him, and he remained consistently and publicly loyal long after the Queen's favour had cooled and after many had found it prudent to forget the Earl.

For the last eighteen years of his life Spenser was what we might call a minor civil servant. His civil-service career was launched on the Irish Sea in 1580, when he was about twenty-seven. In that year, during one of the seamiest passages in English-Irish relations, Spenser became secretary to Arthur, Lord Grey of Wilton, the newly appointed Lord Deputy, and accompanied him to Ireland. Lord Grey was recalled – at his own repeated requests – and sailed from Ireland in August 1582, but Spenser stayed behind, and, except for the occasional visit to England, from then on lived in Ireland and became well embroiled in Irish affairs. From 1581 to 1588 he was the Clerk of the Chancery for Faculties in Dublin, "faculties" being special ecclesiastical dispensations and licences issued formerly by Rome but now by the Anglican Archbishop of Dublin. In 1583 and again in 1584, Spenser was one of the Commissioners of Musters for County Kildare; this job entailed keeping up-to-date records, by district, of the men and military stores available to the English commanders. From 1589 to 1594 he was Clerk of the Council of Munster.[2] Both as a commissioner and as the clerk of a provincial council Spenser would have travelled a good deal. And although he never really came to understand the Irish and their customs, his travels gave him a close knowledge of their difficult existence and of the geography of their country. Many of the scenes and no doubt some of the adventures described in Spenser's poetry were first offered to his imagination in the Irish countryside.

[2]The province of Munster, in the south of Ireland, was made up of the counties of Kerry, Tipperary, Connello (Limerick), Waterford, and Cork. The province was governed by a Council whose President was responsible to the Lord Deputy.

During his eighteen years in Ireland Spenser's means accorded fairly well with his career as a moderately successful, minor civil servant. Gradually he acquired several smallish properties and by 1589 he had become a gentleman undertaker. An undertaker had nothing to do with the burial trade; he was a noble or gentleman who had been granted possession by the Crown of up to twelve thousand acres from the lands of defeated Irish lords and chieftains. In return for his grant an undertaker had to pay annual rent to the Crown and *undertake* to recruit an agreed number of English families, settle them, and supervise the reclaiming, cultivation, and defence of his estate. An undertaker was therefore one of the important instruments of colonization. Spenser joined the plan to resettle the province of Munster with English landowners and farmers. The grant made to him was for the "manor, castle, and lands of Kilcolman", making up an estate of just over three thousand acres. This estate was in the northeast corner of County Cork, about half way between the towns of Limerick and Cork; it comprised a very small part of the rebel Earl of Desmond's lands, forfeited to the Crown in 1583. It is not known whether Spenser's first wife lived long enough to become the mistress of Kilcolman. Spenser married Elizabeth Boyle, his second wife, in June of 1594. She bore him one child,[3] Peregrine – half-brother to Sylvanus and Katherine, children by Spenser's first marriage. Spenser settled one of his lesser properties on Peregrine; it was Sylvanus who eventually inherited Kilcolman.

It is clear from Spenser's poetry that he took deep pleasure in his home and lands of Kilcolman. If he sometimes hankered after life in London, or some important job in England, he was genuinely glad to return to Kilcolman after visits across the water. He seems, too, to have been a fairly competent businessman and a fairly tough estate manager. The boundaries of undertakers' estates were not accurately or promptly surveyed. Spenser and Lord Roche, an Anglo-Irish neighbour of his,[4] had

[3]The story that they had a second child who was killed in the destruction of Kilcolman is a very dubious one.

[4]The Anglo-Irish were a class whose ancestry was English but whose families had lived in Ireland long enough to have well established interests and firm hereditary rights. Amidst the Irish-English troubles their position was understandably difficult. They had as much of an

a long, acrimonious dispute over boundary lines. Roche felt that he had good claim to the better part of the Kilcolman estate and was not slow to go to law to test it. Spenser was just as prompt to enter counter-claims against Roche – claims in which he was not above shedding a doubt or two on Roche's loyalty to the Queen. Neither man was above little campaigns of intimidation against his neighbour's tenants. Though Roche managed to win, or win back, a few ploughlands, Spenser was able to retain almost all of his original grant.

During these years in Ireland Spenser was of course writing poetry. The first three books of his masterwork, *The Faerie Queene*, were published in 1590 and brought him the highest reputation as a poet. This reputation was confirmed by the various works he brought out over the next few years. What with writing his poems, settling and improving his estate, fending off Lord Roche, and holding the clerkship of the Munster Council, Spenser must have been an exceedingly busy man. He had time enough, however, to meet and entertain Sir Walter Raleigh, the grandest of all the Munster settlers. Grandest in every sense, for through some oversight Raleigh was enjoying a grant of about forty thousand acres – more than three times as much as the official maximum of twelve thousand. The contact with Raleigh was useful to Spenser. At Raleigh's invitation, Spenser accompanied him to London in 1589 and it was Raleigh who presented Spenser at the court. When the first three books of *The Faerie Queene* came out shortly after, it was no doubt under the auspices of Raleigh that Spenser was able to present the Queen with a copy of his great poem dedicated to her. Court life both attracted and repelled him. Certainly he hoped that his *Faerie Queene* would bring him some new and distinguished employment from the court; yet more than once he complained (not entirely in a mood of sour grapes) about the frivolity and decadence of the court. Neither in 1590 nor at any other time was Spenser rewarded liberally or given distinguished employment. And he complained about that, too, more than once. But in 1591 the Queen did at least award him an annual pension of

interest in being left alone as the Irish, yet most had little choice but to side with the English.

£50 for life – a mark of royal favour not enjoyed by any other Elizabethan poet.[5] Then seven years later the Privy Council, the Queen's inner circle of advisers, nominated Spenser as the Sheriff of Cork. This was the highest post that came his way. As it happened, Spenser did not live to serve as sheriff; but it was an honour to have been nominated and the honour may have been a belated recognition of the second publication of *The Faerie Queene*, with three books added, in 1596. So although they were modest, Spenser did enjoy rewards of land, money, and position along with his fame as a poet.

During 1596 Spenser wrote a long, unofficial report called *View of the Present State of Ireland*. This work is cast in the form of a prose dialogue between two friends who are discussing what English policy in Ireland should be. Spenser is less concerned with establishing the authenticity of England's claim on Ireland (indeed, that this claim was largely apocryphal troubled Spenser no more than it did his compatriots) than with the perfidy and unreliability of the Irish, the irresolution and inconsistency of English policy, and the bickering incompetence of the English officials trying to execute that policy.[6] Spenser felt that the only way to bring peace, order, and safety to Ireland was to appoint a Lord Lieutenant with the widest possible powers and full responsibility; and to field an army big enough, persistent enough, and carefully enough deployed to force a simple choice upon the Irish: submission or extermination. Submission was not in the Irish air, so, whatever honest hopes Spenser may have had for a settlement in Ireland, the threat of systematic genocide is not far beneath the surface of his prose. For the ruthlessness of his advice Spenser offers no apology, nor, in his time and place, would one have been expected. There is evidence that *View of the Present State of Ireland* came under the eyes of Elizabeth and her councillors. It was a perfectly consistent extension of one variation of their

---

[5]At a very rough approximation, £50 would be worth some $1500 in terms of purchasing power these days.

[6]Ireland was the most crowded graveyard of English reputations, including Lord Grey's. Spenser admired Grey and it is easy to see the *View* as a defence of Grey's policy in Ireland. Grey was one of the models for Artegall, who is the embodiment of Justice in Book V of *The Faerie Queene*.

shifting policy, but it happened to be out of phase at the time and they did not act upon it. In fact it was not published until 1633, so Spenser never saw his only lengthy work of prose in print.

Spenser's career in Ireland came to an abrupt, painful conclusion in Tyrone's great rebellion of 1598. By October of that year Irish insurgents had a grip on large parts of Munster, including County Cork. Probably during this month Spenser's Kilcolman estate was overrun and his home sacked. By early November Spenser and his family were among the English refugees crowding into Cork. Spenser's last act of public service was to be messenger between the officials in Cork and the government in London. He set off in December, probably still unaware that he was now the sheriff-designate of Cork. He died on January 13, 1599, three weeks after delivering his bad news to the government. A story soon got round that he had died in neglected poverty, "for want of bread", as Ben Jonson put it. This seems extremely unlikely, however, since he had just been paid £8 for bearing the dispatches from Cork and it seems improbable that he immediately lost the lot to creditors or footpads. He also had plenty of friendly patrons in London; any one of them would certainly have helped him out. If Spenser did not die for want of bread he did not die of surrender to misfortune either. No doubt the strain of his own shock, disappointment, and loss was very severe. But he was in sufficiently good spirits to be composing his own report on the latest Irish crisis, to be handing it in along with the Cork dispatches, and to be expecting the Queen to read it. His misfortunes probably only made things a little easier for whatever illness it was that killed him. Just four days after Spenser's death a brief reference was made to him in a long, personal letter written by a man called Chamberlain. Just in passing he wrote: "Spenser, our principal poet, coming lately out of Ireland, died at Westminster on Saturday last." Set-piece, public commemorations always tend to be highflown; this estimate of Spenser, private, casual, and disinterested, surely gives him one of the best epitaphs he could have wished.

II

Having reviewed the available information about Spenser's life, our next step in finding out upon what terms his work offers itself to us is to look at some Renaissance ideas about poets and poetry. Just as all Spenser's work was naturally influenced by the times in which he lived and the circumstances of his own life, so it was influenced by the prevailing ideas about literature. In Spenser's time there was plenty of theorizing about the old questions, What is poetry? What is its use? And in many books the theory was mixed with a very practical interest in the rules of composition, in the do's and dont's of how to write poetry. Since his schooldays Spenser would have studied the most influential classical[7] books on the definition, function, and rules of poetry. He certainly knew a number of Renaissance contributions to the subject by English, French, and Italian writers.

Spenser's ideas on the subject were quite typical and had been largely developed from three sources of influence. The first was the Roman poet Horace (65–8 B.C.), whose *Art of Poetry* neatly summarized and passed on much of the classical thought about poets and poetry. The second was the Roman orator Cicero (106–43 B.C.) and the commentaries that grew up round his writings, especially those on orators and oratory. The third was a Renaissance movement, or tendency, that has been called humanism. As used here the term humanism has nothing to do with a secular attitude to life as opposed to a religious one, or with a natural, human frame of reference as opposed to a supernatural one, divinely revealed. For our purposes humanism refers to an intellectual-literary movement concerned with reviving a close study of classical literature. Humanistic love of the ancients sometimes amounted to veneration: "Saint Socrates pray for us", one famous Italian humanist used to say; and he also kept candles burning before

---

[7] In this context "classical" means "pertaining to ancient Greece and Rome". Spenser's knowledge of Latin was first-hand and exceedingly thorough. He knew some Greek but much of his knowledge of Greek literature would have been second-hand, via Latin imitations, references, and translations.

a bust of Plato. Some humanists emphasized textual and linguistic matters; they were most interested in recovering or re-editing texts, in expounding grammar, and in developing a good classical style. Others were most interested in philosophical matters; they were concerned with the thought systems and social ideals of ancient Athens or Rome. Almost all humanists were educators in one fashion or another, but some particularly emphasized pedagogical matters; these last were chiefly interested in the aims and methods of an education grounded on the classics. A few great humanists, such as Erasmus of Rotterdam (1466?–1536), were experts in all these matters.

Humanism as a whole was of course wonderfully served by the invention of the printing press in 1498. It should be stressed, however, that neither Horace, nor Cicero, nor the humanists actually discovered anything; none of their work marks the appearance of any totally new attitude or program. Horace and Cicero had their Greek predecessors – in particular Aristotle;[8] and the Renaissance humanists had their mediaeval predecessors. But it is accurate to say that most literary theorists from 1350 to 1600 found in Horace and Cicero their most convenient, thorough, and elegantly written sources of useful ideas. And they found in the programs of the humanistic educators a support for their views about the usefulness of poetry.

Horace and Renaissance Poetics. Horace's *Art of Poetry* was directly useful to anyone concerned with poetics. As it descended through Horace, the standard Renaissance picture of the poet was of a person who combined a degree of natural talent with three other elements: the divine gift of inspiration; a detailed knowledge of other (especially classical) poets; and an acquired skill in the rules of composition. For example, the most famous and long-lived rule was the rule of decorum,

---

8Aristotle (384-322 B.C.) was a thinker of the very greatest importance in many branches of learning, including philosophy, natural history, and poetics (systematic writing about poetry, dealing especially with the theory and art of writing it). He started as a pupil of Plato (c. 427-348 B.C.), who was the other most important Greek philosopher and who is also mentioned above.

namely, that every subject has its most appropriate form and style of expression: manner must be suitable to matter. Horace was the ancestor of numerous "arts of poetry"; also of numerous "apologies" or "defences" of poetry. Most of these apologies described poetry as much as they defended it, because in defending something it is usually necessary to define it first. The history of these defences of poetry began long before the Renaissance and is still unfolding. Since at least as far back as Plato there has been in western culture an ambiguous attitude toward poets and poetry — uneasiness as well as admiration, hostility as well as praise. The uneasiness and hostility seem to flow from two habits of mind: a kind of overprudent rationality and a kind of over-practical rationality. Over-prudent rationality tends to mistrust the inspired, prophetic, and, therefore, unpredictable element in poetry. Anything touched by the liberties and irrationalities of inspiration, or divine seizure, it finds unsettling. And its strategy has usually been to accuse poets of irresponsibility if not immorality. Over-practical rationality mistrusts poetry because it is fictional. This habit of mind assumes that a fact is inherently superior to a fiction. Confident in the world of factual information, it finds unsettling the idea that fiction may be a way of grasping and expressing truth. Its strategy has usually been to accuse poetry of uselessness if not untruthfulness.

Poets of the Renaissance had many such charges brought against them. Their defenders naturally tried to show that poets, though inspired, are reliable and respectable. They also tried to show that poetry serves a socially useful purpose. The authority of Horace was very helpful because he wrote that the function of poetry is to instruct as well as to please, to edify as well as to entertain. If pleasure alone is not quite respectable enough, then instruction supplies moral ballast and social purpose. If he is a sound teacher as well as an inspired entertainer then the poet can hardly be accused of irresponsibility. To answer the charge that poets are misleading if not downright untruthful, most of their defenders brought forward a particular definition of poetry. On this matter they still used Horace but also fell back on Aristotle's idea of poetry as imitation. According to this definition, what poetry imitates by means of words is nature. Nature is here taken to mean the whole of the natural universe, particularly human nature, experience, and activity. An imitation does not mean an exact or literal copy of nature, which is in any case a practical and logical impossibility. It means rather a selective representation of nature, a world of words imagined powerfully enough and set down accurately enough to persuade readers of its genuine relationship to the world of nature. Since poetry is fictional, the test of a poem is not its literal truthfulness but the general authenticity and persuasiveness of its representation. A poem that passes this test may be said to be serving the truth, or offering a kind of truth. And if this is so, the charge that poets are an untruthful lot becomes almost meaningless.

The definition of poetry as an imitation of nature took it for granted that nature was the poet's primary model. But, following Horace again, Renaissance critics also distinguished two especially important secondary models. One such model, or set of models, was provided by the work of other poets. All the handbooks on writing poetry advised the beginner to study and imitate the work of established poets. Used in connection with the work of other poets, the term "imitation" carried its usual, less specialized meaning of emulating, using as a model, following closely.[9] The authority of the classics was so strong, and the practice of using them so commendable, that one critic felt able to argue that in following Homer or Virgil a poet would be following a second nature.[10] The other secondary model, or set of models, was provided by the poet's own imagination. The recognition of this kind of model allowed for the free, unpredictable play of the poet's imagination and inspiration. It allowed for the fact that a poet's genius may include the power of being fanciful. He deals with things as they are, or seem to be, but also with things as they might have been or

[9]One handbook writer went to the extreme of advising would-be poets to help themselves discreetly to other authors' work. "Steal with due care" was the phrase he used — though even this is not necessarily as straightforwardly larcenous as it sounds.

[10]Homer was the ancient Greek author of two epics: the *Iliad*, about the role of the hero Achilles in the fall of Troy; and the *Odyssey*, about the wanderings of Ulysses (Odysseus) on his way home after the fall of Troy.

might be. Things not in nature or in other authors may occur to him and he can represent them in the form of words. Although the actual world of nature was always the poet's chief model and the chief yardstick of his performance, the critics understood his power to add to the natural world from among his own models. They knew perfectly well that to cut out the products of fancy would be to cut out half the world's best poetry. They knew, too, that fancy as a part of fiction can serve the truth with startling power and persuasiveness.

It was along such lines that Renaissance critics discussed and defended poetry under the wide, general authority of Horace. Some of these critics were also poets of greater or lesser importance. But every poet was fed by, and helped to feed, these "arts" and "defences" of poetry, which tried to give an account of the powers of a poet: what these powers are, what they work with, how they work, and to what purpose.

Cicero and Renaissance Poetics. As it descended through Cicero, the standard picture of the orator was of a civilized, eloquent man trained to give advice in such ways that people would be moved to accept it. The art of oratory was technically known as rhetoric,[11] and it was acquired in the classroom from professional rhetors, or rhetoricians. As an oral art it was used mainly in places of legal, political, and educational assembly; it served lawyers, royal and town councillors, tutors, and schoolteachers. As a written art it could serve almost any subject whatsoever.

There was a threefold link between rhetoric and poetics. First, much of the equipment that the rhetorician was expected to have or acquire was the same as that expected of a poet. Both were supposed to have the power to grasp a subject properly, organize it clearly, and express it elegantly with due attention to the rule of decorum and the kind of audience in view. The technical Latin names for these powers were *inventio*, *dispositio*, and *elocutio*; and they were used for both rhetoric

---

[11]Rhetoric, grammar, and logic made up the Trivium, a standard section of the school curriculum. The Trivium was mediaeval in both name and organization but, with various modifications, it persisted well into the seventeenth century.

and poetry. When it came to such details of *elocutio*[12] as diction or figures of speech, most discussions applied equally well to rhetoric and poetry.

Second, when the writer of a handbook wished to give an illustration of rhetoric in action, more often than not he took his example from a passage or line of poetry so that there was also a kind of specialized working relationship between rhetoric and poetry. The theories of one were most conveniently demonstrated by the practice of the other.

Third, some of the functions assigned to oratory were much like those assigned to poetry. In Ciceronian rhetoric and Horatian poetics the purposes assigned to oratory and poetry overlapped. This is illustrated by a typical and popular book called *The Arte of Rhetorique*, written by Thomas Wilson in 1553. Wilson explains that rhetoric is a strong civilizing force: it instructs men rationally as to the best course to take in a given situation, and also stirs them into actually taking it. But to stir emotions and engage the will rhetoric must give pleasure. Therefore, early in his book Wilson says that the purpose of rhetoric is to please as well as to instruct and persuade. This is very close to what was being written about the purpose of poetry. Poetry may deal in fictional representations, while oratory addresses itself to actual situations; but both have a teaching, civilizing function. And both are effective to the extent that they are also entertaining.

Because of these links, it is not surprising that Renaissance writers did not often feel the need to distinguish carefully between rhetoric and poetics. To be interested in the one was to be interested in the other. Inevitably, Ciceronian rhetoric contributed to theories about poets and their craft.

Humanism and Renaissance Poetics. We have already mentioned that some humanists were especially interested in the aims and methods of an education grounded upon the classics. Cicero's writings on the training of orators were developed by later authors into a whole program of education. First, students were to be thoroughly trained in classical, especially Latin,

[12]Under this heading came all the elements making up what we call style. It applied to written composition as well as to the niceties of oral delivery.

grammar. Then would come further detailed studies in grammar, rhetoric, and logic – studies based on classical texts. The fruits of this program would be men who had mastered Latin language and literature, who could think straight, and who could express themselves fluently and persuasively. The idea was, moreover, to produce men who were not only learned and eloquent but also virtuous and civilized. The Ciceronian ideal was both a good style in Latin and a good style of life.

The humanists we are talking about were committed to this Ciceronian ideal. They were especially attracted to its ethical purpose, to its emphasis upon the civilizing, moral quality of a good education. The texts they chose were ones exemplifying not only a fine classical style but also sound behaviour which would serve citizenship as well as scholarship. As a point of method, the texts chosen were as entertaining as possible so as to bring the pleasure-motive into the learning process: to teach pleasurably. At this point the parallels between the humanist and the poet merge; educational theory makes contact with poetics. Texts of poetry provided scholarly training in grammar and rhetoric; they helped develop moral sensitivity by their representation of varieties of human character in action; and in serving these purposes they furnished entertainment.[13] Most of the poetry used by the humanists was classical, and respect for the classics did not slacken throughout the Renaissance. Some Renaissance poets wrote quite a lot of Latin verse; but others, such as Spenser, wrote only a very little, and well before Spenser's day most important poetry was being written in the vernacular. The defenders of poetry soon claimed the same virtues and uses for contemporary poetry in the vernacular as the humanists claimed for classical poetry.

The humanistic educators looked beyond the classroom. They expected the full fruits of their program to appear in public life. Skill in the arts of eloquence and clear thinking together with powers of good counsel and virtuous action: this was the combination they hoped for in their complete version

[13]We usually limit poetry to verse, as distinct from prose. To Renaissance writers, however, poetry often meant any sort of fiction – any literature of the imagination, including drama, whether in prose or verse. The ideas about poetry that we have been tracing were equally relevant to its narrower or wider meaning.

of the Ciceronian ideal. The end of a humanistic education was to offer the nation good men who could serve it well. This wide, civic purpose was brought neatly into focus by the problem of counsel – the problem of training and advising rulers. When royalty exercises enormous power, stupidity and viciousness in kings can mean enormous disasters. What, then, is the best sort of training for a prince? Who makes the best sort of counsellor? What are the strategies for wedding royal authority to the arts and powers of the humanistic ideal? And – very tricky – how can the king be persuaded to accept good advice, especially if he doesn't like it? Besides standard classical treatments, there were numerous Renaissance works bearing on the problem of counsel. One was Erasmus's *Education of a Christian Prince* (1516). Another was Thomas More's *Utopia* (1516), a debate about counsel which clearly presents the difficulties in the way of a good and effective counsellor. A third was Castiglione's *Book of the Courtier* (1528), in which a group of courtiers builds up a composite definition of an ideal servant of the prince.[14] Erasmus, More, and Castiglione are but a small sampling of the many humanistic authors who had the full Ciceronian ideal in mind.

The poet could help the humanist in shaping the good man who serves his country well. As to art of eloquence, poetry was itself a form of eloquence in action and it could represent in fiction the effects of eloquence. As to the powers of good counsel and virtuous action, the poet in writing his poetry was actually giving his kind of counsel, performing his kind of virtuous action; he could also represent in fiction the operation of these powers. As to getting those in authority to accept good advice, poetry was supposed to entertain as well as instruct; just as poetry might make learning more pleasant to the schoolboy by entertaining as well as teaching, so it might make advice more palatable to the prince by offering it in the form of a pleasant fiction. Thus poetry could claim to be a civilizing force in society and the poet could claim to be a good servant of the prince and his advisers.

14The first two works mentioned were written in Latin. *The Book of the Courtier* was written in Italian; a very popular, influential English translation was completed by Thomas Hoby in 1561.

Sidney, Spenser, and Renaissance Poetics. The best English summary of Renaissance poetics was made by Sir Philip Sidney (1554–86). There is no point raised in our survey which was not in one way or another raised in his *Apology for Poetry*.[15] We mention Sidney not in order to say everything over again in his words, but simply because he cannot be omitted from any discussion involving Elizabethan poetics. On this subject Sidney both practised and preached. He was a major author of fiction in verse and prose; his *Apology* still stands as a most notable piece of literary criticism. In him were combined the Horatian poet-critic, the Ciceronian orator, and the humanistic poet-counsellor. As a courtly writer he produced stylish, entertaining, and instructive fictions. As an active courtier he once suffered the wrath of his queen for giving her frank counsel which she did not like. Interestingly enough, he cast the *Apology*, his masterpiece of poetics, in the form of a classical oration. While not original in its leading ideas, the *Apology* was a thorough, eloquent, and learned summing up of Renaissance poetics. It also showed that Sidney was alert to what was going on in English poetry, and that Spenser was a big part of it.

Unlike Sidney, Spenser was not a critical theorist, but the theory Sidney sums up in his *Apology* reads much as if it were the basis for Spenser's practice. Everything we have said about Renaissance poetics, and which Sidney once said so much better, is continuously demonstrated in Spenser's poetry. When Spenser invokes the Muses at the beginning of a poem, he is following the conventional way of representing the beginning of the creative process. These invocations represent the poet summoning up his own powers and also laying himself open to divine inspiration. Again, nature is Spenser's chief model, but he also follows his own imagination; he goes "hand in hand with nature" but also (in Sidney's words) ranges freely "within the zodiac of his own wit". As we shall see, Spenser takes other poets for models as well. He draws upon mediaeval authors sometimes, fellow Renaissance authors often, classical authors all the time. Classical mythology, for instance, could no more

[15]Though not published until 1595, the *Apology* in manuscript form would have been known to Sidney's acquaintants, including Spenser. An excellent edition of it was brought out recently by Geoffrey Shepherd; see bibliography for details.

be separated out from Spenser's poetry than nerve and muscle tissue could be separated out from a living body. Then again, it is easy to demonstrate Spenser's familiarity with the "arts" of poetry and rhetoric. He can be seen applying everything they mention, from such large, general rules as the observance of decorum to such small poetical or rhetorical devices as the "Paronomasia" or the "pretty Epanorthosis" pointed out to us by the zealous editor of *The Shepheardes Calender*.[16] Finally, Spenser certainly thought of himself as a poet-counsellor, as a good citizen serving his nation by his writing. He takes it for granted that his poetry has a moral, civilizing purpose and that it will best serve this purpose in giving pleasure. He is a courtly poet who represents gentlemen, nobles, and princes in action with the hope that his fiction will be a persuasive model for actual gentlemen, nobles, and princes. He dedicates *The Faerie Queene* to Queen Elizabeth and accompanies it with seventeen dedicatory sonnets to nobles such as Lord Burleigh, the Earl of Oxford, and the Earl of Essex. Of course Spenser wants their patronage – who wouldn't? – but in creating an ideal, exemplary image of them all and offering it to them all, he is also serving his part as poet-counsellor.

Although Spenser's ideas on the subject of poetry were the common, typical ones and he generally worked within the framework they provided, he could be daring and original. In *The Shepheardes Calender* he experimented quite freely in matters of diction and rhythm, translation and adaptation. For *The Faerie Queene* he invented a verse form distinctive and useful enough to become known as the Spenserian stanza. But his genius was not the kind that smashes rules, leaving theorists limp and stranded in the wreckage. That kind of creative force was more a part of the genius of his contemporaries, Shakespeare and Donne. Spenser's genius was of the kind that works old rules and theories to a new perfection. His special quality is that the rules and theories don't use him; he uses them to do many things better than they have ever been done before.

16In his footnotes to the "Januarie" poem. The first device is a form of word-play depending upon the repetition of like sounds; the second is a rhetorical correction or modification of something just said. The *Calender* was Spenser's first major publication; it was edited by a certain unknown E.K. (See pp. 3-13.)

III

The lines of our introduction at this point narrow down to comments and suggestions about the works actually included in this volume. These are meant to be truly and only introductory. Whenever they move from explanation to interpretation they are not intended to yoke the student to any one, dogmatic reading of Spenser's poetry. Above all, they should not be allowed to get in the way of the student who proposes to find out for himself what Spenser's poetry is like.

The Shepheardes Calender (1579)

This was Spenser's first important work, and it came out with enough editorial wrappings to smother a less sturdy work. The editor of *The Shepheardes Calender* is still known only as "E.K.". He is a very academic Spenser fan, full of rather heavy, argumentative enthusiasm as he explains and defends what Spenser is doing. As an editor E.K. has his weaknesses. There is a deliberately antique, rustic flavour to the diction of this poem and he is quite wrong in his remarks about some of Spenser's old-looking words. He is also unhelpful about some mysterious personal allusions in the text though, to be fair, these mystifications were deliberate on Spenser's part. Much of what E.K. says is accurate and helpful, however, so that it still pays to follow him with some care. His introductory matter confirms a good deal of what we have already said about Renaissance views on poetry. Fresh and experimental as it is, Spenser's poem is also a learned contribution to a very old poetic tradition, and E.K.'s response usefully reflects the tastes and standards of learned Elizabethan readers; it indicates the kind of excellences they were on the look-out for. Certainly E.K. was impressed. He thought that the appearance of *The Shepheardes Calender* was quite an event. So did many other readers. The poem was anonymous, but plenty of people knew who the budding author was and, as of 1579, Spenser became a poet to watch.

The Shepheardes Calender is a pastoral poem. It belongs to a class of poetry that is rural in setting and peopled by conventionally simple folk, such as farmers, fishermen, and shepherds. One common subdivision of this class of poetry is called the pastoral eclogue, a short piece usually conducted in the form of reported conversations or songs. Spenser's *Calender* is a carefully organized, unified collection of twelve pastoral eclogues. Above all the pastoral imitates two things in nature: the universal human feeling that life was once delightfully simple, idyllic, and innocent; the universal longing to return to, or recover, such a state of life. These deep-rooted pastoral themes often include regret for the loss of such a happy state and complaint over the way things have gone wrong. When the notes of regret and complaint are strong, the pastoral becomes elegiac, that is, plaintive and mournful in tone. Spenser's eclogues offer the pastoral themes in terms of the joys and sorrows, moods and activities, of shepherds – among whom he includes himself under the name of Colin. He is a shepherd-poet who sings of shepherds clowning among themselves, piping over their flocks, competing for the attention of shepherdesses. But he also laments over the damages caused by wolf or blight, unrequited love, the death of friends, the inescapable onset of winter. He offers the full range of pastoral moods from carefree celebration to bewildered complaint. And since the poem is a twelve-month calendar of eclogues everything takes place within an over-all cycle of seasonal growth, maturity, and decay.

There are pastoral elements in all kinds of literature, but when we speak of the *pastoral*, or pastoral eclogue, we are talking about a distinct, very old tradition of poetry. It is this tradition which provided Spenser with his numerous classical and Renaissance literary models. Even the fact that Spenser chose to begin his career with a pastoral was in the tradition. As E.K. pointed out, it had become customary for fledgling poets to try themselves out first in eclogues.[17] The pastoral tradition was established by two Greek poets of the third century B.C., Theocritus and Bion. It flourished in ancient Latin literature, with Virgil as the most important contributor. It is to

17E.K. distinguishes (mistakenly) between "eclogues" and "aeglogues", insisting that the second term is the proper one for what Spenser is doing. (See pp. 14-15.)

Virgil, among the classical pastoralists, that Spenser owes the most. Of the many Renaissance poets who added to the tradition E.K. names the most important, thus taking care to put Spenser in good company.[18] Many of his modern fellow pastoralists chose to write in Latin but Spenser owes the most to Clément Marot (1497–1544), whose two eclogues were in his native French. In his "November" eclogue Spenser follows Marot so closely as to be more or less translating him for stretches at a time. For the calendar structure of his poem, Spenser's models were English translations of popular almanacs, such as *Kalendar & Compost of Shepherds* and *The Zodiake of Life*. His originality lay in the ingenious application of the calendar structure to a cycle of pastoral eclogues.

Two more things should be said about the pastoral tradition as Spenser inherited it. First, in its post-classical phase the tradition absorbed the pastoral symbolism of the Bible. It was quite natural that Christian pastoralists should use the biblical story of a paradise called Eden: its creation, its loss, and its recovery. It was also quite natural that they should use the New Testament stories of good pastors, or shepherds, who searched out lost sheep and even gave their lives to protect their flocks. Second, there grew up in the pastoral tradition a convention whereby the poet could use the characters and adventures of his shepherds to comment on problematical matters. The convention especially applied if the poet-shepherd was in a solemn or elegiac mood. These comments in pastoral guise might be quite general ones, social, political, or ecclesiastical; or they might be quite personal ones about the poet's own problems. Often the pastoral symbolism of the Bible and the conventional comments went very well together. They are certainly linked in *The Shepheardes Calender* where the dominant, over-all mood is elegiac.

E.K. roughly divides the eclogues of *The Shepheardes Calender* into three kinds:

[18] See E.K.'s introductory letter and note on p. 3. Both E.K. and Spenser pay homage to Chaucer, who is given the pastoral name Tityrus. But Chaucer (*c.* 1340–1400) did not contribute to the tradition of pastoral eclogues as such. Spenser's homage to him is the homage of a confident apprentice to the master storyteller and shaper of the English language.

> For eyther they be Plaintive, as the first, the sixt, the
> eleventh, and the twelfth, or [R]ecreative, such as al those
> be, which conceive matter of love, or commendation of
> special personages, or Moral: which for the most part be
> mixed with some Satyrical bitternesse, namely the second
> of reverence dewe to old age, the fift of coloured deceipt,
> the seventh and ninth of dissolute shepheards and pastours,
> the tenth of contempt of Poetrie and pleasaunt wits.

The eclogues selected for this volume illustrate one of each
kind; "Februarie" is moral, "Aprill" recreative, and "December" plaintive. This selection also shows the early Spenser trying
out several verse-forms. "Februarie" is written in adequate but
undistinguished rhyming couplets with a base-rhythm of nine
syllables. Because of the way it keeps things clattering along
the rhyming couplet of eight to ten syllables has always been a
suitable instrument for narrative, and here we can see Spenser
learning how to tell a tale and keep it moving. This eclogue is
a double-frame poem. The outer frame provides the situation,
which is two shepherds arguing; the inner frame is a self-
contained tale (rudely interrupted) which one of them tells by
way of illustrating his argument. Both frames treat of "the
reverence dewe to old age". The outer frame shows a callow
youngster deriding an old man. The inner one tells how a
social-climbing briar conspires against its neighbour oak and
cons the farmer into chopping it down. In general the fable of
the oak and the briar seems to be presenting the need for a
balance between the dignified civilities of tradition and the
brash enthusiasms of revolution, between the claims of long
experience and those of drastic, instant reform. In particular it
acknowledges the decay and abuses within the life of the old
Catholicism, while also warning against the root-and-branch
doctrines of extreme non-conformity. The tensions between
tradition and enthusiasm, between old and new polity, are
dramatically embodied in the characters of old Thenot and
young Cuddie, as well as the characters of the oak and the briar.

Also a double-frame poem, "Aprill" is recreative in both of
E.K.'s senses. In its outer frame of ten-syllable quatrains two
of Colin's shepherd friends "conceive matter" of his unhappy
love; and the beautiful inner frame is a song of Colin's (sung

by one of the friends) in "commendation of special personages" – a set-piece ode of thirteen stanzas in praise of Queen Elizabeth. The style of this ode is very different from the bluff diction and countrified clump of "Februarie". Here is evidence that this pastoral Colin can sing for queens. This shepherd-poet can be as courtly as you please in diction, theme, and tone. His friends may think he's making a fool of himself in love but they are very impressed by his song in praise of Dame Elisa. The base-rhythm of this ode is pronounced but permissive: each stanza moves between four long lines of ten or eleven syllables and four short lines of four to six syllables towards a concluding medium line of eight or nine syllables. The whole song well displays that chaste exuberance and sedate fluency which characterizes so much of Spenser's poetry.

To give full value to plaintive "December" it is necessary to mention the other plaintive eclogues as well and then to dip briefly into a possible interpretation of the *Calender* as a whole. "December" is one of the four eclogues in which Colin appears in person. Each one finds him complaining and lamenting; each is elegiac in tone. "November" is an actual elegy. "Januarie", "June", and "December" all contain a two-fold lament: the shepherd-poet grieves over his misfortunes in love and also over his disappointments as an artist.[19] This elegiac mood, with its recurrent, two-fold lament, really seems to dominate the whole *Calender*. For one thing, these plaintive eclogues are strategically placed: one at the beginning, one in the middle, and two at the end. For another, Spenser could easily have begun his calendar year of poems in spring; but he didn't, even though in his day the official beginning of the year was March 25. E.K. trots out a lengthy justification for Spenser's decision but surely the simple reason for it is that Spenser wished both to begin and end his calendar with winter, the most appropriately elegiac season.

Pursuing this matter of a personal, elegiac tone, we may note that in "Januarie" Colin breaks his shepherd pipe – though his

---

[19]When the poet is in pastoral guise as a shepherd, his songs and his pipe playing symbolize his poetry; so when the frustrated Colin wants to abandon his pipe, this suggests the poet being tempted to pack it all in and give up composing.

emblem[20] suggests that he has not entirely given up hope of winning his shepherd lass Rosalind. By "June" the shepherd-poet is announcing that Rosalind has definitely abandoned him, a misfortune which threatens his self-confidence and leaves him with almost no hope at all. In the meantime the "Aprill" song has subordinated Rosalind to Queen Elisa and attracted the attention of Calliope herself, the Muse of epic, not pastoral, poetry. In "November", a little pastoral elegy, Colin mourns the death of a shepherdess; but the elegy concludes with an assertion of triumph over death and Colin's emblem here is "Death does not harm". Then in "December" Colin rehearses all his plaintive notes again, abandons his pipes, and bids his flocks and friends a discouraged farewell. But even here all is not black. The emblem of "November" may also apply to "December". Furthermore, there are two Pans in *The Shepheardes Calender*: the classical Pan, piping woodland god of shepherds and goatherds, and the "soveraigne Pan" who, in the glosses to "Maye" and "Julye", is explicitly identified with Christ. And in "December", with the Nativity just off stage, as it were, Colin appeals to the second, greater Pan and repudiates the lesser, classical Pan. This combination of biblical, pastoral symbolism with the convention of personal comment seems to leave even "December" with a muted upswing of hope. The last poem of the cycle implies the birth of the sovereign Pan, the Good Shepherd himself, and so seems to offer the shepherd-poet a way out of his impasse.

With all this in mind we perhaps read the *Calender* as a pastoral account of the first major cycle in the experience of a poet-lover. Rosalind may or may not correspond to an actual woman in Spenser's life; he is deliberately mysterious on the matter. In any case, she is an image of his pastoral Muse in the realm of classical Pan, the minor pastoral deity. The *Calender* seems to present the record of a shift in allegiance from this Pan and the shepherdess Rosalind to the sovereign Pan and

---

[20]The emblem is the little motto, or quotation, with which each eclogue is concluded. Only "December" has no emblem printed, though it is signed off with the words "Colins embleme". This may mean that the emblem was omitted by mistake; but it is rather more likely that Colin's emblem for "November" is supposed to stand duty for "December" as well.

Queen Elisa, whose realm encompasses much more than shepherd-land. Whatever the pleasures and values of this pastoral country, they are shown to have become disillusioning, frustrating, and terminal. The record of this calendar has brought him to the dead of pastoral winter; as pastoral poet he is now old and disappointed. "December" seems to bring this whole first cycle of pastoral experience to an unsatisfactory close. But this very nadir of discontent also seems to contain the possibility of a new vocation, a whole new cycle of experience – perhaps as England's nationalist, Protestant, epic poet in the wider service of Calliope, Elizabeth, and the sovereign Pan. In other words, as the poet of *The Faerie Queene*.

The Faerie Queene, Book I (1590)

A

Spenser himself provided a succinct introduction to his *Faerie Queene*. It took the form of a letter to Sir Walter Raleigh (dated January 1589) which is usually printed in editions of Spenser, and is included here on pages 325 to 331. The letter gives a number of useful hints about *The Faerie Queene*'s general organization and the various models that influenced it: classical, mediaeval, Renaissance, and biblical. For the first part of this discussion we shall simply elaborate on these.

General Organization. Spenser tells Raleigh that his plan calls for a poem whose first part is in twelve books. If this first part is well received he hopes to go on to a second part, also in twelve books. Of this huge project for a poem in twenty-four books we actually have only the first six books and a longish fragment made up of two complete cantos plus two stanzas. What Spenser managed to complete, therefore, was very far short of his grand design. But what is there has body and consistency enough to give all the satisfactions of self-contained completeness. Within this "whole", Book I is, in its turn, perhaps the most self-contained part.

Spenser explains to Raleigh that the first part of his poem is supposed to exhibit the twelve private, moral virtues in action, while the second part will exhibit the twelve public, political virtues in action. The moral virtues are those proper to any good private citizen; the political virtues are those which, in combination with the moral ones, are proper to a good ruler. Each book is to emphasize one virtue as it is displayed in the conduct and adventures of a particular hero. Thus the first book contains "the legende of the Knight of the Red Crosse, or of Holinesse"; the second contains "the legend of Sir Guyon, or of Temperaunce", and so forth. While each book has its hero, the whole poem has a super-hero who makes a sometimes brief but always decisive appearance in each book. This super-hero is the Arthur of Arthurian legend, the Arthur who first appeared in the middle ages and who is still going strong. True to the prophecies about him, he has re-appeared many times – most recently in the Broadway musical "Camelot". Raleigh is told that Arthur displays and sums up in his own person all the virtues which are distributed throughout the poem in the various sub-heroes. In the first part of the poem Arthur is shown exercising the private virtues in the days before he became king – while he was still a private citizen so to speak. Spenser calls Arthur's over-all virtue, the thirteenth one that sums up and includes the other twelve, the virtue of magnificence.

There are also a number of heroines in the poem. In Book I there is Una, who represents truth and is as important to the story as the Redcross knight himself. Or, to take a heroine who actually exemplifies her book's main virtue, there is Britomart in Book III, whose legend is the legend of Chastity. But as there is a super-hero so there is a super-heroine: Gloriana, the Faerie Queene herself. Arthur is betrothed to Gloriana; he ranges through her kingdom in search of her and, in the meantime, demonstrates his worthiness of her. The various heroes of the story are her knights. It is to her court, Spenser tells Raleigh, that people like Una come with their troubles and it is from there that her champions such as the Redcross knight are sent out upon quests to set these troubles right. Gloriana's court is the headquarters of all these chivalric adventurers and she is the ultimate inspiration of all the virtuous energy they display. This is true even though she does not appear "in person" anywhere in the poem as we have it. So although the Redcross knight is the hero of Book I and Una its heroine, it does not do to undervalue the super-hero or to forget the super-heroine. Prince Arthur as well as the Redcross knight serves Una and both of them serve her in Gloriana's name.

Classical Influences. As the letter to Raleigh indicates, it was from Aristotle that Spenser took his idea for the general organization described above. In a treatise called *Nicomachean Ethics* Artistotle had discussed the moral virtues and had written of an inclusive one (usually translated as "magnificence") that summed up all the others.[21] The moral virtues defined by Aristotle are classical ones such as temperance and prudence, whereas the virtue treated in Book I of *The Faerie Queene* is the peculiarly Christian one of holiness. Nevertheless, Book I fits into the general method of organization suggested by the arrangement of Aristotle's argument and his remarks about magnificence. Aristotle's technique of definition also seems to have influenced Spenser. Aristotle defined each virtue as the mean, or middle path, between extremes of excess (too much) and deficiency (too little). Thus courage would be defined as the mean between the excess, foolhardiness, and the deficiency, cowardice. In Book II of *The Faerie Queene* Spenser applies this technique of definition all the time; it is a guiding principle of his narrative and characterization throughout the legend of Sir Guyon. It is not so easy to see this technique working in the legend of the Redcross knight, but it is possible to argue that we see him learning the hard way about Christian holiness as a mean between too much self-confidence and despairing self-contempt, a tension between thrashing about taking providence too much for granted and sinking paralysed into the conviction of being totally beyond the reach of providence.

The Faerie Queene is an epic. Among Spenser's chief models were the three principal epics from ancient Greece and Rome: Homer's *Iliad* and *Odyssey* and Virgil's *Aeneid*. Like these great

[21]It is a little difficult to distinguish precisely twelve moral virtues in the *Nicomachean Ethics*. The exact number of twelve seems to come rather more from later, somewhat schematic commentaries than from Aristotle himself. Spenser was simply following the common assumption that Aristotle had laid down twelve moral virtues.

epics, *The Faerie Queene* is a poem with a serious theme, written in a generally formal, elevated style, and planned on a huge scale, with twenty-four books in all. Like them, it is cosmic in its scope, embracing the heavens, the earth, and the underworld. Like them, it begins with things already well underway, leaving the story's earlier events to emerge in accounts later on. In the case of the incomplete *Faerie Queene* we have to rely on the letter to Raleigh for some help on antecedent events and the ultimate origins of the action. Book I is in itself a small scale epic in twelve cantos. The seriousness of its theme and the elevation of its style are fairly self-evident, but a remark on how it includes the upper, middle, and lower worlds may be called for. To begin at the bottom: the most implacable enemy of Redcross and Una is a witch called Duessa, a formidable expert in lust, deceit, and illusion; in I, v, 19–44 Duessa makes a visit to the underworld, the realm of Night.[22] During this visit it becomes apparent that Duessa's real parents are Deceit and Shame, and that Night is her true ancestor. It is from this underworld of darkness, punishment, and misery that Duessa really comes. This is where she really belongs. In the classical tradition the epic hero usually makes a temporary visit to the underworld. The Redcross knight's descent to the underworld takes place when, thanks to Duessa, he is captured by a giant called Orgoglio and thrown into his dungeons (I, vii, 4–15); these dungeons, in which the knight can only think of how much he wants to die, are explicitly associated with hell (I, viii, 39). In more ways than one this episode marks the nadir, the lowest point, of a quest that has so far had more downs than ups. The main arena of the poem's action is the middle world. Spenser's special poetic version of the middle world is the land of faery. While it is quite recognizable as the natural, earthly world of men and their affairs, Faery land is not quite ordinary; Spenser charges it with special possibilities and a very particular atmosphere. How he does this, and why, will be discussed later. As for the upper world: it does not in Book I suit Spenser's purpose to shift his scene to the heavens as, for instance, Homer sometimes does in his *Iliad*; but the Christian heaven is brought

22The reference I,v,19-44 means Book I, Canto v, stanzas 19 to 44; and so throughout.

into the story, for at a crucial moment in the Redcross knight's quest he is granted a vision of the Heavenly City, the New Jerusalem (I, x, 55–61). Later on, in the *Two Cantos of Mutabilitie*, which seem to be a fragment of an uncompleted Book VII, Spenser does set a heavenly scene among the celestial divinities – classical ones this time: Jove (Zeus), Hermes, and the rest of the Olympians. But in Book I heaven is also present in another, more oblique sense. Classical and Christian traditions both contain stories about divine, supernatural activity in the natural world. In Book I Arthur is chief agent of such supernatural activity in its Christian sense. He seems to be the embodiment, or incarnation, of divine saving grace as it influences men and their affairs. Thus the scene of Arthur defeating Orgoglio and going down into his dungeons to rescue the Redcross knight (I, viii, 1–40) is reminiscent of Christ's defeating Satan and bringing the souls of the righteous up out of their captivity in hell.

The way in which the epics of Homer and Virgil were read also influences the way in which Spenser expected his own epic to be read. Typically, he assumed that his classical predecessors were to be read for moral profit as well as for pleasure. As for *The Faerie Queene*, he tells Raleigh:

> The generall end therefore of all the booke is to fashion a gentleman or noble person in vertuous and gentle discipline . . .

Just as such classical epic heroes as Agamemnon, Ulysses, and Aeneas were customarily taken as examples of good governors and virtuous men, so Arthur is to be taken as

> the image of a brave knight, perfected in the twelve private morall vertues . . . the which is the purpose of these first twelve bookes . . .

Spenser follows Virgil more closely than Homer. One critic has recently reminded readers of *The Faerie Queene* just how explicit Spenser's debt to Virgil actually is.[23] The beginning of *The Faerie Queene* echoes the opening lines of the *Aeneid* as it was known in Renaissance editions, and the wording of the

---

[23]William Nelson, *The Poetry of Edmund Spenser* (New York: Columbia University Press, 1965), pp. 117–18.

letter to Raleigh follows closely one of the most popular sixteenth-century commentaries upon Virgil's epic. In bringing Virgil so clearly to mind Spenser is incidentally announcing that he, like Virgil, began his career by writing pastorals but is now embarked upon the more serious business of writing an epic; that he is writing a nationalistic epic which not only celebrates his country and its ruler but also glorifies them as they could and should be; and that, in so doing, he is performing a heroic labour of public virtue as well as creating a pleasing work of art. There is the implication, moreover, that for this virtue he expects due reward in earthly patronage and preferment as well as the ineffabilities of heaven.

The other Roman poet who most influenced *The Faerie Queene* was Ovid (43 B.C.–A.D. ?18). Ovid was the author of *Metamorphoses*, a work quite as famous as his love poetry and his notorious guide to lovers, *The Art of Love*. All mediaeval and Renaissance poets owed a lot to the *Metamorphoses*. It is a superb collection of tales which still remains the best who's who of Greek and Roman mythology. With regard to its specific influence upon *The Faerie Queene*, it will be most convenient to discuss this when we consider the *Two Cantos of Mutabilitie*. For now it is enough to say that Ovid was by far Spenser's most influential, direct source of tales from classical mythology.

There were also important indirect sources that influenced Spenser's understanding and use of the classical myths. First, there were translations: a few from Greek sources, a great many from Latin. The age of Spenser produced many fructifying, elegant translations. One of the most distinguished of these was Arthur Golding's translation (1565–7) of the *Metamorphoses*. Spenser certainly knew and used this translation, though passages from Ovid in the original would have been part of his mental landscape from his schooldays. Second, there were paintings, woodcuts, and tapestries depicting scenes and figures from classical mythology. These works of art were often interpretations as well as illustrations of the myths. Woodcuts, in particular, were often emblematic; that is, they offered little moral commentaries in pictorial form. Collections of them often appeared in emblem books, with an added verbal commentary under each picture. Spenser was obviously sensitive to the pictorial arts and it is not surprising that many readers have found a markedly visual, picture-like quality in some passages of his work. He was influenced by examples of pictorial art, as well as by the interpretations they suggested and the commentaries that often grew up round them. Third, there were the numerous Renaissance book-length commentaries upon classical mythology and the re-tellings of the myths. For Spenser and his contemporaries the two most important re-tellers and interpreters were Giovanni Boccaccio (1313–75) and Natalis Comes, or Noel Conti (d. 1582). Boccaccio's *Genealogy of the Gods* was not just a handbook of classical mythology; it was also an early Renaissance attempt at a theory of myth, or a science of mythology, and it included a vigorous defence of poetry which Sidney and many other writers were to find exceedingly useful.[24] Comes published his *Mythologies with Commentaries* in 1551. Spenser seems to have used Comes rather more than Boccaccio. When he departs from the usual classical version of a myth, it does not do to accuse Spenser of forgetfulness or inaccuracy; as often as not he is following one of Comes's variations. For example, he accepts Comes's use of "Titan" as a name for the sun as well as for the family name of the twelve titanic children of Uranus, the mythic sky-father.

Spenser's continual use of classical mythology in Book I of *The Faerie Queene* can be briefly illustrated in the person of the Redcross knight himself. Though he is decidedly a Christian hero, Redcross has about him overtones of the mythological hero Herakles, or Hercules. Hercules was once committed to performing twelve labours – nearly impossible tasks – which included ridding the countryside of various monstrous pests. Without being too neat or schematic about it, one can read the Redcross knight's performances and misperformances as a series of preliminary tasks which build up to the near impossible labour of killing a dragon, the monstrous pest who has shut up Una's parents in their castle and is ravaging their kingdom.

[24]We do not have a firm date of first publication for the *Genealogy*. Boccaccio worked on it off and on for thirty years and as late as 1371 was still talking about it as unfinished. It was definitely in print by 1472, having been widely known long since in the form of manuscript copies.

Again, Hercules was once seduced by a princess called Omphale who for a time lured him away from his manly, warlike duties. This is exactly what Redcross allows the false princess, Duessa, to do to him. Immediately after Duessa has delivered Redcross, unmanned and helpless, to Orgoglio, there is a reference to one of the labours of Hercules (I, vii, 17) which rubs in Redcross's ignominy – because for the last while he has been herculean mainly in his weakness for beautiful enchantresses. Hercules' existence, at least his earthly, mortal existence, came to a painful end when he put on a shirt that burned him with a fiery poison. When the dragon's breath nearly roasts the Redcross knight alive in his armour (I, xi, 26–7), Spenser specifically compares him to Hercules in the burning shirt. Spenser is not trying to equate his Christian hero with the classical one; the differences between them are as noticeable as the resemblances. But the resemblances are more than passing and our attention is quite explicitly drawn to them. The use of classical mythology by Christian authors to enrich and amplify their work had been going on since the days of the early Church fathers. Spenser is especially fond of doing this and he is especially good at it; for him it is a fundamental, habitual technique of composition. Perhaps more than any other great English poet, Spenser has to be read with an eye to classical mythology.

Mediaeval Influences. In the far background of *The Faerie Queene* are two great, mediaeval sets of tales. One of these sets is called The Matter of France, the other, The Matter of Britain. The stories in The Matter of France centre upon the emperor Charlemagne (d. 814) and his wars against the Moors; they show the emperor and his knights as the champions of Christendom against encroaching Islam. This theme of militant Christendom engaged in holy wars drew further nourishment from the Crusades, the first of which took place in 1096. Chivalry in these tales is largely of the warrior sort. The chivalric virtues set forth are strength, courage, and skill in battle, loyalty to comrades, and devotion to emperor, the feudal lord. Tales of The Matter of France are usually told with few digressions and a minimum of embroidery. Their plots tend to be simple rather than complex.[25] Their prevailing style is one of austere grandeur; their prevailing tone is highmindedly heroic. Though Charlemagne was an historical figure the stories about him become unabashedly legendary, finding plenty of room for the extraordinary if not the supernatural. The main characters are often presented larger-than-life, capable of wonders of chivalric valour. Most famous among these stories is the *Chanson de Roland* (*Song of Roland*), written in the early twelfth century, not long after the first Crusade. In this epic Charlemagne, after concluding a successful campaign against the Moors, is returning home under cover of a rearguard commanded by his greatest champion, Roland. This rearguard is betrayed to the Moors by Roland's envious uncle, and Roland and his companions die fighting, outnumbered and cut off from the main body of the Christian army. In the course of the action Roland had sounded his fabulous horn as a signal for help; Charlemagne hears it and hurries back in time to avenge his rearguard though too late to save it.

The Matter of Britain centres upon the legendary King Arthur and his knights – particularly Lancelot, Tristan, Gawain, and Percival. These mediaeval stories of Arthur and his court flourished in verse and prose from the twelfth to the fourteenth centuries, with contributions in English and French. Like the Carolingian stories,[26] they describe clashes between the Christian and Islamic worlds. But while the Christian Arthur and his knights do fight the Saracens, this theme is not nearly as important here as it is to The Matter of France. The Arthurian legends also find plenty of room for the extraordinary and the supernatural. In fact they are true romances, that is, they are deliberately set in borderline country where the natural and supernatural worlds overlap. The geography of these stories may be recognizably earthly but their atmosphere is usually numinous – powerfully charged with a sense of the unearthly. Anything can happen and it often does. Marvels are major elements of the typical romantic plot; fabulous beasts are quite

[25]This is not a value judgment. A simple plot can of course be as good as any complex one.
[26]i.e., stories about Carol, or Charles. Charlemagne = Charles the Great.

at home in the typical romantic forest. Much of the action is controlled, in prophecy and in deed, by magicians like Merlin or by enchantresses. The dominant religious motive is not to defeat infidels in political-religious wars but to become sufficiently pure in heart to see the Holy Grail, the sacred chalice said to have been brought to Britain by Joseph of Arimathea.[27] The quest for the Grail is an other-worldly adventure which eventually draws most of Arthur's best knights away from the more mundane quests and duties of the Round Table fellowship. It is a quest attended by mysterious rituals and supernatural manifestations. The Grail is achieved, if at all, in mystical exercises or inexpressible visions. And the moment of complete achievement is also the moment of death.

In The Matter of Britain chivalry is erotic as well as militant. Knights like Lancelot and Tristan are great lovers as well as great warriors. Some of the Arthurian verse romances of the twelfth and thirteenth centuries are love stories of considerable subtlety and intensity. So are some of the episodes in the French prose romances of the fourteenth century, romances that were the source of Malory's wonderful collection, *Morte d'Arthur*, completed about 1470 and first printed by Caxton in 1485. All through this period of the late Middle Ages one of the most popular ways of framing a love story was according to a very potent convention called "Courtly Love". This convention was applied to love stories both inside and outside The Matter of Britain. For our purposes we may note that hardly any Arthurian stories are untouched by the courtly love convention, while some of them, especially the French verse romances of the twelfth century, are examples of the convention in its purest form.

As its name suggests, stories within this convention are about aristocratic lovers. Courtly lovers were expected to be connoisseurs of every degree and strategy of love. They lived by a code that claimed to regulate their behaviour down to the very looks, words, and gestures that passed between them. News of famous lovers was staple castle gossip. Groups of expert lady devotees convened "Courts of Love" in which the code of Courtly Love

[27]See Matthew 27:57.

was expounded and refined, or in which crimes against love were judged and punishment for offenders prescribed. A knightly lover would conduct himself according to the elaborate rules of Courtly Love only in relation to his courtly mistress, not in relation to peasants or middle-class townswomen. He lived – often dangerously and anxiously – in hope of his lady's favour. He undertook the most difficult quests, which were often imposed by her, in her name and for her sake. Desire for his lady included the desire to be worthy of her and was supposed to become for him a school of all the virtues. She for her part was not supposed to be an easy conquest, at least not openly. For a while, at least, she was supposed to be remote, unmelting, and generally hard to get. She might also be capricious, demanding, even fickle. All these qualities in her were supposed to test and refine the devotion of her courtly lover. Such a convention naturally includes the complaints and reproaches of impatient, discouraged lovers as well as the praises of the beauty-struck or the protestations of the hopeful. Indeed each courtly lover might expect to undergo the whole bitter-sweet cycle: from the first, unpredictable moments of attraction and falling in love, through all the tests of devotion and refining obstacles, to the delights of capitulation and con-summation.

The qualities of a love experience to which this convention is best adapted are the heady strangeness, or seeming fateful-ness, of initial attraction and desire, the zest to cultivate a tantalizing pitch of challenge and anticipation, the delicate protocol of the beloved's moves toward complete surrender. Lower-key satisfactions of sustained, post-consummation love remain pretty well outside the convention and are not repre-sented in typical courtly love stories. This is partly because Courtly Love rarely imagines romantic, passionate love as compatible with the contracts, domesticities, and stabilities of marriage. Sometimes a notable mediaeval author such as Chaucer will use the convention in order to tease it, or will even transmute a courtly love story into one of successfully dynamic married love.[28] But most courtly love authors take their con-

---

[28]Chaucer makes considerable use of the courtly love convention, though he is not often concerned with The Matter of Britain.

vention very seriously, including its implication that marriage tends to be dynastic, durable, and dull. Chances are good that at least one of the partners in a courtly love affair will already be married to someone else. Hence a courtly love affair usually begins in potential unfaithfulness to some third party and goes on to adultery. Marital fidelity is the one virtue that courtly lovers are not expected to learn from their desires. They often feel compelled to unlearn it, thus adding to their situation another reason for secrecy, another element of danger. The most famous courtly love stories in The Matter of Britain build these various parts of the convention into situations ranging from delicately balanced tangles of love-etiquette to insoluble, grandly tragic tensions. In the story of Lancelot, he and Queen Guinevere become lovers. Every time they come together Lancelot is party to a double betrayal of King Arthur, who is Guinevere's husband and his liege lord. At one stage Lancelot goes mad under the strain of his situation and the story of this pair of courtly lovers ends in desolate, monastic renunciation. Again, in the story of Tristan, Tristan falls in love with Iseult, but she is already betrothed to King Mark, who is Tristan's liege lord. This story particularly emphasizes the fateful, irresistible quality of romantic love. The lovers are driven into an increasingly wounding conflict with the usual social arrangements for coping with love and its desires. Their situation becomes unbearable and ultimately fatal; repudiating society, then life itself, they embrace death as their only chance of unfrustrated union.

The Grail quest and Courtly Love are two of the strongest themes in The Matter of Britain. It is notable that both imitate an other-worldly, life-denying tendency. In stories where these themes are treated in undiluted form, this tendency builds up to a straining against the bounds of life itself and consummation of desire becomes a deathly, not a living, enterprise. Whether or not this similarity between the stories of the Grail and of Courtly Love is coincidence, there is also a similarity of language. One expects the language of the Grail quest to be religious, to have a cultic, ritualistic, or even mystical, cast. But then so does the language of Courtly Love. According to the convention, courtly lovers are adherents to a religion of love. Eros, or Cupid, is the god of this religion.[29] The beloved is an angel, saint, or priestess; the lover is a worshipper who may be suffering a hell of rejection, or undergoing a purgatory of anxious hope and painful trial, or enjoying a heaven of acceptance. As some great works of religious devotion describe the religious experience in erotic terms, so the courtly love convention describes the erotic experience in religious terms.

The inclusion of romantic love stories in The Matter of Britain is one major, general difference between it and The Matter of France. Another difference lies in the method of telling a story. Some Arthurian verse romances hold to a single, straightforward line of narrative in the fashion of the *Song of Roland*. But most fourteenth-century prose romances manage a story quite differently. Their narratives tend to unfold at a very leisurely tempo. They are built up in an excursive manner; they are not held to a simple line of progression but deployed on several fronts at once. So much use is made of an interrupted or multiple story-line that some of these prose romances consist almost entirely of apparent digressions. A story will start with the adventures of A; quite abruptly he leaves the scene and for a few pages we follow B and C; these two part company and we stay with C; then A reappears and fights with C, whom he mistakes for D; and so on. Mistaken or assumed identities are very important stock in the romancer's trade, as are abrupt exits and unpredictable entrances, together with their resulting complications. These elements combine to produce genuine suspense, but since it is tempered by the leisurely over-all pace of the narrative, it is a kind of low-tension suspense quite peculiar to prose romances.

Another vital influence upon Book I of *The Faerie Queene* is the mediaeval legend of St. George. Spenser's Redcross knight turns out to be St. George; the device on his shield, a red cross on a white background, is the device of St. George. This legend is connected with the actual, historical crusades and the stories they inspired. St. George was a saint of the Near

29Not so much in his playful, cherubic aspect of erotic sportfulness as in his tyrannical aspect of overmastering, passionate desire.

East whose story seems to have been brought West and transplanted in England by Richard I when he returned from his crusade. The legend took firm root in England, where St. George became not only the country's patron saint but also a popular lead figure in masques,[30] town pageants, and village dramas. Early narrative versions of the legend vary in some details, but in general they picture St. George as a veteran opponent of the Saracens who is also noted for his zealous missionary preaching. He rescues a city from the demands of a tribute-hungry dragon by killing the beast just as it approaches its latest, most delectable victim – the king's own daughter. His victory wins him this princess as his bride and gives him the opportunity of preaching to the admiring populace and converting them all, from their king on down. Spenser is silent about Redcross–St. George's preaching skills; he also transposes the princess from a helpless victim awaiting rescue to a vigorous figure, Una, who initiates the campaign against the dragon, and who, in the process of their quest, rescues the saint rather more often than he rescues her. What is important about St. George is that in him Spenser has a figure who is militant, courtly-chivalric, saintly, and patriotic, all at the same time. St. George is the ideal hero for Book I of *The Faerie Queene*, where the religious meaning of the story is historically national as well as timelessly universal. Within Spenser's romantic setting his hero can exemplify both the Christian struggle to be holy and the English nation undergoing the religious-political crises of the Reformation.

Certainly other mediaeval sources echo intermittently in Book I of *The Faerie Queene*; but it is influenced heavily and throughout by the English folklore, literature, and heraldry of St. George, The Matter of France, and The Matter of Britain. Of these three "The Matter of St. George" has the most direct influence. The *direct* influence of the Carolingian epics and the Arthurian romances upon Spenser is limited. Between him and these two great sets of mediaeval stories is another, more

---

[30]Masques were a dramatic form of entertainment, usually amateur, aristocratic, and expensive, combining music, dance, dialogue, and elaborate scenario.

modern set of Renaissance stories. That is why, though the earlier stories are certainly of ultimate importance, they are, as we said earlier, in the far background of *The Faerie Queene*.

Renaissance Influences. In the near background are three works of the Italian Renaissance: Matteo Boiardo's *Orlando Inna-morato* (1484), Ludovico Ariosto's *Orlando Furioso* (final version 1532), and Torquato Tasso's *Gerusalemme Liberata* (authorized edition, 1581).[31] The Orlando of these first two poems is the Roland of the Carolingian epics and in his Italian reincarnations he is still one of the leading warriors in Charlemagne's campaigns against the westward expansion of Islam. Boiardo never completed *Orlando Innamorato*, and Ariosto's poem, though an entirely self-sufficient masterpiece, is in theme and plot a continuation of Boiardo's. *Gerusalemme Liberata* is a romantic epic about the first Crusade.

Boiardo and Ariosto blend The Matter of France with The Matter of Britain. They take the holy war theme and the sternly heroic chivalry of the one and mix it with the love stories, courtly chivalry, and narrative technique of the other. The Roland (Orlando) of *Orlando Furioso*, for example, goes mad out of disappointed love. In this he is like the Arthurian Lancelot and very unlike the Roland of the *Chanson de Roland* who would not, under any circumstances, lose his wits over a lady.

Tasso draws upon history chronicles, not upon The Matter of France and Britain; but even so, he takes the theme of Christian-Islamic wars and mixes it with stories of love and courtly chivalry. In the sixteenth century it was a matter of debate whether or not these three Italian authors had among them produced an entirely new kind of long poem, but their work is

[31]i.e., respectively, *Roland in Love, The Madness of Roland,* and *Jerusalem Delivered. Orlando Furioso* and Malory's *Morte d'Arthur* were written about the same time; but the first is definitely a Renaissance work while the second is usually classified as late mediaeval because, roughly speaking, the Renaissance as a literary phenomenon spread North from Italy and arrived in England over a century later. For a detailed discussion of Boiardo, Ariosto, and Tasso in relation to Spenser, see Graham Hough, *A Preface to "The Faerie Queene",* chaps. i-iv.

certainly distinctive enough to be given a separate classification: the romantic epic in verse. It is with good reason that Spenser mentions Ariosto and Tasso in the letter to Raleigh. Along with Boiardo they provide his closest models for style, for the particular atmosphere and setting of epic romance, and for management of a story. *The Faerie Queene*, too, is a romantic epic in verse.

Of these three Italian authors Spenser seems most indebted to Ariosto. Spenser's poetic version of the middle world, and of the kind of people in it, is very like the world of *Orlando Furioso*. One of the chief models for Duessa is Ariosto's witch, Alcina. The way in which Duessa seduces Redcross, estranging him from Una, is similar to the way in which Alcina seduces Ruggiero, one of Ariosto's heroes, estranging him from his lady Bradamante. The scene of Arthur and Una exposing Duessa for the repulsive witch she actually is (I, viii, 45–50) recalls a like scene in which Bradamante exposes Alcina. Arthur's shield (I, vii, 33–6) may receive the kind of lovingly detailed description that Achilles' tremendous shield is given in Homer, but in its actual looks and qualities it is rather more like one that comes into the possession of Ruggiero. Sometimes Spenser follows Ariosto so closely as to translate whole stanzas from him. Spenser also uses the multiple or interrupted story-line. Redcross and Una are separated by the beginning of Canto ii; from then on the story switches back and forth between them until they are re-united in Canto vii. There were classical precedents for managing a story in this way but Spenser had the special, later example of the mediaeval romances as used and modified by Ariosto. In its setting and atmosphere Spenser's land of faery in many ways resembles Ariosto's world of chivalric romance. When it comes to the tone of what is said and how it's said, however, Ariosto uses a wider tonal scale. He moves back and forth through a scale from burlesque, to irony, to high seriousness. He has an extraordinary versatility which his diffuseness of purpose (as well as his genius) allows him. Spenser's *Faerie Queene* holds much more to a single tone, in keeping with the ruling seriousness of his purpose. He uses touches of irony, even of burlesque, but his prevailing tone is certainly one of high chivalric seriousness.

Biblical Influences. In his letter to Raleigh Spenser refers to the Epistle to the Ephesians, noting that Redcross's armour is "the armour of a Christian man specified by Saint Paul". The Bible and the Christian tradition founded upon it are indispensable to an understanding of *The Faerie Queene*. This assertion applies with particular force to the Legend of Holiness, which is concerned with exhibiting a Christian virtue in action. A glance at the Variorum Edition of Spenser[32] will indicate how many times Book I echoes Scripture, especially passages from the Pauline Epistles and Revelation. There were several English versions of the Bible available to Spenser. Some of them, such as the Geneva Bible of 1560, were supplied with marginal notes distilling considerable scholarship and controversy, and sometimes Spenser is referring as much to these marginal notes as to the biblical text itself.

The Faerie Queene also shows the influence of religious art inspired by the Bible, especially that of the popular emblem books. The figures of Fidelia (Faith), Speranza (Hope), and Charissa (Charity) in Canto x of Book I illustrate this. These ladies, together with their appropriate emblems, derive immediately from biblical commentaries and religious art, and ultimately from such passages of Scripture as I Corinthians 13.

The Bible provided Spenser with much more than a rich fund of detail – verbal echoes, interpretive notes, religious emblems, and the like. It gave him the biblical myth, which exercised his powers of invention with a promising and well-known set of directions.[33] By way of a rough sketch, this myth can be broken down into seven stages, or governing images. (1) The Creation: this culminates in the establishment of man in beatitude, living in close presence to God as his friend and steward of Eden, the unfallen, paradisal world. (2) The Fall: Satan, embodied as a serpent or dragon, offers the primal

[32] Ed. E. Greenlaw *et al.* (10 vols.; Baltimore: Johns Hopkins Press, 1932-49).

[33] A myth is not a fanciful lie or an untruth. As used here, "myth" means a story or set of stories about persons and events that seem ultimately divine in origin and significance. Such events may occur in nature and be experienced in life, but they retain their element of supernatural mystery. A myth can be as true as any other way of organizing and representing the experience of such events; indeed, it may be the only way.

temptation and successfully persuades man to play at being God; as a result man and his whole world with him suffers the fall, the loss of Eden. (3) The Wilderness: excluded from Eden man leads a slavish, wandering, uncertain life in a world turned wilderness. Though cursed with idolatry, sin, and death, man in the wilderness longs persistently for the recovery of Eden and is sustained by prophecies of a saviour-leader who will bring this recovery about. (4) The Incarnation and Redemption: there appears such a saviour, or messiah. He is Christ the god-man who, resisting all temptations, in a final three-day struggle conquers sin and death, in actuality for himself and in principle for the rest of mankind. (5) The Types of Salvation: in the light of the Incarnation man now sees his history, particularly the history of Israel, as the history of salvation. Nation-founders like Abraham, heroes like Samson, priest-kings like David, or prophets like Jonah are seen as forerunners of the Christ to come. In spite of their imperfections they appear in one aspect or another as types of the messiah, the perfect prophet-priest-king. (6) The Apocalypse: a series of increasingly terrible upheavals is climaxed by the second coming of Christ; he defeats Satan again and passes final judgment upon all men.[34] (7) The New Creation: this second triumph of Christ winds up human history and accomplishes the actual, permanent recovery of Eden or entry into the Promised Land. This accomplishment is also expressed as the realization of a new creation, or of the New Jerusalem.

In the Christian tradition understanding of the biblical myth is sharpened by interpreting the experience of Israel in a special way. Israel stands for humanity. The slavery of the Israelites in Egypt is an image of fallen man in bondage to sin and death. The deliverance from Egypt under Moses, who is another type of Christ, is an image of Christ's first victory over Satan. Israel's wandering in the wilderness is an image of the consequences of the fall which persist even though man is now in principle on the way to the Promised Land. The entry into this land under Joshua – again, a type of Christ – is an image of Christ's final,

---

[34]The adjective for these climactic events is "apocalyptic". Another name for Revelation, the last book of the Bible, is The Apocalypse.

apocalyptic victory over Satan and the actual, permanent recovery of beatitude.

Except for Milton (1608–74), who reworks it on a huge scale in *Paradise Lost, Paradise Regain'd,* and *Samson Agonistes,* Spenser draws upon the biblical myth as much as any major English author. The Redcross knight's whole adventure is set in motion by Una, whose parents are described as the King and Queen of Eden. They are types of Adam and Eve, the representatives of all humanity. They have been defeated and are closely besieged by a satanic dragon. So the cause of the Redcross knight's quest is the loss of Eden and the reason for his whole enterprise is to recover it. With this in mind we may expect the other features of the grand biblical myth to be operating in Spenser's story. The knight's first uncertain wanderings bring him under the bondage of experts in evil and illusion, landing him eventually in the "Egypt" of Orgoglio's dungeon. He is redeemed by Arthur who, since he has a divine, not-to-be-resisted quality about him, seems to be a type of Christ. Arthur brings gracious deliverance to Redcross, exposure and destruction to his enemies. After this the Redcross knight's steps are more firmly set towards Eden, though he is still in a wilderness of forest and there are many trials yet to come. Like Moses, he is given a vision of the New Jerusalem, or Promised Land, while still in the wilderness. Finally he destroys the usurping dragon and restores Eden to its rightful king and queen. The apocalyptic notes of decisive battle, judgment, and restoration sound very strongly in the climax of the knight's adventure (I, xi–xii). There he is realized as a biblical-Christian figure, in two senses at least. He fully becomes the type of every redeemed man, in whom Christ's first redemptive victory over Satan is recapitulated, reapplied, and reconfirmed. And he also becomes a type, like Joshua, of the Christ who is still to come, who is to defeat Satan a second, final time and convert paradise regained from an historical possibility into a timeless reality.

One more hint from Spenser's letter to Raleigh still needs to be elaborated. But first a general, cautionary remark about the hints we have explored so far. The classical, mediaeval, Renaissance, and biblical influences of course apply to the whole range of Spenser's work, not just to Book I of *The Faerie Queene*. Almost any work of Spenser's will answer in some degree to all these influences. Discussing them under the heading of *The Faerie Queene* has been a matter of convenience, partly because they are all so well illustrated by Book I of this particular poem. If the commentary on other poems in this selection does not go into questions of influence and tradition, it should not be assumed that these questions are irrelevant.

B

Spenser tells Raleigh that *The Faerie Queene* is a "continued Allegory, or darke conceit". The words "darke conceit" mean a literary concept, or imaginative construct, which does not offer all its meanings at first glance and needs careful reading and interpretation. This is true of many literary constructs, but in the case of an allegory this condition of not being immediately self-evident is built into the original concept. Spenser and his readers inherited a long tradition of reading works allegorically. Within this tradition some works, which to our eyes perhaps do not call for such a reading, were read as allegory. The Song of Songs, for instance, or even Ovid's *Art of Love*, were allegorized so as to yield a set of religious meanings. By Spenser's day there were readers who wanted (as he says) "good discipline delivered plainly in way of precepts, or sermoned at large" in preference to having it "clowdily enwrapped in Allegorical devises". But allegory was still very much a live option for Renaissance authors and in the case of *The Faerie Queene* nobody is left in doubt. It is an allegory, and Spenser's whole point of writing to Raleigh is to ensure that his dark conceit will not be misconstrued.

Spenser's poem is an allegory in two senses, the first of which is technical. He uses all sorts of devices, from the simplest personifications and briefest metaphors to the most complex, sustained symbols, in order to exhibit the nature and meaning of such virtues as holiness. There is more than one way of defining holiness and more than one arena in which it can be exercised. Spenser therefore organizes his fiction so that the same set of narrative facts contains several definitions of holiness and several arenas of its action. In Book I of *The Faerie*

Queene the allegory is fairly systematic; that is, for most of the story all these definitions and arenas are developed simultaneously in that one set of narrative facts. The complexity of the allegory is in itself an imitation of the complexities in understanding and achieving holiness. In the hands of a great allegorist like Spenser apparent obscurities are less likely to be a failure in technique than they are to be a function of knowing that the qualities of holiness are far from self-evident.

The Legend of Holiness is also allegorical in a second, purposive sense. In this book Spenser wants to fashion a fictional gentleman in "vertuous and gentle discipline" for the guidance and inspiration of actual gentlemen. As an aspect of his "plausible and pleasing" fiction, the allegory serves the purpose of attracting readers and conveying a moral to them in an entertaining way. These general purposes alone would qualify Spenser's poem as allegorical for his readers. The allegorical tradition, however, allowed that the difficulties of allegory had a further, double purpose of screening and attracting. While not being difficult and obscure for the sake of difficulty and obscurity, an allegorical text was supposed to screen out frivolous, lazy readers and so preserve the text from misuse or misconstruction. In any good allegory the primary narrative facts could no doubt be read with pleasure for their own sake alone; but, given the general purpose of edification, they weren't supposed to be. For the serious reader, though, allegorical difficulty was no screen but a further attraction. The very challenge of difficulty was itself a part of his pleasure, an entertaining bonus.

The setting of Spenser's allegory is the romantic-chivalric world, mostly as it came to him from mediaeval stories via Ariosto. This world, which Spenser calls the land of faery, we have already described as set in the borderline country where the natural and supernatural worlds overlap. We might say of Spenser's Faery land that it is located by overlapping a vision of an ideal, "golden" world with a vision of the actual, "brazen" world. One frontier of Faery land opens on to an ideal world of things as they should be; the other on to the world of things as they actually are in Tudor England and neighbouring countries. This is the setting for Spenser's narrative, his primary fiction which simultaneously builds up more than one definition of holiness and exhibits more than one arena of its action.

Faery land is useful to Spenser because it is such an appropriate setting in which to imitate tensions between the ideal and the actual. It is a setting finely adapted to display the struggle for moral realization, the struggle to realize possibilities as actualities. If anything can happen in a romance, then there can be movement towards an ideal of holiness. The dream-like, anything-can-happen quality of romance has another use. In such a setting different meanings can attach themselves effortlessly to the same characters and events. You have more than magicians and marvels, more than nightmarish distortions of natural perspective as in the account of the dragon in Cantos xi and xii. The dream-like setting abets continuous multiplicities of significance and various arenas of action can shift and merge with fabulous ease into each other.

The Primary Fiction. Spenser's set of narrative facts is about a romantic quest of chivalry, complete with damsel in distress, wonders, disguises, unexpected entrances and exits, and numerous trials of knightly strength. It is emphasized that Redcross is a Christian knight. The heraldic device on his surcoat and his shield is a red cross on white ground – a sign of the risen Christ. One definition, therefore, that emerges from the story is of the holiness appropriate to a specifically Christian chivalry. From the start chivalric virtues, such as devotion to Una and her cause, have religious overtones. And in the House of Holiness the knight has to submit to the discipline of Christian virtues before being able to carry through with his chivalric quest.

As to the arena in which holiness as a virtue in Christian chivalry is exercised, we have said enough about Spenser's debt to mediaeval and Renaissance authors not to have to go over the subject again. But a few points should be made about Spenser's particular use of the romantic epic and Arthurian legend. First, although his story is very much about Britain and is in the form of an Arthurian romance, Spenser does not employ the usual main characters, except for Arthur himself and Merlin, and he makes surprisingly little use of Malory's *Morte d'Arthur*. Instead, he introduces a new group of characters. This is partly because many of Spenser's characters are images of virtues and vices, and their names provide a first clue to their allegorical role. It is also because of the immediate influence of Ariosto, who did not use the figures of Arthurian legend.

Second, although the Redcross knight's quest is clearly religious as well as chivalric, it is not a Grail quest. Most particularly, it is not a quest in which other-worldly concerns push the knight into a denial of life. His quest is not one that can be fulfilled only in death. If at times he wants to die it is because Orgoglio, or Despair (I, ix, 22–46), has got the better of him – not because he achieves some insupportably intense, mystical ecstasy. He *is* given a visionary glimpse of the New Jerusalem and he does long momentarily for an end to earthly travail. But this vision is not the culmination of his quest. On the contrary, it is granted precisely to enable him to go on with his quest. Even after the dragon-killing his story is unfinished; he still has to find his way back to the court of the Faerie Queene.

Third, although Book I is both a courtly story and a love story, Spenser drastically modifies the convention of Courtly Love. Redcross undergoes many trials for Una's sake and her devotion helps to school him in all the virtues. These virtues, however, include fidelity to one partner within the context of betrothal and the prospect of marriage, so that when he leaves Una and is seduced by Duessa, this is no test of courtly devotion sharp with genuinely tragic tensions but simply a catastrophic blunder. The love between Redcross and Una grows towards betrothal, a festive affirmation of life, not towards an unearthly climax of union in death.

The Historical Allegory. The fiction in Book I also carries a political story which covers, roughly, the period of the Reformation in England from Henry VIII to Elizabeth I. In this allegory Gloriana as Elizabeth is one of the only certain historical identifications. Arthur is probably the Earl of Leicester, Orgoglio is perhaps Philip of Spain. James VI of Scotland felt sure enough that Duessa was an image of Mary Queen of Scots to protest to the English court, in 1596, about this defamation of his mother. Even in historical allegory we are never far from religious meanings because at this time much of politics was religion and *vice versa*. This was an age in which open expression of religious non-conformity could bring a man close to indictment for treason. Depending upon which monarch and ruling group of advisers was in power, Catholics and various sorts of Protestants might have to choose between exile and imprisonment or death. When it came to war between nations, nationalistic fervour did, in many individuals, over-ride their particular religious allegiance. But at least it was an age in which many official policies could be rationalized with some honesty in terms of religious reformation or counter-reformation. There was not too big a credibility gap between announced religious policy and actual power politics.

The war between England and Spain was viewed all over Europe as a holy war, and the Armada expedition seemed for many to be an apocalyptic showdown between the forces of Christ and Antichrist. Who appeared as Antichrist was a matter of which side one was on. Protestant Spenser identifies Duessa – whether she's Mary Tudor, Mary Queen of Scots, or both – with the great harlot "arrayed in purple and scarlet" from Revelation 17. And Book I of *The Faerie Queene* has been described as a Tudor apocalypse. Spenser looks to Elizabeth-Gloriana as the defender of the true faith presiding over "brazen" England's turbulent progress through religious error towards a "golden" England of religious truth, harmony, and security. In this historical allegory Redcross is an image of the religious dimension of English nationality, or of the spiritual condition of England. He can be such an image because he turns out to be St. George, the patron saint of England whose red-cross banner is the same as that of the risen Christ. Holiness as defined by the knight's adventures is the emerging Christian will of a nation trying to follow truth in repudiating the evils of false religion. The arena of this holy action is Faery land as Tudor England. Spenser's fiction presents England as an historical community trying with the help of divine grace to realize its true political-religious destiny. It presents a nation embroiled in the possibility of becoming an actual version of the Promised Land.

The Moral Allegory. Since all the meanings contained in Spenser's fiction are in some degree religious, it seems useful to make a partial distinction by adopting his term "moral allegory". There are at least three (simultaneous) ways of understanding his moral allegory. One way is to take Redcross as the type of every Christian in his struggle to realize the universal vocation to be holy. He is a type of the armed pilgrim, or crusader; he is engaged in a holy war; he wears the "whole armour of God" as prescribed for every Christian by St. Paul in Ephesians 6:10–17. The knight's name, too, does more than identify him in the historical allegory as the patron saint of England. George means "ploughman" or "man of earth". And, as the knight eventually learns (I, x, 66), he was as an infant found and brought up by a ploughman. Redcross therefore embodies men of all stations from farmer to national hero; he also exhibits the possibility of saintliness in men of all stations. "Then come thou man of earth", says Contemplation to the Redcross knight (I, x, 52). This further identifies Redcross as a type of all men: made of frail dust but also made in God's image – divinely created and divinely redeemable. By this reading, holiness emerges as every Christian man's obligation to recognize and cleave to Christian truth (Una). In the arena of everyman's life he has to learn to defeat external enemies presenting the force and attraction of illusion, false doctrine, lawlessness, pride, and despair. Moreover, the achievement of this holiness is a divine as well as a human enterprise. The Christian everyman is not in the slightest excused from his own efforts in the holy conflict, but his best is not good enough. At critical points in his armed pilgrimage he must be saved by divine grace as exhibited in Arthur (I, viii) or symbolized by the well of life (I, xi, 29) and the tree of life (I, xi, 46).

A second way of reading the moral allegory is to take the knight's story as the spiritual history of a single individual. He is not only a type of the armed, Christian everyman; he is also an elaborately characterized individual with a history, name, quest, and destiny of his own. His career through the land of faery is an imitation of a particular Christian life, of one Christian's continuous struggle against everything that frustrates or perverts holiness. The events, people, and places in

Faery land display one man's experience of life, and provide the arena in which he tries to realize the full possibilities implied by his redemption. As with every Christian, so with this particular Christian: divine grace has already saved him in principle and goes on saving him in moments of deepest crisis.

So far we have looked at the Redcross knight from the outside, as one character among many. Helps, hindrances, and temptations have appeared as events and characters largely external to him. A third way of reading the moral allegory is to see the knight as a complex symbol of the innermost self at the centre of an entirely inward moral action. Seen this way the land of faery becomes an internal, psychic landscape; it becomes the arena of the continuous inward activity of a Christian man. All the other characters are images of his own impulses, longings, ideals, and predispositions. Spenser had plenty of precedent for the literary device of distributing a total personality among personifications of its various parts. The inner person of Redcross is thus made visible in the form of other figures; he is defined by what he does with them and what they do to him. But he is also an ultimate someone who is more than just the sum total of all the elements of his personality. He becomes an image of the self partly caught in, partly presiding over, the necessarily difficult process of individuation.[35] Read this way the moral allegory is suggesting that to be holy also has to do with becoming one's full, true self. The structure and dynamics of a person's psychological make up themselves become a means of grace. Spenser did not have modern terminologies of psychology to work with and if he had had them he might not have liked or used them. The point is that his fiction seems in any case to bear this kind of interpretation among others. If it does, then Canto x, usually belaboured as the dullest of the lot, has fair claim to being the climax of Book I. There on the hill of contemplation Redcross, in finding out who he really is, fully accepts himself, his vocation, and his destiny.

---

[35] That is, the process of becoming a whole person, a fully realized, integrated self.

Two Cantos of Mutabilitie
(published posthumously, 1609)

Failing hard evidence to the contrary, it seems best to take the word of the original publisher Ponsonby, that the *Two Cantos* are apparently Cantos vi, vii, and a two-stanza fragment of "some following Booke of the Faerie Queene, under the Legend of Constancie". Some editors assume that the Legend of Constancy was to have been the next following book of *The Faerie Queene*, that is, Book VII. There does not seem much reason to doubt this either, though it has proved very difficult to date the *Two Cantos* with any certainty. Spenser did not necessarily at any time think of the *Two Cantos* as a summing-up, even though the two-stanza fragment does admittedly sound like one. In his approach to these two cantos and their fragment, therefore, the reader should not be entirely controlled by the assumption that they are Spenser's deliberate (or emergency) conclusion to *The Faerie Queene*.

Envy and slander as against open-heartedness and courtesy; deceit and disguise as against truth and openness; change and decay as against stability and repose: whether writing on private or public themes Spenser seems to have had his imagination exercised most often and most powerfully by these three sets of opposites. In Book I, Duessa is the great Spenserian image of deceit; in the *Two Cantos*, Mutabilitie the Titaness is the great Spenserian image of the process of change.

In the last book of Ovid's *Metamorphoses* some four hundred lines are given to the teachings of Pythagoras.[36] Ovid presents the chief doctrine of Pythagoras as the transmigration of souls, with its corollary of vegetarianism – since migrating souls might relocate in any of the animal forms. Embedded in Ovid's account of this doctrine is a celebration of the universal principle of change with its corollaries of decay and renewal, variety and flux, disintegration and recombination. Spenser is not interested in vegetarianism but he is exceedingly interested in Ovid's climactic celebration of change or metamorphosis.

[36] A religious philosopher of the sixth century B.C. A Pythagorean school, based upon his sayings and the books attributed to him, flourished well into the fourth century B.C.

But while Ovid emphasizes the creative aspects of change — renewal, variety, and recombination, Spenser personifies change and begins by stressing her destructive power — the decay, loss, and disintegration she causes, and only then lets her display her presidency over all the natural, orderly processes of renewal and variety-producing change. Ovid shows a kind of stoic, secular confidence in the ultimate balance of the cosmos:

> What we call birth
> Is the beginning of a difference,
> No more than that, and death is only ceasing
> Of what had been before. The parts may vary,
> Shifting from here to there, hither and yon,
> And back again, but the great sum is constant.[37]

The *Two Cantos*, though, do not leave an impression that "the great sum is constant". For Spenser the tensions between Mutabilitie's destructiveness and creativity, between her threatening powers and her various beauties, remain in themselves disturbing and tiring. The fact that Nature makes a judgment against Mutabilitie and confirms "Jove in his imperiall see" does not leave us with the sense of a settled confidence in the ultimate constancy of the great sum. In a way Mutabilitie only loses her case because of a logical technicality: she would have to become something other than she is, that is to say, immutability, in order to be awarded what she claims. In every other respect her case sounds much better than Jove's. She argues it with energetic skill and presents it with orderly brilliance, by pageant. Confronted by her, Jove is reduced to a mumbling bully and the other planetary gods to a huddle of anxious steers. She seems to command the entire action and at the conclusion of the hearing all her present powers, which are as great as she says they are, remain to her. She is one of Spenser's most exuberant, dynamic creations. In the *Two Cantos* only Nature gives off more authority. The two-stanza fragment is not so much an affirmation of an ultimate limit to change as a personal cry of longing for the entire displacement

[37]From Ovid's *Metamorphoses*, trans. Rolfe Humphries (Bloomington: Indiana University Press, 1955).

of change-in-time. At this moment and in this particular mood, at least, the poet looks to exactly what Nature said would happen to Mutabilitie if she were to have things all her own way; he longs for an abstract, eternal stability as against the present actuality of unceasing restlessness in change (vii, 59, 3–5).

In Canto vi, stanzas 38 to 55, Spenser tells a story of the wood-god Faunus and the nymph Molanna. This episode is not as digressive as it looks. It answers in several ways to the larger story of the *Two Cantos*; it is another example of the small variation upon a larger theme, of Spenser's fondness for giving us the whole in a part. First, this episode represents a small debt to Ovid within the larger, general debt: the story of Faunus is based roughly upon Ovid's tale of the hunter Actaeon in Book III of the *Metamorphoses*. Second, there is the rehearsal, in miniature, of an unlooked for intrusion upon the preserve of a god, followed by a trial and the delivery of a verdict. Neither in the larger story nor in the small episode do the offending intruders come off too badly. And in neither case do the winners – the planetary gods – come off too well: in the one, they are reduced to bewildered livestock; in the other, Diana is likened to an outraged dairy-wife. All in all the gods are thrown into a pretty severe state of anxiety. Most important, however, is the way in which the Faunus episode repeats the tension between the power and limited good of mutability, on the one hand, and, on the other, its destructive, wasteful effects. Putting the classical Diana among the unfallen beauties of Ireland, Spenser in effect retells the story of the Fall, complete with temptation and expulsion. He tells why the Irish garden was abandoned by the goddess to become a wilderness overrun by wolves. True, Faunus gets off with only some loss of dignity and the scare of his life, and Molanna, though changed, is united with her reluctant lover as Faunus had promised she would be. But the main point of the episode is to reinforce the theme of harmful change by recounting how Arlo, once the fairest hill, "Was made the most unpleasant and most ill". And the nature and effects of this fall are very much the same as those attributed to Mutabilitie herself right at the beginning of the same canto.

Amoretti (1595)

The *Amoretti* is a collection of sonnets. At one time the term "sonnet" could be applied to any short poem, or lyric, amenable to being set to music. By the middle of the sixteenth century, though, the term was more commonly limited to mean short poems with fourteen decasyllabic lines, using one or another of a definite pattern of rhyme-schemes. The sonnet, in this limited and now usual sense, was brought into English literature mainly by Thomas Wyatt (1503–42) and Henry Howard, Earl of Surrey (*c.* 1517–47). The chief models for both Wyatt and Surrey were Italian sonnets, particularly those of Francesco Petrarca (1304–74). Wyatt generally followed the structure of his Italian models quite closely; he used five sets of rhymes, sometimes only four, and divided his sonnets, Italian style, into two parts: the octave (eight lines) and the sestet (six lines). Though he closed his sonnets with rhyming couplets, these were usually very much a part of the sestet – not set off strongly from it. Surrey was more free with his models and evolved what has since been called the "English" sonnet, or the Shakespearean sonnet, because Shakespeare used it with such huge success. Surrey tended to use seven sets of rhymes. Also, he moved his sonnets through three quatrains and a concluding couplet which was often set off quite distinctly from the rest of the poem, serving as a comment, summary, or unexpected twist on what had gone before. The sonnets in Spenser's *Amoretti* owe something to both Wyatt and Surrey, as well as to the ultimate Italian models. Spenser goes back to Wyatt's five sets of rhymes though he uses a different, even more elaborate, pattern of rhyme schemes; but he follows Surrey's division of four quatrains and a concluding couplet distinctly set off from the rest of the poem. On the whole the Spenserian sonnet can best be described as a modification of Surrey's "English" version.

Most sonnets can be classified as lyrics. That is, they can be classed among those short poems that usually imitate a moment of intensely felt emotion. The typical brevity of a lyric is quite natural: it is a function, or formal expression, of the intensity of the emotion being celebrated – since intensity and duration are not normally co-existent qualities. Its tone is almost always personal, as distinct from impersonal or social. Characteristically it offers a minimum in the way of explicit locale or narrative situation. Trying as it does to seize the brief, intense moment, the typical lyric establishes hardly any history and projects hardly any future. These are generalities, of course. In Elizabethan times, as always, the sonnet was put to public purposes by all sorts of people, including Spenser. While some sonnets are not lyrics at all, but tiny narrative poems, travelogues, and so forth, most are in the lyric class and by the 1580s the sonnet had become domesticated in England primarily as a popular, highly refined instrument for imitating all possible modulations within the emotion of love. The sonnets in *Amoretti* are not exceptional in their theme; they are love lyrics even when Spenser is giving rivals or calumniators the rough side of his tongue.

A single sonnet can do brief, intense justice to an intense moment of emotion. Since it cannot, without tending to defeat itself, run too many intensities together or play upon too many of love's subtleties at once, the English sonneteers domesticated not only the sonnet but the sonnet-cycle as well. Sonnet-cycles allow for intensity within carefully controlled duration; they allow for the arresting moment within a developing and sometimes quite dramatic situation. Occasionally the personal tone of a collection of sonnets begins to shed a deposit of autobiography. But this deposit is incidental — incidental because any good set of sonnets will be self-sufficient. The enjoyment of it will not depend upon our knowing much about the author; its success as poetry will not depend upon how faithfully it squares with the historical facts of the author's life. No author of a sonnet-cycle is committed, even incidentally, to writing versified autobiography. It so happens that the *Amoretti* does deposit some autobiography. Sonnet 74, for instance, celebrates the three Elizabeths in Spenser's life: mother, queen, and (perhaps) wife-to-be. But even here we have to be careful; we are by no means sure, for example, that the lady of Spenser's cycle represents throughout the same, actual, original figure. This autobiographical uncertainty may render his sonnets disappointing as history but it has nothing to do with their excellence as love poems. In contrast to the *Amoretti*, Shakespeare's sonnet-cycle deposits practically no verifiable autobiography; and again, this fact says nothing about its excellence as poetry.

Spenser's sonnet-cycle is among the most obviously conventional of all his works. Conventional here does *not* mean unimaginative, unoriginal, or otherwise undistinguished. A convention is simply a widely agreed upon, persistently effective instrument of articulation and communication. All kinds of authors, of all shades of quality, use conventions. Bad authors may cheapen or blunt a convention; good authors may ennoble, refine, or even transfigure it. In Spenser's age the sonnet-cycle was a virile, pan-European convention, a persistently effective instrument for imitating the experiences of love. When he chose to use this convention Spenser produced a sonnet-cycle rivalled only by Sidney's *Astrophel and Stella* (published posthumously, 1591) and surpassed only by Shakespeare's cycle (1609).

Within the major convention of the sonnet-cycle there were various sub-conventions that Spenser used. One of these is the exploration and expression of the emotions of love using imagery of the hunt. In the course of the *Amoretti* the image of the beloved shifts from one of a beautiful but dangerous and ruthless beast of prey to one of a deer which escapes pursuit but eventually turns back and allows itself to be taken by the hunter. The image of the lover shifts from one of a helpless prey to one of a hunter who, in the moment of greatest discouragement, finds that the yet wild deer has come of its own accord to give itself into his hand. This sub-convention is a versatile device for exploring and celebrating several aspects of love: the ironic complexities in the roles of pursuer and pursued as between the sexes; the elements of raw power and extreme vulnerability in sexual attraction; and the not-so-easy tension in remaining oneself while at the same time belonging deeply to someone else.

The sub-convention of love as a military campaign or siege is another instrument of discovery and expression used in the *Amoretti*. "The battle of the sexes" is a metaphor belonging to this sub-convention, which is so ancient, lively, and well known that it hardly needs further comment. Spenser uses it with chivalric seriousness in the *Amoretti*. Shakespeare uses it with excruciatingly ironic effect in *Othello*; Pope uses it playfully in

The Rape of the Lock; and (in case anyone thinks it has gone out of fashion) Norman Mailer uses it with baleful relentlessness in the technopolitan jungles of *An American Dream*.

One more sub-convention used by Spenser is the casting of love as a religious experience. By this sub-convention the Scriptures and Christian devotional literature supply a good deal of the lover's terminology. Here we may recall the courtly love convention with which we have already dealt at some length in the context of *The Faerie Queene*. Most of the features of Courtly Love are quite plainly to be seen in the *Amoretti* and we mention it again only to point out a couple of changes Spenser makes in transposing Courtly Love into the scheme of his sonnet cycle. First, although courtly love language is markedly religious it sometimes loses its peculiarly Christian flavour. In using the courtly love convention Spenser invariably retains a specifically Christian flavour. Sonnet 68 celebrates Easter, for example, and does so in a way which makes it quite clear that Christian theology informs Spenser's understanding of love. He understands divine love to be the true basis of human love and he understands human love between the sexes to be a model, a foretaste, of divine love. Second, in the courtly love convention love often becomes almost entirely idealized; the lover's devotion to his beloved becomes more and more refined towards love of Love itself. The Spenserian lover is never only in love with Love. The earthy sensuality of his feelings is not consistently idealized, sublimated, or otherwise rarefied. In Spenser's use of the convention the experience of the lover is neither over-idealized nor libertine; it is devoted and refined but with the expectation that the outcome will be marriage and gratification of sexual desire.

Epithalamion (1595)

The *Epithalamion* is Spenser's song in honour of his own wedding. It is the most famous of his shorter poems and perhaps the best known marriage-ode in the language. Ever since its publication in 1595 it has excited admiration for its technical virtuosity, its felicitous blend of classical and Christian motifs, its easy mastery of harmonious tension between solemnity and exuberance, delicacy and desire. Age cannot wither it, nor the custom of innumerable anthologies stale its infinite variety.

The wedding, by which society bears witness to the guarantee of its own perpetuation, is one of the most ancient rituals. And another reason for the success of the *Epithalamion* is that it renders with such exact, fluent sensibility the sub-rituals which make up a whole wedding: the ceremonial preparation and entry of the bride; the wedding procession; the marriage service itself, followed by the marriage feast; the delicate moment when cheery public ritual gives way to private sacrament. The mood of the poem is by turn ceremonious, imperious, worshipful, riotous, sensual, and prayerful. As might be expected from its ritual power, the *Epithalamion* also lives by its drama; although it rehearses the events of a wedding day, it is dramatic rather than simply narrative in mode. The bridegroom speaks throughout, summoning and dismissing attendants, encouraging his bride in the middle of the marriage service, directing the wedding caterers, and invoking the gods. In a sense the whole is a brilliantly handled dramatic monologue, a monologue whose intent and thrust, however, is outward and inclusive, not introspective and exclusive.

The poem falls most naturally into two parts, with the division signalled by a shift in refrain from "That all the woods them answer and their echo ring" to "The woods no more shal answere, nor your echo ring." The first 295 lines concern the wedding day proper, which is presided over by the sun. They trace the course of the day from early morning to sunset – from impatience for day to impatience with day. The sun (daylight) is Phoebus-Apollo, who is also the god of poets and poetry. The bridegroom-poet symbolically identifies himself with the sun; he asks to become Phoebus for this one day. This wedding is the godlike bridegroom's occasion both in the sense that he is the masculine, assertive element in the union and the maker of the poem. The sun-poet's day is imagined as a riot of colour, sound, and movement complete with flowers, music, dancing, shouting, and feasting. This day is given over to public festivity and joy: marriage is a public, social ritual. The second part of the poem concerns the wedding night, which is presided over by the moon. The moon is Phoebe-Cynthia, who is also the goddess presiding over the conception of children. Spenser's bride is symbolically identified with Phoebe – the feminine counterpart of Phoebus – and also to some extent with Hesperus, the star of Venus. It is the goddess-like bride's occasion because she is the feminine, responsive element in the union and also the co-subject of the poem and the recipient of it as a gift. The prayerful wish for the moon-bride's night is untroubled, unembarrassed privacy and quiet. And the night is given over to private joys and to sleep "when it is time to sleep": marriage is also a most personal sacrament between two individuals.

That, in its barest outline, is the dramatic and symbolic structure of the *Epithalamion*. The poem celebrates marriage as both a public and a private event. But that is not quite all. At the beginning of the poem Spenser brings nature, personified in Nymphs and Hours, right into the wedding celebrations. Throughout the whole poem the heroes and divinities of classical mythology are involved. Right at the centre of things, literally in the middle of the poem (lines 204–41), is the Christian marriage service which has been anticipated in deliberate echoes of the "Song of Solomon" (lines 170–80). Then the poem concludes with the hope that this particular, earthly marriage may eventually add to the number of eternal saints in heaven. Spenser manages this mixture of classical and Christian motifs with no incongruity whatever – a considerable technical feat. But quite apart from this, Spenser by his mixture has been adding a third dimension to his poem, a cosmic, theological dimension. He celebrates marriage not only as a private event but also as a social event; and not only as a social event but also as a divinely ordained event within a loving, universal plan of creation and redemption. He believes, without sentimentality, that marriages are made in heaven.

Prothalamion (1596)

This "spousal verse" is in the classical tradition of epideictic odes, that is, odes of formal homage to great personages. The occasion of this poem is the double wedding of Ladies Elizabeth and Katherine Somerset. But Spenser takes this wedding as an occasion also to praise three other great personages: the Earl of Leicester, deceased, but formerly a patron of Spenser; the Earl of Essex, who became patron enough at least to bear the costs of Spenser's funeral; and Queen Elizabeth herself. Marriages involving such a family as the Somersets were state occasions, and the convention of praising a statesman like Essex, or the Queen herself – the virgin bride of England in whom the realm was personified and under whose benign auspices such marriages took place – was natural enough to the *Prothalamion*. Spenser uses other conventions too. One is to heighten his compliments by equating his subjects, metaphorically, with mythical figures: the two brides are swans whiter even than the Jovian swan who ravished Leda; the two bridegrooms are the Dioscuri, the twin sons of Jove. Again, within the spousal song itself there is a special, set-piece song of praise and well-wishing like, for example, the song in praise of Elisa in the "Aprill" poem of *The Shepheardes Calender*.

This piece of formal homage with its conventional, stately, mellifluous praise of great ones sounds as if it should be fairly impersonal and disinterested. In fact it is not. The figure of the poet is firmly if unobtrusively present not only in the beautiful, first-person murmur that concludes each stanza but also at the opening of the poem and again in the eighth stanza. The singer and his situation open the poem and are then merged with, or caught up into, the festive goings-on. He then re-emerges as the aquatic procession reaches "mery London, my most kyndly Nurse", only to merge again with the climactic praise of Essex, Queen Elizabeth, and the betrothal ceremony.

It is almost as if Spenser were blending two conventions, the formal praise of great persons with the elegiac dream-vision. "Almost" because in this poem the melancholy, discouraged poet-figure does not actually fall asleep and dream the rest of the poem. But the way in which he is caught up out of his own troubles into another theme is like enough to the movement from oppressed wakefulness to visionary dreaming that occurs in elegiac dream-visions. At any rate Spenser certainly creates two moods in this poem, the festive and the elegiac. The effect is pleasing if unusual. The mood of celebration dominates the lyric situation but only as a reverie-like holiday from the singer's own troubles. To appreciate Spenser's use of these two apparently incompatible moods, we must remember his conviction that the poet is about the Queen's and country's business just as much as any nobleman, counsellor, or soldier. To him, the composition of a poem like *The Faerie Queene* is as much an affair of state as a Somerset wedding or the recent expedition led by Essex against Cadiz.[38] And London is no more the centre of affairs for high nobility than she is the life and nourishment of the poet and his noble work of poetry. The singer's discouragement, his plaintive mood, stem from a feeling that his contributions to the realm have not attracted their due attention and reward. If his discouraged complaining seems to us inappropriate or graceless we should at least remember that Spenser was not afflicted by silly assumptions about art having nothing to do with "real" life. The only question here is whether or not the note of discouraged complaint is out of place in this particular poem. In attempting both a festive and an elegiac mood Spenser did indeed pose himself a problem of fair difficulty. Some critics, while allowing that the skills and beauties of this poem rival those of the *Epithalamion*, have argued that he did not really bring it off. But on the grounds that there are genuine thematic, even dramatic, links between the poem's two moods, and that his own problems do not becloud his responsive homage to the happiness of those more fortunate, I think it can be argued that he did.

Fowre Hymnes (1596)

The following remarks are clustered around the difficulties in the way of reading all four hymns as closely related parts of a single poem. Spenser himself raises these difficulties both in his dedicatory letter and in the text of the poetry itself. In the letter he plays down the first two hymns as misguided and misguiding products of his youth. He also claims to have made some attempt to call them in, to suppress them. Since too many copies of this first pair of hymns were "scattered abroad" for them to be effectively suppressed, he has by way of amendment and retraction written "in stead of those two Hymnes of earthly or naturall love and beautie, two others of heavenly or celes-

[38]Spenser refers to this expedition in the first half of stanza 9.

tiall". In the second stanza of the third hymn, Spenser seems to be explicitly repudiating his first two hymns.

If Spenser really regretted those first two hymns why did he perpetuate them in print? One answer has been that he must have doctored his original version of them before publishing them in the set as we have it now. It must then be the original, undoctored version that he regrets in his letter and repudiates at the beginning of the third hymn. This is possible though it is perhaps a little strange that none of the numerous copies of the original version "scattered abroad" has survived. Besides, in his letter Spenser does not mention changing the first two hymns. He uses the word "amendment", which denotes both changes and making amends; but, as he puts it, he is making changes and amendment by the addition of two heavenly hymns – not by offering a revised version of the earthly ones. It is true that he uses the phrase "in stead of" but – obviously – the second pair of hymns has not displaced the first. Spenser wanted all four hymns together, and it does not really sound as if he changed the text of the first two.

The problem remains of how seriously we are to take his statements of regret and retraction. These must be taken into account, even if in the end they are not taken too seriously, because our attitude to them will affect our whole reading of the *Fowre Hymnes*. If we emphasize the notes of remorse, we shall tend to read the second pair of hymns as a strong counter-balance, or antidote, to the first. We shall find an entirely unresolved tension if not an actual contrast between the first and second pair. If we soft-pedal the notes of remorse, we shall tend to read the heavenly hymns as a complement or fulfilment of the earthly. There is a quite respectable excuse for this soft-pedalling. All through the Middle Ages and well into the Renaissance many an author publicly offered his regrets for all or part of his work. As far as it is possible to tell, not all these retractions were expressions of genuine regret or repentance. Some simply recorded an evolution to a later, perhaps wiser view of life; others were a kind of formal sop thrown to moralistic critics, real or imagined; others again seem to have been a literary ploy designed to give the work in question a retroactive twist, an ironic or mock-serious dimension. Some no doubt contained elements of all these motives. So many retractions were made that it has become customary to think of them as conventional and it is often hard to decide, in any given case, just what weight to give them.

In Spenser's case, the retraction probably has something of all three motives. The first, least important motive is to reassure the two friendly countesses to whom he dedicates his hymns while he goes ahead and prints the first two anyway. The second, more important motive is to express genuine regret for the way in which the first two hymns apparently roused misgivings about Spenser's purpose and character as they circulated by themselves in manuscript form. And surely one meaning of his dedicatory letter is that he fully expects the publication of all four hymns to allay such misgivings. The third, most important motive is to give a conventional signal that the whole set of hymns is going to record, to imitate, a kind of experience which in itself contains certain unavoidable tensions. Our hypothesis will be that there are tensions, but no disruptive contrasts between the first and second pair of hymns.

The *Fowre Hymnes* is a love poem, a philosophical-religious love poem. At least three things make it this particular kind of love poem. First, its argument clearly rests upon metaphysical and theological propositions. Second, the content of this argument has a good deal to do with the poem's actual tone and shape. Third, at least part of the poem's intent is to make a demonstration, or bring about conviction. Spenser's over-all imitation of certain love experiences is more impressive than the quality of particular arguments he uses; he is a poet, not a philosopher or theologian. But in the *Fowre Hymnes* argument is part of imitation and therefore we must look at the sort of philosophical and religious equipment he is using.

Spenser's philosophical equipment comes from a fund of commonplace Renaissance ideas of love derived ultimately from Plato. For such ideas the two most important Platonic sources were the *Symposium*, or *Dinner Party* (c. 385 B.C.), and the *Phaedrus* (c. 370 B.C.). Both these philosophical dialogues were concerned with the nature, dynamics, and effects of love. So many later commentators interpreted Plato in so many ways that it is extremely difficult to describe accurately Renaissance

Platonism as Spenser found it. Nevertheless, it is possible to follow him as he goes over this large, unsystematic fund of ideas, selecting what is useful to him for the purposes of the *Fowre Hymnes*. Two texts of Renaissance Platonism were most useful to him: a long commentary on the *Symposium* by Marsilio Ficino (1433–99) and the fourth part of *The Courtier* by Baldassare Castiglione (1478–1529), whose book achieved enormous popularity in England through Thomas Hoby's translation of 1561. Directly and indirectly such texts as these provided Spenser with a set of ideas concerning, so to speak, the pure theory of love. Love is a primal, creative force in the universe; it expresses itself in a superabundance or overflow of creative activity. Love's creativity brings warmth, order, and beauty out of the cold anarchy of chaos. In the eternal, spiritual state in which Love dwells, Beauty, Goodness, and Wisdom are essentially the same; they are the Forms, or Ideas, of a single principle, a spirit often called "the One". Love is often defined as the desire for Beauty, the drive towards Beauty. Hence it is also the drive towards Goodness, Wisdom, and – ultimately – union with the One.

Spenser uses another set of ideas concerning, as it were, the practice of love, the operation of love within the human condition. Among the beings created by Love were immortal human souls. These souls were originally in a state of beatitude, that is, in the close presence of the eternal One. There they were hardly distinct from the divine Goodness, Wisdom, and Beauty which they contemplated. But they suffered a fall, or separation, into the world of time where they are to some extent imprisoned in mortal bodies. The human soul is nevertheless still capable of apprehending the eternal forms. The process of apprehension is through either direct inspiration or the careful exercise of intellectual contemplation, or both. In any case it is love that inspires and love that provides the grounds of contemplation. Love is thus the means whereby the human soul may begin the long, difficult process of reunion with the One from which it finds itself divided. Awakening in his soul as the desire for physical beauty, Love not only reminds the lover of his original, eternal home but also puts him on the way to recovering that home. The stages on this way were often described metaphorically as the Platonic ladder of love. Here, briefly, is a composite account of this ladder as found in such Renaissance documents as the fourth book of Castiglione's *Courtier*: (1) the lover is visually attracted by the physical beauty of his lady; (2) out of this attraction there grows a process of idealization and purification in which the lover's rational soul moves from contemplating this beauty for its own sake to forming an idea of universal beauty; (3) the lover realizes that both his soul and the idea it now entertains are informed with power and beauty; he realizes that this is because they are both reflections, however brokenly, of eternal Beauty itself; (4) he then ascends from the desire of this rarefied, idealized beauty to the contemplation of its heavenly original; (5) he finally regains beatitude in the close presence of the divine One. The Platonic ladder helps to express a doctrine of love as a continuing, divine strategy of recovery and reunion.

Spenser's theological equipment for the *Fowre Hymnes* is simply orthodox Christian doctrine. This comes most clearly to the surface in the third hymn, which is a meditation on the Incarnation: its cause, its occurrence, and its consequences. God is love and, in the energy of his love, created a divine race of angels. A fair number of these angels tried to repudiate their dependent, creaturely nature and so disenfranchised themselves from heaven. God's loving creativity made good this loss by calling man and his new, paradisal world into being. Man in his turn played at being God, so he too forfeited beatitude and fell into a separation from God and from his first, proper home. But God's loving activity again manifested itself, this time in the Incarnation. This event demonstrates what divine love is like. It should kindle man's repentance in reawakening responsive human love; it becomes the means of redemption, the divine strategy for a recovery of beatitude.

In writing the *Fowre Hymnes* Spenser obviously selected the most pronounced coincidences between his philosophical and theological equipment. Philosophy provides the dominant terminology for the first pair of hymns, Christian theology the dominant terminology for the second. Both supply him with an argument about divine and human love set in a cycle of creation, fall, separation, recovery, and reunion. This is a strong clue that all four hymns should be read as a single poem. Few Renaissance authors would have felt obliged to stress *either* Platonism *or* Christian theology. (The whole point of much of Ficino's work, for example, was to reconcile the two.) Spenser shared with most Renaissance authors an assumption that there was an affinity between Platonism and Christian philosophy, and he expressed this assumption by Christianizing his Platonism.

All four hymns imitate the initiative of divine love and the response of human love. The human lover undergoes an experience which, as he comes to realize more and more clearly, is grounded in the creativity of the divine lover himself. The hymns also imitate the human lover's whole experience, understood as a process tending towards reunion with the divine lover. This, too, suggests that *Fowre Hymnes* may be read as a single poem. In the first hymn the divine lover is celebrated under his Platonic name, Eros, the creator-god of physical desire. The human lover's response is one of helpless surrender to the overmastering power of love. Here the terms of Renaissance Platonism are mingled with those of Courtly Love, because the lover comes to understand his pains and difficulties as agents in a refining, ennobling process. If we are looking for the Platonic ladder, this first hymn also records the lover's ascent through the first step (lines 120 ff.) to the second (lines 184–96). The second hymn celebrates the divine lover under another Platonic name, Venus, the creator-goddess of beauty. The lover responds to the attraction of his lady's beauty – her physical beauty and her inner, moral beauty. And he comes to understand that all her beauties are teaching him something about eternal Beauty itself. This hymn goes over the second step of the Platonic ladder again before coming to the third (lines 211–24).

The hymn to Heavenly Love celebrates the divine lover as the Christian God whose loving activity appears in both creation and redemption. He made men as rational beings who could love him in beatitude and, when they lost beatitude, he made possible its recovery. In this hymn the human lover contemplates the Incarnation wherein the divine-human lover undergoes a redemptive trial for his sake and on his behalf. And in contemplating this he comes to grasp the possibility of beatitude in his loving response to the divine lover's redemptive activity. The fourth hymn celebrates God's loving activity by reviewing the whole of creation in its ascending orders of beauty and grandeur. This review raises the human lover to a final, almost inexpressible vision of the possibility of recovered bliss. The climax of the *Fowre Hymnes* imitates a visionary reunion with the god of love, the absolute, eternal source of all Beauty, Goodness, and Wisdom.

Having sketched the matter of Spenser's imitation, we should turn briefly to his manner of deploying it. Here, it seems, is the decisive clue that the four hymns are not a fractured set; they not only may be, but should be, read as a single poem. Spenser deploys his verse in a series of recapitulations. The first movement of the set is a hymn to creation and love which brings the human lover to the second step of the Platonic ladder. The next hymn celebrates creation again and recapitulates the lover's attainment to the second Platonic step before leaving him at the third. But this hymn of beauty does not stop there; instead of readying the lover for the next step up, it firmly returns him to the first, that is, to the attractiveness of his lady's physical beauties. The third movement of the set is yet another hymn to loving creativity. Here the human lover's purifying, testing experience of the first two hymns is recapitulated and definitively amplified in the divine lover's incarnation. This "descent" into humanity also echoes and amplifies the human lover's return to the first step of the Platonic ladder earlier on. Seen against these large recapitulative rhythms, lines 8 to 14 of the third hymn are not necessarily the announcement of a complete break with what has gone before. They are rather the signal that a new element, best expressed in Christian terms, is about to enter the same process with which the first two hymns are concerned. It is still the human lover's intensifying response to divine love that is being imitated. Moreover, the earlier Platonic terminology is not entirely abandoned. In the last stanza of the third hymn it is clearly present, though Christianized.

Thus, the rhythm established by the first three hymns is not one of a series of straightforwardly linear, ascending movements. It is a rhythm of strongly recapitulative movements. Each of the second and third hymns, while reaching higher than its predecessor, also turns back and recapitulates it – as if reaffirming and gathering up what has gone before. The three hymns to creating love celebrate a kind of increasing seniority – Eros, Venus, the Christian God. The second hymn amplifies the first; then the third, with God as the grand first cause, gathers up and amplifies the first and the second.

The fourth hymn grandly supersedes the first three, but also affirms them, gathers them up, by exhibiting the results of all this loving creativity in their full splendour. The Platonic Ideas, or Eternal Forms, are there in Spenser's vision of all creation (lines 82–4) and he gives them a high place in the scale of being. The final hymn is an inspired meditation, an ecstatic contemplation leading to a visionary affirmation of recovered beatitude. This last great recapitulation lifts the lover to what is his original and his ultimate home: the close presence of Sapience in the bosom of God. Sapience, though feminine, is an image of God-the-Son "by whom all things were made"; she is also Spenser's image for the divine unity of Beauty, Goodness, and Wisdom made visible. Even at this climactic moment, Spenser's Renaissance Platonism is gathered up in and fused with his Christian theology. The *Fowre Hymnes* does not fall apart in the middle. The poem's master rhythm is not one-two, one-two; it is not even a simple ascending one-two-three-four. It is more like one, one-two, two-three, four, with the last movement going over, gathering up, and heightening the first three into an astonishingly intense, vibrant climax.

One more thing needs to be said. Even when read as an organic whole, the poem does embody a tension which is not entirely resolved or integrated. Spenser imitates the process whereby a human lover comes to experience the undiluted power of divine love in climactic, inspired moments of longing, meditation, and vision. In such intense moments and from such a heightened perspective even the best of human desire and beauty may appear as insignificant or misleading. At such moments the experience of human love may compare unfavourably with knowledge of divine love. Such notes of unfavourable comparison sound clearly at the end of both the third and fourth hymns and they cannot be dismissed lightly, for in spite of the divine-human incarnation in the third hymn, they do seem to maintain the old dichotomy between human, bodily love and divine, spiritual love. One answer may be that although these tensions indeed appear in such exalted moments of vision, even the most inspired lovers must come back down to earth. Therefore Spenser is only imitating quite accurately the tension that the best of human lovers may sometimes feel. But since Spenser did not choose (except in the second hymn) to imitate the experience of having to come back down to earth, this answer is a bit too neat. A better one, perhaps, is that Spenser unflinchingly imitates a tension in the human situation that even his Christian understanding of love cannot fully resolve. That is, precisely because there is so much divinity in it, human love may give rise to longings which, within the human limitations of this life, it cannot always satisfy.

Historical and Biographical Data

1533–1547   HENRY VIII (King since 1509)

1533   Henry VIII excommunicated. Cranmer made Archbishop of Canterbury. Henry marries Anne Boleyn. Birth of Elizabeth.

1534   Act of Succession. Act of Supremacy styling Henry as "only Supreme Head in earth of the Church of England called *Anglicana Ecclesia*".

1535   Visitation of the monasteries. Execution of Thomas More and John Fisher.

1536   Execution of Anne Boleyn. Henry marries Jane Seymour. New Act of Succession. The Pilgrimage of Grace. Calvin, *Institutio*. Death of Erasmus; Tyndale.

1537   Death of Jane Seymour. Suppression of abbeys. Cranmer, *Institution of a Christian Man*, also known as "The Bishop's Book".

1538   Order to place authorized version of English Bible in every parish church.

1539   Act of Six Articles provides for death penalty on anyone denying Transubstantiation, necessity of auricular confession, and clerical celibacy. Suppression of abbeys continues. Persecution and burning of Protestants continues. The "Great Bible".

1540   Henry invades Scotland. He marries Anne of Cleves; has marriage annulled; marries Catherine Howard. French version of Calvin's *Institutio*.

1542   Execution of Catherine Howard.

1543   Henry marries Catherine Parr. Copernicus, *De Revolutionibus*.

1545   Council of Trent begins.

1546   Death of Luther.

1547   Death of Henry VIII.

1547–1553   EDWARD VI

1547   Accession of Edward VI at age of nine. Somerset becomes Protector. Birth of Cervantes.

1548   Latimer's "Plough Sermon". Nicholas Udall translates Erasmus's Paraphrase of the New Testament. The arrest of Stephen Gardiner.

1549   War with France. Somerset pursues policy of religious toleration; encourages Parliament to repeal the Statutes of Treason and Act of Six Articles. Somerset overthrown by the rising Dudley, Earl of Warwick. *Book of Common Prayer*. Act of Uniformity. Kett's rebellion over enclosures.

1550   Treaty of Boulogne. Removal of Roman Catholic bishops. Cranmer, *Defense of the True Doctrine of the Sacrament*.

1551   Second session of the Council of Trent begins. Treaty of Angers. Dudley created Duke of Northumberland. Coverdale made Bishop of Exeter. Cranmer, *An Answer to Stephen Gardiner*. Robynson's translation of More's *Utopia*.

1552   Execution of Somerset. Revision of 1549 *Book of Common Prayer*. Second Act of Uniformity. Birth of Walter Raleigh(?).
Edmund Spenser born to Elizabeth Spenser of London. The name and occupation of his father is not known, nor is the date of his birth certain – 1553 and 1554 being other possible dates. His family is distantly related to the Spencers, wealthy nobility of Wormleighton (Warwickshire) and Althorp (Northamptonshire).

1553   Death of Edward VI.

1553–1558   MARY TUDOR

1553   Accession of Mary. Voyage of Willoughby and Chancellor. Thomas Wilson, *The Arte of Rhetorique*. Nicholas Udall, *Ralph Roister Doister*(?). More, *A Dialogue of Comfort Against Tribulation*. Death of Rabelais.

1554   The Wyatt Rebellion. Execution of Northumberland's

daughter-in-law, Lady Jane Grey. Queen Mary marries Philip of Spain and reconciles England with Rome but neither resigns the title of "Supreme Head" nor restores Church lands. Coverdale allowed to leave England. Birth of Fulke Greville; Richard Hooker; Philip Sidney.

1555 Latimer and Ridley burnt. Birth of Lancelot Andrewes.

1556 Cranmer burnt. Death of Aretino.

1557 War with France. Stationers' Company incorporated; its Register, while accumulating invaluable records for future researchers, becomes a handy and potent device of royal censorship. Surrey, *Certain Books of Virgil's Aeneis. Courte of Venus*. Tottel, *Songs and Sonnets*, also known as "Tottel's Miscellany". W. Rastell publishes More's English works.

1558 Death of Mary Tudor.

1558–1603   ELIZABETH I

1558 Accession of Elizabeth. Loss of Calais. William Cecil, later Lord Burghley, made Secretary of State. John Knox, *First Blast of the Trumpet against the Monstrous Regiment of Women*. Birth of Robert Greene; Thomas Lodge.

1559 Mary Stuart marries the Dauphin Francis. Treaty of Château-Cambrésis. Death of Henry II of France and accession of Francis II. Revolt in Scotland against French protectorate is assisted by Elizabeth. Matthew Parker made Archbishop of Canterbury. Acts of Uniformity and Supremacy. Second revision of the *Book of Common Prayer*. First extant edition of *Mirror for Magistrates*.

1560 Treaty of Edinburgh. The Geneva Bible. Death of Melanchthon.

1561 Trouble in Ulster over Shane O'Neill's claim to the earldom of Tyrone. Norton and Sackville, *Gorboduc*. Thomas Hoby translates Castiglione's *The Book of the Courtier*. Thomas Norton translates Calvin's *Institutes*. Stow's edition of Chaucer. Birth of Francis Bacon.

1562 Third Session of the Council of Trent begins. Civil war in France. Secret Treaty of Richmond with the Huguenots. Hawkins begins his voyage. Elizabeth's grave illness sharply increases anxieties about the succession. Latimer, *Twenty Seven Sermons*. John Jewel, *Apologia pro Ecclesia Anglicana*. Birth of Lope de Vega.

1562?–69 **Shortly after its foundation in 1561 Spenser enters the Merchant Taylors School. Here he is under the régime of the first headmaster, Richard Mulcaster, a famous educator who has a sturdy patriotic and pedagogic confidence in the vernacular: "I love Rome but London better, I favour Italy but England more, I honour Latin but worship English."**

1563　The Second Book of Homilies. The Thirty-nine Articles. Elizabeth's first Poor Law. John Foxe, *Acts and Monuments*, also known as "Foxe's Book of Martyrs". English surrender at Le Havre.

1564　Treaty of Troyes by which Elizabeth loses all effective claims to Calais. Death of Calvin; Michelangelo; Vesalius. Birth of Galileo; Marlowe; Shakespeare(?).

1565　Mary Queen of Scots creates Darnley Duke of Albany and marries him. Murray's rebellion in Scotland aided by Elizabeth. William Allen, *Defence and Declaration*. Cooper, *Thesaurus Linguae Romanae et Britannicae*. Arthur Golding translates the "Fyrst Fower Bookes" of Ovid's *Metamorphoses*. The Louvain edition of More's Latin works.

1566　Birth of Prince James in Scotland. Renewed anxieties over the English succession; marriage for Elizabeth a major topic of debate in her third Parliament. Murder of Rizzio in Scotland. Shane O'Neill's effective control of Ulster broken by a strong punitive expedition.

1567　Revolt of the Netherlands. Murder of Darnley. Queen Mary marries Bothwell; she is defeated, imprisoned, and deposed. Prince James crowned James VI. William Allen, *Treatise in Defense of the Power of the Priesthood*. Golding publishes translation of Ovid's *Metamorphoses*, I–XV.

1568　Queen Mary escapes, is defeated again, takes refuge in England. Establishment of the English College of Douai.

The "Bishops' Bible". *The Pithy . . . Works of Master Skelton*. Death of Roger Ascham; Coverdale.

1569   Elizabeth imprisons Mary. Mercantile, religious, and political rivalry with Spain becoming increasingly sharp. Northern Rebellion broken; Norfolk imprisoned.

Spenser employed to make some twenty-two brief verse translations for inclusion in a volume of Protestant piety and anti-Catholic propaganda brought out by Jan Van der Noot: *A Theatre wherein be represented as wel the miseries & calamities that follow the voluptuous Worldlings, As also the greate ioyes and plesures which the faithfull do enioy.* **Spenser's reworking of seventeen of these pieces appears twenty-two years later in his** *Complaints*.

1569–1576: **Spenser at Cambridge as a Sizar of Pembroke Hall. Graduates a Bachelor of Arts in 1573 and a Master of Arts in 1576. At Cambridge Spenser forms what is to be a lifelong friendship with Gabriel Harvey (1545–1630), a Fellow of Pembroke Hall, University Praelector in Rhetoric, and Lecturer in Greek. Friendship persists in spite of sharply different temperaments, divergent literary theories and interests, and Harvey's distinct lack of enthusiasm for** *The Faerie Queene*.

At this time Cambridge was one of the intellectual strongholds of an increasingly articulate Puritanism whose exponents were beginning to alarm Elizabeth and her ministers at least as much as the Roman Catholics. During this period occurred the controversy between the parties of Cartwright (1535–1603) and Whitgift (1530?–1604) over Church discipline and doctrine. The *Admonition to Parliament, A Second Admonition* (ascribed to Cartwright), and Whitgift's first reply thereto were all published in 1572. Spenser could have watched from close quarters the process by which Whitgift and his party prevented the Presbyterian Cartwright from receiving the expected award of a Doctorate in Divinity (1570), deprived him of his Professorship in Divinity (1570) and his Fellowship in

Trinity College (1572), and forced him to flee the country to avoid a summons issued by the Ecclesiastical Commissioners for his arrest (1574).

1570   Papal Bull excommunicating and deposing Elizabeth. Roger Ascham, *The Scholemaster*.

1571   Negotiations over the conditions upon which Mary may return to Scotland break down. The Battle of Lepanto. Active consideration of a possible match between Elizabeth and the Duke of Anjou. The Ridolfi Conspiracy. Statutes passed that it is treasonable to declare Elizabeth a heretic or usurper and to introduce or act in accordance with papal Bulls. Death of Jewel. Birth of Keppler.

1572   Treaty of Blois. Massacre of St. Bartholomew. *Admonition to Parliament. A Second Admonition.* Whitgift, *Answer to a Libel entitled an Admonition.* Death of Knox. Birth of John Donne; Ben Jonson.

1573   Siege of La Rochelle. English attempts in Ireland to colonize and pacify continue to go badly, especially in Ulster, Munster, and Connaught. Cartwright, *Reply to an Answer.*

1574   Treaty of Bristol between England and Spain. Walter Travers, *Ecclesiasticae Disciplinae Explicatio* and Cartwright's translation of this work under the title *A Full and Plain Declaration.* Whitgift, *Defence of an Answer.* Birth of Joseph Hall.

1575   Further settlement with Spain over trading rights in Antwerp and English refugees in the Netherlands. Philip II of Spain goes bankrupt. Edmund Grindal made Archbishop of Canterbury. Cartwright, *Second Reply.* Tasso, *Gerusalemme Liberata.* Death of Matthew Parker. Birth of Jacob Boehme; Thomas Heywood(?); John Marston(?); Cyril Tourneur.

1576   Spaniards sack Antwerp. Pacification of Ghent, confirming William of Orange's stadholderate of Holland and Zeeland. Frobisher's voyage begins. Death of Titian.

1577   Don John of Austria, governor of Spanish Netherlands, seizes Namur. Drake's voyage round the world begins.

Opening of Blackfriars Theatre. Cartwright, *The Rest of the Second Reply*. Holinshed, *The First Volume of the Chronicles* and *The Last Volume* . . . Birth of Robert Burton.

1578 Don John has several successes against the army of the States-General. Pressure on Elizabeth to intervene in the Low Countries. The Pope commissions Thomas Stukeley's expedition to Ireland; expedition collapses. Lyly, *Euphues, the Anatomy of Wit*. Birth of William Harvey.

Spenser becomes secretary to John Young, lately elevated to the Bishopric of Rochester. Young had been Master of Pembroke Hall while Spenser was a student there.

1579 Jesuit mission to England. Project of Elizabeth's marriage to the Duke of Anjou re-opened, carried forward, then in effect abandoned. James Fitzmaurice raises Munster against the English. Gosson, *School of Abuse*. Thomas North translates Plutarch's *Lives*.

Evidence is good, but not compelling, that Spenser makes his first marriage, to a certain Machabyas Chylde, on October 27 of this year. Two children come of this marriage: Sylvanus and Katherine. Publication of *The Shepheardes Calender*, dedicated to Philip Sidney.

1580 Collapse of Fitzmaurice's uprising in Munster; systematic devastation of Munster by English. The two Jesuits, Campion and Parsons (Persons), arrive in England. Stow, *Chronicles*. Death of Camoens; Breughel(?). Birth of John Webster(?).

By now Spenser has some connection with the Earl of Leicester and is perhaps in his employ.

Publication – not by Spenser – of some correspondence between Spenser and Harvey. These letters give evidence of Spenser's passing interest in the application of Latin quantitative principles of metre to English verse; also of Spenser's friendly, though not close, relations with Sidney (1554–86) and his circle. The correspondence also refers by title to several works of

Spenser which have not survived; and it shows that by 1580 Spenser was already at work on *The Faerie Queene*.

In the summer of this year Spenser becomes one of the secretaries to the new Lord Deputy of Ireland, Lord Grey of Wilton. Lord Grey arrives at Dublin in August with Spenser presumably among his company. They arrive shortly after a particularly savage passage of the Irish uprisings – the rape of the Desmond lands in Limerick and Kerry.

1581   Duke of Anjou visits England. Secret recusant press established in East Ham, Essex; to help avoid discovery, its products are given the imprint "Douai". Edmund Campion executed. Arthur Hall's translation of the *Iliad*, I–X. Mulcaster, *Positions*. Tasso's *Gerusalemme Liberata*, authorized edition.

Spenser is granted the post of Clerk of the Chancery for Faculties. He holds this post for seven years.

1582   Attempt to assassinate William of Orange. Duke of Parma, new Governor of the Spanish Netherlands, wins several major victories against an ineffective combination of the States-General with the Duke of Anjou. Spanish fleet, under Santa Cruz, defeats a French naval force at Terceira. Allen, *Brief History of the Martyrdom of XII Priests*. Anthony Munday, *The English Roman Life*. The "Rheims" New Testament. Gosson, *Plays Refuted*. Mulcaster, *First Part of the Elementary*.

Spenser leases, for an annual rental of £3, a property called New Abbey in County Kildare, about twenty-five miles from Dublin.

1583   Walsingham sent to Scotland to offset the influence of the anti-English faction there, but fails. Arrest of Throckmorton exposes the Guise conspiracy in favour of Mary. Desmond captured and killed near Tralee. Whitgift made Archbishop of Canterbury (Grindal having been under suspension since 1577). Death of the explorer Humphrey Gilbert; Grindal. Birth of Philip Massinger.

Spenser appointed a Commissioner of Musters for County Kildare. He holds this post for two years.

1584   Mendoza expelled from England. Assassination of William of Orange. Death of the Duke of Anjou. Parma recovers Ypres, Bruges, and Ghent for Spain. Raleigh's first attempt to organize the colony of Virginia. Giordano Bruno, *De l'infinito*. Birth of Francis Beaumont.

Some evidence that in this year Spenser is appointed as Deputy to Ludovick Bryskett, Clerk of the Munster Council.

1585   Secret Treaty of Joinville between Guise of France and Philip of Spain. Elizabeth refuses the proffered sovereignty of the Netherlands but commits an English army, under Leicester, to the campaign against Parma. The Parry Plot; execution of Parry. Mary moved to new quarters and subjected to more and more careful surveillance. John Davis makes his first attempt to find "the north-west passage". Drake's raid on Vigo, the Canaries, the Cape Verde Islands, and the Spanish Indies. Death of Ronsard.

Spenser is appointed Prebendary of Limerick Cathedral.

1586   Battle of Zutphen; death of Philip Sidney. Failure of Leicester's campaign and his return to England. Treaty of Berwick. Babington Plot; trial and execution of Babington. Trial of Mary at Fotheringay Castle. The Holy See contracts to pay Philip of Spain a million crowns if and when he successfully invades England. Kyd's *Spanish Tragedy* performed(?). Knox, *History of the Reformation in Scotland*. Warner, *Albion's England*, I–IV. Birth of John Ford.

1587   William Allen made a Cardinal. The Pope proclaims a Crusade against England. Execution of Mary Queen of Scots. Leicester back in the Netherlands with another English force; he fails again and is recalled. Drake's raid on Cadiz. Beginning of Raleigh's second unsuccessful attempt to establish a colony in Virginia. Marlowe's *Tamburlaine*, Parts I and II, performed. Death of Foxe.

1588   The Armada. Conference between Elizabeth's representatives and Parma at Brussels. Cardinal Allen publishes manifesto calling upon English Catholics to co-operate with invading Spanish forces. Greene, *Pandosto*. "Martin Marprelate", *O Read over Dr. Bridges*. Death of Leicester; Veronese. Birth of Thomas Hobbes.

Late in this year, or early in the next, Spenser occupies Kilcolman, an estate of more than three thousand acres. Spenser's actual grant of possession was passed on October 26, 1590. Kilcolman becomes his home for the rest of his life.

1589   Unsuccessful expedition, led by Drake and Sir John Norreys, against Spain. Several anonymous anti-Marprelate tracts: *Countercuff by Pasquil*; *MarMartin*; *Martin's Months Mind*; *Return of Pasquil*. Cooper, *Admonition to the People of England*. Lyly, *Pap with a Hatchet*. "Martin Marprelate", *Ha' ye any Work for a Cooper?*; *Theses Martinianae*. George Puttenham, *Art of English Poesy*. Nashe, *Anatomy of Absurdity*. Marlowe's *Dr. Faustus* performed(?).

Spenser makes the first of several trips back to London, this time probably in the company of his "Irish" neighbour, Sir Walter Raleigh, and seems, through Raleigh, to have been granted audience with the Queen and to have presented her with *The Faerie Queene*, I–III. The poem is entered in the Stationers' Register by Spenser's publisher, Ponsonby, on December 1.

1590   In France, Henry IV (Henry of Navarre) wins the Battle of Ivry against the Catholic League. Spanish forces reinforce the Catholic League. Sidney, *The Countesse of Pembrokes Arcadia*. Henry Holland, *Treatise Against Witchcraft*.

Spenser publishes the first three books of *The Faerie Queene*. The formal grant of Kilcolman to Spenser could perhaps be the Queen's first gift in response to the presentation and dedication of the poem to her.

1591   Elizabeth aids Henry IV of France against the Spanish-Catholic League coalition; Essex reinforces Dieppe. Increasingly severe measures taken against both Recusants and Puritan dissenters. Shakespeare's *Henry VI* performed(?). Greene, *Notable Discovery of Couzenage*; *Second Part of Coney-Catching*. John Harington's translation of Ariosto, *Orlando Furioso*. Birth of Robert Herrick.

On February 25, Queen Elizabeth grants Spenser a pension for life of £50 annually.

Publication of Spenser's *Daphnaida*, an elegy on Douglas Howard, daughter of Henry Lord Howard; and a collection of poems, some of which had been written earlier but never before published: *Complaints, Containing sundrie Small Poemes of the Worlds Vanitie*. The poems here collected are: *The Ruines of Time*; *The Teares of the Muses*; *Virgils Gnat*; *Prosopopoia, or Mother Hubberds Tale*; *The Ruines of Time: by Bellay*; *Muiopotmos, or The Tale of the Butterflie*; *Visions of the Worlds vanitie*; *Bellayes visions*; *Petrarches visions*. Some of the vanities of which Spenser complains are lack of critical and literary acumen in high places, and the lag between promise and performance when it comes to rewards and patronage. There are contemporary references to parts or all of the *Complaints* being called in, i.e., suppressed, presumably because of the attacks on Lord Burghley in *The Ruines of Time* and *Mother Hubberds Tale*.

1592   Conventicle Act. Essex recalled from France. Opening of Rose Theatre. Greene's *Friar Bacon and Friar Bungay* performed. Marlowe's *Edward II* performed(?). Samuel Daniel, *Delia*. Greene, *Quip for an Upstart Courtier*; *Groatsworth of Wit*. Gabriel Harvey, *Four Letters and certain Sonnets*. Nashe, *Pierce Penniless*; *Strange News*. Warner, *Albion's England*, I–VIII. Death of Greene; Montaigne.

1593   O'Donnell appeals to Philip of Spain, offering his army for a common cause against the English in Ireland. Henry IV of France publicly renounces his protestantism and embraces Roman Catholicism. Attendance at Anglican service enforced on pain of banishment. Agrarian Law of 1563 repealed. Theatres closed.

Michael Drayton, *Idea*. Giffard, *Dialogue concerning Witches*. Richard Hooker, *Of the Laws of Ecclesiastical Polity*, I–IV. Shakespeare, *Venus and Adonis*. Death of Marlowe. Birth of George Herbert; Izaak Walton.

1594   Tyrone starts to treat directly with Spain. First of a series of bad harvests in England. Nashe, *The Unfortunate Traveller*. Shakespeare, *The Rape of Lucrece*. Death of Allen; Mercator; Tintoretto.

Spenser sits as one of the Queen's Justices for the County of Cork.

In June, probably of this year, Spenser is married again, this time to Elizabeth Boyle who is also distantly related to the Spencers of Wormleighton and Althorp. There is one child of this marriage, Peregrine.

1595   Raleigh's voyage to Guiana. Drake and Hawkins both die during an unsuccessful expedition to the West Indies. George Chapman, *Ovid's Banquet of Sense*. Collected edition of Montaigne's *Essais*. Daniel, *Civil Wars*, I–IV. Shakespeare's *Midsummer Night's Dream* performed(?). Sidney, *Defense of Poesie* (also printed by a second publisher as *An Apology for Poetry*). Death of Tasso.

Spenser brings out *Amoretti and Epithalamion* and *Colin Clouts Come Home Againe*. Bound in the same volume with *Colin Clouts* is a group of elegies, of which Spenser's *Astrophel* is the first, mourning the death of Sir Philip Sidney.

1596   Philip of Spain commits considerable supplies of money and munitions to the assistance of O'Donnell and Tyrone. Philip's fleet bearing Spanish soldiery for the "Irish enterprise" is dispersed and decisively crippled by a storm. Essex, Howard, and Vere conduct the assault on Cadiz; the sack of Cadiz, Faro, and Loulé. Shakespeare's *Merchant of Venice* performed(?). John Davies, *Orchestra*. Nashe, *Have with you to Saffron Walden*. Raleigh, *Discovery of Guiana*. Warner, *Albion's England*, I–XII. Thomas Deloney, *The Pleasant History of John Winchcomb*. Death of Peele. Birth of Descartes.

Spenser brings out the first edition of *The Faerie

Queene, IV–VI, together with the second edition of books I–III. Later this year he publishes the *Fowre Hymnes* together with a second edition of *Daphnaida*; and the *Prothalamion*, composed in honour of the double wedding for the Earl of Worcester's two eldest daughters.

1597   Unsuccessful attempt by Essex, Vere, and Raleigh to destroy the Spanish fleet assembling at Ferrol. This fleet, Philip's second armada against England, is dispersed and partially destroyed by a storm. Francis Bacon, *Essays*. Keppler, *Mysterium Cosmographicum*. John Donne writes *The Storm* and *The Calm* as verse-letters. Hooker, *On the Laws of Ecclesiastical Polity*, Book V. James VI (later James I of England), *Demonology*.

1598   Edict of Nantes; end of the French civil war. Bacon, *Essays* (second edition). *Hero and Leander*, as begun by Christopher Marlowe and completed by George Chapman. Jonson's *Every Man in His Humour* performed. Shakespeare's *Much Ado About Nothing* performed(?). John Marston, *The Scourge of Villany*. Thomas Speght's edition of Chaucer. Death of Philip II; Burghley.

Spenser's prose work, *View of the Present State of Ireland*, is entered in the Stationers' Register on April 14. Though circulated in manuscript at this time the *View* is not actually published until 1633.

By June, Tyrone's Great Rebellion is under way; in August he sharply defeats the English at the Battle of the Yellow Ford. In October the rebels move into Munster; Kilcolman is sacked and Spenser, along with many fellow undertakers and settlers, takes refuge in Cork. (About this time, ironically enough, Spenser is recommended for the post of Sheriff of Cork.) In December Spenser carries reports from Lord General Norris to the Privy Council and delivers them at Whitehall on December 24.

1599   Essex sent as Lord Lieutenant to Ireland; after several months of indecisive campaigning he enters into unauthorized parleys with Tyrone and, in an effort to justify his actions before the Queen, returns to London against her explicit orders. Opening of the Globe Theatre. Performances of Dekker's *Shoemakers' Holiday*; Jonson's *Every Man Out of His Humour*; Shakespeare's *Henry V* and *Julius Caesar*. Birth of Cromwell; Velasquez.

On January 13 Spenser dies in Westminster. He is buried in Westminster Abbey, "Nere to Chaucer," according to an early seventeenth century account, "at the charges of the Earl of Essex: his Hearse being carried by Poets, and mournfull Verses and Pomes, throwne into his Tombe". Spenser's "Mutabilitie Cantos", the only surviving, hitherto unpublished parts of *The Faerie Queene*, appeared for the first time in the 1609 edition of the poem – ten years after Spenser's death. The first collected (folio) edition of Spenser's works appeared in 1611.

1600   Battle of Nieuport. Lord Mountjoy appointed Lord Deputy of Ireland. Essex tried by a special commission and deprived of his offices. Foundation of the East India Company. Fortune Theatre opened. Jonson's *Cynthia's Revels* performed. William Gilbert, *De Magnete*. Publication of *England's Helicon* and of *England's Parnassus*. Edward Fairfax translates Tasso's *Gerusalemme Liberata* under the title of *Godfrey of Bouloigne*. Birth of Prince Charles (later Charles I); Calderon. Death of Hooker; Nashe; Giordano Bruno (burnt as a heretic).

1601   Mountjoy suppresses the rebellion in Munster. The Spanish land 3000 men in Ireland but are unable effectively to link up with Tyrone. Unsuccessful attempt by Essex to raise London and the court against the Queen; his trial and execution. Shakespeare's *Merry Wives of Windsor* and *Twelfth Night* performed(?). Jonson's *Poetaster* performed.

1602   Proclamation ordering all Jesuits and secular priests to leave the realm. Consistent English successes against Tyrone. Opening of the Bodleian Library. Shakespeare's

Hamlet entered in the Stationers' Register; *Troilus and Cressida* and *All's Well that Ends Well* performed.

1603   Mountjoy forces the surrender of Tyrone. Florio translates the *Essais* of Montaigne. Jonson's *Sejanus* performed. Death of Cartwright; Gilbert. Death of Elizabeth I in the forty-fifth year of her reign and the accession of James.

Note on the Text

This selection of Spenser's poetry has been arranged so that, wherever possible, every page is a self-contained combination of text, running glossary, and notes. The system is a compromise: it leaves the actual text clear of markings but forfeits the clean-looking page of nothing but text; it tries to offer instant, minimal aid at the bottom of each page in place of more systematic and thorough – but harder to get at – information at the back of the book.

As to the text: thanks are due to the Johns Hopkins Press for permission to use the text of its Variorum Edition of Spenser. The only changes that have been made reflect the modern use of the letters u, v, i, and j; retention of the Elizabethan convention in the case of these letters would seem to impose an entirely gratuitous difficulty upon the modern reader.

As to the glossary: the hope is that readers will be able fairly quickly, and without undue irritation, to train themselves in dropping the eye to the bottom of the page for help with strange words and phrases. The assumption going with this hope is that readers will hold themselves to the text at a fairly high pitch of concentration for fairly lengthy stretches of time, thus coming to know the difficult words and becoming more and more independent of the glossary. Difficult words in the shorter poems are glossed up to three or four times and with each new poem the glossary starts over again; in Book One of *The Faerie Queene* difficult words, especially those used in more than one sense, may be glossed as many as eight times. In the shorter poems the numbers in the glossary refer to lines of the text; in *The Faerie Queene* the glossary first gives the number of the stanza, then (in brackets) the number of the relevant line. For the most part the glossary offers simple synonyms; but for some strange words and phrases it will offer a paraphrase.

As to the notes: these are not used for interpretation. Some interpretation has been included in the Introduction but most of it has been hopefully left to lecture-room exchanges between teachers and students. As a rule, then, the notes are used either to give explanations or paraphrases that are too long to be handled in the glossary or to give information about names, places, and events – especially concerning the body of classical mythology.

Acknowledgements are due to G. P. Putnam's Sons for permission to quote from *The Bestiary*, as translated and edited by T. H. White for Capricorn Books; and to Rolfe Humphries and the Indiana University Press for permission to quote from Mr. Humphries's translation of Ovid's *Metamorphoses*. It is a pleasure to acknowledge the free use I have made of Jay Macpherson's elegant and usefully arranged retelling of the classical myths, *Four Ages of Man* (Macmillan of Canada, 1962). Finally, thanks are due to my colleagues Jean MacIntyre, for advice on terms in archery, and Anne Wilson, for a suggestion about Spenser's contribution to the literature on the lechery of goats.

THE
Shepheardes Calender

Conteyning twelve Æglogues proportionable
to the twelve monethes.

Entitled
TO THE NOBLE AND VERTU
ous Gentleman most worthy of all titles
both of learning and chevalrie M.
Philip Sidney.
(∵)

AT LONDON

Printed by Hugh Singleton, dwelling in
Creede Lane neere unto Ludgate at the
signe of the golden Tunne, and
are there to be solde.
1579.

TO HIS BOOKE

Goe little booke: thy selfe present,
As child whose parent is unkent:
To him that is the president
Of noblesse and of chevalree,
And if that Envie barke at thee,   5
As sure it will, for succoure flee
   Under the shadow of his wing,
And asked, who thee forth did bring,
A shepheards swaine saye did thee sing,
All as his straying flocke he fedde: 10
And when his honor has thee redde,
Crave pardon for my hardyhedde.
   But if that any aske thy name,
Say thou wert base begot with blame:
For thy thereof thou takest shame.   15
And when thou art past jeopardee,
Come tell me, what was sayd of mee:
And I will send more after thee.

                           Immeritô

2. **unkent:** unknown.
9. **swaine:** boy.
12. **hardyhedde:** boldness.
15. **For thy:** because; **thereof:** of which.

19. **Immeritô:** i.e., Unworthy (Spenser's name for himself).

TO THE MOST EXCELLENT AND LEARNED BOTH
Orator and Poete, Mayster Gabriell Harvey, his

VERIE SPECIAL AND SINGULAR GOOD FREND E. K. COMMEN- §
DETH THE GOOD LYKING OF THIS HIS LABOUR,
AND THE PATRONAGE OF THE
NEW POETE

Uncouthe unkiste, Sayde the olde famous Poete
Chaucer: whom for his excellencie and wonderfull
skil in making, his scholler Lidgate, a worthy scholler
of so excellent a maister, calleth the Loadestarre of
our Language: and whom our Colin clout in his   *5*
Æglogue calleth Tityrus the God of shepheards, comparing hym to the worthines of the Roman Tityrus
Virgile. Which proverbe, myne owne good friend
Ma. Harvey, as in that good old Poete it served well
Pandares purpose, for the bolstering of his baudy   *10* §
brocage, so very well taketh place in this our new
Poete, who for that he is uncouthe (as said Chaucer)
is unkist, and unknown to most men, is regarded but
of few. But I dout not, so soone as his name shall
be sounded in the tromp of fame, but that he shall be
come into the knowledg of men, and his worthines   *15*
not onely kiste, but also beloved of all, embraced of

1. **Uncouthe:** unknown.
3. **making:** writing poetry,
   composing; **scholler:**
   pupil.
5. **Colin clout:** i.e., another
   of Spenser's names for
   himself.
11. **brocage:** pimping; **taketh
    place in:** applies to.
12. **for that:** because.

§ *good frend E.K.:* The identity of E.K. has not been proven. Some
have suggested Edward Kirke (or Kerke), who was a contemporary
of Spenser's at Pembroke Hall, Cambridge; others have suggested that
E.K. is a pseudonym for Spenser himself. It seems most likely that
E.K. was an actual person, other than Spenser, who collaborated with
him on the critical apparatus of the poem.
§ *Pandares purpose:* The reference is to Chaucer's *Troilus and Criseyde*
(Cressida) in which Pandarus, Cressida's uncle, becomes the go-
between for Troilus and Cressida.

the most, and wondred at of the best. No lesse I
thinke, deserveth his wittinesse in devising, his pithi-
nesse in uttering, his complaints of love so lovely,   *20*
his discourses of pleasure so pleasantly, his pastorall
rudenesse, his morall wisenesse, his dewe observing
of Decorum everye where, in personages, in seasons,
in matter, in speach, and generally in al seemely sim-
plycitie of handeling his matter, and framing his   *25*
words: the which of many thinges which in him be
straunge, I know will seeme the straungest, the words
them selves being so auncient, the knitting of them
so short and intricate, and the whole Periode and
compasse of speache so delightsome for the round-   *30*
nesse, and so grave for the straungenesse. And firste
of the wordes to speake, I graunt they be something
hard, and of most men unused, yet both English, and
also used of most excellent Authors and most famous
Poetes. In whom whenas this our Poet hath bene   *35*
much traveiled and throughly redd, how could it be,
(as that worthy Oratour sayde) but that walking in
the sonne although for other cause he walked, yet
needes he mought be sunburnt; and having the sound
of those auncient Poetes still ringing in his eares, he   *40*
mought needes in singing hit out some of theyr tunes.
But whether he useth them by such casualtye and
custome, or of set purpose and choyse, as thinking
them fittest for such rusticall rudenesse of shepheards, eyther for that theyr rough sounde would   *45*
make his rymes more ragged and rustical, or els because such olde and obsolete wordes are most used
of country folke, sure I think, and think I think not

19. **devising:** skill in the in-
    vention and shaping of
    his matter.
22. **rudenesse:** lack of polish.
23. **Decorum:** i.e., the prin-
    ciple of suiting all matters
    of style to the subject.
29. **Periode:** deployment of
    clauses and sentences.
30. **compasse:** range.
31. **straungenesse:** newness,
    originality.
35. **whenas:** when, since.
39. **needes he mought:** he can-
    not but.
42. **casualtye:** chance.

amisse, that they bring great grace and, as one would
say, auctoritie to the verse. For albe amongst many   50
other faultes it specially be objected of Valla against   §
Livie, and of other against Saluste, that with over
much studie they affect antiquitie, as coveting thereby credence and honor of elder yeeres, yet I am of
opinion, and eke the best learned are of the lyke,   55
that those auncient solemne wordes are a great ornament both in the one and in the other; the one labouring to set forth in hys worke an eternall image
of antiquitie, and the other carefully discoursing matters of gravitie and importaunce. For if my memory   60
fayle not, Tullie in that booke, wherein he endev-
oureth to set forth the paterne of a perfect Oratour,
sayth that ofttimes an auncient worde maketh the
style seeme grave, and as it were reverend: no otherwise then we honour and reverence gray heares for   65
a certein religious regard, which we have of old age.
yet nether every where must old words be stuffed in,
nor the commen Dialecte and maner of speaking so
corrupted therby, that as in old buildings it seme disorderly and ruinous. But all as in most exquisite pic-   70
tures they use to blaze and portraict not onely the
daintie lineaments of beautye, but also rounde about
it to shadow the rude thickets and craggy clifts, that

50. **albe:** although.
52. **of other:** by someone else.
55. **eke:** also, even.
65. **heares:** hairs.

70-8. **But all as . . . Even so:**
   But just as . . . Even so.
71. **blaze:** depict.

§ *Valla*: Lorenzo Valla (1405-57) was a famous Italian humanist who,
in the course of his interest in classical philology, published suggested
emendations to the text of *Livy*, i.e., Titus Livius (57 B.C.-A.D. 17),
the Roman historian. *Saluste*: Sallust (86 - c.34 B.C.), a Roman
politician, general, author, and amateur historian. *Tullie* (line 61):
Marcus Tullius Cicero (106-43 B.C.), jurist, consul, and one of Rome's
greatest authors and orators; a superb stylist, he was one of the chief
literary models for the Renaissance humanists. *Alceus* (line 83):
There were three Greek poets of this name (which E.K. is recalling
via Cicero) and the works of all of them survive only in fragments;
but the reference is probably to Alcaeus of Lesbos (*fl.* 600-580 B.C.),
a lyric poet and the countryman and contemporary of the poetess
Sappho.

by the basenesse of such parts, more excellency may
accrew to the principall; for oftimes we fynde our-   75
selves, I knowe not how, singularly delighted with the
shewe of such naturall rudenesse, and take great pleasure in that disorderly order. Even so doe those rough
and harsh termes enlumine and make more clearly to
appeare the brightnesse of brave and glorious words.   80
So oftentimes a dischorde in Musick maketh a comely
concordaunce: so great delight tooke the worthy
Poete Alceus to behold a blemish in the joynt of a
wel shaped body. But if any will rashly blame such
his purpose in choyse of old and unwonted words,   85
him may I more justly blame and condemne, or of
witlesse headinesse in judging, or of heedelesse hardinesse in condemning. for not marking the compasse   §
of hys bent, he wil judge of the length of his cast.
for in my opinion it is one special prayse, of many   90
why⌐h are dew to this Poete, that he hath laboured
to restore, as to theyr rightfull heritage such good
and naturall English words, as have ben long time
out of use and almost cleane disherited. Which is the
onely cause, that our Mother tonge, which truely of   95
it self is both ful enough for prose and stately enough
for verse, hath long time ben counted most bare and
barrein of both. which default when as some endev-
oured to salve and recure, they patched up the holes
with peces and rags of other languages, borrowing   100
here of the french, there of the Italian, every where

85. **unwonted:** unusual,   94. **cleane:** entirely.
    strange.   99. **salve:** remedy; **recure:**
86-7. **or . . . or:** either . . . **or.**   heal.
87. **headinesse:** rashness.

§ *compasse and cast*: Terms from archery. The *compass* is the curved
path described by an arrow in flight, or the angle of elevation when
aiming which determines this path. The *cast* is the ability of a bow
to propel an arrow; it also refers to the distance over which a bow
will drive an arrow. *Hys* and *his* are pronoun references to Spenser.

of the Latine, not weighing how il those tongues accorde with themselves, but much worse with ours:
So now they have made our English tongue, a gal-
limaufray or hodgepodge of al other speches. Other   *105*
some not so wel seene in the English tonge as perhaps in other languages, if them happen to here an
olde word albeit very naturall and significant, crye
out streight way, that we speak no English, but gib-
brish, or rather such, as in old time Evanders mother   *110* §
spake. whose first shame is, that they are not
ashamed, in their own mother tonge straungers to be
counted and alienes. The second shame no lesse then
the first, that what so they understand not, they
streight way deeme to be sencelesse, and not at al   *115*
to be understode. Much like to the Mole in Æsopes
fable, that being blynd her selfe, would in no wise be
perswaded, that any beast could see. The last more
shameful then both, that of their owne country and
natural speach, which together with their Nources   *120*
milk they sucked, they have so base regard and bas-
tard judgement, that they will not onely themselves
not labor to garnish and beautifie it, but also repine,
that of other it shold be embellished. Like to the
dogge in the maunger, that him selfe can eate no   *125*
hay, and yet barketh at the hungry bullock, that so
faine would feede: whose currish kind though cannot
be kept from barking, yet I conne them thanke that
they refrain from byting.

102. **accorde with:** agree
     among.
105. **Other:** or.
106. **seene:** skilled.

107. **them:** they.
123. **repine:** sulk, grumble.
128. **conne:** can.

§ *Evanders mother*: Evander, son of the prophetic goddess Carmentis,
was a Greek who migrated to Italy before the founding of Rome.
He and/or his mother were supposed to have taught the pre-Roman
inhabitants the use of written language. Thus to speak or write "like
Evander's mother" seems to have been a proverbial phrase for speaking or writing in a very antiquated manner.

Now for the knitting of sentences, whych they call   *130*
the joynts and members therof, and for al the compasse of the speach, it is round without roughnesse,
and learned wythout hardnes, such indeede as may
be perceived of the leaste, understoode of the moste,
but judged onely of the learned. For what in most   *135*
English wryters useth to be loose, and as it were
ungyrt, in this Authour is well grounded, finely
framed, and strongly trussed up together. In regard
wherof, I scorne and spue out the rakehellye route
of our ragged rymers (for so themselves use to hunt   *140*
the letter) which without learning boste, without
judgement jangle, without reason rage and fome, as
if some instinct of Poeticall spirite had newly ravished them above the meanenesse of commen capa-
citie. And being in the middest of all theyr bravery,   *145*
sodenly eyther for want of matter, or of ryme, or
having forgotten theyr former conceipt, they seeme
to be so pained and traveiled in theyr remembrance,
as it were a woman in childebirth or as that same
Pythia, when the traunce came upon her.   *150 §*

Os rabidum fera corda domans &c.

Nethelesse let them a Gods name feede on theyr

136. **useth:** is habitually.
137. **ungyrt:** slack.
139. **rakehellye route:** rascally lot.
140. **use to hunt the letter:** i.e., habitually strive for alliterative effects.
142. **jangle:** carp, bicker.
143. **ravished:** inspired, en-tranced.
144. **meanenesse:** average level.
145. **bravery:** i.e., showing off.
147. **former conceipt:** original conception.
148. **traveiled:** troubled, laboured.
152. **a Gods:** in God's.

§ *Pythia*: One of the names of Apollo's sacred priestess, through whom he delivered oracles in his shrine at Delphi. The Latin quotation is from a passage in Book VI of Virgil's *Aeneid* in which the priestess is being seized by a prophetic trance; the more she tries to resist the seizure, the more the god "overmasters her frenzied lips and curbs her wild heart".

owne folly, so they seeke not to darken the beames
of others glory. As for Colin, under whose person
the Authour selfe is shadowed, how furre he is from   *155*
such vaunted titles and glorious showes, both him
selfe sheweth, where he sayth.

   Of Muses Hobbin. I conne no skill.
And,

  Enough is me to paint out my unrest, &c.   *160*

And also appeareth by the basenesse of the name,
wherein, it semeth, he chose rather to unfold great
matter of argument covertly, then professing it, not   §
suffice thereto accordingly. which moved him rather
in Æglogues, then other wise to write, doubting per-   *165*
haps his habilitie, which he little needed, or mynding
to furnish our tongue with this kinde, wherein it faulteth, or following the example of the best and most
auncient Poetes, which devised this kind of wryting,
being both so base for the matter, and homely for   *170*
the manner, at the first to trye theyr habilities: and
as young birdes, that be newly crept out of the nest,
by little first to prove theyr tender wyngs, before
they make a greater flyght. So flew Theocritus, as   §
you may perceive he was all ready full fledged. So   *175*
flew Virgile, as not yet well feeling his winges. So
flew Mantuane, as being not full somd. So Petrarque.

153. **so:** as long as.
158. **conne:** know, have.
161. **basenesse:** lowliness.
163. **covertly:** secretly.

166. **habilitie:** ability.
167. **this kinde:** this genre;
 faulteth: is lacking.
177. **full somd:** full fledged.

§ *then professing it . . . accordingly*: "Than, after declaring it openly,
to fail to live up to it".
§ *Theocritus*: Greek poet (*c.* 310-250 B.C.) whose works included pastoral poems called "Idylls". *Virgile*: Virgil (70-19 B.C.), Roman poet
whose early works included pastoral poems called "Eclogues" or
"Bucolics". *Mantuane*: So called after his birthplace, Mantua, was
Baptista Spanuoli (1448-1516). Spanuoli, *Petrarque* (Petrarca, 1304-

So Boccace; So Marot, Sanazarus, and also divers
other excellent both Italian and French Poetes, whose
foting this Author every where followeth, yet so as   *180*
few, but they be wel sented can trace him out. So
finally flyeth this our new Poete, as a bird, whose
principals be scarce growen out, but yet as that in
time shall be hable to keepe wing with the best.

Now as touching the generall dryft and purpose of   *185*
his Æglogues, I mind not to say much, him selfe
labouring to conceale it. Onely this appeareth, that
his unstayed yougth had long wandred in the common Labyrinth of Love, in which time to mitigate
and allay the heate of his passion, or els to warne   *190*
(as he sayth) the young shepheards .s. his equalls
and companions of his unfortunate folly, he com-
piled these xii. Æglogues, which for that they be proportioned to the state of the xii. monethes, he termeth
the SHEPHEARDS CALENDAR, applying an olde name to   *195 §*
a new worke. Hereunto have I added a certain Glosse
or scholion for thexposition of old wordes and harder
phrases: which maner of glosing and commenting,
well I wote, wil seeme straunge and rare in our
tongue: yet for somuch as I knew many excellent   *200*

180. **foting:** footsteps; **yet so as few, but:** yet in such a way that few (readers), unless.
181. **wel sented:** sharp of scent.
183. **principals:** primary feathers.
188. **unstayed:** unstable.
191. **.s.:** namely, that is (abbr. of Latin "scilicet").
196. **Glosse or scholion:** annotation or commentary.
199. **wote:** know.

74), *Boccace* (Boccaccio, 1313-75), and *Sanazarus* (Sannazaro, 1458-
1530) were all scholars and poets of the Italian Renaissance whose
works included pastoral poems in Latin. Clément *Marot* (1497-1544)
was a French poet whose works included two Eclogues in the vernacular. Of all these pastoralists Spenser was especially indebted to
Virgil, the Mantuan Spanuoli, and Marot.
§ SHEPHEARDS CALENDAR: Though Spenser put the form of the Calendar
to his own original use, he did not invent his title; the "olde name"
was *Kalendar & Compost of Shepherds*, a popular country almanac
long since translated from the original French and still selling well in
Spenser's day.

and proper devises both in wordes and matter would
passe in the speedy course of reading, either as unknowen, or as not marked, and that in this kind, as
in other we might be equal to the learned of other
nations, I thought good to take the paines upon me,   *205*
the rather for that by meanes of some familiar acquaintaunce I was made privie to his counsell and
secret meaning in them, as also in sundry other works
of his. which albeit I know he nothing so much
hateth, as to promulgate, yet thus much have I ad-   *210*
ventured upon his frendship, him selfe being for long
time furre estraunged, hoping that this will the rather
occasion him, to put forth divers other excellent works
of his, which slepe in silence, as his Dreames, his
Legendes, his Court of Cupide, and sondry others;   *215*
whose commendations to set out, were verye vayne;
the thinges though worthy of many, yet being knowen
to few. These my present paynes if to any they be
pleasurable or profitable, be you judge, mine own
good Maister Harvey, to whom I have both in re-   *220*
spect of your worthinesse generally, and otherwyse
upon some particular and special considerations voued
this my labour, and the maydenhead of this our commen frends Poetrie, himselfe having already in the
beginning dedicated it to the Noble and worthy   *225*
Gentleman, the right worshipfull Ma. Phi. Sidney, a
special favourer and maintainer of all kind of learning. Whose cause I pray you Sir, yf Envie shal stur
up any wrongful accusasion, defend with your mighty

201. **devises:** ingenuities.
203. **and that in:** and so that
in.
206. **the rather for that:** all the
more because.
207. **made privie to:** put in the
know concerning; **coun-
sell:** plan.
209. **albeit:** although.
210-11. **promulgate:** advertise;
adventured upon: risked

trespassing upon.
212. **the rather:** all the more.
213. **occasion:** spur, open the
way for.
216. **commendations:** good
points.
218. **paynes:** efforts.
222. **voued:** dedicated.
223. **maydenhead:** i.e., first offering.

Rhetorick and other your rare gifts of learning, as   *230*
you can, and shield with your good wil, as you ought,
against the malice and outrage of so many enemies,
as I know wilbe set on fire with the sparks of his
kindled glory. And thus recommending the Author
unto you, as unto his most special good frend, and   *235*
my selfe unto you both, as one making singuler account of two so very good and so choise frends, I
bid you both most hartely farwel, and commit you
and your most commendable studies to the tuicion
of the greatest.   *240*

Your owne assuredly to
be commaunded E. K.

Post scr.

Now I trust M. Harvey, that upon sight of your speciall frends and fellow Poets doings, or els for envie   *245*
of so many unworthy Quidams, which catch at the
garlond, which to you alone is dewe, you will be perswaded to pluck out of the hateful darknesse, those
so many excellent English poemes of yours, which lye
hid, and bring them forth to eternall light. Trust me   *250*
you doe both them great wrong, in depriving them
of the desired sonne, and also your selfe, in smooth-
ering your deserved prayses, and all men generally,
in withholding from them so divine pleasures, which
they might conceive of your gallant English verses,   *255*
as they have already doen of your Latine Poemes,

239. **tuicion:** care, guidance.
246. **Quidams:** certain types, you-know-whos.
252. **sonne:** sun, i.e., publica-tion.
256. **doen:** done.

which in my opinion both for invention and Elocu- §
tion are very delicate, and superexcellent. And thus
againe, I take my leave of my good Mayster Harvey.
from my lodging at London thys 10. of Aprill. 1579. *260*

§ *invention and Elocution*: These are terms inherited by the Renaissance
from classical rhetoric and literary theory. Renaissance critics would
generally think of *inventio* as the power of discovering and selecting
what is to be said; and of *elecutio* as the power of best expressing
what is to be said. For some later critics of the English Renaissance
elocutio came to be a pejorative term meaning unnecessary frills or
mere ornamental niceties of diction. E.K. is not using the term in this
pejorative sense.

THE GENERALL ARGUMENT OF
the whole booke

Little I hope, needeth me at large to discourse the
first Originall of Æglogues, having alreadie touched
the same. But for the word Æglogues I know is unknowen to most, and also mistaken of some the best
learned (as they think) I wyll say somewhat thereof,   5
being not at all impertinent to my present purpose.

They were first of the Greekes the inventours of
them called Æglogai as it were αἴγων or αἰγονόμων.
λόγοι. that is Goteheards tales. For although in Virgile and others the speakers be more shepheards,   10
then Goteheards, yet Theocritus in whom is more
ground of authoritie, then in Virgile, this specially
from that deriving, as from the first head and wel-
spring the whole Invencion of his Æglogues, maketh
Goteheards the persons and authors of his tales. This   15
being, who seeth not the grossenesse of such as by
colour of learning would make us beleeve that they
are more rightly termed Eclogai, as they would say,   §
extraordinary discourses of unnecessarie matter, which
difinition albe in substaunce and meaning it agree   20
with the nature of the thing, yet nowhit answereth

1. **Little . . . needeth me:**
There is little need, I
hope, for me.
6. **impertinent:** irrelevant.

12-13. **this . . . that:** i.e., Virgil . . . Theocritus.
15. **This being:** this being so.
21. **answereth with:** answers
to.

---

§ *Eclogai:* In trying to distinguish between "Aeglogue" and "Eclogue"
E.K. is following an old but mistaken etymology. In any case
"Eclogue" (literally, "a selection") has become one of the special
terms for what we generally call a Pastoral, or a pastoral poem.

with the ἀνάλυσις and interpretation of the word.
For they be not termed Eclogues, but Æglogues.
which sentence this authour very well observing, upon good judgement, though indeede few Goteheards   25
have to doe herein, nethelesse doubteth not to cal
them by the used and best knowen name. Other curious discourses hereof I reserve to greater occasion.
These xii. Æclogues every where answering to the
seasons of the twelve monthes may be well devided   30
into three formes orranckes. For eyther they be
Plaintive, as the first, the sixt, the eleventh, and the
twelfth, or recreative, such as al those be, which conceive matter of love, or commendation of special
personages, or Moral: which for the most part be   35
mixed with some Satyrical bitternesse, namely the
second of reverence dewe to old age, the fift of coloured deceipt, the seventh and ninth of dissolute
shepheards and pastours, the tenth of contempt of
Poetrie and pleasaunt wits. And to this division may   40
every thing herein be reasonably applyed: a few onely
except, whose speciall purpose and meaning I am not
privie to. And thus much generally of these xii. Æclogues. Now will we speake particularly of all, and
first of the first. which he calleth by the first monethes   45
name Januarie: wherein to some he may seeme
fowly to have faulted, in that he erroniously beginneth with that moneth, which beginneth not the
yeare. For it is wel known, and stoutely mainteyned
with strong reasons of the learned, that the yeare   50
beginneth in March. for then the sonne reneweth his
finished course, and the seasonable spring refresheth
the earth, and the plesaunce thereof being buried in
the sadnesse of the dead winter now worne away,

24. **sentence:** precise inter-
    pretation, meaningful dis-
    tinction.
26. **doubteth not:** is not
    afraid.

27. **curious:** elaborate.
37. **coloured:** hidden, dis-
    guised.
47. **fowly . . . faulted:** to have
    blundered badly.

reliveth. This opinion maynteine the olde Astrologers   *55*
and Philosophers, namely the reverend Andalo, and   §
Macrobius in his holydayes of Saturne, which ac-
coumpt also was generally observed both of Grecians
and Romans. But saving the leave of such learned
heads, we mayntaine a custome of coumpting the   *60*
seasons from the moneth January, upon a more speciall cause, then the heathen Philosophers ever coulde
conceive, that is, for the incarnation of our mighty
Saviour and eternall redeemer the L. Christ, who as
then renewing the state of the decayed world, and   *65*
returning the compasse of expired yeres to theyr
former date and first commencement, left to us his
heires a memoriall of his birth in the ende of the last
yeere and beginning of the next. which reckoning, beside that eternall monument of our salvation, leaneth   *70*
also uppon good proofe of special judgement. For albeit that in elder times, when as yet the coumpt of
the yere was not perfected, as afterwarde it was by
Julius Cæsar, they began to tel the monethes from
Marches beginning, and according to the same God   *75*
(as is sayd in Scripture) comaunded the people of
the Jewes to count the moneth Abib, that which we
call March, for the first moneth, in remembraunce
that in that moneth he brought them out of the land
of Ægipt: yet according to tradition of latter times   *80*
it hath bene otherwise observed, both in government
of the church, and rule of Mightiest Realmes. For
from Julius Cæsar who first observed the leape yeere

75. **according . . . God:** in
    accordance with . . . God
    who.

§ *Andalo, and Macrobius:* Andalo de Negro, an astronomer who in
  1475 published a book on astrolabes, the instruments for obtaining
  the altitudes of planets and stars. *Macrobius:* A fifth-century encyclo-
  pedist who wrote the *Saturnalia,* a seven-volume compendium of all
  kinds of lore. E.K. proceeds to follow him closely on the subject of
  calendar years.

which he called Bissextilem Annum, and brought in
to a more certain course the odde wandring dayes   *85*
which of the Greekes were called ὑπερβαίνοντες. of
the Romanes intercalares (for in such matter of
learning I am forced to use the termes of the learned)
the monethes have bene nombred xii. which in the
first ordinaunce of Romulus were but tenne, count-   *90 §*
ing but CCCiiii. dayes in every yeare, and beginning
with March. But Numa Pompilius, who was the father
of al the Romain ceremonies and religion, seeing that
reckoning to agree neither with the course of the
sonne, nor of the Moone, thereunto added two   *95*
monethes, January and February: wherin it seemeth,
that wise king minded upon good reason to begin the
yeare at Januarie, of him therefore so called tan-
quam Janua anni the gate and entraunce of the yere,
or of the name of the god Janus, to which god for   *100 §*
that the old Paynims attributed the byrth and beginning of all creatures new comming into the
worlde, it seemeth that he therfore to him assigned
the beginning and first entraunce of the yeare. which
account for the most part hath hetherto continued.   *105*
Notwithstanding that the Ægiptians beginne theyr
yeare at September, for that according to the opinion
of the best Rabbins, and very purpose of the scripture selfe, God made the worlde in that Moneth,
that is called of them Tisri. And therefore he com-   *110*
maunded them, to keepe the feast of Pavilions in the   *§*
end of the yeare, in the xv. day of the seventh
moneth, which before that time was the first.

101. **Paynims:** pagans.

---

§ *Romulus*: The legendary founder and first king of Rome. *Numa
   Pompilius*: Traditionally Romulus' successor as king of Rome; he
   seems to be a semi-historical (as opposed to a purely legendary)
   figure.
§ *Janus*: The Roman god of doorways, city-gates, and beginnings. Being
   two-faced, he can see backwards and forwards at the same time.
§ *feast of Pavilions*: See Leviticus 23:33-43.

But our Authour respecting nether the subtiltie of thone parte, nor the antiquitie of thother, thinketh *115* it fittest according to the simplicitie of commen understanding, to begin with Januarie, wening it perhaps no decorum, that Shepheard should be seene in matter of so deepe insight, or canvase a case of so doubtful judgment. So therefore beginneth he, and *120* so continueth he throughout.

115. **thone . . . thother:** the one . . . the other.
117. **wening:** thinking.
118. **no decorum:** inappropriate.
119. **canvase:** discuss.

Februarie

Ægloga Secunda

ARGUMENT

*This Æglogue is rather morall and generall, then bent
to any secrete or particular purpose. It specially contey-
neth a discourse of old age, in the persone of* Thenot *an
olde Shepheard, who for his crookednesse and unlusti-
nesse, is scorned of* Cuddie *an unhappy Heardmans
boye. The matter very well accordeth with the season of* §
*the moneth, the yeare now drouping, and as it were,
drawing to his last age. For as in this time of yeare, so
then in our bodies there is a dry and withering cold,
which congealeth the crudled blood, and frieseth the
wetherbeaten flesh, with stormes of Fortune, and hoare
frosts of Care. To which purpose the olde man telleth a
tale of the Oake and the Bryer, so lively and so feelingly, as if the thing were set forth in some Picture before our eyes, more plainly could not appeare.*

§ *The matter very well accordeth . . . age*: This suggests that Spenser
originally meant to begin his "Calender" in March. Though for this
poem January eventually suited his purpose best, elsewhere he certainly thinks of March as the year's beginning. See, for instance, the
Two Cantos of Mutabilitie, Canto VII, stanzas 32-43, where the
parade of months begins with March and ends with February. Right
up until 1752 the legal, official beginning of the year was March 25.

CUDDIE   THENOT

A h for pittie, wil rancke Winters rage,
   These bitter blasts never ginne tasswage?
The kene cold blowes through my beaten hyde,
All as I were through the body gryde.
My ragged rontes all shiver and shake,   5
As doen high Towers in an earthquake:
They wont in the wind wagge their wrigle tailes,
Perke as Peacock: but nowe it avales.

THENOT

Lewdly complainest thou laesie ladde,
Of Winters wracke, for making thee sadde.   10
Must not the world wend in his commun course
From good to badd, and from badde to worse,
From worse unto that is worst of all,
And then returne to his former fall?
Who will not suffer the stormy time,   15
Where will he live tyll the lusty prime?
Selfe have I worne out thrise threttie yeares,
Some in much joy, many in many teares:
Yet never complained of cold nor heate,
Of Sommers flame, nor of Winters threat: 20
Ne ever was to Fortune foeman,
But gently tooke, that ungently came.
And ever my flocke was my chiefe care,
Winter or Sommer they mought well fare.

2. **ginne:** begin; **tasswage:** to abate.
4. **gryde:** pierced.
5. **rontes:** cattle of small breed.
6. **doen:** do.
7. **wont:** usually, are accustomed to.
8. **Perke:** pert; **it avales:** it droops.
9. **Lewdly:** basely, ignorantly.
10. **wracke:** violence.
11. **wend:** proceed.
14. **fall:** case, condition.
17. **threttie:** thirty.
24. **mought:** must.

CUDDIE

No marveile *Thenot,* if thou can beare   25
Cherefully the Winters wrathfull cheare:
For Age and Winter accord full nie,
This chill, that cold, this crooked, that wrye.
And as the lowring Wether lookes downe,
So semest thou like good fryday to frowne.   30
But my flowring youth is foe to frost,
My shippe unwont in stormes to be tost.

THENOT

The soveraigne of seas he blames in vaine,
That once seabeate, will to sea againe.
So loytring live you little heardgroomes,   35
Keeping your beastes in the budded broomes:
And when the shining sunne laugheth once,
You deemen, the Spring is come attonce.
Tho gynne you, fond flyes, the cold to scorne,
And crowing in pypes made of greene corne,   40
You thinken to be Lords of the yeare.
But eft, when ye count you freed from feare,
Comes the breme winter with chamfred browes,
Full of wrinckles and frostie furrowes:
Drerily shooting his stormy darte,   45
Which cruddles the blood, and pricks the harte.
Then is your careless corage accoied,
Your carefull heards with cold bene annoied.
Then paye you the price of your surquedrie,
With weeping, and wayling, and misery.   50

26. **cheare:** mood, aspect.
32. **unwont:** (is) unaccustomed.
35. **heardgroomes:** herdsmen.
38. **deemen:** consider, imagine; **attonce:** already.
42. **eft:** afterwards.
43. **breme:** chilly, rough;
    chamfred: creased.
46. **cruddles:** curdles.
47. **careless corage:** carefree nature; **accoied:** dampened, daunted.
48. **carefull:** gloomy, anxious.
49. **surquedrie:** arrogance.

CUDDIE

Ah foolish old man, I scorne thy skill,
That wouldest me, my springing youngth to spil.
I deeme, thy braine emperished bee
Through rusty elde, that hath rotted thee:
Or sicker thy head veray tottie is,   55
So on thy corbe shoulder it leanes amisse.
Now thy selfe hast lost both lopp and topp,
Als my budding braunch thou wouldest cropp:
But were thy yeares greene, as now bene myne,
To other delights they would encline.   60
Tho wouldest thou learne to caroll of Love,
And hery with hymnes thy lasses glove.
Tho wouldest thou pype of *Phyllis* prayse:
But *Phyllis* is myne for many dayes:
I wonne her with a gyrdle of gelt,   65
Embost with buegle about the belt.
Such an one shepheards woulde make full faine:
Such an one would make thee younge againe.

THENOT

Thou art a fon, of thy love to boste,
All that is lent to love, wyll be lost.   70

CUDDIE

Seest, howe brag yond Bullocke beares,
So smirke, so smoothe, his pricked eares?
His hornes bene as broade, as Rainebowe bent,
His dewelap as lythe, as lasse of Kent.
See howe he venteth into the wynd.   75

51. **skill:** judgment.
52. **wouldest:** wishes(t); **spil:** sour, spoil.
54. **elde:** old age.
55. **sicker:** surely; **veray tottie:** really giddy.
56. **corbe:** crooked.
57. **lopp and topp:** i.e., all your branches (including lopp - the twigs).
58. **Als:** also.
61. **Tho:** then.
62. **hery:** celebrate.
65. **gelt:** gold.
67. **full faine:** very glad.
69. **fon:** dolt.
71. **brag:** proudly.
72. **smirke:** trim.
75. **venteth:** snuffs.

Weenest of love is not his mynd?
Seemeth thy flocke thy counsell can,
So lustlesse bene they, so weake so wan,
Clothed with cold, and hoary wyth frost.
Thy flocks father his corage hath lost: *80*
Thy Ewes, that wont to have blowen bags,
Like wailefull widdowes hangen their crags:
The rather Lambes bene starved with cold,
All for their Maister is lustlesse and old.

THENOT

Cuddie, I wote thou kenst little good,   *85*
So vainely tadvaunce thy headlesse hood.
For Youngth is a bubble blown up with breath,
Whose witt is weakenesse, whose wage is death,
Whose way is wildernesse, whose ynne Penaunce,
And stoopegallaunt Age the hoste of Greevaunce. *90* §
But shall I tel thee a tale of truth,
Which I cond of *Tityrus* in my youth,
Keeping his sheepe on the hils of Kent?

CUDDIE

To nought more *Thenot,* my mind is bent,
Then to heare novells of his devise: *95*
They bene so well thewed, and so wise,
What ever that good old man bespake.

76. **Weenest:** do you suppose.
77. **can:** knows.
80. **corage:** i.e., zest.
81. **blowen bags:** swelling udders.
82. **crags:** necks.
83. **rather:** earlier.
85. **kenst:** know(est).
86. **tadvaunce:** to put forward; **headlesse hood:** (?)

vacant notions.
89. **ynne:** (final) abode.
92. **cond of:** learned from; **Tityrus:** i.e., Chaucer.
94. **bent:** inclined, disposed.
95. **novells:** novelle, short tales; **devise:** devising, invention.
96. **well thewed:** i.e., edifying.

§ *stoopegallaunt Age*: I.e., "Old age, which lays the gallant low". "Stoopgallant" was one of the colloquial names for the plague-fever. The whole line is rendered by Warton (one of Spenser's editors) thus: "The tamer of whose gay gallantries is Old Age, the guest or companion of Misery".

THENOT

Many meete tales of youth did he make,
And some of love, and some of chevalrie:
But none fitter then this to applie. *100*
Now listen a while, and hearken the end.

There grewe an aged Tree on the greene,
    A goodly Oake sometime had it bene,
With armes full strong and largely displayd,
But of their leaves they were disarayde: *105*
The bodie bigge, and mightely pight,
Throughly rooted, and of wonderous hight:
Whilome had bene the King of the field,
And mochell mast to the husband did yielde,
And with his nuts larded many swine. *110*
But now the gray mosse marred his rine,
His bared boughes were beaten with stormes,
His toppe was bald, and wasted with wormes,
His honor decayed, his braunches sere.

    Hard by his side grewe a bragging brere, *115*
Which proudly thrust into Thelement,
And seemed to threat the Firmament.
Yt was embellisht with blossomes fayre,
And thereto aye wonned to repayre
The shepheards daughters, to gather flowres, *120*
To peinct their girlonds with his colowres.
And in his small bushes used to shrowde
The sweete Nightingale singing so lowde:
Which made this foolish Brere wexe so bold,
That on a time he cast him to scold, *125*

98. **meete:** proper.
104. **largely displayd:** widely spread.
106. **pight:** fixed, grounded.
108. **Whilome:** once.
109. **mochell mast:** much fodder; **husband:** husbandman.
111. **rine:** bark.
114. **sere:** withered.
115. **brere:** briar.
116. **Thelement:** the air.
119. **wonned:** were in the habit of; **repayre:** go(ing).
121. **peinct:** paint.
125. **cast:** decided.

And snebbe the good Oake, for he was old.
  Why standst there (quoth he) thou brutish blocke?
Nor for fruict, nor for shadowe serves thy stocke:
Seest, how fresh my flowers bene spredde,
Dyed in Lilly white, and Cremsin redde,   *130*
With Leaves engrained in lusty greene,
Colours meete to clothe a mayden Queene.
Thy wast bignes but combers the grownd,
And dirks the beauty of my blossomes rownd.
The mouldie mosse, which thee accloieth,   *135*
My Sinamon smell too much annoieth.
Wherefore soone I rede thee, hence remove,
Least thou the price of my displeasure prove.
So spake this bold brere with great disdaine:
Little him answered the Oake againe,   *140*
But yielded, with shame and greefe adawed,
That of a weede he was overawed.
  Yt chaunced after upon a day,
The Husbandman selfe to come that way,
Of custome for to servewe his grownd,   *145*
And his trees of state in compasse rownd.
Him when the spitefull brere had espyed,
Causlesse complained, and lowdly cryed
Unto his Lord, stirring up sterne strife:
O my liege Lord, the God of my life,   *150*
Pleaseth you ponder your Suppliants plaint,
Caused of wrong, and cruell constraint,
Which I your poore Vassall dayly endure:
And but your goodnes the same recure,
Am like for desperate doole to dye,   *155*

126. **snebbe:** reprove, tell off.
131. **engrained:** dyed.
133. **wast:** useless.
134. **dirks:** darkens.
135. **accloieth:** smothers.
137. **rede:** advise.
138. **prove:** experience, feel.
141. **adawed:** daunted.
145. **servewe:** survey.
146. **trees of state:** noble, stately trees.
152. **Caused of:** caused by; **contraint:** hardship.
154. **but:** unless; **recure:** remedy.
155. **doole:** sorrow.

Through felonous force of mine enemie.
   Greatly aghast with this piteous plea,
Him rested the goodman on the lea,
And badde the Brere in his plaint proceede.
With painted words tho gan this proude weede,   *160*
(As most usen Ambitious folke:)
His colowred crime with craft to cloke.
   Ah my soveraigne, Lord of creatures all,
Thou placer of plants both humble and tall,
Was not I planted of thine owne hand,   *165*
To be the primrose of all thy land,
With flowring blossomes, to furnish the prime,
And scarlot berries in Sommer time?
How falls it then, that this faded Oake,
Whose bodie is sere, whose braunches broke,   *170*
Whose naked Armes stretch unto the fyre,
Unto such tyrannie doth aspire:
Hindering with his shade my lovely light,
And robbing me of the swete sonnes sight?
So beate his old boughes my tender side,   *175*
That oft the bloud springeth from wounds wyde:
Untimely my flowres forced to fall,
That bene the honor of your Coronall.
And oft he lets his cancker wormes light
Upon my braunches, to worke me more spight: *180*
And oft his hoarie locks downe doth cast,
Where with my fresh flowretts bene defast.
For this, and many more such outrage,
Craving your goodlihead to aswage
The ranckorous rigour of his might,   *185*
Nought aske I, but onely to hold my right:

158. **Him:** himself.
161. **most usen:** use for the most part.
162. **colowred:** concealed, disguised.
167. **prime:** springtime.
169. **falls:** happens.
177. **Untimely:** before their time.
178. **honor:** glory; **Coronall:** garland.
182. **defast:** destroyed.
184. **your goodlihead:** (you of) your goodness.

Submitting me to your good sufferance,
And praying to be garded from greevance.
  To this the Oake cast him to replie
Well as he couth: but his enemie   *190*
Had kindled such coles of displeasure,
That the good man noulde stay his leasure,
But home him hasted with furious heate,
Encreasing his wrath with many a threate.
His harmefull Hatchet he hent in hand,   *195*
(Alas, that it so ready should stand)
And to the field alone he speedeth.
(Ay little helpe to harme there needeth)   §
Anger nould let him speake to the tree,
Enaunter his rage mought cooled bee: *200*
But to the roote bent his sturdy stroke,
And made many wounds in the wast Oake.
The Axes edge did oft turne againe,
As halfe unwilling to cutte the graine:
Semed, the sencelesse yron dyd feare,   *205*
Or to wrong holy eld did forbeare.
For it had bene an auncient tree,
Sacred with many a mysteree,
And often crost with the priestes crewe,
And often halowed with holy water dewe.   *210*
But sike fancies weren foolerie,
And broughten this Oake to this miserye.

187. **sufferance:** patience.
189. **cast:** attempted.
190. **couth:** could.
192. **noulde:** would not; **stay his leasure:** wait to hear him (the Oak) out.
195. **hent:** snatched up.
200. **Enaunter:** in case; **mought:** might.

205. **Semed:** it seemed; **dyd feare,/Or . . . forbeare:** did (either) fear or forbear.
206. **holy eld:** sacrosanct old age.
211. **sike:** such; **foolerie:** foolishness.

§ (*Ay little helpe . . . needeth*): "The will to do harm never needs very much *help*" (if you apply the phrase to the Briar) or "*encouragement*" (if you apply the phrase to the husbandman).

For nought mought they quitten him from decay:
For fiercely the good man at him did laye.
The blocke oft groned under the blow,　　　　　215
And sighed to see his neare overthrow.
In fine the steele had pierced his pitth,
Tho downe to the earth he fell forthwith:
His wonderous weight made the grounde to quake,
Thearth shronke under him, and seemed to shake.
There lyeth the Oake, pitied of none.　　　　　221
　　Now stands the Brere like a Lord alone,
Puffed up with pryde and vaine pleasaunce:
But all this glee had no continuaunce.
For eftsones Winter gan to approche,　　　　　225
The blustring Boreas did encroche,
And beate upon the solitarie Brere:
For nowe no succoure was seene him nere.
Now gan he repent his pryde to late:
For naked left and disconsolate,　　　　　　　230
The byting frost nipt his stalke dead,
The watrie wette weighed downe his head,
And heaped snowe burdned him so sore,
That nowe upright he can stand no more:
And being downe, is trodde in the durt　　　　235
Of cattell, and brouzed, and sorely hurt.
Such was thend of this Ambitious brere,
For scorning Eld

CUDDIE

　　Now I pray thee shepheard, tel it not forth:
Here is a long tale, and little worth.　　　　　240
So longe have I listened to thy speche,
That graffed to the ground is my breche:
My hartblood is welnigh frorne I feele,

213. **nought mought:** in no way
could; **quitten:** exempt;
decay: destruction.
217. **In fine:** finally.
225. **eftsones:** immediately.

226. **Boreas:** i.e., the North
Wind.
229. **gan:** did.
237. **thend:** the end.
242. **graffed:** grafted.
243. **frorne:** frozen.

And my galage growne fast to my heele:
But little ease of thy lewd tale I tasted.   *245*
Hye thee home shepheard, the day is nigh wasted.

THENOTS EMBLEME   §

Iddio perche è vecchio,
Fa suoi al suo essempio.

CUDDIES EMBLEME

Niuno vecchio,
Spaventa Iddio.

GLOSSE   §

3 Kene) sharpe.
4 Gride) perced: an olde word much used of Lidgate, but not
    found (that I know of) in Chaucer. 5 Ronts) young
    bullockes.
10 Wracke) ruine or Violence, whence commeth shipwracke:
    and not wreake, that is vengeaunce or wrath. 21 Foe-
    man) a foe.
25 Thenot) the name of a shepheard in Marot his Æglogues.
33 The soveraigne of Seas) is Neptune the God of the seas. The
    saying is borowed of Mimus Publianus, which used this
    proverb in a verse. Improbè Neptunum accusat, qui iterum
    naufragium facit.
35 Heardgromes) Chaucers verse almost whole.
39 Fond Flyes) He compareth carelesse sluggardes or ill hus-

---

244. **galage:** (wooden) shoe.   245. **lewd:** stupid.

---

§ *Thenots Embleme*: "God, because he is old, creates his own in his
own image." *Cuddies Embleme*: "No old man fears God."
§ E.K.'s Glosse has been included because of its interest as an example
of an Elizabethan editorial apparatus. It has been included without
annotation of any kind; a gloss upon a gloss seemed a bit outside
the scope of this volume. The reader should know, however, that
although many of E.K.'s remarks are helpful, accurate, and well put,
some of them are quite wrong and a few, it seems, deliberately baff-
ling.

bandmen to flyes, that so soone as the sunne shineth, or yt wexeth any thing warme, begin to flye abroade, when sodeinly they be overtaken with cold.

42 But eft when) A verye excellent and lively description of Winter, so as may bee indifferently taken, eyther for old Age, or for Winter season.

43 Breme) chill, bitter. *43* Chamfred) chapt, or wrinckled.

47 Accoied) plucked down and daunted. *49* Surquedrie) pryde.

54 Elde) olde age. *55* Sicker) sure. *55* Tottie) wavering.

56 Corbe) crooked. *62* Herie) worshippe.

63 Phyllis) the name of some mayde unknowen, whom Cuddie, whose person is secrete, loved. The name is usuall in Theocritus, Virgile, and Mantuane.

66 Belte) a girdle or wast band. *69* A fon) a foole. *74* lythe) soft and gentile.

75 Venteth) snuffeth in the wind. *80* Thy flocks Father) the Ramme.

82 Crags) neckes.

83 Rather Lambes) that be ewed early in the beginning of the yeare.

87 Youth is) A verye moral and pitthy Allegorie of youth, and the lustes thereof, compared to a wearie wayfaring man.

92 Tityrus) I suppose he meane Chaucer, whose prayse for pleasaunt tales cannot dye, so long as the memorie of hys name shal live, and the name of Poetrie shal endure.

96 Well thewed) that is, Bene moratæ, full of morall wisenesse.

102 There grew) This tale of the Oake and the Brere, he telleth as learned of Chaucer, but it is cleane in another kind, and rather like to Æsopes fables. It is very excellente for pleasaunt descriptions, being altogether a certaine Icon or Hypotyposis of disdainfull younkers.

118 Embellisht) beautified and adorned. *119* To wonne) to haunt or frequent. *126* Sneb) checke.

127 Why standst) The speach is scornefull and very presumptuous. *131* Engrained) dyed in grain.

135 Accloieth) encombreth. *141* Adawed) daunted and confounded.

146 Trees of state) taller trees fitte for timber wood. *149* Sterne strife) said Chaucer .s. fell and sturdy. *150* O my liege) A maner of supplication, wherein is kindly coloured the affection and speache of Ambitious men.

166 The Primrose) The chiefe and worthiest.

171 Naked armes) metaphorically ment of the bare boughes, spoyled of leaves. This colourably he speaketh, as adjudging hym to the fyre.

176 The blood) spoken of a blocke, as it were of a living creature, figuratively, and (as they saye) κατ᾽ εἱκασμόν.

178 Coronall) Garlande.

181 Hoarie lockes) metaphorically for withered leaves.

182 Flourets) young blossomes. *195* Hent) caught. *198* Ay)
evermore.

199 Nould) for would not. *200* Enaunter) least that.

202 Wounds) gashes.

209 The priestes crewe) holy water pott, wherewith the popishe
priest used to sprinckle and hallowe the trees from mischaunce. Such blindnesse was in those times, which the
Poete supposeth, to have bene the finall decay of this auncient Oake.

215 The blocke oft groned) A livelye figure, whiche geveth sence
and feeling to unsensible creatures, as Virgile also sayeth:
Saxa gemunt gravido &c.

224 Glee) chere and jollitie.

226 Boreas) The Northerne wynd, that bringeth the moste stormie
weather.

238 For scorning Eld) And minding (as shoulde seme) to have
made ryme to the former verse, he is conningly cutte of by
Cuddye, as disdayning to here any more. *244* Galage) a
startuppe or clownish shoe.

Embleme

This embleme is spoken of Thenot, as a moral of his former
tale: namelye, that God, which is himselfe most aged, being before
al ages, and without beginninge, maketh those, whom he loveth
like to himselfe, in heaping yeares unto theyre dayes, and blessing
them wyth longe lyfe. For the blessing of age is not given to all,
but unto those, whome God will so blesse: and albeit that many
evil men reache unto such fulnesse of yeares, and some also wexe
olde in myserie and thraldome, yet therefore is not age ever the
lesse blessing. For even to such evill men such number of yeares
is added, that they may in their last dayes repent, and come to
their first home. So the old man checketh the rashheaded boy, for
despysing his gray and frostye heares.

Whom Cuddye doth counterbuff with a byting and bitter proverbe, spoken indeede at the first in contempt of old age generally.
for it was an old opinion, and yet is continued in some mens conceipt, that men of yeares have no feare of god at al, or not so
much as younger folke. For that being rypened with long experience, and having passed many bitter brunts and blastes of veng-

eaunce, they dread no stormes of Fortune, nor wrathe of Gods, nor daunger of menne, as being eyther by longe and ripe wisedome armed against all mischaunces and adversitie, or with much trouble hardened against all troublesome tydes: lyke unto the Ape, of which is sayd in Æsops fables, that oftentimes meeting the Lyon, he was at first sore aghast and dismayed at the grimnes and austeritie of hys countenance, but at last being acquainted with his lookes, he was so furre from fearing him, that he would familiarly gybe and jest with him: Suche longe experience breedeth in some men securitie. Although it please Erasmus a great clerke and good old father, more fatherly and favourablye to construe it in his Adages for his own behoofe, That by the proverbe Nemo Senex metuit Jovem, is not meant, that old men have no feare of God at al, but that they be furre from superstition and Idolatrous regard of false Gods, as is Jupiter. But his greate learning notwithstanding, it is to plaine, to be gainsayd, that olde men are muche more enclined to such fond fooleries, then younger heades.

Aprill

Ægloga Quarta

ARGUMENT

This Æglogue is purposely intended to the honor and prayse of our most gracious sovereigne, Queene Elizabeth. The speakers herein be Hobbinoll and Thenott, § two shepheardes: the which Hobbinoll being before mentioned, greatly to have loved Colin, is here set forth more largely, complayning him of that boyes great misadventure in Love, whereby his mynd was alienate and with drawen not onely from him, who moste loved him, but also from all former delightes and studies, aswell in pleasaunt pyping, as conning ryming and singing, and other his laudable exercises. Whereby he taketh occasion, for proofe of his more excellencie and skill in poetrie, to recorde a songe, which the sayd Colin sometime made in honor of her Majestie, whom abruptly he termeth Elysa.

conning: studying (the arts of); **abruptly:** (?) by way of abbreviation.

§ *Hobbinoll*: A pastoral name which designates Spenser's friend Gabriel Harvey. It is not known whom *Thenott* stands for, if indeed it stands for any actual person at all. *Colin* (Colin Clout) is Spenser's most consistent name for himself here and elsewhere.

THENOT   HOBBINOLL

Tell me good Hobbinoll, what garres thee greete?
  What? hath some Wolfe thy tender Lambes ytorne?
Or is thy Bagpype broke, that soundes so sweete?
Or art thou of thy loved lasse forlorne?

Or bene thine eyes attempred to the yeare,   5
Quenching the gasping furrowes thirst with rayne?
Like April shoure, so stremes the trickling teares
Adowne thy cheeke, to quenche thy thristye payne.

HOBBINOLL

Nor thys, nor that, so muche doeth make me mourne,
But for the ladde, whome long I lovd so deare,   10
Nowe loves a lasse, that all his love doth scorne:
He plongd in payne, his tressed locks dooth teare.

Shepheards delights he dooth them all forsweare,
Hys pleasaunt Pipe, whych made us meriment,
He wylfully hath broke, and doth forbeare   15
His wonted songs, wherein he all outwent.

THENOT

What is he for a Ladde, you so lament?
Ys love such pinching payne to them, that prove?
And hath he skill to make so excellent,
Yet hath so little skill to brydle love?   20

HOBBINOLL

Colin thou kenst, the Southerne shepheardes boye:
Him Love hath wounded with a deadly darte.
Whilome on him was all my care and joye,
Forcing with gyfts to winne his wanton heart.

1. **garres:** is making; **greete:**
   weep.
4. **forlorne:** jilted, forsaken.
5. **attempred:** attuned.
8. **thristye:** thirsty.
12. **tressed:** braided.

16. **wonted:** usual; **outwent:**
    surpassed.
17. **What . . . Ladde:** what sort
    of lad is he.
18. **prove:** try (it).
19. **make:** compose.

But now from me hys madding mynd is starte,   25
And woes the Widdowes daughter of the glenne: §
So nowe fayre *Rosalind* hath bredde hys smart,
So now his frend is chaunged for a frenne.

THENOT

But if hys ditties bene so trimly dight,
I pray thee *Hobbinoll*, recorde some one: 30
The whiles our flockes doe graze about in sight,
And we close shrowded in thys shade alone.

HOBBINOL

Contented I: then will I singe his laye
Of fayre *Elisa*, Queene of shepheardes all:
Which once he made, as by a spring he laye,   35
And tuned it unto the Waters fall.

Ye dayntye Nymphs, that in this blessed Brooke
    doe bathe your brest,
For sake your watry bowres, and hether looke,
    at my request: 40
And eke you Virgins, that on *Parnasse* dwell,   §
Whence floweth *Helicon* the learned well,

25. **madding:** frenzied.
26. **woes:** woos.
27. **bredde:** caused; **smart:** pain.
28. **frenne:** stranger.
29. **trimly dight:** neatly made, elegantly turned.
33. **laye:** song.
39. **bowres:** bowers.
41. **eke:** also.

§ *glenne*: Spenser may have thought, with E.K., that here "glen" means "hamlet" or "borough". In the 1580s, however, Spenser was using the word in its usual sense of "uncultivated valley". *Rosalind*: There have been attempts to supply this lady (along with E.K.) with an historical identity, but as in the case of E.K., none of them is conclusive.

§ *Virgins*: The nine Muses, daughters of Jove (Zeus) and Mnemosyne (Memory), and patronesses, under Apollo, of the arts. The Romans assigned an art to each one: *Calliope* (line 100) is the Muse of epic poetry; Clio of history; Erato of lyric poetry; Euterpe of music; Melpomene of tragedy; Polyhymnia of rhetoric; Terpsichore of the dance; Thalia of comedy; and Urania of astronomy. Their usual haunts are mountains, especially *Parnasse* (Parnassus) and *Helicon*, with its sacred stream Hippocrene. Spenser is following a medieval tradition in making Helicon the stream rather than the mountain.

Helpe me to blaze
Her worthy praise,
Which in her sexe doth all excell.   45

Of fayre *Elisa* be your silver song,
    that blessed wight:
The flowre of Virgins, may shee florish long,
    In princely plight.
For shee is *Syrinx* daughter without spotte,   50 §
Which *Pan* the shepheards God of her begot:
    So sprong her grace
    Of heavenly race,
No mortall blemishe may her blotte.

See, where she sits upon the grassie greene,   55
    (O seemely sight)
Yclad in Scarlot like a mayden Queene,
    And Ermines white.
Upon her head a Cremosin coronet,
With Damaske roses and Daffadillies set: 60
    Bayleaves betweene,
    And Primroses greene
Embellish the sweete Violet.

Tell me, have ye seene her angelick face,
    Like *Phœbe* fayre?   65 §

43. **blaze:** extol.   49. **plight:** state, condition.
47. **wight:** person.   59. **Cremosin:** crimson.

§ *Syrinx*: To suit his purpose Spenser here modifies the classical myth.
See the Glosse for E.K.'s retelling of the story in its usual form and
for his explanation of Spenser's reference to it. *Pan*: The son of
Hermes (Mercury) is the god of herdsmen and their herds and is
himself half goatish in shape, having goat's horns, ears, and legs.
§ *Phœbe*: The "bright one". Though originally quite distinct from each
of them, Phoebe comes to be identified by the poets with Artemis
(Diana), the virgin huntress, goddess of forests, and to take over the
name and function of Selene (Luna), the moon-goddess. *Cynthia*
(line 82), so called from her birthplace Mount Cynthus, is another
name for Phoebe-Artemis. This composite goddess is celebrated in
one or more of three aspects: as the moon – particularly the bright
of the moon; as giver of fertility in women; as virgin huntress and
mistress of woods and forests. In this particular passage Spenser is
careful to distinguish between these various names and aspects.

Her heavenly haveour, her princely grace
    can you well compare?
The Redde rose medled with the White yfere,
In either cheeke depeincten lively chere.
    Her modest eye,   70
    Her Majestie,
Where have you seene the like, but there?

I sawe *Phœbus* thrust out his golden hedde,   §
    upon her to gaze:
But when he sawe, how broade her beames did spredde,
    it did him amaze.   76
He blusht to see another Sunne belowe,
Ne durst againe his fyrye face out showe:
    Let him, if he dare,
    His brightnesse compare   80
With hers, to have the overthrowe.

Shewe thy selfe *Cynthia* with thy silver rayes,
    and be not abasht:
When shee the beames of her beauty displayes,
    O how art thou dasht?   85
But I will not match her with *Latonaes* seede,   §
Such follie great sorow to *Niobe* did breede.
    Now she is a stone,
    And makes dayly mone,
Warning all other to take heede.   90

66. **haveour:** bearing.   **chere:** mood, disposition.
68. **medled:** mingled; **yfere:**   86. **seede:** children.
    together.   87. **breede:** cause.
69. **depeincten:** show, depict;

§ *Phœbus*: Also the "bright one". He is identified with and absorbs
  Helios, the ancient sun-god, much as Phoebe absorbs Selene, the
  ancient moon-goddess. He is the sun, masculine counterpart of Phoebe,
  the moon; he is also identified with Apollo, the bright archer who is
  the brother of Artemis and the god of music, poetry, and prophecy.
§ *Latonaes seede*: Latona (Leto), a Titaness, was once with child by
  Jove (Zeus); in spite of delays caused by Jove's jealous consort Juno
  (Hera), Latona was eventually delivered of two children, Apollo and
  Artemis. In his Glosse E.K. retells the story of the rivalry between
  Latona and *Niobe* very well.

> *Pan* may be proud, that ever he begot
>   such a Bellibone,
> And *Syrinx* rejoyse, that ever was her lot
>   to beare such an one.
> Soone as my younglings cryen for the dam,   *95*
> To her will I offer a milkwhite Lamb:
>   Shee is my goddesse plaine,
>   And I her shepherds swayne,
> Albee forswonck and forswatt I am.
>
> I see *Calliope* speede her to the place,   *100*
>   where my Goddesse shines:
> And after her the other Muses trace,
>   with their Violines.
> Bene they not Bay braunches, which they doe beare,
> All for *Elisa* in her hand to weare?   *105*
>   So sweetely they play,
>   And sing all the way,
> That it a heaven is to heare.
>
> Lo how finely the graces can it foote   §
>   to the Instrument: *110*
> They dauncen deffly, and singen soote,
>   in their meriment.
> Wants not a fourth grace, to make the daunce even?
> Let that rowme to my Lady be yeven:
>   She shalbe a grace,   *115*
>   To fyll the fourth place,
> And reigne with the rest in heaven.

92. **Bellibone:** comely wench.
98. **swayne:** boy, youth.
99. **Albee:** although; **forswonck and forswatt:** sweaty and tired.

109. **it foote:** foot it, i.e., dance.
111. **deffly:** deftly; **soote:** sweetly.
114. **rowme:** place (in the dance); **yeven:** given.

§ *the graces*: The three beautiful daughters of Zeus and Eurynome. Their main function in mythology is to wait upon Aphrodite (Venus). For the rest, see E.K.'s useful description of them in his Glosse.

And whither rennes this bevie of Ladies bright,
    raunged in a rowe?
They bene all Ladyes of the lake behight,   *120*
    that unto her goe.
Chloris, that is the chiefest Nymph of al,
Of Olive braunches beares a Coronall:
    Olives bene for peace,
    When wars doe surcease: *125*
Such for a Princesse bene principall.

Ye shepheards daughters, that dwell on the greene,
    hye you there apace:
Let none come there, but that Virgins bene,
    to adorne her grace.   *130*
And when you come, whereas shee is in place,
See, that your rudenesse doe not you disgrace:
    Binde your fillets faste,
    And gird in your waste,
For more finesse, with a tawdrie lace.   *135 §*

Bring hether the Pincke and purple Cullambine,
    With Gelliflowres:
Bring Coronations, and Sops in wine,
    worne of Paramoures.
Strowe me the ground with Daffadowndillies,   *140*
And Cowslips, and Kingcups, and loved Lillies:
    The pretie Pawnce,
    And the Chevisaunce,
Shall match with the fayre flowre Delice.

---

118. **rennes:** runs.
120. **behight:** called, named.
128. **hye:** hasten; **apace:** quickly.
131. **whereas:** where.
132. **rudenesse:** rusticity, lack of polish.

138. **Sops in wine:** garden pinks.
140. **Strowe me:** strew . . . for me.
143. **Chevisaunce:** (?) wall-flower.
144. **flowre Delice:** lily or iris.

---

§ *tawdrie lace*: This phrase comes from "St. Audrey's Lace", meaning a neck-piece or stomacher of silk as sold at St. Audrey's Fair in Ely, England. "Tawdry" does not here mean, as it now does, showy in a cheap and tasteless way.

Now ryse up *Elisa*, decked as thou art,   *145*
  in royall aray:
And now ye daintie Damsells may depart
  echeone her way.
I feare, I have troubled your troupes to longe:
Let dame *Eliza* thanke you for her song.   *150*
    And if you come hether,
    When Damsines I gether,
I will part them all you among.

THENOT

And was thilk same song of *Colins* owne making?
Ah foolish boy, that is with love yblent: *155*
Great pittie is, he be in such taking,
For naught caren, that bene so lewdly bent.   §

HOBBINOL

Sicker I hold him, for a greater fon,
That loves the thing, he cannot purchase.
But let us homeward: for night draweth on,   *160*
And twincling starres the daylight hence chase.

THENOTS EMBLEME

O quam te memorem virgo?   §

HOBBINOLS EMBLEME

O dea certe.

154. **thilk:** this.   156. **such taking:** such a state.
155. **yblent:** dazzled.   158. **Sicker:** certainly; **fon:**
                                 fool.

§ *For naught caren . . . bent*: "For those who are foolishly set on love
disregard everything else."
§ The emblems are quoted from Virgil's *Aeneid*, I, 327-8. *Thenots
Embleme*: "What title shall I give you, maiden?" *Hobbinols Embleme*: "A goddess, surely."

GLOSSE

1 Gars thee greete) causeth thee weepe and complain.

4 Forlorne) left and forsaken.

5 Attempred to the yeare) agreeable to the season of the yeare, that is Aprill, which moneth is most bent to shoures and seasonable rayne: to quench, that is, to delaye the drought, caused through drynesse of March wyndes.

10 The Ladde) Colin Clout.   *11* The Lasse) Rosalinda.

12 Tressed locks) wrethed and curled.

17 Is he for a ladde) A straunge manner of speaking .s. what maner of Ladde is he?

19 To make) to rime and versifye. For in this word making, our olde Englishe Poetes were wont to comprehend all the skil of Poetrye, according to the Greeke woorde ποιεῖν, to make, whence commeth the name of Poets.

21 Colin thou kenst) knowest. Seemeth hereby that Colin perteyneth to some Southern noble man, and perhaps in Surrye or Kent, the rather bicause he so often nameth the Kentish downes, and before, As lythe as lasse of Kent.

26 The Widowes) He calleth Rosalind the Widowes daughter of the glenne, that is, of a country Hamlet or borough, which I thinke is rather sayde to coloure and concele the person, then simply spoken. For it is well knowen, even in spighte of Colin and Hobbinoll, that shee is a Gentle woman of no meane house, nor endewed with anye vulgare and common gifts both of nature and manners: but suche indeede, as neede nether Colin be ashamed to have her made knowne by his verses, nor Hobbinol be greved, that so she should be commended to immortalitie for her rare and singular Vertues: Specially deserving it no lesse, then eyther Myrto the most excellent Poete Theocritus his dearling, or Lauretta the divine Petrarches Goddesse, or Himera the worthye Poete Stesichorus hys Idole: Upon whom he is sayd so much to have doted, that in regard of her excellencie, he scorned and wrote against the beauty of Helena. For which his præsumptuous and unheedie hardinesse, he is sayde by vengeaunce of the Gods, thereat being offended, to have lost both his eyes.

28 Frenne) a straunger. The word I thinke was first poetically put, and afterwarde used in commen custome of speach for forenne.

29 Dight) adorned.   *33* Laye) a songe. as Roundelayes and

Virelayes. In all this songe is not to be respected, what the worthinesse of her Majestie deserveth, nor what to the highnes of a Prince is agreeable, but what is moste comely for the meanesse of a shepheards witte, or to conceive, or to utter. And therefore he calleth her Elysa, as through rudenesse tripping in her name: and a shepheards daughter, it being very unfit, that a shepheards boy brought up in the shepefold, should know, or ever seme to have heard of a Queenes roialty.

37 Ye daintie) is, as it were an Exordium ad preparandos animos.

41 Virgins) the nine Muses, daughters of Apollo and Memorie, whose abode the Poets faine to be on Parnassus, a hill in Grece, for that in that countrye specially florished the honor of all excellent studies.

42 Helicon) is both the name of a fountaine at the foote of Parnassus, and also of a mounteine in Bæotia, out of which floweth the famous Spring Castalius, dedicate also to the Muses: of which spring it is sayd, that when Pegasus the winged horse of Perseus (whereby is meant fame and flying renowme) strooke the grownde with his hoofe, sodenly thereout sprange a wel of moste cleare and pleasaunte water, which fro thence forth was consecrate to the Muses and Ladies of learning.

46 Your silver song) seemeth to imitate the lyke in Hesiodus ἀργυρέον μέλος.

50 Syrinx) is the name of a Nymphe of Arcadie, whom when Pan being in love pursued, she flying from him, of the Gods was turned into a reede. So that Pan catching at the Reedes in stede of the Damosell, and puffing hard (for he was almost out of wind) with hys breath made the Reedes to pype: which he seeing, tooke of them, and in remembraunce of his lost love, made him a pype thereof. But here by Pan and Syrinx is not to bee thoughte, that the shephearde simplye meante those Poetical Gods: but rather supposing (as seemeth) her graces progenie to be divine and immortall (so as the Paynims were wont to judge of all Kinges and Princes, according to Homeres saying.

Θυμὸς δὴ μέγας ἐστὶ διοτρεφέως βασιλῆως,
τιμὴ δ' ἐκ διός ἐστι φιλεῖ δε ὁ μητίετα Ζεύς.)

could devise no parents in his judgement so worthy for her, as Pan the shepheards God, and his best beloved Syrinx. So that by Pan is here meant the most famous and victorious King, her highnesse Father, late of worthy memorye K. Henry the eyght. And by that name, oftymes (as hereafter appeareth) be noted kings and mighty Potentates: And in some place Christ himself, who is the verye Pan and god of Shepheardes.

59 Cremosin coronet) he deviseth her crowne to be of the finest and most delicate flowers, instede of perles and precious stones, wherewith Princes Diademes use to bee adorned and embost. 63 Embellish) beautifye and set out.

65 Phebe) the Moone, whom the Poets faine to be sister unto Phæbus, that is the Sunne. 68 Medled) mingled.

68 Yfere) together. By the mingling of the Redde rose and the White, is meant the uniting of the two principall houses of Lancaster and of Yorke: by whose longe discord and deadly debate, this realm many yeares was sore traveiled, and almost cleane decayed. Til the famous Henry the seventh, of the line of Lancaster, taking to wife the most vertuous Princesse Elisabeth, daughter to the fourth Edward of the house of Yorke, begat the most royal Henry the eyght aforesayde, in whom was the firste union of the Whyte Rose and the Redde.

73 I saw Phæbus) the sunne. A sensible Narration, and present view of the thing mentioned, which they call παρουσία.

82 Cynthia) the Moone so called of Cynthus a hyll, where she was honoured.

86-7 Latonaes seede) Was Apollo and Diana. Whom when as Niobe the wife of Amphion scorned, in respect of the noble fruict of her wombe, namely her seven sonnes, and so many daughters, Latona being therewith displeased, commaunded her sonne Phœbus to slea al the sonnes, and Diana all the daughters: whereat the unfortunate Niobe being sore dismayed, and lamenting out of measure, was feigned of the Poetes, to be turned into a stone upon the sepulchre of her children. for which cause the shepheard sayth, he will not compare her to them, for feare of like mysfortune.

92 A Bellibone) or a Bonibell. homely spoken for a fayre mayde or Bonilasse.

99 Forswonck and forswatt) overlaboured and sunneburnt.

100 Calliope) one of the nine Muses: to whome they assigne the honor of all Poetical Invention, and the firste glorye of the Heroicall verse. other say, that shee is the Goddesse of Rhetorick: but by Virgile it is manifeste, that they mystake the thyng. For there in hys Epigrams, that arte semeth to be

attributed to Polymnia, saying:

Signat cuncta manu, loquiturque Polymnia gestu.

which seemeth specially to be meant of Action and elocution, both special partes of Rhetorick: besyde that her name, which (as some construe it) importeth great remembraunce, conteineth another part. But I holde rather with them, which call her Polymnia or Polyhymnia of her good singing.

104 Bay branches) be the signe of honor and victory, and therfore of myghty Conquerors worn in theyr triumphes, and eke of famous Poets, as saith Petrarch in hys Sonets.

Arbor vittoriosa triomphale,
Honor d' Imperadori & di Poëti, &c.

109 The Graces) be three sisters, the daughters of Jupiter, (whose names are Aglaia, Thalia, Euphrosyne, and Homer onely addeth a fourth .s. Pasithea) otherwise called Charites, that is thanks. whom the Poetes feyned to be the Goddesses of al bountie and comelines, which therefore (as sayth Theodontius) they make three, to wete, that men first ought to be gracious and bountiful to other freely, then to receive benefits at other mens hands curteously, and thirdly to requite them thankfully; which are three sundry Actions in liberalitye. And Boccace saith, that they be painted naked, (as they were indeede on the tombe of C. Julius Cæsar) the one having her backe toward us, and her face fromwarde, as proceeding from us: the other two toward us, noting double thanke to be due to us for the benefit, we have done.

111 Deaffly) Finelye and nimbly.   *111* Soote) Sweete.

112 Meriment) Mirth.

118 Bevie) A beavie of Ladyes, is spoken figuratively for a company or troupe. the terme is taken of Larkes. For they say a Bevie of Larkes, even as a Covey of Partridge, or an eye of Pheasaunts.

120 Ladyes of the lake) be Nymphes. For it was an olde opinion amongste the Auncient Heathen, that of every spring and fountaine was a goddesse the Soveraigne. Whiche opinion stucke in the myndes of men not manye yeares sithence, by meanes of certain fine fablers and lowd lyers, such as were the Authors of King Arthure the great and such like, who tell many an unlawfull leasing of the Ladyes of the Lake, that is, the Nymphes. For the word Nymphe in Greeke signifieth Well water, or otherwise a Spouse or Bryde.

120 Behight) called or named.

122 Chloris) the name of a Nymph, and signifieth greenesse, of whome is sayd, that Zephyrus the Westerne wind being in love with her, and coveting her to wyfe, gave her for a dowrie, the chiefedome and soveraigntye of al flowres and greene herbes, growing on earth.

124 Olives bene) The Olive was wont to be the ensigne of Peace and quietnesse, eyther for that it cannot be planted and pruned, and so carefully looked to, as it ought, but in time of peace: or els for that the Olive tree, they say, will not growe neare the Firre tree, which is dedicate to Mars the God of battaile, and used most for speares and other instruments of warre. Whereupon is finely feigned, that when Neptune and Minerva strove for the naming of the citie of Athens, Neptune striking the ground with his mace, caused a horse to come forth, that importeth warre, but at Minervaes stroke sprong out an Olive, to note that it should be a nurse of learning, and such peaceable studies.

133 Binde your) Spoken rudely, and according to shepheardes simplicitye.

136 Bring) all these be names of flowers. Sops in wine a flowre in colour much like to a Coronation, but differing in smel and quantitye. Flowre delice, that which they use to misterme, Flowre de luce, being in Latine called Flos delitiarum.

145 Now rise) is the conclusion. For having so decked her with prayses and comparisons, he returneth all the thanck of hys laboure to the excellencie of her Majestie.

152 When Damsins) A base reward of a clownish giver.

155 Yblent) Y, is a poeticall addition. blent blinded.

Embleme

This Poesye is taken out of Virgile, and there of him used in the person of Æneas to his mother Venus, appearing to him in likenesse of one of Dianaes damosells: being there most divinely set forth. To which similitude of divinitie Hobbinoll comparing the excelency of Elisa, and being through the worthynes of Colins song, as it were, overcome with the hugenesse of his imagination, brusteth out in great admiration, (O quam te memorem virgo?) being otherwise unhable, then by soddein silence, to expresse the worthinesse of his conceipt. Whom Thenot answereth with another part of the like verse, as confirming by his graunt and approvaunce, that Elisa is nowhit inferiour to the Majestie of her, of whome that Poete so boldly pronounced, O dea certe.

December

Ægloga Duodecima

ARGUMENT

This Æglogue (even as the first beganne) is ended with a complaynte of Colin to God Pan. wherein as weary of his former wayes, he proportioneth his life to the foure seasons of the yeare, comparing hys youthe to the spring time, when he was fresh and free from loves follye. His manhoode to the sommer, which he sayth, was consumed with greate heate and excessive drouth caused throughe a Comet or blasinge starre, by which hee meaneth love, which passion is comenly compared to such flames and immoderate heate. His riper yeares hee resembleth to an unseasonable harveste wherein the fruites fall ere they be rype. His latter age to winters chyll and frostie season, now drawing neare to his last ende.

The gentle shepheard satte beside a springe,
　　All in the shadowe of a bushye brere,
That *Colin* hight, which wel could pype and singe,
For he of *Tityrus* his songs did lere.
　　There as he satte in secreate shade alone,　　　5
　　Thus gan he make of love his piteous mone.

O soveraigne *Pan* thou God of shepheards all,　　§
Which of our tender Lambkins takest keepe:
And when our flocks into mischaunce mought fall,
Doest save from mischiefe the unwary sheepe:　　10
　　Als of their maisters hast no lesse regarde,
　　Then of the flocks, which thou doest watch and
　　　　ward:

I thee beseche (so be thou deigne to heare,
Rude ditties tund to shepheards Oaten reede,
Or if I ever sonet song so cleare,　　　　　　　15
As it with pleasaunce mought thy fancie feede)
　　Hearken awhile from thy greene cabinet,
　　The rurall song of carefull Colinet.

Whilome in youth, when flowrd my joyfull spring,
Like Swallow swift I wandred here and there:　　20
For heate of heedlesse lust me so did sting,
That I of doubted daunger had no feare.
　　I went the wastefull woodes and forest wyde,
　　Withouten dreade of Wolves to bene espyed.

2. **brere:** briar.
3. **hight:** (was) called.
4. **of Tityrus:** from Tityrus, i.e., Chaucer (and/or) Virgil; **lere:** learn.
8. **Which . . . takest keepe:** who looks after.
9. **mought:** might
11. **Als:** and also.
12. **ward:** guard
15. **sonet:** song; **song:** sung.
17. **cabinet:** arbour.
18. **carefull:** sorrowful.
19. **Whilome:** once.
22. **doubted:** formidable.
23. **went:** ranged; **wastefull:** waste.

§ *soveraigne Pan*: Within the Christianized pastoral convention this is probably an appeal to Christ; if so, this Pan is to be distinguished from the Pan of lines 46-52. (See E.K.'s final remarks concerning Syrinx and Pan in his Glosse to the Aprill poem.)

I wont to raunge amydde the mazie thickette,   25
And gather nuttes to make me Christmas game:
And joyed oft to chace the trembling Pricket,
Or hunt the hartlesse hare, til shee were tame.
 What wreaked I of wintrye ages waste,
 Tho deemed I, my spring would ever laste.   30

How often have I scaled the craggie Oke,
All to dislodge the Raven of her neste:
Howe have I wearied with many a stroke,
The stately Walnut tree, the while the rest
 Under the tree fell all for nuts at strife: 35
 For ylike to me was libertee and lyfe.

And for I was in thilke same looser yeares,
(Whether the Muse so wrought me from my birth,
Or I tomuch beleeved my shepherd peres)
Somedele ybent to song and musicks mirth,   40
 A good olde shepherde, *Wrenock* was his name,   §
 Made me by arte more cunning in the same.

Fro thence I durst in derring doe compare
With shepheards swayne, what ever fedde in field:
And if that *Hobbinol* right judgement bare,   45
To *Pan* his owne selfe pype I neede not yield.
 For if the flocking Nymphes did folow *Pan*,
 The wiser Muses after *Colin* ranne.

25. **wont to:** used to; **mazie:** maze-like.
27. **Pricket:** buck in its second year.
29. **wreaked:** recked, cared; **waste:** devastation, desolation.
30. **Tho deemed I:** I thought then.
32. **of her neste:** from her nest.
37. **thilke:** those.
39. **peres:** peers, fellows.
40. **Somedele ybent to:** somewhat attracted, or given to.

§ *Wrenock*: This might be Spenser's old schoolmaster Richard Mulcaster, though the case for making the identification has not been really proven.

But ah such pryde at length was ill repayde,
The shepheards God (perdie God was he none)   50
My hurtlesse pleasaunce did me ill upbraide,
My freedome lorne, my life he lefte to mone.   §
    Love they him called, that gave me checkmate,
    But better mought they have behote him Hate.

Tho gan my lovely Spring bid me farewel,   55
And Sommer season sped him to display
(For love then in the Lyons house did dwell)
The raging fyre, that kindled at his ray.
    A comett stird up that unkindly heate,
    That reigned (as men sayd) in *Venus* seate.   60

Forth was I ledde, not as I wont afore,
When choise I had to choose my wandring waye:
But whether luck and loves unbridled lore
Would leade me forth on Fancies bitte to playe: 64
    The bush my bedde, the bramble was my bowre,
    The Woodes can witnesse many a wofull stowre.

Where I was wont to seeke the honey Bee,
Working her formall rowmes in Wexen frame:
The grieslie Todestoole growne there mought I see
And loathed Paddocks lording on the same.   70
    And where the chaunting birds luld me a sleepe,
    The ghastlie Owle her grievous ynne doth keepe.

Then as the springe gives place to elder time,
And bringeth forth the fruite of sommers pryde:

50. **perdie:** truly, indeed.
51. **hurtlesse pleasaunce:** harmless pleasure.
54. **behote:** called.
57. **Lyons house:** i.e., the zodiacal sign of Leo.
59. **unkindly:** unnatural.
60. **Venus seate:** i.e., star of Venus, Hesperus.
63. **lore:** teaching.
66. **stowre:** peril, crisis.
70. **Paddocks:** toads.
72. **ynne:** abode, haunt.

§ *My freedome lorne . . . mone*: "He left me, my freedom gone, to bemoan my wretched existence."

Also my age now passed youngthly pryme,　　　75
To thinges of ryper reason selfe applyed.
　　And learnd of lighter timber cotes to frame,
　　Such as might save my sheepe and me fro shame.

To make fine cages for the Nightingale,
And Baskets of bulrushes was my wont:　　　80
Who to entrappe the fish in winding sale
Was better seene, or hurtful beastes to hont?
　　I learned als the signes of heaven to ken,
　　How *Phœbe* fayles, where *Venus* sittes and when.

And tryed time yet taught me greater thinges,　　85
The sodain rysing of the raging seas:
The soothe of byrds by beating of their wings,
The power of herbs, both which can hurt and ease:
　　And which be wont tenrage the restlesse sheepe,
　　And which be wont to worke eternall sleepe.　　90

But ah unwise and witlesse *Colin cloute*,
That kydst the hidden kinds of many a wede:
Yet kydst not ene to cure thy sore hart roote,
Whose ranckling wound as yet does rifelye bleede.
　　Why livest thou stil, and yet hast thy deathes wound?
　　Why dyest thou stil, and yet alive art founde?　　96

Thus is my sommer worne away and wasted,
Thus is my harvest hastened all to rathe:
The eare that budded faire, is burnt and blasted,
And all my hoped gaine is turnd to scathe.　　　100
　　Of all the seede, that in my youth was sowne,
　　Was nought but brakes and brambles to be mowne.

75. **youngthly:** youthful.
77. **cotes:** huts, shelters.
81. **sale:** net (of willow stems).
82. **hont:** hunt.
84. **fayles:** wanes.
85. **tryed:** faithful, trusty.
87. **soothe:** i.e., identification.
89. **tenrage:** to madden.

92. **kydst:** knew(est); **kinds:** nature, qualities.
93. **ene:** even.
94. **rifelye:** copiously.
98. **rathe:** soon.
100. **hoped:** hoped for; **scathe:** loss.

My boughes with bloosmes that crowned were at firste,
And promised of timely fruite such store,
Are left both bare and barrein now at erst: *105*
The flattring fruite is fallen to grownd before,
   And rotted, ere they were halfe mellow ripe:
   My harvest wast, my hope away dyd wipe.

The fragrant flowres, that in my garden grewe,
Bene withered, as they had bene gathered long.   *110*
Theyr rootes bene dryed up for lacke of dewe,
Yet dewed with teares they han be ever among.
   Ah who has wrought my *Rosalind* this spight
   To spil the flowres, that should her girlond dight?

And I, that whilome wont to frame my pype,   *115*
Unto the shifting of the shepheards foote:
Sike follies nowe have gathered as too ripe,
And cast hem out, as rotten and unsoote.
   The loser Lasse I cast to please nomore,
   One if I please, enough is me therefore.   *120*

And thus of all my harvest hope I have
Nought reaped but a weedye crop of care:
Which, when I thought have thresht in swelling sheave,
Cockel for corne, and chaffe for barley bare.
   Soone as the chaffe should in the fan be fynd,   *125*
   All was blowne away of the wavering wynd.

So now my yeare drawes to his latter terme,
My spring is spent, my sommer burnt up quite:
My harveste hasts to stirre up winter sterne,   *129*
And bids him clayme with rigorous rage hys right.

105. **at erst:** at length.
108. **wast:** wasted, useless.
110. **as:** as if.
112. **han be ever:** have been always.
114. **dight:** bedeck.
115. **frame:** direct, adapt.
117. **Sike:** such.

118. **unsoote:** bitter.
119. **loser:** looser; **cast:** attempt.
124. **Cockel:** e.g. darnel (a weed that grows among grain).
125. **fan:** winnowing-fan; **fynd:** separated out.

So nowe he stormes with many a sturdy stoure,
So now his blustring blast eche coste doth scoure.

The carefull cold hath nypt my rugged rynde,
And in my face deepe furrowes eld hath pight:
My head besprent with hoary frost I fynd,　　　*135*
And by myne eie the Crow his clawe dooth wright.
　　Delight is layd abedde, and pleasure past,
　　No sonne now shines, cloudes han all overcast.

Now leave ye shepheards boyes your merry glee,
My Muse is hoarse and weary of thys stounde:　*140*
Here will I hang my pype upon this tree,
Was never pype of reede did better sounde.
　　Winter is come, that blowes the bitter blaste,
　　And after Winter dreerie death does hast.

Gather ye together my little flocke,　　　　*145*
My little flock, that was to me so liefe:
Let me, ah lette me in your folds ye lock,
Ere the breme Winter breede you greater griefe.
　　Winter is come, that blowes the balefull breath,
　　And after Winter commeth timely death.　*150*

Adieu delightes, that lulled me asleepe,
Adieu my deare, whose love I bought so deare:
Adieu my little Lambes and loved sheepe,
Adieu ye Woodes that oft my witnesse were:
　　Adieu good *Hobbinol*, that was so true,　　*155*
　　Tell *Rosalind*, her *Colin* bids her adieu.

131. **stoure:** gust, tumult.　　　135. **besprent:** rimed.
132. **eche coste:** i.e., in every　140. **thys stounde:** this noise.
　　　direction.　　　　　　　　　146. **liefe:** dear.
133. **carefull:** sad.　　　　　　148. **breme:** chill, harsh;
134. **eld:** age; **pight:** scored.　　　　**breede:** cause.

COLINS EMBLEME §

GLOSSE

4 Tityrus) Chaucer: as hath bene oft sayd. *8* Lambkins) young lambes.

11 Als of their) Semeth to expresse Virgils verse

Pan curat oves oviumque magistros.

13 Deigne) voutchsafe. *17-8* Cabinet) Colinet) diminutives.

25 Mazie) For they be like to a maze whence it is hard to get out agayne.

39 Peres) felowes and companions.

40 Musick) that is Poetry as Terence sayth Qui artem tractant musicam, speking of Poetes. *43* Derring doe) aforesayd.

57 Lions house) He imagineth simply that Cupid, which is love, had his abode in the whote signe Leo, which is in middest of somer; a pretie allegory, whereof the meaning is, that love in him wrought an extraordinarie heate of lust.

58 His ray) which is Cupides beame or flames of Love.

59 A Comete) a blasing starre, meant of beautie, which was the cause of his whote love.

---

§ *Colins Embleme*: None of the primary editions of *The Shepheardes Calender* prints anything in the way of a motto after the words "Colins Embleme". In his edition (1715) of the works of Spenser, John Hughes supplied a suitable quotation for this emblem from an edition of Virgil which Spenser no doubt knew. Since then some editors have printed Hughes' emblem (with or without comment) and some have not. Since *The Shepheardes Calender* went through five editions in Spenser's lifetime, thus leaving plenty of time for authoritative, corrective additions, it seems most likely that the omission was deliberate. If this is so, the reader was presumably expected to refer back a few pages to the end of the November poem, which gives the last of the three emblems assigned to Colin in the course of the *Calender*. This November emblem is "La Mort ny Mord" – "Death does not harm" – which is nearly as suitable for the December poem as it is for its own.

60 Venus) the goddesse of beauty or pleasure. Also a signe in heaven, as it is here taken. So he meaneth that beautie, which hath alwayes aspect to Venus, was the cause of all his unquietnes in love.

67 Where I was) a fine discription of the chaunge of hys lyfe and liking; for all things nowe seemed to hym to have altered their kindly course.

70 Lording) Spoken after the maner of Paddocks and Frogges sitting which is indeed Lordly, not removing nor looking once a side, unlesse they be sturred.

73 Then as) The second part. That is his manhoode.

77 Cotes) sheepecotes. for such be the exercises of shepheards.

81 Sale) or Salow a kind of woodde like Wyllow, fit to wreath and bynde in leapes to catch fish withall.

84 Phæbe fayles) The Eclipse of the Moone, which is alwayes in Cauda or Capite Draconis, signes in heaven.

84 Venus) .s. Venus starre otherwise called Hesperus and Vesper and Lucifer, both because he seemeth to be one of the brightest starres, and also first ryseth and setteth last. All which skill in starres being convenient for shepheardes to knowe as Theocritus and the rest use.

86 Raging seaes) The cause of the swelling and ebbing of the sea commeth of the course of the Moone, sometime encreasing, sometime wayning and decreasing.

87 Sooth of byrdes) A kind of sooth saying used in elder tymes, which they gathered by the flying of byrds; First (as is sayd) invented by the Thuscanes, and from them derived to the Romanes, who (as is sayd in Livie) were so supersticiously rooted in the same, that they agreed that every Noble man should put his sonne to the Thuscanes, by them to be brought up in that knowledge.

88 Of herbes) That wonderous thinges be wrought by herbes, aswell appeareth by the common working of them in our bodies, as also by the wonderful enchauntments and sorceries that have bene wrought by them; insomuch that it is sayde that Circe a famous sorceresse turned men into sondry kinds of beastes and Monsters, and onely by herbes: as the Poete sayth Dea sæva potentibus herbis &c.

92 Kidst) knewest. *97-8* Thus is my) The thyrde parte wherein is set forth his ripe yeres as an untimely harvest, that bringeth little fruite.

99 Eare) of corne. *100* Scathe) losse hinderaunce.

109 The fragraunt flowres) sundry studies and laudable partes of learning, wherein how our Poete is seene, be they witnesse which are privie to his study.

112 Ever among) Ever and anone. *127* So now my yeere) The last part, wherein is described his age by comparison of wyntrye stormes.

133 Carefull cold) for care is sayd to coole the blood.

135 Hoary frost) A metaphore of hoary heares scattred lyke to a gray frost.

139 Glee) mirth. *148* Breeme) sharpe and bitter.

151 Adiew delights) is a conclusion of all. where in six verses he comprehendeth briefly all that was touched in this booke. In the first verse his delights of youth generally. in the second, the love of Rosalind, in the thyrd, the keeping of sheepe, which is the argument of all Æglogues. In the fourth his complaints. And in the last two his professed frendship and good will to his good friend Hobbinoll.

Embleme

The meaning whereof is that all thinges perish and come to theyr last end, but workes of learned wits and monuments of Poetry abide for ever. And therefore Horace of his Odes a work though ful indede of great wit and learning, yet of no so great weight and importaunce boldly sayth.

> Exegi monimentum ære perennius,
> Quod nec imber nec aquilo vorax &c.

Therefore let not be envied, that this Poete in his Epilogue sayth he hath made a Calendar, that shall endure as long as time &c. folowing the ensample of Horace and Ovid in the like.

> Grande opus exegi quod nec Jovis ira nec ignis,
> Nec ferrum poterit nec edax abolere vetustas &c.

Loe I have made a Calender for every yeare,
That steele in strength, and time in durance shall outweare:
And if I marked well the starres revolution,
  It shall continewe till the worlds dissolution.
To teach the ruder shepheard how to feede his sheepe,   5
And from the falsers fraud his folded flocke to keepe.
  Goe lyttle Calender, thou hast a free passeporte,
Goe but a lowly gate emongste the meaner sorte.
Dare not to match thy pype with Tityrus hys style,
  Nor with the Pilgrim that the Ploughman playde a whyle: §
But followe them farre off, and their high steppes adore, 11
The better please, the worse despise, I aske nomore.

Merce non mercede

5. **ruder:** rougher, untutored.
6. **falsers:** deceiver's.
8. **meaner:** more common, lowlier.
9. **Tityrus hys style:** Tityrus' (i.e., Chaucer's) style.
10. **Pilgrim . . . a whyle:** Ploughman who played the part of a pilgrim for a time.

§ *Pilgrim that the Ploughman playde a whyle*: A reference either to William Langland and his *Piers Plowman* (composed over the years *c.* 1362-90) or to *The Plowman's Tale*, one of the spurious additions once included among Chaucer's *Canterbury Tales*. If Tityrus (line 9) is Chaucer rather than Virgil, and if Spenser's reference is in fact to *The Plowman's Tale*, then his distinguishing it from Chaucer's "hys style" suggests that Spenser suspected it did not belong among the *Canterbury Tales*.

THE FAERIE
QUEENE

Disposed into twelve bookes,
Fashioning
XII. Morall vertues.

LONDON
Printed for William Ponsonbie.
1596.

TO
THE MOST HIGH,
MIGHTIE
And
MAGNIFICENT
EMPRESSE RENOW-
MED FOR PIETIE, VER-
TUE, AND ALL GRATIOUS
GOVERNMENT ELIZABETH BY
THE GRACE OF GOD QUEENE
OF ENGLAND FRAUNCE AND
IRELAND AND OF VIRGI-
NIA, DEFENDOUR OF THE
FAITH, &c. HER MOST
HUMBLE SERVAUNT
EDMUND SPENSER
DOTH IN ALL HU-
MILITIE DEDI-
CATE, PRE-
SENT
AND CONSECRATE THESE
HIS LABOURS TO LIVE
WITH THE ETERNI-
TIE OF HER
FAME.

THE FIRST BOOKE OF

The Faerie Queene

CONTAYNING

THE LEGENDE OF THE
KNIGHT OF THE RED CROSSE,

OR

OF HOLINESSE

1 L o I the man, whose Muse whilome did maske,
  As time her taught in lowly Shepheards weeds, §
  Am now enforst a far unfitter taske, §
  For trumpets sterne to chaunge mine Oaten reeds,
  And sing of Knights and Ladies gentle deeds;
  Whose prayses having slept in silence long,
  Me, all too meane, the sacred Muse areeds
  To blazon broad emongst her learned throng:
 Fierce warres and faithfull loves shall moralize my song.

(Note: The first number indicates the stanza; the number in
brackets indicates the line.)

 1. (1) **whilome:** once, formerly; (1) **maske:** disguise (herself);
  (2) **weeds:** clothing; (7) **areeds:** teaches, instructs.

§ *lowly Shepheards weeds*: The Muse in lowly shepherd's clothing sym-
 bolizes pastoral poetry or the pastoral poet; Spenser's precise reference is to his poem *The Shepheardes Calender* (1579). The *Oaten
 reeds* are shepherd's pipes and hence also stand for pastoral poetry.
§ *enforst a far unfitter taske*: "Driven to a task for which it is far more
 difficult to fit oneself", i.e., writing epic rather than pastoral poetry.

2   Helpe then, O holy Virgin chiefe of nine,   §
        Thy weaker Novice to performe thy will,
        Lay forth out of thine everlasting scryne
        The antique rolles, which there lye hidden still,
        Of Faerie knights and fairest *Tanaquill*,   §
        Whom that most noble Briton Prince so long
        Sought through the world, and suffered so much ill,
        That I must rue his undeserved wrong:
    O helpe thou my weake wit, and sharpen my dull tong.

3   And thou most dreaded impe of highest Jove,   §
        Faire *Venus* sonne, that with thy cruell dart
        At that good knight so cunningly didst rove,
        That glorious fire it kindled in his hart,
        Lay now thy deadly Heben bow apart,
        And with thy mother milde come to mine ayde:
        Come both, and with you bring triumphant *Mart*,
        In loves and gentle jollities arrayd,
    After his murdrous spoiles and bloudy rage allayd.

2. (3) **scryne:** covered shelf, book-chest; (8) **rue:** pity.
3. (1) **impe:** offspring; (3) **rove:** shoot; (5) **Heben:** (of) ebony;
    (7) **Mart:** Mars.

§ *holy Virgin chiefe of nine*: Calliope, the Muse of epic poetry, or perhaps Clio, the Muse of history. In classical sources sometimes
Calliope seems to be senior among the nine Muses, sometimes Clio.
Among Renaissance poets and critics epic poetry (Calliope) was certainly the senior, most important kind of poetry.
§ *Tanaquill*: The consort of Tarquinius Priscus, traditionally the fifth
king of Rome. As a type of the virtuous and noble queen she provides one of Spenser's names for Queen Elizabeth. The *Briton Prince*
is Arthur, hero of *The Faerie Queene* as a whole.
§ *Jove*: In mythology the sky-god, king and father of the younger race
of gods known as the Olympians; identified with Zeus, who is usually given as the son of the Titan Cronus (Saturn) and thus grand-
son of Gaia (Earth-mother) and Uranus (Sky-father). Spenser
sometimes thinks of Jove in this precise genealogical sense but often
simply as the highest universal god – sometimes Christianized but very
often not. *Venus* (Aphrodite) is the goddess of love, beauty, generation, and fertility; her "sonne" is Cupid (Eros). *Mart*: Mars (Ares),
the god of war and Venus' paramour.

4   And with them eke, O Goddesse heavenly bright,
       Mirrour of grace and Majestie divine,
       Great Lady of the greatest Isle, whose light
       Like *Phœbus* lampe throughout the world   §
           doth shine,
     Shed thy faire beames into my feeble eyne,
     And raise my thoughts too humble and too vile,
     To thinke of that true glorious type of thine,
     The argument of mine afflicted stile:
   The which to heare, vouchsafe, O dearest dred a-while.

4. (1-3) **Goddesse . . . Great Lady:** Queen Elizabeth; (1) **eke:**
   also; (5) **eyne:** eyes; (8) **stile:** composition, literary work.

---

§ *Phœbus lampe*: The lamp of Phoebus is the sun. Phoebus Apollo
absorbed the ancient sun-god Helios, and hence is often identified
with the sun itself.

Canto I

The Patron of true Holinesse,
Foule Errour doth defeate:
Hypocrisie him to entrape,
Doth to his home entreate.

1 A Gentle Knight was pricking on the plaine,
   Y cladd in mightie armes and silver shielde,
   Wherein old dints of deepe wounds did remaine,
   The cruell markes of many' a bloudy fielde;
   Yet armes till that time did he never wield:
   His angry steede did chide his foming bitt,
   As much disdayning to the curbe to yield:
   Full jolly knight he seemd, and faire did sitt,
As one for knightly giusts and fierce encounters fitt.

2 But on his brest a bloudie Crosse he bore,
   The deare remembrance of his dying Lord,
   For whose sweete sake that glorious badge he wore,
   And dead as living ever him ador'd:
   Upon his shield the like was also scor'd,
   For soveraine hope, which in his helpe he had:
   Right faithfull true he was in deede and word,
   But of his cheere did seeme too solemne sad;
Yet nothing did he dread, but ever was ydrad.

1. (1) **Gentle:** wellborn (hence) of gentlemanly qualities; (1) **pricking:** riding; (8) **jolly:** gallant (with possible suggestion of) overconfident; (9) **giusts:** jousts.
2. (5) **scor'd:** engraved; (8) **cheere:** mood, expression; (8) **sad:** serious; (9) **ydrad:** held in dread.

3   Upon a great adventure he was bond,
      That greatest *Gloriana* to him gave,   §
      That greatest Glorious Queene of *Faerie* lond,
      To winne him worship, and her grace to have,
      Which of all earthly things he most did crave;
      And ever as he rode, his hart did earne
      To prove his puissance in battell brave
      Upon his foe, and his new force to learne;
  Upon his foe, a Dragon horrible and stearne.

4   A lovely Ladie rode him faire beside,
      Upon a lowly Asse more white then snow,
      Yet she much whiter, but the same did hide
      Under a vele, that wimpled was full low,
      And over all a blacke stole she did throw,
      As one that inly mournd: so was she sad,
      And heavie sat upon her palfrey slow;
      Seemed in heart some hidden care she had,
  And by her in a line a milke white lambe she lad.

5   So pure an innocent, as that same lambe,
      She was in life and every vertuous lore,
      And by descent from Royall lynage came
      Of ancient Kings and Queenes, that had of yore
      Their scepters stretcht from East to Westerne shore,
      And all the world in their subjection held;
      Till that infernall feend with foule uprore
      Forwasted all their land, and them expeld:
  Whom to avenge, she had this Knight from far compeld.

3. (4) **worship:** honour; (6) **earne:** yearn; (7) **puissance:** prowess, might.
4. (9) **lad:** led.
5. (3) **lynage:** lineage; (8) **Forwasted:** ravaged.

§ *Gloriana*: Heroine of *The Faerie Queene* as a whole and, in the historical aspect of the poem, Spenser's chief name for Queen Elizabeth.

6   Behind her farre away a Dwarfe did lag,
        That lasie seemd in being ever last,
        Or wearied with bearing of her bag
        Of needments at his backe. Thus as they past,
        The day with cloudes was suddeine overcast,
        And angry *Jove* an hideous storme of raine
        Did poure into his Lemans lap so fast,
        That every wight to shrowd it did constrain,
    And this faire couple eke to shrowd themselves were fain.

7   Enforst to seeke some covert nigh at hand,
        A shadie grove not far away they spide,
        That promist ayde the tempest to withstand:
        Whose loftie trees yclad with sommers pride,
        Did spred so broad, that heavens light did hide,
        Not perceable with power of any starre:
        And all within were pathes and alleies wide,
        With footing worne, and leading inward farre:
    Faire harbour that them seemes; so in they entred arre.

8   And foorth they passe, with pleasure forward led,
        Joying to heare the birdes sweete harmony,
        Which therein shrouded from the tempest dred,
        Seemd in their song to scorne the cruell sky.
        Much can they prayse the trees so straight and hy,
        The sayling Pine, the Cedar proud and tall,
        The vine-prop Elme, the Poplar never dry,
        The builder Oake, sole king of forrests all,
    The Aspine good for staves, the Cypresse funerall.

6. (7) **Lemans:** lover's, i.e., earth's; (8) **wight:** person; (8) **shrowd:**
    take cover; (9) **eke:** also (too, as well); (9) **fain:** glad.
7. (1) **covert:** shelter; (9) **them seemes:** seems to them.
8. (5) **can:** did.

9 The Laurell, meed of mightie Conquerours
  And Poets sage, the Firre that weepeth still,
  The Willow worne of forlorne Paramours,
  The Eugh obedient to the benders will,
  The Birch for shaftes, the Sallow for the mill,
  The Mirrhe sweete bleeding in the bitter wound,
  The warlike Beech, the Ash for nothing ill,
  The fruitfull Olive, and the Platane round,
 The carver Holme, the Maple seeldom inward sound.

10 Led with delight, they thus beguile the way,
  Untill the blustring storme is overblowne;
  When weening to returne, whence they did stray,
  They cannot finde that path, which first was showne,
  But wander too and fro in wayes unknowne,
  Furthest from end then, when they neerest weene,
  That makes them doubt, their wits be not their owne:
  So many pathes, so many turnings seene,
 That which of them to take, in diverse doubt they been.

11 At last resolving forward still to fare,
  Till that some end they finde or in or out,
  That path they take, that beaten seemd most bare,
  And like to lead the labyrinth about;
  Which when by tract they hunted had throughout,
  At length it brought them to a hollow cave,
  Amid the thickest woods. The Champion stout
  Eftsoones dismounted from his courser brave,
 And to the Dwarfe a while his needlesse spere he gave.

 9. (1) **meed:** reward; (4) **Eugh:** yew; (9) **carver:** (good for) carving; (9) **Holme:** holme-oak.
10. (3) **weening:** thinking; (6) **weene:** think (themselves to be); (7) **doubt:** suspect; (9) **diverse:** distracting.
11. (1) **fare:** go; (4) **like:** likely; (4) **about:** out of (from); (8) **Eftsoones:** thereupon, forthwith.

12   Be well aware, quoth then that Ladie milde,
      Least suddaine mischiefe ye too rash provoke:
      The danger hid, the place unknowne and wilde,
      Breedes dreadfull doubts: Oft fire is without smoke,
      And perill without show: therefore your stroke
      Sir knight with-hold, till further triall made.
      Ah Ladie (said he) shame were to revoke
      The forward footing for an hidden shade:
   Vertue gives her selfe light, through darkenesse for to
        wade.

13   Yea but (quoth she) the perill of this place
      I better wot then you, though now too late
      To wish you backe returne with foule disgrace,
      Yet wisedome warnes, whilest foot is in the gate,
      To stay the steppe, ere forced to retrate.
      This is the wandring wood, this *Errours den*,
      A monster vile, whom God and man does hate:
      Therefore I read beware. Fly fly (quoth then
   The fearefull Dwarfe:) this is no place for living men.

14   But full of fire and greedy hardiment,
      The youthfull knight could not for ought be staide,
      But forth unto the darksome hole he went,
      And looked in: his glistring armor made
      A litle glooming light, much like a shade,
      By which he saw the ugly monster plaine,
      Halfe like a serpent horribly displaide,
      But th'other halfe did womans shape retaine,
   Most lothsom, filthie, foule, and full of vile disdaine.

12. (1) **aware:** on guard; (7) **revoke:** hold back.
13. (2) **wot:** know; (8) **read:** advise.
14. (1) **hardiment:** audacity, hardihood; (9) **disdaine:** hatefulness.

15   And as she lay upon the durtie ground,
    Her huge long taile her den all overspred,
    Yet was in knots and many boughtes upwound,
    Pointed with mortall sting. Of her there bred
    A thousand yong ones, which she dayly fed,
    Sucking upon her poisonous dugs, eachone
    Of sundry shapes, yet all ill favored:
    Soone as that uncouth light upon them shone,
  Into her mouth they crept, and suddain all were gone.

16   Their dam upstart, out of her den effraide,
    And rushed forth, hurling her hideous taile
    About her cursed head, whose folds displaid
    Were stretcht now forth at length without entraile.
    She lookt about, and seeing one in mayle
    Armed to point, sought backe to turne againe;
    For light she hated as the deadly bale,
    Ay wont in desert darknesse to remaine,
  Where plaine none might her see, nor she see any plaine.

17   Which when the valiant Elfe perceiv'd, he lept   §
    As Lyon fierce upon the flying pray,
    And with his trenchand blade her boldly kept
    From turning backe, and forced her to stay:
    Therewith enrag'd she loudly gan to bray,
    And turning fierce, her speckled taile advaunst,
    Threatning her angry sting, him to dismay:
    Who nought aghast, his mightie hand enhaunst:
  The stroke down from her head unto her shoulder
      glaunst.

15. (3) **boughtes:** folds, coils; (7) **ill favored:** repulsive; (8) **uncouth:** unusual.
16. (4) **entraile:** twisting; (6) **to point:** completely; (7) **bale:** harm, grief; (8) **wont:** accustomed.
17. (3) **trenchand:** sharp; (7) **Threatning:** brandishing; (8) **enhaunst:** lifted.

§ *Elfe:* The Redcross knight is often referred to as the Elfe, or the elfin knight, or the faery knight. In Book I at least, Spenser does not distinguish between elfin-kind and faery-kind. He does distinguish between elfin- or faery-kind and human-kind, since the Redcross knight turns out to be not of elfin-kind but of "English blood", of mortal human-kind (Canto X, stanzas 60 and 64-6).

18 Much daunted with that dint, her sence was dazd,
    Yet kindling rage, her selfe she gathered round,
    And all attonce her beastly body raizd
    With doubled forces high above the ground:
    Tho wrapping up her wrethed sterne arownd,
    Lept fierce upon his shield, and her huge traine
    All suddenly about his body wound,
    That hand or foot to stirre he strove in vaine:
God helpe the man so wrapt in *Errours* endlesse traine.

19 His Lady sad to see his sore constraint,
    Cride out, Now now Sir knight, shew what ye bee,
    Add faith unto your force, and be not faint:
    Strangle her, else she sure will strangle thee.
    That when he heard, in great perplexitie,
    His gall did grate for griefe and high disdaine,
    And knitting all his force got one hand free,
    Wherewith he grypt her gorge with so great paine,
That soone to loose her wicked bands did her constraine.

20 Therewith she spewd out of her filthy maw
    A floud of poyson horrible and blacke,
    Full of great lumpes of flesh and gobbets raw,
    Which stunck so vildly, that it forst him slacke
    His grasping hold, and from her turne him backe:
    Her vomit full of bookes and papers was,
    With loathly frogs and toades, which eyes did lacke,
    And creeping sought way in the weedy gras:
Her filthy parbreake all the place defiled has.

18. (1) **dint:** blow; (5) **Tho:** then; (5) **wrethed:** coiled; (6) **traine:** length (literally, tail).
19. (6) **disdaine:** indignation; (9) **constraine:** force.
20. (1) **maw:** stomach, gullet; (3) **gobbets:** chunks (of food); (9) **parbreake:** vomit.

21 As when old father *Nilus* gins to swell
        With timely pride above the *Aegyptian* vale,
        His fattie waves do fertile slime outwell,
        And overflow each plaine and lowly dale:
        But when his later spring gins to avale,
        Huge heapes of mudd he leaves, wherein there breed
        Ten thousand kindes of creatures, partly male
        And partly female of his fruitfull seed;
    Such ugly monstrous shapes elswhere may no man reed.

22 The same so sore annoyed has the knight,
        That welnigh choked with the deadly stinke,
        His forces faile, ne can no longer fight.
        Whose corage when the feend perceiv'd to shrinke,
        She poured forth out of her hellish sinke
        Her fruitfull cursed spawne of serpents small,
        Deformed monsters, fowle, and blacke as inke,
        Which swarming all about his legs did crall,
    And him encombred sore, but could not hurt at all.

23 As gentle Shepheard in sweete even-tide,
        When ruddy *Phœbus* gins to welke in west,
        High on an hill, his flocke to vewen wide,
        Markes which do byte their hasty supper best;
        A cloud of combrous gnattes do him molest,
        All striving to infixe their feeble stings,
        That from their noyance he no where can rest,
        But with his clownish hands their tender wings
    He brusheth oft, and oft doth mar their murmurings.

21. (1) **Nilus:** Nile; (2) **timely:** seasonal; (3) **fattie:** fructive;
    (5) **spring:** flood-source; (5) **avale:** sink, abate; (9) **reed:** see.
22. (3) **ne can no:** nor can he; (4) **corage:** courage (mind, heart);
    (5) **sinke:** cesspool, i.e., filthy insides; (6) **fruitfull:** abundant.
23. (2) **welke:** wane, set; (5) **combrous:** troublesome; (7) **noyance:**
    annoyance; (8) **clownish:** coarse.

24   Thus ill bestedd, and fearefull more of shame,
      Then of the certaine perill he stood in,
      Halfe furious unto his foe he came,
      Resolv'd in minde all suddenly to win,
      Or soone to lose, before he once would lin;
      And strooke at her with more then manly force,
      That from her body full of filthie sin
      He raft her hatefull head without remorse;
   A streame of cole black bloud forth gushed from her
      corse.

25   Her scattred brood, soone as their Parent deare
      They saw so rudely falling to the ground,
      Groning full deadly, all with troublous feare,
      Gathred themselves about her body round,
      Weening their wonted entrance to have found
      At her wide mouth: but being there withstood
      They flocked all about her bleeding wound,
      And sucked up their dying mothers blood,
   Making her death their life, and eke her hurt their good.

26   That detestable sight him much amazde,
      To see th'unkindly Impes of heaven accurst,
      Devoure their dam; on whom while so he gazd,
      Having all satisfide their bloudy thurst,
      Their bellies swolne he saw with fulnesse burst,
      And bowels gushing forth: well worthy end
      Of such as drunke her life, the which them nurst;
      Now needeth him no lenger labour spend,
   His foes have slaine themselves, with whom he should
      contend.

24. (1) **bestedd:** beset; (5) **lin:** give up, cease; (8) **raft:** severed; (9) **corse:** corpse, body.
25. (2) **rudely:** unceremoniously; (5) **Weening:** thinking; (5) **wonted:** usual, accustomed.
26. (2) **unkindly:** unnatural; (2) **Impes:** children.

27 His Ladie seeing all, that chaunst, from farre
  Approcht in hast to greet his victorie,
  And said, Faire knight, borne under happy starre,
  Who see your vanquisht foes before you lye:
  Well worthy be you of that Armorie,
  Wherein ye have great glory wonne this day,
  And proov'd your strength on a strong enimie,
  Your first adventure: many such I pray,   §
And henceforth ever wish, that like succeed it may.

28 Then mounted he upon his Steede againe,
  And with the Lady backward sought to wend;
  That path he kept, which beaten was most plaine,
  Ne ever would to any by-way bend,
  But still did follow one unto the end,
  The which at last out of the wood them brought.
  So forward on his way (with God to frend)
  He passed forth, and new adventure sought;
Long way he travelled, before he heard of ought.

29 At length they chaunst to meet upon the way
  An aged Sire, in long blacke weedes yclad,
  His feete all bare, his beard all hoarie gray,
  And by his belt his booke he hanging had;
  Sober he seemde, and very sagely sad,
  And to the ground his eyes were lowly bent,
  Simple in shew, and voyde of malice bad,
  And all the way he prayed, as he went,
And often knockt his brest, as one that did repent.

27. (1) **chaunst:** took place; (5) **Armorie:** (set of) armour.
28. (2) **wend:** make his way.
29. (2) **weedes:** garments; (5) **sad:** pensive; (7) **shew:** appearance.

§ *many such I pray . . . it may:* "I pray that you will have many
such similarly successful adventures."

30 He faire the knight saluted, louting low,
  Who faire him quited, as that courteous was:
  And after asked him, if he did know
  Of straunge adventures, which abroad did pas.
  Ah my deare Sonne (quoth he) how should, alas,
  Silly old man, that lives in hidden cell,
  Bidding his beades all day for his trespas,
  Tydings of warre and worldly trouble tell?
 With holy father sits not with such things to mell.   §

31 But if of daunger which hereby doth dwell,
  And homebred evill ye desire to heare,
  Of a straunge man I can you tidings tell,
  That wasteth all this countrey farre and neare.
  Of such (said he) I chiefly do inquere,
  And shall you well reward to shew the place,
  In which that wicked wight his dayes doth weare:
  For to all knighthood it is foule disgrace,
 That such a cursed creature lives so long a space.

32 Far hence (quoth he) in wastfull wildernesse
  His dwelling is, by which no living wight
  May ever passe, but thorough great distresse.
  Now (sayd the Lady) draweth toward night,
  And well I wote, that of your later fight
  Ye all forwearied be: for what so strong,
  But wanting rest will also want of might?
  The Sunne that measures heaven all day long,
 At night doth baite his steedes the *Ocean* waves emong.

30. (1) **louting:** bowing; (2) **faire him quited:** returned his greeting decently; (6) **Silly:** simple, harmless; (7) **Bidding his beades:** saying his prayers; (9) **sits:** befits.
31. (4) **wasteth:** lays waste to; (7) **wight:** creature; (7) **weare:** spend.
32. (1) **wastfull:** desolate; (3) **thorough:** through; (5) **wote:** know; (5) **later:** recent; (7) **wanting:** lacking; (9) **baite:** stop to feed and refresh.

§ *With holy father . . . to mell:* "It is not fitting for a holy father to meddle in such matters."

33   Then with the Sunne take Sir, your timely rest,
      And with new day new worke at once begin:
      Untroubled night they say gives counsell best.
      Right well Sir knight ye have advised bin,
      (Quoth then that aged man;) the way to win
      Is wisely to advise: now day is spent;
      Therefore with me ye may take up your In
      For this same night. The knight was well content:
  So with that godly father to his home they went.

34   A little lowly Hermitage it was,
      Downe in a dale, hard by a forests side,
      Far from resort of people, that did pas
      In travell to and froe: a little wyde
      There was an holy Chappell edifyde,
      Wherein the Hermite dewly wont to say
      His holy things each morne and eventyde:
      Thereby a Christall streame did gently play,
  Which from a sacred fountaine welled forth alway.

35   Arrived there, the little house they fill,
      Ne looke for entertainement, where none was:
      Rest is their feast, and all things at their will;
      The noblest mind the best contentment has.
      With faire discourse the evening so they pas:
      For that old man of pleasing wordes had store,
      And well could file his tongue as smooth as glas;
      He told of Saintes and Popes, and evermore
  He strowd an *Ave-Mary* after and before.

33. (4) **bin**: been; (6) **advise**: consider; (7) **In**: lodging, shelter.
34. (4) **wyde**: way off; (5) **edifyde**: built; (6) **wont to**: (was) in the habit of.
35. (6) **store**: a good supply; (7) **file**: polish, i.e., sound very plausible; (8) **evermore**: continually; (9) **strowd**: scattered.

36   The drouping Night thus creepeth on them fast,
        And the sad humour loading their eye liddes,   §
        As messenger of *Morpheus* on them cast   §
        Sweet slombring deaw, the which to sleepe them
                biddes.
        Unto their lodgings then his guestes he riddes:
        Where when all drownd in deadly sleepe he findes,
        He to his study goes, and there amiddes
        His Magick bookes and artes of sundry kindes,
    He seekes out mighty charmes, to trouble sleepy mindes.

37   Then choosing out few wordes most horrible,
        (Let none them read) thereof did verses frame,
        With which and other spelles like terrible,
        He bad awake blacke *Plutoes* griesly Dame,   §
        And cursed heaven, and spake reprochfull shame
        Of highest God, the Lord of life and light;
        A bold bad man, that dar'd to call by name
        Great *Gorgon*, Prince of darknesse and dead night,
    At which *Cocytus* quakes, and *Styx* is put to flight.

36. (2) **sad humour:** i.e., heavy sleepiness; (5) **riddes:** sends; (6)
    deadly: death-like.
37. (2) **frame:** put together.

§ *sad humour*: Here *sad* means "heavy" in the sense of irresistible
  drowsiness. In physiology *humour* was the term for body-fluids; here
  it means "moisture" and the notion of "heavy moisture" goes with
  "deaw", meaning drops from Lethe, the river of forgetfulness.
§ *Morpheus*: The Roman god of sleep and dreams. He is sometimes
  thought of more precisely as the one of all the thousand sons of
  Sleep (Somnus, Hypnos) who best counterfeits the human form in
  dreams.
§ *Plutoes griesly Dame*: Proserpina (Persephone). She is called *griesly*
  because although originally the beautiful, innocent Spring-maiden, she
  had come to be associated with infernal spells and the sinister phases
  of the moon. *Great Gorgon*: Demogorgon, here referred to in his
  later, medieval aspect as a sinister primal deity who controls the
  spirits of the lower world. *Cocytus* and *Styx*, the rivers of lamentation
  and hatefulness respectively, are two of the five rivers that encircle
  and flow through the kingdom of the dead.

38 And forth he cald out of deepe darknesse dred
  Legions of Sprights, the which like little flyes
  Fluttring about his ever damned hed,
  A-waite whereto their service he applyes,
  To aide his friends, or fray his enimies:
  Of those he chose out two, the falsest twoo,
  And fittest for to forge true-seeming lyes;
  The one of them he gave a message too,
 The other by him selfe staide other worke to doo.

39 He making speedy way through spersed ayre,
  And through the world of waters wide and deepe,
  To *Morpheus* house doth hastily repaire.
  Amid the bowels of the earth full steepe,
  And low, where dawning day doth never peepe,
  His dwelling is; there *Tethys* his wet bed §
  Doth ever wash, and *Cynthia* still doth steepe
  In silver deaw his ever-drouping hed,
 Whiles sad Night over him her mantle black doth spred.

40 Whose double gates he findeth locked fast, §
  The one faire fram'd of burnisht Yvory,
  The other all with silver overcast;
  And wakefull dogges before them farre do lye,
  Watching to banish Care their enimy,
  Who oft is wont to trouble gentle Sleepe.
  By them the Sprite doth passe in quietly,
  And unto *Morpheus* comes, whom drowned deepe
 In drowsie fit he findes: of nothing he takes keepe.

38. (2) **Sprights:** spirits; (4) **applyes:** employs; (5) **fray:** terrify;
(9) **staide:** (he) kept.
39. (1) **spersed:** widespread; (3) **repaire:** make his way; (8) **deaw:**
dew.
40. (7) **Sprite:** spirit; (9) **fit:** condition; (9) **keepe:** notice, care.

§ *Tethys*: Wife of Oceanus (the Ocean) oldest of the Titans, and the
mother of Nymphs and rivers. *Cynthia*: the moon-goddess.
§ *double gates*: False dreams issued through the ivory gate, true ones
through the gate of horn – here silvered over by Spenser.

41   And more, to lulle him in his slumber soft,
      A trickling streame from high rocke tumbling downe
      And ever-drizling raine upon the loft,
      Mixt with a murmuring winde, much like the sowne
      Of swarming Bees, did cast him in a swowne:
      No other noyse, nor peoples troublous cryes,
      As still are wont t'annoy the walled towne,
      Might there be heard: but carelesse Quiet lyes,
  Wrapt in eternall silence farre from enemyes.

42   The messenger approching to him spake,
      But his wast wordes returnd to him in vaine:
      So sound he slept, that nought mought him awake.
      Then rudely he him thrust, and pusht with paine,
      Whereat he gan to stretch: but he againe
      Shooke him so hard, that forced him to speake.
      As one then in a dreame, whose dryer braine   §
      Is tost with troubled sights and fancies weake,
  He mumbled soft, but would not all his silence breake.

43   The Sprite then gan more boldly him to wake,
      And threatned unto him the dreaded name
      Of *Hecate*: whereat he gan to quake,   §
      And lifting up his lumpish head, with blame
      Halfe angry asked him, for what he came.
      Hither (quoth he) me *Archimago* sent,
      He that the stubborne Sprites can wisely tame,
      He bids thee to him send for his intent
  A fit false dreame, that can delude the sleepers sent.

41. (3) **loft**: upper floor; (5) **swowne**: swoon, trance; (7) **still**:
always; (8) **carelesse**: unconscious, free from care.
42. (2) **wast**: wasted; (3) **mought**: could; (4) **paine**: exertion,
force.
43. (6) **Archimago**: i.e., the "aged sire", the hermit; (9) **fit**:
appropriate, suitable; (9) **sent**: senses.

§ *dryer braine*: The condition of light or troubled sleep was supposed
to be the result of a deficiency of moisture in the brain.
§ *Hecate*: Originally the dark Titan-goddess to whom Zeus gave great
powers over earth, sea, and sky. Spenser refers to her in her later,
rather narrower aspects as the patroness of witches and the goddess
of the dark of the moon, enchantment, and black magic.

44   The God obayde, and calling forth straight way
  A diverse dreame out of his prison darke,
  Delivered it to him, and downe did lay
  His heavie head, devoide of carefull carke,
  Whose sences all were straight benumbd and starke.
  He backe returning by the Yvorie dore,
  Remounted up as light as chearefull Larke,
  And on his litle winges the dreame he bore
In hast unto his Lord, where he him left afore.

45   Who all this while with charmes and hidden artes,
  Had made a Lady of that other Spright,
  And fram'd of liquid ayre her tender partes
  So lively, and so like in all mens sight,
  That weaker sence it could have ravisht quight:
  The maker selfe for all his wondrous witt,
  Was nigh beguiled with so goodly sight:
  Her all in white he clad, and over it
Cast a blacke stole, most like to seeme for *Una* fit.

46   Now when that ydle dreame was to him brought,
  Unto that Elfin knight he bad him fly,
  Where he slept soundly void of evill thought,
  And with false shewes abuse his fantasy,
  In sort as he him schooled privily:
  And that new creature borne without her dew,
  Full of the makers guile, with usage sly
  He taught to imitate that Lady trew,
Whose semblance she did carrie under feigned hew.

44. (2) **diverse:** distracting; (4) **carefull:** anxious; (4) **carke:** grief, trouble; (5) **starke:** stiff.

45. (4) **like:** lifelike; (9) **Una:** i.e., the "lovely Ladie" of "Royall lynage" here named for the first time; (9) **fit:** proper, fitting for.

46. (4) **fantasy:** fancy (in the sense of a tendency to delusive imagination); (5) **privily:** secretly; (6) **without her dew:** unnaturally; (9) **hew:** shape, hue.

47   Thus well instructed, to their worke they hast,
     And comming where the knight in slomber lay,
     The one upon his hardy head him plast,
     And made him dreame of loves and lustfull play,
     That nigh his manly hart did melt away,
     Bathed in wanton blis and wicked joy:
     Then seemed him his Lady by him lay,
     And to him playnd, how that false winged boy,   §
Her chast hart had subdewd, to learne Dame pleasures
     toy.

48   And she her selfe of beautie soveraigne Queene,
     Faire *Venus* seemde unto his bed to bring
     Her, whom he waking evermore did weene,
     To be the chastest flowre, that ay did spring
     On earthly braunch, the daughter of a king,
     Now a loose Leman to vile service bound:
     And eke the *Graces* seemed all to sing,   §
     Hymen ĩō Hymen, dauncing all around,   §
Whilst freshest *Flora* her with Yvie girlond crownd.

47. (3) **him plast:** placed himself; (8) **playnd:** complained;
    (9) **toy:** game, play.
48. (3) **weene:** consider; (6) **Leman:** mistress.

§ *false winged boy*: Cupid (Eros), here seen in his aspect as the desire
  for erotic pleasure; sometimes called the *blind God* (stanza 51) – his
  blindness being a metaphor for both the random unpredictability of
  sexual attraction and also the irrationality of passion (sight usually
  being associated with reason).
§ *the Graces*: Aglaia, Euphrosyne, and Thalia; they almost always
  appear with Aphrodite (Venus) as her ladies-in-waiting.
§ *Hymen io Hymen*: A ritual cry raised during wedding processions in
  praise and glorification of Hymen, the Roman god of marriage. *Flora*:
  the Roman goddess of flowering and blossoming plants.

49   In this great passion of unwonted lust,
    Or wonted feare of doing ought amis,
    He started up, as seeming to mistrust
    Some secret ill, or hidden foe of his:
    Lo there before his face his Lady is,
    Under blake stole hyding her bayted hooke,
    And as halfe blushing offred him to kis,
    With gentle blandishment and lovely looke,
Most like that virgin true, which for her knight him took.

50   All cleane dismayd to see so uncouth sight,
    And halfe enraged at her shamelesse guise,
    He thought have slaine her in his fierce despight:
    But hasty heat tempring with sufferance wise,
    He stayde his hand, and gan himselfe advise
    To prove his sense, and tempt her faigned truth.
    Wringing her hands in wemens pitteous wise,
    Tho can she weepe, to stirre up gentle ruth,
Both for her noble bloud, and for her tender youth.

51   And said, Ah Sir, my liege Lord and my love,
    Shall I accuse the hidden cruell fate,
    And mightie causes wrought in heaven above,
    Or the blind God, that doth me thus amate,
    For hoped love to winne me certaine hate?
    Yet thus perforce he bids me do, or die.
    Die is my dew: yet rew my wretched state
    You, whom my hard avenging destinie
Hath made judge of my life or death indifferently.

49. (1) **unwonted:** unlooked for; (2) **wonted:** typical, customary;
   (3) **mistrust:** suspect.
50. (1) **uncouth:** strange, unusual; (2) **guise:** behaviour; (4) **sufferance:** patience; (6) **prove:** make sure of; (6) **tempt:** test out;
   (8) **Tho:** then; (8) **can:** did; (8) **ruth:** pity.
51. (4) **amate:** dismay; (7) **rew:** take pity on; (9) **indifferently:**
   equally.

52   Your owne deare sake forst me at first to leave
        My Fathers kingdome, There she stopt with teares;
        Her swollen hart her speach seemd to bereave,
        And then againe begun, My weaker yeares
        Captiv'd to fortune and frayle worldly feares,
        Fly to your faith for succour and sure ayde:
        Let me not dye in languor and long teares.
        Why Dame (quoth he) what hath ye thus dismayd?
    What frayes ye, that were wont to comfort me affrayd?

53   Love of your selfe, she said, and deare constraint
        Lets me not sleepe, but wast the wearie night
        In secret anguish and unpittied plaint,
        Whiles you in carelesse sleepe are drowned quight.
        Her doubtfull words made that redoubted knight
        Suspect her truth: yet since no'untruth he knew,
        Her fawning love with foule disdainefull spight
        He would not shend, but said, Deare dame I rew,
    That for my sake unknowne such griefe unto you grew.

54   Assure your selfe, it fell not all to ground;
        For all so deare as life is to my hart,
        I deeme your love, and hold me to you bound;
        Ne let vaine feares procure your needlesse smart,
        Where cause is none, but to your rest depart.
        Not all content, yet seemd she to appease
        Her mournefull plaintes, beguiled of her art,
        And fed with words, that could not chuse but please,
    So slyding softly forth, she turnd as to her ease.

52. (3) **bereave:** deprive (her) of.
53. (1) **deare constraint:** grievous distress; (5) **doubtfull:** questionable; (8) **shend:** put to shame; (8) **rew:** am sorry; (9) **unknowne:** i.e., unknown to me.
54. (4) **smart:** pain; (6) **appease:** check; (7) **beguiled:** foiled; (9) **as:** as if (going).

55 Long after lay he musing at her mood,
      Much griev'd to thinke that gentle Dame so light,
      For whose defence he was to shed his blood.
      At last dull wearinesse of former fight
      Having yrockt a sleepe his irkesome spright,
      That troublous dreame gan freshly tosse his braine,
      With bowres, and beds, and Ladies deare delight:
      But when he saw his labour all was vaine,
    With that misformed spright he backe returnd againe.

55. (5) **irkesome spright:** restless mind.

Canto II

*The guilefull great Enchaunter parts
The Redcrosse Knight from Truth:
Into whose stead faire falshood steps,
And workes him wofull ruth.*

1   By this the Northerne wagoner had set   §
        His sevenfold teme behind the stedfast starre,
     That was in Ocean waves yet never wet,
     But firme is fixt, and sendeth light from farre
     To all, that in the wide deepe wandring arre:
     And chearefull Chaunticlere with his note shrill
     Had warned once, that *Phœbus* fiery carre
     In hast was climbing up the Easterne hill,
  Full envious that night so long his roome did fill.

2   When those accursed messengers of hell,
        That feigning dreame, and that faire-forged Spright
     Came to their wicked maister, and gan tell
     Their bootelesse paines, and ill succeeding night:
     Who all in rage to see his skilfull might
     Deluded so, gan threaten hellish paine
     And sad *Proserpines* wrath, them to affright.   §
     But when he saw his threatning was but vaine,
  He cast about, and searcht his balefull bookes againe.

ruth: trouble.
  1. (2) **stedfast starre:** Pole Star; (6) **Chaunticlere:** i.e., rooster.
  2. (4) **bootelesse:** fruitless, ineffective; (4) **ill succeeding:** unsuccessful; (9) **balefull:** dreadful, deadly.

§ *Northerne wagoner*: The constellation Boötes, also called either the
  Wagoner or the Bear Keeper depending upon whether the constellation forming the *sevenfold teme* was called Charles' Wain (Wagon)
  or the Great Bear.
§ *sad Proserpines wrath*: Proserpina (Persephone), daughter of Jove
  and his sister-wife Ceres (Demeter) who was the goddess of corn
  and the other fruits of the earth. Pluto (Hades) kidnapped Proserpina

3   Eftsoones he tooke that miscreated faire,
        And that false other Spright, on whom he spred
        A seeming body of the subtile aire,
        Like a young Squire, in loves and lusty-hed
        His wanton dayes that ever loosely led,
        Without regard of armes and dreaded fight:
        Those two he tooke, and in a secret bed,
        Covered with darknesse and misdeeming night,
Them both together laid, to joy in vaine delight.

4   Forthwith he runnes with feigned faithfull hast
        Unto his guest, who after troublous sights
        And dreames, gan now to take more sound repast,
        Whom suddenly he wakes with fearefull frights,
        As one aghast with feends or damned sprights,
        And to him cals, Rise rise unhappy Swaine,
        That here wex old in sleepe, whiles wicked wights
        Have knit themselves in *Venus* shamefull chaine;
Come see, where your false Lady doth her honour staine.

5   All in amaze he suddenly up start
        With sword in hand, and with the old man went;
        Who soone him brought into a secret part,
        Where that false couple were full closely ment
        In wanton lust and lewd embracement:
        Which when he saw, he burnt with gealous fire,
        The eye of reason was with rage yblent,
        And would have slaine them in his furious ire,
But hardly was restreined of that aged sire.

3. (1) **Eftsoones:** forthwith; (4) **lusty-hed:** lasciviousness; (8) **misdeeming:** misleading.
4. (3) **repast:** repose; (6) **Swaine:** young man; (7) **wights:** persons.
5. (4) **ment:** entwined; (7) **yblent:** blinded; (9) **But . . . of:** but for being barely restrained by.

to be his queen in the underworld. *Sad* is used both in the sense of "grieving" and also of "sombre", "gloomy". As in Canto I, stanza 37, Spenser is associating Proserpina with sinister powers and spells.

6   Returning to his bed in torment great,
      And bitter anguish of his guiltie sight,
      He could not rest, but did his stout heart eat,
      And wast his inward gall with deepe despight,
      Yrkesome of life, and too long lingring night.
      At last faire *Hesperus* in highest skie
      Had spent his lampe, and brought forth dawning light,
      Then up he rose, and clad him hastily;
    The Dwarfe him brought his steed: so both away do fly.

7   Now when the rosy-fingred Morning faire,
      Weary of aged *Tithones* saffron bed,   §
      Had spred her purple robe through deawy aire,
      And the high hils *Titan* discovered,
      The royall virgin shooke off drowsy-hed,
      And rising forth out of her baser bowre,
      Lookt for her knight, who far away was fled,
      And for her Dwarfe, that wont to wait each houre;
    Then gan she waile and weepe, to see that woefull
        stowre.

8   And after him she rode with so much speede
      As her slow beast could make; but all in vaine:
      For him so far had borne his light-foot steede,
      Pricked with wrath and fiery fierce disdaine,
      That him to follow was but fruitlesse paine;
      Yet she her weary limbes would never rest,
      But every hill and dale, each wood and plaine
      Did search, sore grieved in her gentle brest,
    He so ungently left her, whom she loved best.

6. (4) **wast**: fretted; (4) **despight**: anger; (5) **Yrkesome**: impatient, weary; (6) **Hesperus**: the Evening Star.
7. (4) **Titan**: the sun; (5) **drowsy-hed**: drowsiness; (6) **baser bowre**: lower chamber; (8) **wont**: was accustomed; (9) **stowre**: predicament, peril.
8. (4) **disdaine**: scorn; (9) **ungently**: rudely, ignobly.

§ *aged Tithones*: Eos (Aurora), the goddess of dawn and morning, fell in love with the mortal Tithonus and asked for him the gift of immortality from Zeus. Her request was honoured but unfortunately she had forgotten also to ask for eternal youth, so that Tithonus eventually became old, decrepit, and repulsive. To put him in some fashion out of his misery Eos turned him into a grasshopper or cicada.

9   But subtill *Archimago*, when his guests
        He saw divided into double parts,
        And *Una* wandring in woods and forrests,
        Th'end of his drift, he praisd his divelish arts,
        That had such might over true meaning harts;
        Yet rests not so, but other meanes doth make,
        How he may worke unto her further smarts:
        For her he hated as the hissing snake,
    And in her many troubles did most pleasure take.

10   He then devisde himselfe how to disguise;
        For by his mightie science he could take
        As many formes and shapes in seeming wise,
        As ever *Proteus* to himselfe could make: §
        Sometime a fowle, sometime a fish in lake,
        Now like a foxe, now like a dragon fell,
        That of himselfe he oft for feare would quake,
        And oft would flie away. O who can tell
    The hidden power of herbes, and might of Magicke
        spell?

 9. (2) **double parts:** two parties; (4) **Th'end:** the aim, purpose;
    (4) **drift:** plot; (7) **smarts:** sorrows.
10. (1) **devisde:** considered; (6) **fell:** fierce.

§ *Proteus*: The guardian of Poseidon's (Neptune's) herds of sea-
creatures, Proteus had the power of prophecy. Under questioning, he
would change himself into many various shapes; but if the ques-
tioner hung onto him until he resumed his true shape Proteus would
have to answer questions truthfully.

11 But now seemde best, the person to put on
      Of that good knight, his late beguiled guest:
      In mighty armes he was yclad anon,
      And silver shield: upon his coward brest
      A bloudy crosse, and on his craven crest
      A bounch of haires discolourd diversly:
      Full jolly knight he seemde, and well addrest,
      And when he sate upon his courser free,   §
Saint George himself ye would have deemed him to be.

12 But he the knight, whose semblaunt he did beare,
      The true *Saint George* was wandred far away,
      Still flying from his thoughts and gealous feare;
      Will was his guide, and griefe led him astray.
      At last him chaunst to meete upon the way
      A faithlesse Sarazin all arm'd to point,
      In whose great shield was writ with letters gay
      Sans foy: full large of limbe and every joint
He was, and cared not for God or man a point.

13 He had a faire companion of his way,
      A goodly Lady clad in scarlot red,
      Purfled with gold and pearle of rich assay,
      And like a *Persian* mitre on her hed
      She wore, with crownes and owches garnished,
      The which her lavish lovers to her gave;
      Her wanton palfrey all was overspred
      With tinsell trappings, woven like a wave,
Whose bridle rung with golden bels and bosses brave.

11. (1-2) **person . . . Of:** to impersonate; (2) **beguiled:** disappointed; (3) **anon:** very soon; (5) **craven:** cowardly; (6) **discolourd diversly:** multicoloured; (7) **addrest:** appointed; (8) **free:** willing, spirited.
12. (1) **semblaunt:** likeness; (4) **Will:** passion; (6) **arm'd to point:** fully armed; (9) **point:** jot.
13. (3) **Purfled:** bordered decoratively; (3) **assay:** quality; (5) **owches:** ornamental brooches; (7) **wanton:** playful; (9) **bosses:** ornamental rivets of a shield.

§ *free*: Spenser is also using the word with its earlier connotation of "noble". The courser is noble in the sense of being mettlesome and finely bred.

14 With faire disport and courting dalliaunce
      She intertainde her lover all the way:
      But when she saw the knight his speare advaunce,
      She soone left off her mirth and wanton play,
      And bad her knight addresse him to the fray:
      His foe was nigh at hand. He prickt with pride
      And hope to winne his Ladies heart that day,
      Forth spurred fast: adowne his coursers side
    The red bloud trickling staind the way, as he did ride.

15 The knight of the *Redcrosse* when him he spide,
      Spurring so hote with rage dispiteous,
      Gan fairely couch his speare, and towards ride:
      Soone meete they both, both fell and furious,
      That daunted with their forces hideous,
      Their steeds do stagger, and amazed stand,
      And eke themselves too rudely rigorous,
      Astonied with the stroke of their owne hand,
    Do backe rebut, and each to other yeeldeth land.

16 As when two rams stird with ambitious pride,
      Fight for the rule of the rich fleeced flocke,
      Their horned fronts so fierce on either side
      Do meete, that with the terrour of the shocke
      Astonied both, stand sencelesse as a blocke,
      Forgetfull of the hanging victory:
      So stood these twaine, unmoved as a rocke,
      Both staring fierce, and holding idely
    The broken reliques of their former cruelty.

14. (1) **disport:** entertainment; (1) **courting:** love-making (adj.);
      (5) **addresse him:** ready himself.
15. (2) **dispiteous:** pitiless; (4) **fell:** implacable; (8) **Astonied:**
      stunned; (9) **rebut:** recoil.

17   The *Sarazin* sore daunted with the buffe
     Snatcheth his sword, and fiercely to him flies;
     Who well it wards, and quyteth cuff with cuff:
     Each others equall puissaunce envies,   §
     And through their iron sides with cruell spies
     Does seeke to perce: repining courage yields
     No foote to foe. The flashing fier flies
     As from a forge out of their burning shields,
  And streames of purple bloud new dies the verdant fields.

18   Curse on that Crosse (quoth then the *Sarazin*)
     That keepes thy body from the bitter fit;
     Dead long ygoe I wote thou haddest bin,
     Had not that charme from thee forwarned it:
     But yet I warne thee now assured sitt,
     And hide thy head. Therewith upon his crest
     With rigour so outrageous he smitt,
     That a large share it hewd out of the rest,
  And glauncing downe his shield, from blame him fairely
      blest.

19   Who thereat wondrous wroth, the sleeping spark
     Of native vertue gan eftsoones revive,
     And at his haughtie helmet making mark,
     So hugely stroke, that it the steele did rive,
     And cleft his head. He tumbling downe alive,
     With bloudy mouth his mother earth did kis,
     Greeting his grave: his grudging ghost did strive
     With the fraile flesh; at last it flitted is,
  Whither the soules do fly of men, that live amis.

17. (1) **buffe:** buffet, blow; (3) **quyteth:** repays; (6) **repining:** wrathful.
18. (2) **fit:** attack; (3) **wote:** know; (4) **forwarned:** deflected; (5) **assured sitt:** (to) brace yourself; (8) **share:** part, piece; (9) **from . . . blest:** i.e., which happily preserved him from injury.
19. (3) **making mark:** taking aim; (4) **rive:** cut through.

§ *Each others . . . seeke to perce*: "Each begrudges the other's equal valour and searches with cruel looks for a weak point in his armour."

20 The Lady when she saw her champion fall,
  ⌐ e the old ruines of a broken towre,
  Staid not to waile his woefull funerall,
  But from him fled away with all her powre;
  Who after her as hastily gan scowre,
  Bidding the Dwarfe with him to bring away
  The *Sarazins* shield, signe of the conqueroure.
  Her soone he overtooke, and bad to stay,
For present cause was none of dread her to dismay.

21 She turning backe with ruefull countenaunce,
  Cride, Mercy mercy Sir vouchsafe to show
  On silly Dame, subject to hard mischaunce,
  And to your mighty will. Her humblesse low
  In so ritch weedes and seeming glorious show,
  Did much emmove his stout heroïcke heart,
  And said, Deare dame, your suddein overthrow
  Much rueth me; but now put feare apart,
And tell, both who ye be, and who that tooke your part.

22 Melting in teares, then gan she thus lament;
  The wretched woman, whom unhappy howre
  Hath now made thrall to your commandement,
  Before that angry heavens list to lowre,
  And fortune false betraide me to your powre,
  Was, (O what now availeth that I was!)
  Borne the sole daughter of an Emperour,
  He that the wide West under his rule has,
And high hath set his throne, where *Tiberis* doth pas.

20. (5) **gan scowre:** began to pursue; (8) **stay:** stop.
21. (1) **ruefull:** pitiful; (3) **silly:** harmless; (5) **weedes:** clothing;
  (6) **emmove:** move; (8) **rueth:** grieves.
22. (4) **list:** chose; (4) **lowre:** frown, lour; (6) **availeth:** does it
  avail; (9) **Tiberis:** the river Tiber.

23 He in the first flowre of my freshest age,
    Betrothed me unto the onely haire
    Of a most mighty king, most rich and sage;
    Was never Prince so faithfull and so faire,
    Was never Prince so meeke and debonaire;
    But ere my hoped day of spousall shone,
    My dearest Lord fell from high honours staire,
    Into the hands of his accursed fone,
And cruelly was slaine, that shall I ever mone.

24 His blessed body spoild of lively breath,
    Was afterward, I know not how, convaid
    And fro me hid: of whose most innocent death
    When tidings came to me unhappy maid,
    O how great sorrow my sad soule assaid.
    Then forth I went his woefull corse to find,
    And many yeares throughout the world I straid,
    A virgin widow, whose deepe wounded mind
With love, long time did languish as the striken hind.

25 At last it chaunced this proud *Sarazin*,
    To meete me wandring, who perforce me led
    With him away, but yet could never win
    The Fort, that Ladies hold in soveraigne dread.
    There lies he now with foule dishonour dead,
    Who whiles he liv'de, was called proud *Sans foy*,
    The eldest of three brethren, all three bred
    Of one bad sire, whose youngest is *Sans joy*,
And twixt them both was borne the bloudy bold *Sans loy*.

23. (5) **debonaire:** gallantly courteous; (8) **fone:** foes.
24. (2) **convaid:** taken away; (5) **assaid:** afflicted; (9) **hind:** doe.
25. (4) **dread:** reverence.

26   In this sad plight, friendlesse, unfortunate,
       Now miserable I *Fidessa* dwell,
       Craving of you in pitty of my state,
       To do none ill, if please ye not do well.
       He in great passion all this while did dwell,
       More busying his quicke eyes, her face to view,
       Then his dull eares, to heare what she did tell;
       And said, Faire Lady hart of flint would rew
    The undeserved woes and sorrowes, which ye shew.

27   Henceforth in safe assuraunce may ye rest,
       Having both found a new friend you to aid,
       And lost an old foe, that did you molest:
       Better new friend then an old foe is said.
       With chaunge of cheare the seeming simple maid
       Let fall her eyen, as shamefast to the earth,
       And yeelding soft, in that she nought gain-said,
       So forth they rode, he feining seemely merth,
    And she coy lookes: so dainty they say maketh derth.

28   Long time they thus together traveiled,
       Till weary of their way, they came at last,
       Where grew two goodly trees, that faire did spred
       Their armes abroad, with gray mosse overcast,
       And their greene leaves trembling with every blast,
       Made a calme shadow far in compasse round:
       The fearefull Shepheard often there aghast
       Under them never sat, ne wont there sound
    His mery oaten pipe, but shund th'unlucky ground.

26. (4) **if please ye not:** if it is not your pleasure to; (8) **rew:** pity.
27. (5) **cheare:** countenance; (7) **gain-said:** opposed; (8) **feining:** putting on; (8) **seemely:** comely; (9) **so . . . derth:** thus coy daintiness, they say, creates desire.
28. (7) **aghast:** terrified; (8) **ne wont:** nor was in the habit of.

29   But this good knight soone as he them can spie,
        For the coole shade him thither hastly got:
        F · golden *Phœbus* now ymounted hie,
        From fiery wheeles of his faire chariot
        Hurled his beame so scorching cruell hot,
        That living creature mote it not abide;
        And his new Lady it endured not.
        There they alight, in hope themselves to hide
From the fierce heat, and rest their weary limbs a tide.

30   Faire seemely pleasaunce each to other makes,
        With goodly purposes there as they sit:
        And in his falsed fancy he her takes
        To be the fairest wight, that lived yit;
        Which to expresse, he bends his gentle wit,
        And thinking of those braunches greene to frame
        A girlond for her dainty forehead fit,
        He pluckt a bough; out of whose rift there came
Small drops of gory bloud, that trickled downe the same.

31   Therewith a piteous yelling voyce was heard,
        Crying, O spare with guilty hands to teare
        My tender sides in this rough rynd embard,
        But fly, ah fly far hence away, for feare
        Least to you hap, that happened to me heare,
        And to this wretched Lady, my deare love,
        O too deare love, love bought with death too deare.
        Astond he stood, and up his haire did hove,
And with that suddein horror could no member move.

29. (6) **mote:** could; (9) **tide:** while.
30. (1) **pleasaunce:** pleasing courtesies; (3) **falsed:** deceived, abused.
31. (3) **rynd:** bark; (3) **embard:** confined; (5) **hap:** should happen; (8) **Astond:** thunderstruck; (8) **hove:** rise.

32   At last whenas the dreadfull passion
        Was overpast, and manhood well awake,
        Yet musing at the straunge occasion,
        And doubting much his sence, he thus bespake;
        What voyce of damned Ghost from *Limbo* lake,   §
        Or guilefull spright wandring in empty aire,
        Both which fraile men do oftentimes mistake,
        Sends to my doubtfull eares these speaches rare,
    And ruefull plaints, me bidding guiltlesse bloud to spare?

33   Then groning deepe, Nor damned Ghost, (quoth he,)
        Nor guilefull sprite to thee these wordes doth speake,
        But once a man *Fradubio*, now a tree,
        Wretched man, wretched tree; whose nature weake,
        A cruell witch her cursed will to wreake,
        Hath thus transformd, and plast in open plaines,
        Where *Boreas* doth blow full bitter bleake,
        And scorching Sunne does dry my secret vaines:
    For though a tree I seeme, yet cold and heat me paines.

34   Say on *Fradubio* then, or man, or tree,
        Quoth then the knight, by whose mischievous arts
        Art thou misshaped thus, as now I see?
        He oft finds med'cine, who his griefe imparts;
        But double griefs afflict concealing harts,   §
        As raging flames who striveth to suppresse.
        The author then (said he) of all my smarts,
        Is one *Duessa* a false sorceresse,
    That many errant knights hath brought to wretchednesse.

32. (5) **Limbo lake:** the lake of Limbo; (8) **doubtfull:** apprehensive; (8) **rare:** thin sounding; (9) **ruefull:** pitiful.
33. (7) **Boreas:** the north wind.

§ *Limbo lake*: In theology Limbo is the region bordering or encircling hell in which the souls of unbaptized infants, and of the righteous who died before the coming of Christ, await the resurrection. Spenser seems to be using "lake of limbo" simply in the general sense of the underworld of lost souls.
§ *But double griefs . . . to suppresse*: "But as a fire grows fiercer in the attempt to smother it, so grief is doubled in the effort to conceal it."

35   In prime of youthly yeares, when corage hot
         The fire of love and joy of chevalree
         First kindled in my brest, it was my lot
         To love this gentle Lady, whom ye see,
         Now not a Lady, but a seeming tree;
         With whom as once I rode accompanyde,
         Me chaunced of a knight encountred bee,
         That had a like faire Lady by his syde,
      Like a faire Lady, but did fowle *Duessa* hyde.

36   Whose forged beauty he did take in hand,
         All other Dames to have exceeded farre;
         I in defence of mine did likewise stand,
         Mine, that did then shine as the Morning starre:
         So both to battell fierce arraunged arre,
         In which his harder fortune was to fall
         Under my speare: such is the dye of warre:
         His Lady left as a prise martiall,
      Did yield her comely person, to be at my call.

37   So doubly lov'd of Ladies unlike faire,
         Th'one seeming such, the other such indeede,
         One day in doubt I cast for to compare,
         Whether in beauties glorie did exceede;
         A Rosy girlond was the victors meede:
         Both seemde to win, and both seemde won to bee,
         So hard the discord was to be agreede.
         Frælissa was as faire, as faire mote bee,
      And ever false *Duessa* seemde as faire as shee.

35. (1) **corage**: heart; (8) **like**: similarly; (9) **Like a**: in the likeness of.
36. (1) **did . . . hand**: was willing to assert (in knightly trial by battle); (7) **dye**: hazard; (8) **prise martiall**: spoil of war.
37. (3) **cast**: planned; (4) **Whether**: which one (exceeded) the other; (8) **mote**: could.

38   The wicked witch now seeing all this while
       The doubtfull ballaunce equally to sway,
       What not by right, she cast to win by guile,
       And by her hellish science raisd streight way
       A foggy mist, that overcast the day,
       And a dull blast, that breathing on her face,
       Dimmed her former beauties shining ray,
       And with foule ugly forme did her disgrace:
Then was she faire alone, when none was faire in place.

39   Then cride she ⟨ ⟩, Fye, fye, deformed wight,
       Whose borrowed beautie now appeareth plaine
       To have before bewitched all mens sight;
       O leave her soone, or let her soone be slaine.
       Her loathly visage viewing with disdaine,
       Eftsoones I thought her such, as she me told,
       And would have kild her; but with faigned paine,
       The false witch did my wrathfull hand with-hold;
So left her, where she now is turnd to treen mould.

40   Thens forth I tooke *Duessa* for my Dame,
       And in the witch unweeting joyd long time,
       Ne ever wist, but that she was the same,
       Till on a day (that day is every Prime,
       When Witches wont do penance for their crime)
       I chaunst to see her in her proper hew,
       Bathing her selfe in origane and thyme:
       A filthy foule old woman I did vew,
That ever to have toucht her, I did deadly rew.

38. (3) **cast:** resolved.
39. (1) **wight:** creature; (5) **disdaine:** disgust; (6) **Eftsoones:** immediately; (9) **treen:** (of) trees; (9) **mould:** shape.
40. (2) **unweeting:** unsuspecting; (2) **joyd:** took pleasure; (3) **wist:** knew; (3) **same:** i.e., a witch; (4) **Prime:** spring-time; (6) **proper hew:** own true form; (9) **rew:** repent.

41   Her neather partes misshapen, monstruous,
      Were hidd in water, that I could not see,
      But they did seeme more foule and hideous,
      Then womans shape man would beleeve to bee.
      Thens forth from her most beastly companie
      I gan refraine, in minde to slip away,
      Soone as appeard safe oportunitie:
      For danger great, if not assur'd decay
  I saw before mine eyes, if I were knowne to stray.

42   The divelish hag by chaunges of my cheare
      Perceiv'd my thought, and drownd in sleepie night,
      With wicked herbes and ointments did besmeare
      My bodie all, through charmes and magicke might,
      That all my senses were bereaved quight:
      Then brought she me into this desert waste,
      And by my wretched lovers side me pight,
      Where now enclosd in wooden wals full faste,
  Banisht from living wights, our wearie dayes we waste.

43   But how long time, said then the Elfin knight,
      Are you in this misformed house to dwell?
      We may not chaunge (quoth he) this evil plight,
      Till we be bathed in a living well;
      That is the terme prescribed by the spell.
      O how, said he, mote I that well out find,
      That may restore you to your wonted well?
      Time and suffised fates to former kynd
  Shall us restore, none else from hence may us unbynd.

41. (6) **gan:** did.
42. (1) **cheare:** countenance, looks; (5) **bereaved:** made away with; (7) **pight:** fixed; (8) **faste:** securely.
43. (7) **wonted well:** accustomed well-being; (8) **suffised:** satisfied; (8) **kynd:** nature.

44   The false *Duessa*, now *Fidessa* hight,
         Heard how in vaine *Fradubio* did lament,
         And knew well all was true. But the good knight
         Full of sad feare and ghastly dreriment,
         When all this speech the living tree had spent,
         The bleeding bough did thrust into the ground,
         That from the bloud he might be innocent,
         And with fresh clay did close the wooden wound:
     Then turning to his Lady, dead with feare her found.

45   Her seeming dead he found with feigned feare,
         As all unweeting of that well she knew,
         And paynd himselfe with busie care to reare
         Her out of carelesse swowne. Her eylids blew
         And dimmed sight with pale and deadly hew
         At last she up gan lift: with trembling cheare
         Her up he tooke, too simple and too trew,
         And oft her kist. At length all passed feare,
     He set her on her steede, and forward forth did beare.

44. (1) **hight:** called; (4) **dreriment:** dolefulness.
45. (2) **As:** as if; (2) **unweeting:** in ignorance; (4) **carelesse:** unconscious; (5) **hew:** appearance.

Canto III

Forsaken Truth long seekes her love,
And makes the Lyon mylde,
Marres blind Devotions mart, and fals
In hand of leachour vylde.

1 Nought is there under heav'ns wide hollownesse,
    That moves more deare compassion of mind,
  Then beautie brought t'unworthy wretchednesse
  Through envies snares or fortunes freakes unkind:
  I, whether lately through her brightnesse blind,
  Or through alleageance and fast fealtie,   §
  Which I do owe unto all woman kind,
  Feele my heart perst with so great agonie,
When such I see, that all for pittie I could die.

2 And now it is empassioned so deepe,
    For fairest *Unaes* sake, of whom I sing,
  That my fraile eyes these lines with teares do steepe,
  To thinke how she through guilefull handeling,
  Though true as touch, though daughter of a king,
  Though faire as ever living wight was faire,
  Though nor in word nor deede ill meriting,
  Is from her knight divorced in despaire
And her due loves deriv'd to that vile witches share.

mart: profit, profitable scheme.
vylde: vile.
1. (3) **unworthy:** undeserved; (6) **fast fealtie:** true loyalty; (8)
perst: pierced.
2. (3) **steepe:** stain; (9) **deriv'd:** diverted, drawn off.

§ *fealtie:* Fealty was the feudal vassal's or tenant's sworn acknowledg-
ment of fidelity and personal obligation to his lord. The term was
easily appropriated to the chivalric courtly-love vocabulary of the
knightly lover's relationship to his lady.

3   Yet she most faithfull Ladie all this while
        Forsaken, wofull, solitarie mayd
        Farre from all peoples prease, as in exile,
        In wildernesse and wastfull deserts strayd,
        To seeke her knight; who subtilly betrayd
        Through that late vision, which th'Enchaunter
            wrought,
        Had her abandond. She of nought affrayd,
        Through woods and wastnesse wide him daily sought;
    Yet wished tydings none of him unto her brought.

4   One day nigh wearie of the yrkesome way,
        From her unhastie beast she did alight,
        And on the grasse her daintie limbes did lay
        In secret shadow, farre from all mens sight:
        From her faire head her fillet she undight,
        And laid her stole aside. Her angels face
        As the great eye of heaven shyned bright,
        And made a sunshine in the shadie place;
    Did never mortall eye behold such heavenly grace.

5   It fortuned out of the thickest wood
        A ramping Lyon rushed suddainly,
        Hunting full greedie after salvage blood;
        Soone as the royall virgin he did spy,
        With gaping mouth at her ran greedily,
        To have attonce devour'd her tender corse:
        But to the pray when as he drew more ny,
        His bloudie rage asswaged with remorse,
    And with the sight amazd, forgat his furious forse.

3. (3) **prease:** crowd, press.
4. (1) **yrkesome:** troublesome; (5) **fillet:** hair-ribbon; (5) **undight:**
   undid, unbound.
5. (1) **fortuned:** happened; (3) **salvage:** wild, i.e., of wild beasts;
   (6) **attonce:** at once; (6) **corse:** body.

6   In stead thereof he kist her wearie feet,
        And lickt her lilly hands with fawning tong,
        As he her wronged innocence did weet.
        O how can beautie maister the most strong,
        And simple truth subdue avenging wrong?
        Whose yeelded pride and proud submission,
        Still dreading death, when she had marked long,
        Her hart gan melt in great compassion,
   And drizling teares did shed for pure affection.

7   The Lyon Lord of every beast in field,
        Quoth she, his princely puissance doth abate,
        And mightie proud to humble weake does yield,
        Forgetfull of the hungry rage, which late
        Him prickt, in pittie of my sad estate:
        But he my Lyon, and my noble Lord,
        How does he find in cruell hart to hate
        Her that him lov'd, and ever most adord,
   As the God of my life? why hath he me abhord?

8   Redounding teares did choke th'end of her plaint,
        Which softly ecchoed from the neighbour wood;
        And sad to see her sorrowfull constraint
        The kingly beast upon her gazing stood;
        With pittie calmd, downe fell his angry mood.
        At last in close hart shutting up her paine,
        Arose the virgin borne of heavenly brood,
        And to her snowy Palfrey got againe,
   To seeke her strayed Champion, if she might attaine.

6. (3) **As:** as if; (3) **weet:** understand; (5) **avenging:** vengeful.
7. (2) **puissance:** power; (5) **estate:** state.
8. (3) **constraint:** distress; (7) **brood:** parentage, race.

9   The Lyon would not leave her desolate,
        But with her went along, as a strong gard
        Of her chast person, and a faithfull mate
        Of her sad troubles and misfortunes hard:
        Still when she slept, he kept both watch and ward,
        And when she wakt, he waited diligent,
        With humble service to her will prepard:
        From her faire eyes he tooke commaundement,
    And ever by her lookes conceived her intent.

10   Long she thus traveiled through deserts wyde,
        By which she thought her wandring knight shold pas,
        Yet never shew of living wight espyde;
        Till that at length she found the troden gras,
        In which the tract of peoples footing was,
        Under the steepe foot of a mountaine hore;
        The same she followes, till at last she has
        A damzell spyde slow footing her before,
    That on her shoulders sad a pot of water bore.

11   To whom approching she to her gan call,
        To weet, if dwelling place were nigh at hand;
        But the rude wench her answer'd nought at all,
        She could not heare, nor speake, nor understand;
        Till seeing by her side the Lyon stand,
        With suddaine feare her pitcher downe she threw,
        And fled away: for never in that land
        Face of faire Ladie she before did vew,
    And that dread Lyons looke her cast in deadly hew.

9. (5) **ward:** guard; (9) **conceived:** understood.
10. (5) **tract:** trace, mark; (6) **hore:** grey or frost-topped; (9) **sad:** heavy, firm.
11. (1) **gan:** did; (2) **weet:** learn; (3) **rude:** unkempt, wild; (9) **deadly hew:** deathly state.

12   Full fast she fled, ne ever lookt behynd,
     As if her life upon the wager lay,
     And home she came, whereas her mother blynd
     Sate in eternall night: nought could she say,
     But suddaine catching hold, did her dismay
     With quaking hands, and other signes of feare:
     Who full of ghastly fright and cold affray,
     Gan shut the dore. By this arrived there
Dame *Una*, wearie Dame, and entrance did requere.

13   Which when none yeelded, her unruly Page
     With his rude clawes the wicket open rent,
     And let her in; where of his cruell rage
     Nigh dead with feare, and faint astonishment,
     She found them both in darkesome corner pent;
     Where that old woman day and night did pray
     Upon her beades devoutly penitent;
     Nine hundred *Pater nosters* every day,
And thrise nine hundred *Aves* she was wont to say.

14   And to augment her painefull pennance more,
     Thrise every weeke in ashes she did sit,
     And next her wrinkled skin rough sackcloth wore,
     And thrise three times did fast from any bit:
     But now for feare her beads she did forget.
     Whose needlesse dread for to remove away,
     Faire *Una* framed words and count'nance fit:
     Which hardly doen, at length she gan them pray,
That in their cotage small, that night she rest her may.

12. (2) **upon . . . lay:** were at stake; (7) **affray:** terror.
13. (2) **wicket:** small gate; (5) **pent:** penned, confined.
14. (4) **bit:** bite of food; (8) **hardly doen:** (having been) accomplished with difficulty.

15   The day is spent, and commeth drowsie night,
  When every creature shrowded is in sleepe;
  Sad *Una* downe her laies in wearie plight,
  And at her feet the Lyon watch doth keepe:
  In stead of rest, she does lament, and weepe
  For the late losse of her deare loved knight,
  And sighes, and grones, and evermore does steepe
  Her tender brest in bitter teares all night,
 All night she thinks too long, and often lookes for light.

16   Now when *Aldeboran* was mounted hie   §
  Above the shynie *Cassiopeias* chaire,
  And all in deadly sleepe did drowned lie,
  One knocked at the dore, and in would fare;
  He knocked fast, and often curst, and sware,
  That readie entrance was not at his call:
  For on his backe a heavy load he bare
  Of nightly stelths and pillage severall,
 Which he had got abroad by purchase criminall.

17   He was to weete a stout and sturdie thiefe,
  Wont to robbe Churches of their ornaments,
  And poore mens boxes of their due reliefe,
  Which given was to them for good intents;
  The holy Saints of their rich vestiments
  He did disrobe, when all men carelesse slept,
  And spoild the Priests of their habiliments,
  Whiles none the holy things in safety kept;
 Then he by cunning sleights in at the window crept.

15. (9) **All night . . . too long:** she spends the night thinking the night is too long.
16. (3) **deadly:** deathlike; (4) **fare:** go; (8) **stelths:** thefts; (8) **severall:** different kinds (of); (9) **purchase:** dealings.
17. (1) **to weete:** to wit; (6) **carelesse:** free of care; (7) **habiliments:** vestments.

§ *Aldeboran*: Aldebaran, a star of the first magnitude; Alpha in the constellation Taurus. *Cassiopeias chaire*: the constellation named after the Queen of Ethiopia whose daughter Andromeda was rescued from the sea-monster by Perseus.

18   And all that he by right or wrong could find,
      Unto this house he brought, and did bestow
      Upon the daughter of this woman blind,
      Abessa daughter of *Corceca* slow,
      With whom he whoredome usd, that few did know,
      And fed her fat with feast of offerings,
      And plentie, which in all the land did grow;
      Ne spared he to give her gold and rings:
    And now he to her brought part of his stolen things.

19   Thus long the dore with rage and threats he bet,
      Yet of those fearefull women none durst rize,
      The Lyon frayed them, him in to let:
      He would no longer stay him to advize,
      But open breakes the dore in furious wize,
      And entring is; when that disdainfull beast
      Encountring fierce, him suddaine doth surprize,
      And seizing cruell clawes on trembling brest,
    Under his Lordly foot him proudly hath supprest.

20   Him booteth not resist, nor succour call,
      His bleeding hart is in the vengers hand,
      Who streight him rent in thousand peeces small,
      And quite dismembred hath: the thirstie land
      Drunke up his life; his corse left on the strand.
      His fearefull friends weare out the wofull night,
      Ne dare to weepe, nor seeme to understand
      The heavie hap, which on them is alight,
    Affraid, least to themselves the like mishappen might.

19. (1) **bet:** beat; (3) **frayed:** terrified; (4) **stay him:** hold (himself) back; (4) **advize:** consider; (6) **disdainfull:** indignant.
20. (1) **Him booteth not:** it does him no good to; (2) **vengers:** avenger's; (5) **corse:** body, corpse; (8) **hap:** fate, fortune.

21   Now when broad day the world discovered has,
       Up *Una* rose, up rose the Lyon eke,
       And on their former journey forward pas,
       In wayes unknowne, her wandring knight to seeke,
       With paines farre passing that long wandring
             Greeke,   §
       That for his love refused deitie;
       Such were the labours of this Lady meeke,
       Still seeking him, that from her still did flie,
    Then furthest from her hope, when most she weened nie.

22   Soone as she parted thence, the fearefull twaine,
       That blind old woman and her daughter deare
       Came forth, and finding *Kirkrapine* there slaine,
       For anguish great they gan to rend their heare,
       And beat their brests, and naked flesh to teare.
       And when they both had wept and wayld their fill,
       Then forth they ranne like two amazed deare,
       Halfe mad through malice, and revenging will,
    To follow her, that was the causer of their ill.

21. (5) **paines:** trouble, difficulties; (9) **most . . . nie:** when she thought herself nearest.
22. (4) **heare:** hair; (7) **amazed:** crazed.

§ *long wandring Greeke*: The wily, "never-at-a-loss" Odysseus (Ulysses) who, due to the anger of Poseidon (Neptune), took ten years to find his way home after the fall of Troy. Seven of these ten years he spent on the island of Ogygia with the nymph Calypso, who tempted him with the offer of immortality to stay with her as her husband. For love of his queen Penelope and his island-kingdom Ithaca, Odysseus refused her offer.

23   Whom overtaking, they gan loudly bray,
      With hollow howling, and lamenting cry,
      Shamefully at her rayling all the way,
      And her accusing of dishonesty,
      That was the flowre of faith and chastity;
      And still amidst her rayling, she did pray,   §
      That plagues, and mischiefs, and long misery
      Might fall on her, and follow all the way,
  And that in endlesse error she might ever stray.

24   But when she saw her prayers nought prevaile,
      She backe returned with some labour lost;
      And in the way as she did weepe and waile,
      A knight her met in mighty armes embost,
      Yet knight was not for all his bragging bost,
      But subtill *Archimag*, that *Una* sought
      By traynes into new troubles to have tost:
      Of that old woman tydings he besought,
  If that of such a Ladie she could tellen ought.

25   Therewith she gan her passion to renew,
      And cry, and curse, and raile, and rend her heare,
      Saying, that harlot she too lately knew,
      That causd her shed so many a bitter teare,
      And so forth told the story of her feare:
      Much seemed he to mone her haplesse chaunce,
      And after for that Ladie did inquire;
      Which being taught, he forward gan advaunce
  His faire enchaunted steed, and eke his charmed launce.

23. (6) **her rayling:** i.e., Corceca's.
24. (1) **nought prevaile:** (were) having no effect; (4) **embost:** encased; (5) **bost:** boast, claim; (7) **traynes:** wiles.
25. (6) **haplesse:** unlucky; (9) **launce:** lance, spear.

§ An abrupt shift in pronouns (from "they" to "her" and "she") of which one editor complains, "It would have been more clear had Spenser written *'their* rayling – *they* did pray'." But Spenser has already told us that Abessa cannot speak. She is not completely mute; she can make sad and angry noises; but she can't speak – which leaves Corceca to do the intelligible scolding and praying.

26   Ere long he came, where *Una* traveild slow,
         And that wilde Champion wayting her besyde:
      Whom seeing such, for dread he durst not show
      Himselfe too nigh at hand, but turned wyde
      Unto an hill; from whence when she him spyde,
      By his like seeming shield, her knight by name
      She weend it was, and towards him gan ryde:
      Approching nigh, she wist it was the same,
   And with faire fearefull humblesse towards him shee
         came.

27   And weeping said, Ah my long lacked Lord,
         Where have ye bene thus long out of my sight?
      Much feared I to have bene quite abhord,
      Or ought have done, that ye displeasen might,
      That should as death unto my deare hart light:
      For since mine eye your joyous sight did mis,
      My chearefull day is turnd to chearelesse night,
      And eke my night of death the shadow is;
   But welcome now my light, and shining lampe of blis.

28   He thereto meeting said, My dearest Dame,
         Farre be it from your thought, and fro my will,
      To thinke that knighthood I so much should shame,
      As you to leave, that have me loved still,
      And chose in Faery court of meere goodwill,
      Where noblest knights were to be found on earth:
      The earth shall sooner leave her kindly skill
      To bring forth fruit, and make eternall derth,
   Then I leave you, my liefe, yborne of heavenly berth.

26. (2) **wayting:** in attendance; (7) **weend:** thought; (8) **wist:**
knew, felt sure.
27. (4) **ought:** anything; (5) **deare:** sore, (and/or) fond; (5) **light:**
fall, come upon.
28. (2) **fro:** from; (4) **still:** constantly; (5) **meere:** perfect; (8)
derth: barrenness, scarcity; (9) **liefe:** beloved.

29   And sooth to say, why I left you so long,
      Was for to seeke adventure in strange place,
      Where *Archimago* said a felon strong
      To many knights did daily worke disgrace;
      But knight he now shall never more deface:
      Good cause of mine excuse; that mote ye please
      Well to accept, and evermore embrace
      My faithfull service, that by land and seas
    Have vowd you to defend, now then your plaint appease.

30   His lovely words her seemd due recompence
      Of all her passed paines: one loving howre
      For many yeares of sorrow can dispence:
      A dram of sweet is worth a pound of sowre:
      She has forgot, how many a wofull stowre
      For him she late endur'd; she speakes no more
      Of past: true is, that true love hath no powre
      To looken backe; his eyes be fixt before.
    Before her stands her knight, for whom she toyld so sore.

31   Much like, as when the beaten marinere,
      That long hath wandred in the *Ocean* wide,
      Oft soust in swelling *Tethys* saltish teare,
      And long time having tand his tawney hide
      With blustring breath of heaven, that none can bide,
      And scorching flames of fierce *Orions* hound,   §
      Soone as the port from farre he has espide,
      His chearefull whistle merrily doth sound,
    And *Nereus* crownes with cups; his mates him pledg
      around.

29. (1) **sooth:** truth; (5) **deface:** destroy; (6) **mote:** might; (9)
appease: cease.
30. (3) **dispence:** make up for; (5) **stowre:** peril.
31. (5) **bide:** withstand.

---

§ *fierce Orions hound*: The brightest of all stars, Sirius, also called the
Dog-star; Alpha in the constellation Canis Major. Orion is a giant
hunter and Sirius is his dog. On earth Orion pursued the Pleiades
for five years and this chase continues in the heavens. *Nereus* is a
sea-god who, under Poseidon, rules the Mediterranean. The phrase
And Nereus crownes with cups means "And returns thanks to Nereus
with drink-offerings".

32 Such joy made *Una*, when her knight she found;
  And eke th'enchaunter joyous seemd no lesse,
  Then the glad marchant, that does vew from ground
  His ship farre come from watrie wildernesse,
  He hurles out vowes, and *Neptune* oft doth blesse: §
  So forth they past, and all the way they spent
  Discoursing of her dreadfull late distresse,
  In which he askt her, what the Lyon ment:
Who told her all that fell in journey as she went.

33 They had not ridden farre, when they might see
  One pricking towards them with hastie heat,
  Full strongly armd, and on a courser free,
  That through his fiercenesse fomed all with sweat,
  And the sharpe yron did for anger eat,
  When his hot ryder spurd his chauffed side;
  His looke was sterne, and seemed still to threat
  Cruell revenge, which he in hart did hyde,
And on his shield *Sans loy* in bloudie lines was dyde.

34 When nigh he drew unto this gentle payre
  And saw the Red-crosse, which the knight did beare,
  He burnt in fire, and gan eftsoones prepare
  Himselfe to battell with his couched speare.
  Loth was that other, and did faint through feare,
  To taste th'untryed dint of deadly steele;
  But yet his Lady did so well him cheare,
  That hope of new good hap he gan to feele;
So bent his speare, and spurnd his horse with yron heele.

32. (9) **told her all that fell:** told all that befell her.
33. (2) **pricking:** spurring; (3) **free:** willing, spirited; (6) **chauffed:** chafed, torn by the rowel on the spur.
34. (6) **th'untryed dint:** the unfamiliar stroke; (8) **hap:** fortune; (9) **bent:** aimed.

§ *Neptune*: Also called Poseidon. He is the trident-bearing earth-shaker, chief god of the sea and one of Zeus' two older brothers.

35   But that proud Paynim forward came so fierce,
        And full of wrath, that with his sharp-head speare
        Through vainely crossed shield he quite did pierce,
        And had his staggering steede not shrunke for feare,
        Through shield and bodie eke he should him beare:
        Yet so great was the puissance of his push,
        That from his saddle quite he did him beare:
        He tombling rudely downe to ground did rush,
    And from his gored wound a well of bloud did gush.

36   Dismounting lightly from his loftie steed,
        He to him lept, in mind to reave his life,
        And proudly said, Lo there the worthie meed
        Of him, that slew *Sansfoy* with bloudie knife;
        Henceforth his ghost freed from repining strife,
        In peace may passen over *Lethe* lake,   §
        When morning altars purgd with enemies life,
        The blacke infernall *Furies* doen aslake:
    Life from *Sansfoy* thou tookst, *Sansloy* shall from thee
        take.

37   Therewith in haste his helmet gan unlace,
        Till *Una* cride, O hold that heavie hand,
        Deare Sir, what ever that thou be in place:
        Enough is, that thy foe doth vanquisht stand
        Now at thy mercy: Mercie not withstand:
        For he is one the truest knight alive,
        Though conquered now he lie on lowly land,
        And whilest him fortune favour, faire did thrive
    In bloudie field: therefore of life him not deprive.

35. (1) **Paynim**: pagan; (5) **beare**: thrust; (6) **puissance**: force, power; (7) **beare**: carry.
36. (2) **reave**: take; (3) **meed**: reward; (5) **repining**: complaining, fretful; (8) **doen aslake**: (do) appease, satisfy.
37. (3) **place**: rank; (5) **withstand**: reject, withhold.

§ *Lethe* lake: The waters of forgetfulness. The Lethe is one of five rivers that encircle and flow through the underworld. The *Furies* (Erinyes) are three frightful sisters, the goddesses of vengeance.

38 Her piteous words might not abate his rage,
　　　But rudely rending up his helmet, would
　　　Have slaine him straight: but when he sees his age,
　　　And hoarie head of *Archimago* old,
　　　His hastie hand he doth amazed hold,
　　　And halfe ashamed, wondred at the sight:
　　　For that old man well knew he, though untold,
　　　In charmes and magicke to have wondrous might,
　Ne ever wont in field, ne in round lists to fight.

39 And said, Why *Archimago*, lucklesse syre,
　　　What doe I see? what hard mishap is this,
　　　That hath thee hither brought to taste mine yre?
　　　Or thine the fault, or mine the error is,
　　　In stead of foe to wound my friend amis?
　　　He answered nought, but in a traunce still lay,
　　　And on those guilefull dazed eyes of his
　　　The cloud of death did sit. Which doen away,
　He left him lying so, ne would no lenger stay.

40 But to the virgin comes, who all this while
　　　Amased stands, her selfe so mockt to see
　　　By him, who has the guerdon of his guile,
　　　For so misfeigning her true knight to bee:
　　　Yet is she now in more perplexitie,
　　　Left in the hand of that same Paynim bold,
　　　From whom her booteth not at all to flie;
　　　Who by her cleanly garment catching hold,
　Her from her Palfrey pluckt, her visage to behold.

38. (5) **hold:** check; (9) **round:** enclosed.
39. (3) **yre:** wrath; (5) **amis:** in error; (8) **doen away:** once it (i.e., the trance) had passed off.
40. (3) **guerdon:** reward; (7) **booteth:** it avails.

41   But her fierce servant full of kingly awe
        And high disdaine, whenas his soveraine Dame
        So rudely handled by her foe he sawe,
        With gaping jawes full greedy at him came,
        And ramping on his shield, did weene the same
        Have reft away with his sharpe rending clawes:
        But he was stout, and lust did now inflame
        His corage more, that from his griping pawes
He hath his shield redeem'd, and foorth his swerd he
        drawes.

42   O then too weake and feeble was the forse
        Of salvage beast, his puissance to withstand:
        For he was strong, and of so mightie corse,
        As ever wielded speare in warlike hand,
        And feates of armes did wisely understand.
        Eftsoones he perced through his chaufed chest
        With thrilling point of deadly yron brand,
        And launcht his Lordly hart: with death opprest
He roar'd aloud, whiles life forsooke his stubborne brest.

43   Who now is left to keepe the forlorne maid
        From raging spoile of lawlesse victors will?
        Her faithfull gard remov'd, her hope dismaid,
        Her selfe a yeelded pray to save or spill.
        He now Lord of the field, his pride to fill,
        With foule reproches, and disdainfull spight
        Her vildly entertaines, and will or nill,
        Beares her away upon his courser light:
Her prayers nought prevaile, his rage is more of might.

41. (1) **awe**: awfulness; (5) **ramping**: raging; (8) **corage**: heart,
    courage.
42. (2) **salvage**: wild; (6) **chaufed**: angry; (7) **thrilling**: piercing;
    (7) **brand**: sword; (8) **launcht**: penetrated.
43. (2) **spoile**: ravin, ruination; (7) **vildly**: vilely; (7) **entertaines**:
    treats; (9) **more of might**: stronger (than her prayers).

44   And all the way, with great lamenting paine,
  And piteous plaints she filleth his dull eares,
  That stony hart could riven have in twaine,
  And all the way she wets with flowing teares:
  But he enrag'd with rancor, nothing heares.
  Her servile beast yet would not leave her so,
  But followes her farre off, ne ought he feares,
  To be partaker of her wandring woe,
More mild in beastly kind, then that her beastly foe.

44. (3) **riven:** split; (9) **kind:** nature; (9) **then:** than.

Canto IV

To sinfull house of Pride, Duessa
    guides the faithfull knight,
Where brothers death to wreak Sansjoy
    doth chalenge him to fight.

1　Young knight, what ever that dost armes professe,
　　　And through long labours huntest after fame,
　　　Beware of fraud, beware of ficklenesse,
　　　In choice, and change of thy deare loved Dame,
　　　Least thou of her beleeve too lightly blame,
　　　And rash misweening doe thy hart remove:
　　　For unto knight there is no greater shame,
　　　Then lightnesse and inconstancie in love;
　　That doth this *Redcrosse* knights ensample plainly prove.

2　Who after that he had faire *Una* lorne,
　　　Through light misdeeming of her loialtie,
　　　And false *Duessa* in her sted had borne,
　　　Called *Fidess'*, and so supposd to bee;
　　　Long with her traveild, till at last they see
　　　A goodly building, bravely garnished,
　　　The house of mightie Prince it seemd to bee:
　　　And towards it a broad high way that led,
　　All bare through peoples feet, which thither traveiled.

wreak: avenge.
1. (6) **misweening:** misjudgment; (6) **remove:** alienate.
2. (1) **lorne:** deserted; (2) **light:** overhasty; (3) **borne:** taken up with; (6) **bravely garnished:** splendidly decorated.

3   Great troupes of people traveild thitherward
      Both day and night, of each degree and place,
      But few returned, having scaped hard,
      With balefull beggerie, or foule disgrace,
      Which ever after in most wretched case,
      Like loathsome lazars, by the hedges lay.
      Thither *Duessa* bad him bend his pace:
      For she is wearie of the toilesome way,
  And also nigh consumed is the lingring day.

4   A stately Pallace built of squared bricke,
      Which cunningly was without morter laid,
      Whose wals were high, but nothing strong, nor thick,
      And golden foile all over them displaid,
      That purest skye with brightnesse they dismaid:
      High lifted up were many loftie towres,
      And goodly galleries farre over laid,
      Full of faire windowes, and delightfull bowres;
  And on the top a Diall told the timely howres.

5   It was a goodly heape for to behould,
      And spake the praises of the workmans wit;
      But full great pittie, that so faire a mould
      Did on so weake foundation ever sit:
      For on a sandie hill, that still did flit,
      And fall away, it mounted was full hie,
      That every breath of heaven shaked it:
      And all the hinder parts, that few could spie,
  Were ruinous and old, but painted cunningly.

---

3. (2) **place:** rank; (3) **hard:** barely; (6) **lazars:** lepers; (7) **pace:** step(s).
4. (5) **dismaid:** outfaced.
5. (1) **heape:** pile, mass of building; (5) **still:** continuously; (5) **flit:** crumble.

6   Arrived there they passed in forth right;
        For still to all the gates stood open wide,
        Yet charge of them was to a Porter hight
        Cald *Malvenù*, who entrance none denide:
        Thence to the hall, which was on every side
        With rich array and costly arras dight:
        Infinite sorts of people did abide
        There waiting long, to win the wished sight
    Of her, that was the Lady of that Pallace bright.

7   By them they passe, all gazing on them round,
        And to the Presence mount; whose glorious vew
        Their frayle amazed senses did confound:
        In living Princes court none ever knew
        Such endlesse richesse, and so sumptuous shew;
        Ne *Persia* selfe, the nourse of pompous pride
        Like ever saw. And there a noble crew
        Of Lordes and Ladies stood on every side,
    Which with their presence faire, the place much
        beautifide.

8   High above all a cloth of State was spred,
        And a rich throne, as bright as sunny day,
        On which there sate most brave embellished
        With royall robes and gorgeous array,
        A mayden Queene, that shone as *Titans* ray,
        In glistring gold, and peerelesse pretious stone:
        Yet her bright blazing beautie did assay
        To dim the brightnesse of her glorious throne,
    As envying her selfe, that too exceeding shone.

6. (2) **still:** always; (4) **Malvenù:** i.e., ill-come, unwelcome; (6) **arras:** tapestry; (6) **dight:** decked out.
7. (2) **Presence:** i.e., ceremonial attendance upon royalty; hence, often, the royal person himself.
8. (3) **brave:** splendidly; (7) **assay:** try.

9 Exceeding shone, like *Phœbus* fairest childe,
  That did presume his fathers firie wayne,
  And flaming mouthes of steedes unwonted wilde
  Through highest heaven with weaker hand to rayne;
  Proud of such glory and advancement vaine,
  While flashing beames do daze his feeble eyen,
  He leaves the welkin way most beaten plaine,
  And rapt with whirling wheels, inflames the skyen,
With fire not made to burne, but fairely for to shyne.

10 So proud she shyned in her Princely state,
  Looking to heaven; for earth she did disdayne,
  And sitting high; for lowly she did hate:
  Lo underneath her scornefull feete, was layne
  A dreadfull Dragon with an hideous trayne,
  And in her hand she held a mirrhour bright,
  Wherein her face she often vewed fayne,
  And in her selfe-lov'd semblance tooke delight;
For she was wondrous faire, as any living wight.

11 Of griesly *Pluto* she the daughter was,
  And sad *Proserpina* the Queene of hell;
  Yet did she thinke her pearelesse worth to pas
  That parentage, with pride so did she swell,
  And thundring *Jove*, that high in heaven doth dwell,
  And wield the world, she claymed for her syre,
  Or if that any else did *Jove* excell: §
  For to the highest she did still aspyre,
Or if ought higher were then that, did it desyre.

9. (1) **childe:** i.e., Phaëton; (2) **presume:** took the liberty of; (2) **wayne:** chariot; (3) **unwonted:** unexpectedly; (6) **eyen:** eyes; (7) **welkin way:** path through the heavens; (8) **skyen:** skies.
10. (5) **trayne:** tail; (7) **fayne:** with pleasure.

§ The drift of these last three lines is this: because she always aspires to the highest possible parentage, Lucifera reserves filial claim to whichever power might be above Jove, or to whichever super-power might be beyond *that* power, and so on.

12   And proud *Lucifera* men did her call,
  That made her selfe a Queene, and crownd to be,
  Yet rightfull kingdome she had none at all,
  Ne heritage of native soveraintie,
  But did usurpe with wrong and tyrannie
  Upon the scepter, which she now did hold:
  Ne ruld her Realme with lawes, but pollicie,
  And strong advizement of six wisards old,
That with their counsels bad her kingdome did uphold.

13   Soone as the Elfin knight in presence came,
  And false *Duessa* seeming Lady faire,
  A gentle Husher, *Vanitie* by name
  Made rowme, and passage for them did prepaire:
  So goodly brought them to the lowest staire
  Of her high throne, where they on humble knee
  Making obeyssance, did the cause declare,
  Why they were come, her royall state to see,
To prove the wide report of her great Majestee.

14   With loftie eyes, halfe loth to looke so low,
  She thanked them in her disdainefull wise,
  Ne other grace vouchsafed them to show
  Of Princesse worthy, scarse them bad arise.
  Her Lordes and Ladies all this while devise
  Themselves to setten forth to straungers sight:
  Some frounce their curled haire in courtly guise,
  Some prancke their ruffes, and others trimly dight
Their gay attire: each others greater pride does spight.

12. (7) **pollicie:** statecraft that is politic rather than just.
13. (3) **Husher:** usher; (5) **goodly;** courteously; (9) **To prove:** to confirm for themselves.
14. (2) **wise:** manner; (5) **devise:** contrive; (7) **guise:** fashion (of the court); (8) **prancke:** pleat; (8) **dight:** adorn; (9) **each others . . . spight:** each despises what he takes to be the greater pride of everyone else.

15   Goodly they all that knight do entertaine,
        Right glad with him to have increast their crew:
        But to *Duess'* each one himselfe did paine
        All kindnesse and faire courtesie to shew;
        For in that court whylome her well they knew:
        Yet the stout Faerie mongst the middest crowd
        Thought all their glorie vaine in knightly vew,
        And that great Princesse too exceeding prowd,
     That to strange knight no better countenance allowd.

16   Suddein upriseth from her stately place
        The royall Dame, and for her coche doth call:
        All hurtlen forth, and she with Princely pace,
        As faire *Aurora* in her purple pall,
        Out of the East the dawning day doth call:
        So forth she comes: her brightnesse brode doth blaze;
        The heapes of people thronging in the hall,
        Do ride each other, upon her to gaze:
     Her glorious glitterand light doth all mens eyes amaze.

17   So forth she comes, and to her coche does clyme,
        Adorned all with gold, and girlonds gay,
        That seemd as fresh as *Flora* in her prime,
        And strove to match, in royall rich array,
        Great *Junoes* golden chaire, the which they say
        The Gods stand gazing on, when she does ride
        To *Joves* high house through heavens bras-paved way
        Drawne of faire Pecocks, that excell in pride,
     And full of *Argus* eyes their tailes dispredden wide.   §

15. (3) **himself did paine:** went out of his way; (5) **whylome:** long
    since; (6) **mongst the middest:** in the midst of.
16. (3) **hurtlen:** rush; (6) **brode:** abroad; (9) **glitterand:** glittering.
17. (9) **dispredden:** fanned out.

§ *Argus eyes*: Once when Zeus was enjoying his latest mortal love, Io,
he sensed the approach of his wife Hera (Juno), and in an attempt
to avoid a scene he turned Io into a fine white heifer. But the sus-
picious Hera asked for the heifer as a present and assigned it to one
of her servants, the hundred-eyed monster Argus, to guard. At the
command of Zeus, Hermes (Mercury) killed Argus after charming
him into such a deep sleep that every one of his hundred eyes closed.
Hera took the eyes of Argus and set them in the tail of the peacock,
her own special bird.

18   But this was drawne of six unequall beasts,
      On which her six sage Counsellours did ryde,
      Taught to obay their bestiall beheasts,
      With like conditions to their kinds applyde:
      Of which the first, that all the rest did guyde,
      Was sluggish *Idlenesse* the nourse of sin;
      Upon a slouthfull Asse he chose to ryde,
      Arayd in habit blacke, and amis thin,
Like to an holy Monck, the service to begin.

19   And in his hand his Portesse still he bare,
      That much was worne, but therein little red,
      For of devotion he had little care,
      Still drownd in sleepe, and most of his dayes ded;
      Scarse could he once uphold his heavie hed,
      To looken, whether it were night or day:
      May seeme the wayne was very evill led,
      When such an one had guiding of the way,
That knew not, whether right he went, or else astray.

20   From worldly cares himselfe he did esloyne,
      And greatly shunned manly exercise,
      From every worke he chalenged essoyne,
      For contemplation sake: yet otherwise,
      His life he led in lawlesse riotise;
      By which he grew to grievous malady;
      For in his lustlesse limbs through evill guise
      A shaking fever raignd continually:
Such one was *Idlenesse*, first of this company.

18. (3) **beheasts:** commands; (4) **With like . . . applyde:** the coun-
sellors were in character, or nature, like the beasts they rode;
(8) **amis:** cape trimmed with fur.
19. (1) **Portesse:** portable breviary; (7) **wayne:** chariot, coach.
20. (1) **esloyne:** withdraw; (3) **chalenged essoyne:** claimed exemp-
tion; (5) **riotise:** extravagance; (7) **lustlesse:** listless; (7) **through
evill guise:** thanks to an evil way of life.

21   And by his side rode loathsome *Gluttony*,
      Deformed creature, on a filthie swyne,
      His belly was up-blowne with luxury,
      And eke with fatnesse swollen were his eyne,
      And like a Crane his necke was long and fyne,
      With which he swallowd up excessive feast,
      For want whereof poore people oft did pyne;
      And all the way, most like a brutish beast,
  He spued up his gorge, that all did him deteast.

22   In greene vine leaves he was right fitly clad;
      For other clothes he could not weare for heat,
      And on his head an yvie girland had,
      From under which fast trickled downe the sweat:
      Still as he rode, he somewhat still did eat,
      And in his hand did beare a bouzing can,
      Of which he supt so oft, that on his seat
      His dronken corse he scarse upholden can,
  In shape and life more like a monster, then a man.

23   Unfit he was for any worldly thing,
      And eke unhable once to stirre or go,
      Not meet to be of counsell to a king,
      Whose mind in meat and drinke was drowned so,
      That from his friend he seldome knew his fo:
      Full of diseases was his carcas blew,
      And a dry dropsie through his flesh did flow,
      Which by misdiet daily greater grew:
  Such one was *Gluttony*, the second of that crew.

21. (5) **fyne:** slender.
22. (3) **yvie:** ivy; (6) **bouzing can:** drinking mug.
23. (3) **meet:** fit.

24   And next to him rode lustfull *Lechery*,
      Upon a bearded Goat, whose rugged haire,
      And whally eyes (the signe of gelosy,)   §
      Was like the person selfe, whom he did beare:
      Who rough, and blacke, and filthy did appeare,
      Unseemely man to please faire Ladies eye;
      Yet he of Ladies oft was loved deare,
      When fairer faces were bid standen by:
  O who does know the bent of womens fantasy?

25   In a greene gowne he clothed was full faire,
      Which underneath did hide his filthinesse,
      And in his hand a burning hart he bare,
      Full of vaine follies, and new fanglenesse:
      For he was false, and fraught with ficklenesse,
      And learned had to love with secret lookes,
      And well could daunce, and sing with ruefulnesse,
      And fortunes tell, and read in loving bookes,
  And thousand other wayes, to bait his fleshly hookes.

26   Inconstant man, that loved all he saw,
      And lusted after all, that he did love,
      Ne would his looser life be tide to law,
      But joyd weake wemens hearts to tempt, and prove
      If from their loyall loves he might them move;
      Which lewdnesse fild him with reprochfull paine
      Of that fowle evill, which all men reprove,
      That rots the marrow, and consumes the braine:
  Such one was *Lecherie*, the third of all this traine.

25. (5) **fraught with:** full of; (7) **could:** knew (how to) dance . . .
and a thousand other ways; (7) **ruefulnesse:** pathos.

26. (4) **prove:** set about testing.

§ *whally eyes*: For *whally* one editor gives "marked with streaks". Perhaps the phrase means "wall-eyed" which, in turn, can mean "having a whitish eye". But neither streaky nor whitish eyes are particularly associated with jealousy and lechery. Spenser may conceivably have known the Anglo-Saxon word *hwall* (hence *whall*), meaning "wanton".

27   And greedy *Avarice* by him did ride,
     Upon a Camell loaden all with gold;   §
     Two iron coffers hong on either side,
     With precious mettall full, as they might hold,
     And in his lap an heape of coine he told;
     For of his wicked pelfe his God he made,
     And unto hell him selfe for money sold;
     Accursed usurie was all his trade,
  And right and wrong ylike in equall ballaunce waide.

28   His life was nigh unto deaths doore yplast,
     And thred-bare cote, and cobled shoes he ware,
     Ne scarse good morsell all his life did tast,
     But both from backe and belly still did spare,
     To fill his bags, and richesse to compare;
     Yet chylde ne kinsman living had he none
     To leave them to; but thorough daily care
     To get, and nightly feare to lose his owne,
  He led a wretched life unto him selfe unknowne.

29   Most wretched wight, whom nothing might suffise,
     Whose greedy lust did lacke in greatest store,
     Whose need had end, but no end covetise,
     Whose wealth was want, whose plenty made him pore,
     Who had enough, yet wished ever more;
     A vile disease, and eke in foote and hand
     A grievous gout tormented him full sore,
     That well he could not touch, nor go, nor stand:
  Such one was *Avarice*, the fourth of this faire band.

27. (5) **told:** counted; (6) **pelfe:** wealth.
28. (1) **yplast:** placed; (2) **cobled:** much or clumsily mended;
    (5) **richesse:** wealth; (5) **compare:** amass, acquire.
29. (3) **covetise:** covetousness.

§ *Upon a Camell*: Perhaps Avarice rides a camel because of its associations with the proverbially wealthy and exotic caravans of the near
East. Perhaps Spenser is remembering a story in the *History* of
Herodotus, in which a certain tribe of India uses camels to carry off
gold thrown up by the diggings of great desert ants that are "not as
big as dogs but bigger than foxes".

30 And next to him malicious *Envie* rode,
  Upon a ravenous wolfe, and still did chaw
  Betweene his cankred teeth a venemous tode,
  That all the poison ran about his chaw;
  But inwardly he chawed his owne maw
  At neighbours wealth, that made him ever sad;
  For death it was, when any good he saw,
  And wept, that cause of weeping none he had,
But when he heard of harme, he wexed wondrous glad.

31 All in a kirtle of discolourd say
  He clothed was, ypainted full of eyes;
  And in his bosome secretly there lay
  An hatefull Snake, the which his taile uptyes
  In many folds, and mortall sting implyes.
  Still as he rode, he gnasht his teeth, to see
  Those heapes of gold with griple Covetyse,
  And grudged at the great felicitie
Of proud *Lucifera*, and his owne companie.

32 He hated all good workes and vertuous deeds,
  And him no lesse, that any like did use,
  And who with gracious bread the hungry feeds,
  His almes for want of faith he doth accuse;
  So every good to bad he doth abuse:
  And eke the verse of famous Poets witt
  He does backebite, and spightfull poison spues
  From leprous mouth on all, that ever writt:
Such one vile *Envie* was, that fifte in row did sitt.

30. (3) **cankred:** rotten; (4) **chaw:** jaw.
31. (1) **kirtle:** gown, tunic; (1) **discolourd:** variously coloured;
(1) **say:** fine (woollen) cloth; (4) **uptyes:** winds up; (5) **implyes:**
envelops; (7) **griple:** greedy; (7) **Covetyse:** i.e., Avarice, his
fellow-counsellor.
32. (2) **use:** practise; (9) **fifte:** fifth.

33   And him beside rides fierce revenging *Wrath*,
        Upon a Lion, loth for to be led;
        And in his hand a burning brond he hath,
        The which he brandisheth about his hed;
        His eyes did hurle forth sparkles fiery red,
        And stared sterne on all, that him beheld,
        As ashes pale of hew and seeming ded;
        And on his dagger still his hand he held,
Trembling through hasty rage, when choler in him sweld.

34   His ruffin raiment all was staind with blood,
        Which he had spilt, and all to rags yrent,
        Through unadvized rashnesse woxen wood;
        For of his hands he had no governement,
        Ne car'd for bloud in his avengement:
        But when the furious fit was overpast,
        His cruell facts he often would repent;
        Yet wilfull man he never would forecast,
How many mischieves should ensue his heedlesse hast.

35   Full many mischiefes follow cruell *Wrath*;
        Abhorred bloudshed, and tumultuous strife,
        Unmanly murder, and unthrifty scath,
        Bitter despight, with rancours rusty knife,
        And fretting griefe the enemy of life;
        All these, and many evils moe haunt ire,
        The swelling Splene, and Frenzy raging rife,
        The shaking Palsey, and Saint *Fraunces* fire:
Such one was *Wrath*, the last of this ungodly tire.

33. (9) **choler:** anger.
34. (1) **ruffin:** disorderly; (3) **woxen wood:** (having) become insanely angry; (5) **avengement:** vengeance; (7) **facts:** deeds; (9) **ensue:** result from.
35. (3) **unthrifty scath:** reckless damage; (6) **moe:** more; (8) **Saint Fraunces fire:** i.e., erysipelas, a disease producing a deep red colour on the skin; (9) **tire:** row, series (of figures).

36   And after all, upon the wagon beame
            Rode *Sathan*, with a smarting whip in hand,
            With which he forward lasht the laesie teme,
            So oft as *Slowth* still in the mire did stand.
            Huge routs of people did about them band,
            Showting for joy, and still before their way
            A foggy mist had covered all the land;
            And underneath their feet, all scattered lay
Dead sculs and bones of men, whose life had gone astray.

37   So forth they marchen in this goodly sort,
            To take the solace of the open aire,
            And in fresh flowring fields themselves to sport;
            Emongst the rest rode that false Lady faire,
            The fowle *Duessa*, next unto the chaire
            Of proud *Lucifera*, as one of the traine:
            But that good knight would not so nigh repaire,
            Him selfe estraunging from their joyaunce vaine,
Whose fellowship seemd far unfit for warlike swaine.

38   So having solaced themselves a space
            With pleasaunce of the breathing fields yfed,
            They backe returned to the Princely Place;
            Whereas an errant knight in armes ycled,
            And heathnish shield, wherein with letters red
            Was writ *Sans joy*, they new arrived find:
            Enflam'd with fury and fiers hardy-hed,
            He seemd in hart to harbour thoughts unkind,
And nourish bloudy vengeaunce in his bitter mind.

36. (2) **Sathan:** Satan; (5) **routs:** crowds.

37. (1) **sort:** fashion; (7) **repaire:** go; (9) **swaine:** young man.
38. (7) **hardy-hed:** boldness.

39 Who when the shamed shield of slaine *Sans foy*
    He spide with that same Faery champions page,
    Bewraying him, that did of late destroy
    His eldest brother, burning all with rage
    He to him leapt, and that same envious gage
    Of victors glory from him snatcht away:
    But th'Elfin knight, which ought that warlike wage,
    Disdaind to loose the meed he wonne in fray,
And him rencountring fierce, reskewd the noble pray.

40 Therewith they gan to hurtlen greedily,
    Redoubted battaile ready to darrayne,
    And clash their shields, and shake their swords on hy,
    That with their sturre they troubled all the traine;
    Till that great Queene upon eternall paine
    Of high displeasure, that ensewen might,
    Commaunded them their fury to refraine,
    And if that either to that shield had right,
In equall lists they should the morrow next it fight.

41 Ah dearest Dame, (quoth then the Paynim bold,)
    Pardon the errour of enraged wight,
    Whom great griefe made forget the raines to hold
    Of reasons rule, to see this recreant knight,
    No knight, but treachour full of false despight
    And shamefull treason, who through guile hath slayn
    The prowest knight, that ever field did fight,
    Even stout *Sans foy* (O who can then refrayn?)
Whose shield he beares renverst, the more to heape
      disdayn.

39. (3) **Bewraying:** betraying; (5) **envious gage:** enviable pledge;
(7) **ought:** owned; (7) **wage:** reward; (8) **meed:** prize; (9)
rencountring: engaging.
40. (1) **hurtlen:** spar and jostle; (2) **Redoubted:** fearful; (2)
darrayne: fight out; (6) **ensewen:** follow.
41. (1) **Paynim:** pagan; (5) **despight:** malice; (7) **prowest:** bravest;
(9) **renverst:** reversed.

42   And to augment the glorie of his guile,
          His dearest love the faire *Fidessa* loe
          Is there possessed of the traytour vile,
          Who reapes the harvest sowen by his foe,
          Sowen in bloudy field, and bought with woe:
          That brothers hand shall dearely well requight
          So be, O Queene, you equall favour showe.
          Him litle answerd th'angry Elfin knight;
     He never meant with words, but swords to plead
          his right.

43   But threw his gauntlet as a sacred pledge,
          His cause in combat the next day to try:
          So been they parted both, with harts on edge,
          To be aveng'd each on his enimy.
          That night they pas in joy and jollity,
          Feasting and courting both in bowre and hall;
          For Steward was excessive *Gluttonie*,
          That of his plenty poured forth to all;
     Which doen, the Chamberlain *Slowth* did to rest
          them call.

44   Now whenas darkesome night had all displayd
          Her coleblacke curtein over brightest skye,
          The warlike youthes on dayntie couches layd,
          Did chace away sweet sleepe from sluggish eye,
          To muse on meanes of hoped victory.
          But whenas *Morpheus* had with leaden mace
          Arrested all that courtly company,
          Up-rose *Duessa* from her resting place,
     And to the Paynims lodging comes with silent pace.

42. (2) **loe:** behold; (6) **requight:** revenge; (7) **So be:** if so be.
43. (9) **doen:** (being) done, brought to an end.
44. (3) **dayntie:** fine, choice.

45   Whom broad awake she finds, in troublous fit,
        Forecasting, how his foe he might annoy,
        And him amoves with speaches seeming fit:
        Ah deare *Sans joy*, next dearest to *Sans foy*,
        Cause of my new griefe, cause of my new joy,
        Joyous, to see his ymage in mine eye,
        And greev'd, to thinke how foe did him destroy,
        That was the flowre of grace and chevalrye;
   Lo his *Fidessa* to thy secret faith I flye.

46   With gentle wordes he can her fairely greet,
        And bad say on the secret of her hart.
        Then sighing soft, I learne that litle sweet
        Oft tempred is (quoth she) with muchell smart:
        For since my brest was launcht with lovely dart
        Of deare *Sansfoy*, I never joyed howre,
        But in eternall woes my weaker hart
        Have wasted, loving him with all my powre,
   And for his sake have felt full many an heavie stowre.

47   At last when perils all I weened past,
        And hop'd to reape the crop of all my care,
        Into new woes unweeting I was cast,
        By this false faytor, who unworthy ware
        His worthy shield, whom he with guilefull snare
        Entrapped slew, and brought to shamefull grave.
        Me silly maid away with him he bare,
        And ever since hath kept in darksome cave,
   For that I would not yeeld, that to *Sans-foy* I gave.

45. (1) **fit:** condition; (3) **seeming fit:** apparently sincere.
46. (1) **can:** did; (4) **muchell:** much; (5) **launcht:** pierced; (6)
joyed howre: had an hour of joy; (9) **stowre:** peril.
47. (3) **unweeting:** unknowing; (4) **faytor:** rogue; (4) **ware:** wore;
(5) **His:** i.e., Sansfoy's; (7) **silly:** innocent, helpless.

48   But since faire Sunne hath sperst that lowring clowd,
      And to my loathed life now shewes some light,
      Under your beames I will me safely shrowd,
      From dreaded storme of his disdainfull spight:
      To you th'inheritance belongs by right
      Of brothers prayse, to you eke longs his love.
      Let not his love, let not his restlesse spright
      Be unreveng'd, that calles to you above
  From wandring *Stygian* shores, where it doth
      endlesse move.

49   Thereto said he, Faire Dame be nought dismaid
      For sorrowes past; their griefe is with them gone:
      Ne yet of present perill be affraid;
      For needlesse feare did never vantage none,
      And helplesse hap it booteth not to mone.
      Dead is *Sans-foy*, his vitall paines are past,
      Though greeved ghost for vengeance deepe do grone:
      He lives, that shall him pay his dewties last,
  And guiltie Elfin bloud shall sacrifice in hast.

50   O but I feare the fickle freakes (quoth shee)
      Of fortune false, and oddes of armes in field.
      Why dame (quoth he) what oddes can ever bee,
      Where both do fight alike, to win or yield?
      Yea but (quoth she) he beares a charmed shield,
      And eke enchaunted armes, that none can perce,
      Ne none can wound the man, that does them wield.
      Charmd or enchaunted (answerd he then ferce)
  I no whit reck, ne you the like need to reherce.

48. (1) **sperst:** dispersed; (3) **shrowd:** take shelter; (6) **longs:** belongs; (9) **Stygian:** of the river Styx.
49. (4) **vantage none:** bring any advantage (or) benefit anyone; (5) **helplesse hap:** unavoidable chance; (6) **vitall paines:** troubles of life; (8) **dewties last:** last rites.
50. (9) **reck:** care about.

51   But faire *Fidessa*, sithens fortunes guile,
        Or enimies powre hath now captived you,
        Returne from whence ye came, and rest a while
        Till morrow next, that I the Elfe subdew,
        And with *Sans-foyes* dead dowry you endew.
        Ay me, that is a double death (she said)
        With proud foes sight my sorrow to renew:
        Where ever yet I be, my secret aid
    Shall follow you. So passing forth she him obaid.

51. (1) **sithens:** since; (4) **that I:** when I (shall); (5) **endew:**
     endow.

Canto V

> *The faithfull knight in equall field*
> *subdewes his faithlesse foe,*
> *Whom false Duessa saves, and for*
> *his cure to hell does goe.*

1   The noble hart, that harbours vertuous thought,
    And is with child of glorious great intent,
    Can never rest, untill it forth have brought
    Th'eternall brood of glorie excellent:
    Such restlesse passion did all night torment
    The flaming corage of that Faery knight,
    Devizing, how that doughtie turnament
    With greatest honour he atchieven might;
Still did he wake, and still did watch for dawning light.

2   At last the golden Orientall gate
    Of greatest heaven gan to open faire,
    And *Phœbus* fresh, as bridegrome to his mate,
    Came dauncing forth, shaking his deawie haire:
    And hurld his glistring beames through gloomy aire.
    Which when the wakeful Elfe perceiv'd, streight way
    He started up, and did him selfe prepaire,
    In sun-bright armes, and battailous array:
For with that Pagan proud he combat will that day.

1. (6) **corage:** heart; (7) **Devizing:** considering; (8) **atchieven:** win.
2. (1) **Orientall:** eastern; (8) **battailous:** warlike.

3   And forth he comes into the commune hall,
          Where earely waite him many a gazing eye,
          To weet what end to straunger knights may fall.
          There many Minstrales maken melody,
          To drive away the dull melancholy,
          And many Bardes, that to the trembling chord
          Can tune their timely voyces cunningly,
          And many Chroniclers, that can record
      Old loves, and warres for Ladies doen by many a Lord.

4   Soone after comes the cruell Sarazin,
          In woven maile all armed warily,
          And sternly lookes at him, who not a pin
          Does care for looke of living creatures eye.
          They bring them wines of *Greece* and *Araby*,
          And daintie spices fetcht from furthest *Ynd*,
          To kindle heat of corage privily:
          And in the wine a solemne oth they bynd
      T'observe the sacred lawes of armes, that are assynd.

5   At last forth comes that far renowmed Queene,
          With royall pomp and Princely majestie;
          She is ybrought unto a paled greene,
          And placed under stately canapee,
          The warlike feates of both those knights to see.
          On th'other side in all mens open vew
          Duessa placed is, and on a tree
          Sans-foy his shield is hangd with bloudy hew:
      Both those the lawrell girlonds to the victor dew.

3. (2) **waite**: there awaits; (7) **timely**: correctly rhythmical.
4. (2) **warily**: carefully; (6) **Ynd**: India; (7) **corage**: courage;
(7) **privily**: internally; (9) **assynd**: pointed out, i.e., formally
rehearsed by heralds.
5. (3) **paled greene**: grassy field marked and fenced for a
tournament; (4) **canapee**: canopy; (9) **those**: i.e., both
Duessa and Sansfoy's shield; (9) **lawrell girlonds**: i.e., prizes.

6 A shrilling trompet sownded from on hye,
  And unto battaill bad them selves addresse:
  Their shining shieldes about their wrestes they tye,
  And burning blades about their heads do blesse,
  The instruments of wrath and heavinesse:
  With greedy force each other doth assayle,
  And strike so fiercely, that they do impresse
  Deepe dinted furrowes in the battred mayle;
 The yron walles to ward their blowes are weake and
   fraile.

7 The Sarazin was stout, and wondrous strong,
  And heaped blowes like yron hammers great:
  For after bloud and vengeance he did long.
  The knight was fiers, and full of youthly heat,
  And doubled strokes, like dreaded thunders threat:
  For all for prayse and honour he did fight.
  Both stricken strike, and beaten both do beat,
  That from their shields forth flyeth firie light,
 And helmets hewen deepe, shew marks of eithers might.

8 So th'one for wrong, the other strives for right:
  As when a Gryfon seized of his pray,
  A Dragon fiers encountreth in his flight,
  Through widest ayre making his ydle way,   §
  That would his rightfull ravine rend away:
  With hideous horrour both together smight,
  And souce so sore, that they the heavens affray:
  The wise Southsayer seeing so sad sight,
 Th'amazed vulgar tels of warres and mortall fight.

6. (3) **wrestes:** wrists; (4) **blesse:** brandish.
7. (4) **fiers:** fierce and proud.
8. (2) **Gryfon:** griffin or vulture; (2) **seized of:** that has seized;
  (5) **ravine:** prey; (7) **souce:** pounce; (9) **vulgar:** common man.

---

§ *ydle way*: This could mean "idle" in the sense that the dragon is just beating along with nothing particular in mind, or "empty" in the sense of carrying no prey in its claws at the moment.

9   So th'one for wrong, the other strives for right,
        And each to deadly shame would drive his foe:
        The cruell steele so greedily doth bight
        In tender flesh, that streames of bloud down flow,
        With which the armes, that earst so bright did show,
        Into a pure vermillion now are dyde:
        Great ruth in all the gazers harts did grow,
        Seeing the gored woundes to gape so wyde,
    That victory they dare not wish to either side.

10   At last the Paynim chaunst to cast his eye,
        His suddein eye, flaming with wrathfull fyre,
        Upon his brothers shield, which hong thereby:
        Therewith redoubled was his raging yre,
        And said, Ah wretched sonne of wofull syre,   §
        Doest thou sit wayling by black *Stygian* lake,
        Whilest here thy shield is hangd for victors hyre,
        And sluggish german doest thy forces slake,
    To after-send his foe, that him may overtake?

11   Goe caytive Elfe, him quickly overtake,
        And soone redeeme from his long wandring woe;
        Goe guiltie ghost, to him my message make,
        That I his shield have quit from dying foe.
        Therewith upon his crest he stroke him so,
        That twise he reeled, readie twise to fall;
        End of the doubtfull battell deemed tho
        The lookers on, and lowd to him gan call
    The false *Duessa*, Thine the shield, and I, and all.

9. (7) **ruth:** pity, compassion.
10. (4) **yre:** anger; (7) **victors hyre:** the victor's taking; (8) **german:** brother; (8) **slake:** slacken; (9) **To after-send his foe:** i.e., to send the Redcross Knight to follow after Sansjoy's dead brother.
11. (1) **caytive:** base, ignoble; (3) **make:** deliver; (4) **quit:** recovered, redeemed; (7) **deemed:** discerned; (7) **tho:** then.

§ In lines 5-7 of this stanza Sansjoy invokes his dead brother; in lines 8-9 he chides himself; in lines 1-4 of the next stanza he addresses the Redcross knight.

12 Soone as the Faerie heard his Ladie speake,
  Out of his swowning dreame he gan awake,
  And quickning faith, that earst was woxen weake,
  The creeping deadly cold away did shake:
  Tho mov'd with wrath, and shame, and Ladies sake,
  Of all attonce he cast avengd to bee,
  And with so'exceeding furie at him strake,
  That forced him to stoupe upon his knee;
 Had he not stouped so, he should have cloven bee.

13 And to him said, Goe now proud Miscreant,
  Thy selfe thy message doe to german deare,
  Alone he wandring thee too long doth want:
  Goe say, his foe thy shield with his doth beare.
  Therewith his heavie hand he high gan reare,
  Him to have slaine; when loe a darkesome clowd
  Upon him fell: he no where doth appeare,
  But vanisht is. The Elfe him cals alowd,
 But answer none receives: the darknes him does
  shrowd.

14 In haste *Duessa* from her place arose,
  And to him running said, O prowest knight,
  That ever Ladie to her love did chose,
  Let now abate the terror of your might,
  And quench the flame of furious despight,
  And bloudie vengeance; lo th'infernall powres
  Covering your foe with cloud of deadly night,
  Have borne him hence to *Plutoes* balefull bowres.
 The conquest yours, I yours, the shield, and glory yours.

12. (6) **cast:** resolved.
13. (1) **Miscreant:** villain, unbeliever; (3) **want:** miss.
14. (2) **prowest:** bravest; (8) **bowres:** chambers, halls.

15   Not all so satisfide, with greedie eye
        He sought all round about, his thirstie blade
        To bath in bloud of faithlesse enemy;
        Who all that while lay hid in secret shade:
        He standes amazed, how he thence should fade.
        At last the trumpets, Triumph sound on hie,
        And running Heralds humble homage made,
        Greeting him goodly with new victorie,
     And to him brought the shield, the cause of enmitie.

16   Wherewith he goeth to that soveraine Queene,
        And falling her before on lowly knee,
        To her makes present of his service seene:
        Which she accepts, with thankes, and goodly gree,
        Greatly advauncing his gay chevalree.
        So marcheth home, and by her takes the knight,
        Whom all the people follow with great glee,
        Shouting, and clapping all their hands on hight,
     That all the aire it fils, and flyes to heaven bright.

17   Home is he brought, and laid in sumptuous bed:
        Where many skilfull leaches him abide,
        To salve his hurts, that yet still freshly bled.
        In wine and oyle they wash his woundes wide,
        And softly can embalme on every side.
        And all the while, most heavenly melody
        About the bed sweet musicke did divide,
        Him to beguile of griefe and agony:
     And all the while *Duessa* wept full bitterly.

15. (6) **Triumph:** i.e., a salute to the winner; (8) **goodly:** courteously.
16. (3) **seene:** skilled; (4) **gree:** favour; (5) **advauncing:** extolling;
(5) **gay:** brilliant; (8) **on hight:** aloud, i.e., loudly.
17. (2) **leaches:** physicians; (2) **abide:** attend; (5) **can:** do; (7)
divide: move in brilliant (ornamental) passages.

18   As when a wearie traveller that strayes
         By muddy shore of broad seven-mouthed *Nile*,
         Unweeting of the perillous wandring wayes,
         Doth meet a cruell craftie Crocodile,
         Which in false griefe hyding his harmefull guile,
         Doth weepe full sore, and sheddeth tender teares:
         The foolish man, that pitties all this while
         His mournefull plight, is swallowd up unwares,
Forgetfull of his owne, that mindes anothers cares.

19   So wept *Duessa* untill eventide,
         That shyning lampes in *Joves* high house were light:
         Then forth she rose, ne lenger would abide,
         But comes unto the place, where th'Hethen knight
         In slombring swownd nigh voyd of vitall spright,
         Lay cover'd with inchaunted cloud all day:
         Whom when she found, as she him left in plight,
         To wayle his woefull case she would not stay,
But to the easterne coast of heaven makes speedy way.

20   Where griesly *Night*, with visage deadly sad,
         That *Phœbus* chearefull face durst never vew,
         And in a foule blacke pitchie mantle clad,
         She findes forth comming from her darkesome mew,
         Where she all day did hide her hated hew.
         Before the dore her yron charet stood,
         Alreadie harnessed for journey new;
         And coleblacke steedes yborne of hellish brood,
That on their rustie bits did champ, as they were wood.

18. (8) **unwares:** suddenly.
19. (5) **nigh . . . spright:** with the spark of life almost out.
20. (4) **mew:** den; (6) **charet:** chariot; (8) **brood:** parentage; (9)
wood: berserk.

21   Who when she saw *Duessa* sunny bright,
         Adornd with gold and jewels shining cleare,
         She greatly grew amazed at the sight,
         And th'unacquainted light began to feare:
         For never did such brightnesse there appeare,
         And would have backe retyred to her cave,
         Untill the witches speech she gan to heare,
         Saying, Yet O thou dreaded Dame, I crave
    Abide, till I have told the message, which I have.

22   She stayd, and foorth *Duessa* gan proceede,
         O thou most auncient Grandmother of all,
         More old then *Jove*, whom thou at first didst   §
              breede,
         Or that great house of Gods cælestiall,
         Which wast begot in *Dæmogorgons* hall,
         And sawst the secrets of the world unmade,
         Why suffredst thou thy Nephewes deare to fall
         With Elfin sword, most shamefully betrade?
    Lo where the stout *Sansjoy* doth sleepe in deadly shade.

21. (4) **unacquainted:** unaccustomed; (7) **gan:** began.
22. (3) **breede:** cause, give birth to; (6) **unmade:** (which was as
    yet) unformed from chaos; (7) **suffredst:** allow(est); (7)
    Nephewes: grandchildren.

---

§ This is another of Spenser's variations, for whatever reason, on the
usual classical cosmogony. Usually Night (Nyx) is given as the daughter of Chaos, as the sister of Erebus (the Depth), and as the mother
of Aether (Sky) and Hemera (Day); while the Titans Cronus
(Saturn) and Rhea (Ops) are usually given as the parents of Zeus
(Jove).

23   And him before, I saw with bitter eyes
         The bold *Sansfoy* shrinke underneath his speare;
         And now the pray of fowles in field he lyes,
         Nor wayld of friends, nor laid on groning beare,
         That whylome was to me too dearely deare.
         O what of Gods then boots it to be borne,
         If old *Aveugles* sonnes so evill heare?   §
         Or who shall not great *Nightes* children scorne,
      When two of three her Nephews are so fowle forlorne?

24   Up then, up dreary Dame, of darknesse Queene,
         Go gather up the reliques of thy race,
         Or else goe them avenge, and let be seene,
         That dreaded *Night* in brightest day hath place,
         And can the children of faire light deface.
         Her feeling speeches some compassion moved
         In hart, and chaunge in that great mothers face:
         Yet pittie in her hart was never proved
      Till then: for evermore she hated, never loved.

25   And said, Deare daughter rightly may I rew
         The fall of famous children borne of mee,
         And good successes, which their foes ensew:
         But who can turne the streame of destinee,
         Or breake the chayne of strong necessitee,
         Which fast is tyde to *Joves* eternall seat?
         The sonnes of Day he favoureth, I see,
         And by my ruines thinkes to make them great:
      To make one great by others losse, is bad excheat.

23. (4) **groning beare:** i.e., sorrowful bier; (5) **dearely:** injuriously;
    (7) **so evill heare:** are so ill spoken of; (or perhaps) are in
    such a bad way.
24. (2) **reliques:** remnants; (2) **race:** family; (8) **proved:** really
    felt.
25. (3) **And good . . . ensew:** and the good successes which
    follow (i.e., accrue to) their foes; (or perhaps) which their
    foes follow after – strive for; (9) **bad excheat:** an unfair profit.

---

§ *Aveugles sonnes*: i.e., the three Sans brothers. Aveugle=Blind One.

26 Yet shall they not escape so freely all;
 For some shall pay the price of others guilt:
 And he the man that made *Sansfoy* to fall,
 Shall with his owne bloud price that he hath spilt.
 But what art thou, that telst of Nephews kilt?
 I that do seeme not I, *Duessa* am,
 (Quoth she) how ever now in garments gilt,
 And gorgeous gold arayd I to thee came;
Duessa I, the daughter of Deceipt and Shame.

27 Then bowing downe her aged backe, she kist
 The wicked witch, saying; In that faire face
 The false resemblance of Deceipt, I wist
 Did closely lurke; yet so true-seeming grace
 It carried, that I scarse in darkesome place
 Could it discerne, though I the mother bee
 Of falshood, and root of *Duessaes* race.
 O welcome child, whom I have longd to see,
And now have seene unwares. Lo now I go with thee.

28 Then to her yron wagon she betakes,
 And with her beares the fowle welfavourd witch:
 Through mirkesome aire her readie way she makes.
 Her twyfold Teme, of which two blacke as pitch,
 And two were browne, yet each to each unlich,
 Did softly swim away, ne ever stampe,
 Unlesse she chaunst their stubborne mouths to twitch;
 Then foming tarre, their bridles they would champe,
And trampling the fine element, would fiercely rampe.

26. (4) **price:** pay the price of (the blood); (5) **kilt:** killed.
27. (9) **unwares:** unexpectedly.
28. (2) **welfavourd:** good looking; (4) **twyfold:** twofold; (5) **unlich:** unlike; (6) **ne:** nor; (7) **chaunst:** happened; (8) **foming tarre:** frothing foam as black as tar; (9) **fine element:** air; (9) **rampe:** rear.

29 So well they sped, that they be come at length
        Unto the place, whereas the Paynim lay,
        Devoid of outward sense, and native strength,
        Coverd with charmed cloud from vew of day,
        And sight of men, since his late luckelesse fray.
        His cruell wounds with cruddy bloud congealed,
        They binden up so wisely, as they may,
        And handle softly, till they can be healed:
    So lay him in her charet, close in night concealed.

30 And all the while she stood upon the ground,
        The wakefull dogs did never cease to bay,
        As giving warning of th'unwonted sound,
        With which her yron wheeles did them affray,
        And her darke griesly looke them much dismay;
        The messenger of death, the ghastly Owle
        With drearie shriekes did also her bewray;
        And hungry Wolves continually did howle,
    At her abhorred face, so filthy and so fowle.

31 Thence turning backe in silence soft they stole,
        And brought the heavie corse with easie pace
        To yawning gulfe of deepe *Avernus* hole.   §
        By that same hole an entrance darke and bace
        With smoake and sulphure hiding all the place,
        Descends to hell: there creature never past,
        That backe returned without heavenly grace;
        But dreadfull *Furies*, which their chaines have brast,
    And damned sprights sent forth to make ill men aghast.

29. (6) **cruddy:** clotted.
30. (7) **her bewray:** betray her presence.
31. (2) **corse:** body; (4) **bace:** low; (8) **brast:** burst, broken.

§ *Avernus hole*: Beside Lake Avernus is a cavern from which leads one
  of the pathways to the underworld. In Virgil's *Aeneid* Aeneas, taking
  the due precautions and enjoying the heavenly grace of his mother
  Venus, uses this entrance for his visit to the underworld.

32   By that same way the direfull dames doe drive
        Their mournefull charet, fild with rusty blood,
        And downe to *Plutoes* house are come bilive:
        Which passing through, on every side them stood
        The trembling ghosts with sad amazed mood,
        Chattring their yron teeth, and staring wide
        With stonie eyes; and all the hellish brood
        Of feends infernall flockt on every side,
    To gaze on earthly wight, that with the Night durst ride.

33   They pas the bitter waves of *Acheron*,   §
        Where many soules sit wailing woefully,
        And come to fiery flood of *Phlegeton*,
        Whereas the damned ghosts in torments fry,
        And with sharpe shrilling shriekes doe bootlesse cry,
        Cursing high *Jove*, the which them thither sent.
        The house of endlesse paine is built thereby,
        In which ten thousand sorts of punishment
    The cursed creatures doe eternally torment.

34   Before the threshold dreadfull *Cerberus*   §
        His three deformed heads did lay along,
        Curled with thousand adders venemous,
        And lilled forth his bloudie flaming tong:
        At them he gan to reare his bristles strong,
        And felly gnarre, untill dayes enemy
        Did him appease; then downe his taile he hong
        And suffered them to passen quietly:
    For she in hell and heaven had power equally.

32. (1) **direfull:** dreadful; (3) **bilive:** quickly.
33. (5) **bootlesse:** uselessly, hopelessly.
34. (4) **lilled:** lolled; (6) **felly gnarre:** cruelly snarl; (8) **suffered:** allowed.

§ *Acheron* and *Phlegeton*: The rivers of Sorrow and Fire respectively; two of the five rivers of Hades.
§ *Cerberus*: The three-headed, snaky-tailed watchdog of the underworld, one of the pestiferous brood of the snake-woman Echidna and the monster Typhon.

35   There was *Ixion* turned on a wheele,   §
          For daring tempt the Queene of heaven to sin;
          And *Sisyphus* an huge round stone did reele
          Against an hill, ne might from labour lin;
          There thirstie *Tantalus* hong by the chin;
          And *Tityus* fed a vulture on his maw;
          Typhœus joynts were stretched on a gin,
          Theseus condemned to endlesse slouth by law,
    And fifty sisters water in leake vessels draw.

35. (4) **lin**: cease; (6) **maw**: liver; (7) **gin**: rack; (8) **slouth**: idleness;
    (9) **leake**: leaky.

§ *Ixion*: The king of Thessaly who enjoyed the friendship and banquets of the gods; he returned this hospitality with the gross insult
of attempting to carry off Hera, wife of Zeus himself. The sin of
Sisyphus was that he betrayed the whereabouts of Aegina, whom Zeus
was secretly visiting, to her father Aesopus; then when Zeus sent
Death (Thanatos) as a punishment, Sisyphus outwitted him twice and
contrived to live to a ripe old age. *Tantalus*, who also enjoyed the
friendship of the gods, once returned their hospitality by serving
them with the flesh of his own son Pelops to see if they could detect
that it was not the flesh of a beast; in Tartarus, the place of punishment, Tantalus is always thirsty because the water round him recedes
whenever he bends to drink. *Tityus* is a giant thus punished for assault-
ing Leto, the mother of Apollo and Artemis. *Typhœs*, or Typhon,
is a monster with a hundred dragon heads who warred against Zeus.
Spenser does not give the usual account of his punishment, namely,
that Zeus buried him under the volcano Aetna where Hephaestus
(Vulcan), the artificer-god, uses his neck as an anvil. During an
attempt to carry off Persephone from the underworld *Theseus* was
inveigled into sitting in the Chair of Forgetfulness (hence into endless inactivity) but was eventually rescued by Herakles (Hercules).
The *fifty sisters* are the Danaids – daughters of Danaus – thus punished for the simultaneous mass-murder of their respective husbands
on their wedding-night. Only one sister refused to take part in the
plot and helped her husband to escape.

36 They all beholding worldly wights in place,
        Leave off their worke, unmindfull of their smart,
        To gaze on them; who forth by them doe pace,
        Till they be come unto the furthest part:
        Where was a Cave ywrought by wondrous art,
        Deepe, darke, uneasie, dolefull, comfortlesse,
        In which sad *Æsculapius* farre a part
        Emprisond was in chaines remedilesse,
    For that *Hippolytus* rent corse he did redresse.

37 *Hippolytus* a jolly huntsman was,
        That wont in charet chace the foming Bore;
        He all his Peeres in beautie did surpas,
        But Ladies love as losse of time forbore:
        His wanton stepdame loved him the more,
        But when she saw her offred sweets refused
        Her love she turnd to hate, and him before
        His father fierce of treason false accused,
    And with her gealous termes his open eares abused.

38 Who all in rage his Sea-god syre besought,
        Some cursed vengeance on his sonne to cast:
        From surging gulf two monsters straight were
                brought,
        With dread whereof his chasing steedes aghast,
        Both charet swift and huntsman overcast.
        His goodly corps on ragged cliffs yrent,
        Was quite dismembred, and his members chast
        Scattered on every mountaine, as he went,
    That of *Hippolytus* was left no moniment.

36. (1) **worldly:** i.e., living, from the upper world; (1) **in place:**
present, at hand; (2) **smart:** agony; (8) **remedilesse:** without
hope of release.
37. (4) **forbore:** refrained from; (5) **stepdame:** Phaedra.
38. (1) **Sea-god syre:** Poseidon (Neptune); (9) **moniment:** i.e.,
identifiable traces.

39   His cruell stepdame seeing what was donne,
     Her wicked dayes with wretched knife did end,
     In death avowing th'innocence of her sonne.
     Which hearing his rash Syre, began to rend
     His haire, and hastie tongue, that did offend:
     Tho gathering up the relicks of his smart
     By *Dianes* meanes, who was *Hippolyts* frend,
     Them brought to *Æsculape*, that by his art
Did heale them all againe, and joyned every part.

40   Such wondrous science in mans wit to raine
     When *Jove* avizd, that could the dead revive,
     And fates expired could renew againe,
     Of endlesse life he might him not deprive,
     But unto hell did thrust him downe alive,
     With flashing thunderbolt ywounded sore:
     Where long remaining, he did alwaies strive
     Himselfe with salves to health for to restore,
And slake the heavenly fire, that raged evermore.

41   There auncient Night arriving, did alight
     From her nigh wearie waine, and in her armes
     To *Æsculapius* brought the wounded knight:
     Whom having softly disarayd of armes,
     Tho gan to him discover all his harmes,
     Beseeching him with prayer, and with praise,
     If either salves, or oyles, or herbes, or charmes
     A fordonne wight from dore of death mote raise,
He would at her request prolong her nephews daies.

40. (2) **avizd:** noticed; (3) **fates:** i.e., destined term of life.
41. (2) **waine:** chariot; (4) **disarayd:** stripped; (5) **discover:** point out; (8) **fordonne:** far gone.

42   Ah Dame (quoth he) thou temptest me in vaine,
     To dare the thing, which daily yet I rew,
     And the old cause of my continued paine
     With like attempt to like end to renew.
     Is not enough, that thrust from heaven dew
     Here endlesse penance for one fault I pay,
     But that redoubled crime with vengeance new
     Thou biddest me to eeke? Can Night defray
  The wrath of thundring *Jove*, that rules both night and
     day?

43   Not so (quoth she) but sith that heavens king
     From hope of heaven hath thee excluded quight,
     Why fearest thou, that canst not hope for thing,
     And fearest not, that more thee hurten might,
     Now in the powre of everlasting Night?
     Goe to then, O thou farre renowmed sonne
     Of great *Apollo*, shew thy famous might
     In medicine, that else hath to thee wonne
  Great paines, and greater praise, both never to be
     donne.

44   Her words prevaild: And then the learned leach
     His cunning hand gan to his wounds to lay,
     And all things else, the which his art did teach:
     Which having seene, from thence arose away
     The mother of dread darknesse, and let stay
     Aveugles sonne there in the leaches cure,
     And backe returning tooke her wonted way,
     To runne her timely race, whilst *Phœbus* pure
  In westerne waves his wearie wagon did recure.

---

42. (4) **end:** result; (5) **dew:** duly, (or perhaps) my rights of
heaven; (8) **eeke:** compound.
43. (1) **sith that:** since; (3) **thing:** anything; (6) **Goe to:** set to,
begin; (8) **else:** already; (9) **donne:** outdone.
44. (6) **cure:** care; (9) **wagon:** team; (9) **recure:** restore.

45   The false *Duessa* leaving noyous Night,
     Returnd to stately pallace of dame Pride;
     Where when she came, she found the Faery knight
     Departed thence, albe his woundes wide
     Not throughly heald, unreadie were to ride.
     Good cause he had to hasten thence away;
     For on a day his wary Dwarfe had spide,
     Where in a dongeon deepe huge numbers lay
Of caytive wretched thrals, that wayled night and day.

46   A ruefull sight, as could be seene with eie;
     Of whom he learned had in secret wise
     The hidden cause of their captivitie,
     How mortgaging their lives to *Covetise*,
     Through wastfull Pride, and wanton Riotise,
     They were by law of that proud Tyrannesse
     Provokt with *Wrath*, and *Envies* false surmise,
     Condemned to that Dongeon mercilesse,
Where they should live in woe, and die in
       wretchednesse.

47   There was that great proud king of *Babylon*,
     That would compell all nations to adore,
     And him as onely God to call upon,
     Till through celestiall doome throwne out of dore,
     Into an Oxe he was transform'd of yore:
     There also was king *Crœsus*, that enhaunst
     His heart too high through his great riches store;
     And proud *Antiochus*, the which advaunst
His cursed hand gainst God, and on his altars daunst.

45. (1) **noyous:** unwholesome; (5) **throughly:** completely, i.e., were not really in a condition which permitted riding; (9) **caytive:** captive; (9) **thrals:** slaves.
47. (1) **king of Babylon:** Nebuchadnezzar (see Daniel 4); (3) **onely God:** the only God; (4) **doome:** decree; (6) **enhaunst:** lifted up; (9) **daunst:** danced.

48 And them long time before, great *Nimrod* was,
 That first the world with sword and fire warrayd;
 And after him old *Ninus* farre did pas
 In princely pompe, of all the world obayd;
 There also was that mightie Monarch layd
 Low under all, yet above all in pride,
 That name of native syre did fowle upbrayd,
 And would as *Ammons* sonne be magnifide,
Till scornd of God and man a shamefull death he dide.

49 All these together in one heape were throwne,
 Like carkases of beasts in butchers stall.
 And in another corner wide were strowne
 The antique ruines of the *Romaines* fall:
 Great *Romulus* the Grandsyre of them all,
 Proud *Tarquin*, and too lordly *Lentulus*,
 Stout *Scipio*, and stubborne *Hanniball*,
 Ambitious *Sylla*, and sterne *Marius*,
High *Cæsar*, great *Pompey*, and fierce *Antonius*.

50 Amongst these mighty men were wemen mixt,
 Proud wemen, vaine, forgetfull of their yoke:
 The bold *Semiramis*, whose sides transfixt
 With sonnes owne blade, her fowle reproches spoke;
 Faire *Sthenobœa*, that her selfe did choke
 With wilfull cord, for wanting of her will;
 High minded *Cleopatra*, that with stroke
 Of Aspes sting her selfe did stoutly kill:
And thousands moe the like, that did that dongeon fill.

48. (2) **warrayd:** afflicted, attacked; (5) **mightie Monarch:** Alexander the Great.

51   Besides the endlesse routs of wretched thralles,
          Which thither were assembled day by day,
          From all the world after their wofull falles,
          Through wicked pride, and wasted wealthes decay.
          But most of all, which in that Dongeon lay
          Fell from high Princes courts, or Ladies bowres,
          Where they in idle pompe, or wanton play,
          Consumed had their goods, and thriftlesse howres,
    And lastly throwne themselves into these heavy stowres.

52   Whose case when as the carefull Dwarfe had tould,
          And made ensample of their mournefull sight
          Unto his maister, he no lenger would
          There dwell in perill of like painefull plight,
          But early rose, and ere that dawning light
          Discovered had the world to heaven wyde,
          He by a privie Posterne tooke his flight,
          That of no envious eyes he mote be spyde:
    For doubtlesse death ensewd, if any him descryde.

53   Scarse could he footing find in that fowle way,
          For many corses, like a great Lay-stall
          Of murdred men which therein strowed lay,
          Without remorse, or decent funerall:
          Which all through that great Princesse pride did fall
          And came to shamefull end. And them beside
          Forth ryding underneath the castell wall,
          A donghill of dead carkases he spide,
    The dreadfull spectacle of that sad house of *Pride*.

51. (4) **decay:** destruction; (9) **stowres:** misfortunes.
52. (1) **carefull:** worried; (7) **privie:** hidden; (7) **Posterne:** private
gate or exit way, often underground; (9) **descryde:** discovered.
53. (2) **Lay-stall:** offal-heap.

Canto VI

From lawlesse lust by wondrous grace
fayre Una is releast:
Whom salvage nation does adore,
and learnes her wise beheast.

1
A s when a ship, that flyes faire under saile,
    An hidden rocke escaped hath unwares,
  That lay in waite her wrack for to bewaile,   §
  The Marriner yet halfe amazed stares
  At perill past, and yet in doubt ne dares
  To joy at his foole-happie oversight:
  So doubly is distrest twixt joy and cares
  The dreadlesse courage of this Elfin knight,
Having escapt so sad ensamples in his sight.

2
  Yet sad he was that his too hastie speed
    The faire *Duess'* had forst him leave behind;
  And yet more sad, that *Una* his deare dreed
  Her truth had staind with treason so unkind;
  Yet crime in her could never creature find,
  But for his love, and for her owne selfe sake,
  She wandred had from one to other *Ynd*,
  Him for to seeke, ne ever would forsake,
Till her unwares the fierce *Sansloy* did overtake.

salvage nation: wild, uncivilized folk; **beheast:** bidding.
1. (3) **bewaile:** (?) bring about; (5) **in doubt:** fearful; (5) **ne:** not;
   (6) **foole-happie:** lucky; (9) **ensamples:** warning examples.
2. (3) **dreed:** object of reverence; (9) **unwares:** without warning.

§ *bewaile*: The Oxford English Dictionary has a special entry for this
use of *bewaile*, remarking that it is either "very forced (? suggested
by the consequences of a wreck), or it is a mere error".

3   Who after *Archimagoes* fowle defeat,
         Led her away into a forrest wilde,
         And turning wrathfull fire to lustfull heat,
         With beastly sin thought her to have defilde,
         And made the vassall of his pleasures vilde.
         Yet first he cast by treatie, and by traynes,
         Her to perswade, that stubborne fort to yilde:
         For greater conquest of hard love he gaynes,
    That workes it to his will, then he that it constraines.

4   With fawning wordes he courted her a while,
         And looking lovely, and oft sighing sore,
         Her constant hart did tempt with diverse guile:
         But wordes, and lookes, and sighes she did abhore,
         As rocke of Diamond stedfast evermore.
         Yet for to feed his fyrie lustfull eye,
         He snatcht the vele, that hong her face before;
         Then gan her beautie shine, as brightest skye,
    And burnt his beastly hart t'efforce her chastitye.

5   So when he saw his flatt'ring arts to fayle,
         And subtile engines bet from batteree,
         With greedy force he gan the fort assayle,
         Whereof he weend possessed soone to bee,
         And win rich spoile of ransackt chastetee.
         Ah heavens, that do this hideous act behold,
         And heavenly virgin thus outraged see,
         How can ye vengeance just so long withhold,
    And hurle not flashing flames upon that Paynim bold?

3. (5) **vilde:** vile; (6) **cast by treatie:** went about it by trying to secure her agreement; (6) **traynes:** wily propositions; (8) **hard love:** i.e., love that is hard to win.
4. (2) **lovely:** amorously; (9) **t'efforce:** to force, violate.
5. (2) **bet:** beaten; (2) **batteree:** emplacements, siege-positions.

6   The pitteous maiden carefull comfortlesse,
        Does throw out thrilling shriekes, and shrieking cryes,
        The last vaine helpe of womens great distresse,
        And with loud plaints importuneth the skyes,
        That molten starres do drop like weeping eyes;
        And *Phœbus* flying so most shamefull sight,
        His blushing face in foggy cloud implyes,
        And hides for shame. What wit of mortall wight
    Can now devise to quit a thrall from such a plight?

7   Eternall providence exceeding thought,
        Where none appeares can make her selfe a way:
        A wondrous way it for this Lady wrought,
        From Lyons clawes to pluck the griped pray.
        Her shrill outcryes and shriekes so loud did bray,
        That all the woodes and forestes did resownd;
        A troupe of *Faunes* and *Satyres* far away   §
        Within the wood were dauncing in a rownd,
    Whiles old *Sylvanus* slept in shady arber sownd.

8   Who when they heard that pitteous strained voice,
        In hast forsooke their rurall meriment,
        And ran towards the far rebownded noyce,
        To weet, what wight so loudly did lament.
        Unto the place they come incontinent:
        Whom when the raging Sarazin espide,
        A rude, misshapen, monstrous rablement,
        Whose like he never saw, he durst not bide,
    But got his ready steed, and fast away gan ride.

6. (4) **importuneth:** urgently beseeches; (7) **implyes:** wraps; (9) **thrall:** captive.
7. (2) **her selfe:** i.e., providence; (4) **griped:** firm-grasped; (5) **bray:** sound out; (8) **rownd:** circle (also, perhaps, name of a dance); (9) **sownd:** soundly.
8. (3) **rebownded:** re-echoing, resounding; (4) **weet:** find out; (5) **incontinent:** forthwith; (7) **rablement:** rabble.

§ *Faunes* and *Satyres*: Wild creatures of woods and fields, half man and half goat, who are followers of Pan (Faunus). *Sylvanus*: Silvanus, the Roman god of woods and uncultivated, semi-wild land; he is cheerful but a bit uncanny and dangerous. He, too, is associated with Fauns and Satyrs and is sometimes actually identified with Pan.

9   The wyld woodgods arrived in the place,
      There find the virgin dolefull desolate,
      With ruffled rayments, and faire blubbred face,
      As her outrageous foe had left her late,
      And trembling yet through feare of former hate;
      All stand amazed at so uncouth sight,
      And gin to pittie her unhappie state,
      All stand astonied at her beautie bright,
    In their rude eyes unworthie of so wofull plight.

10   She more amaz'd, in double dread doth dwell;
      And every tender part for feare does shake:
      As when a greedie Wolfe through hunger fell
      A seely Lambe farre from the flocke does take,
      Of whom he meanes his bloudie feast to make,
      A Lyon spyes fast running towards him,
      The innocent pray in hast he does forsake,
      Which quit from death yet quakes in every lim
    With chaunge of feare, to see the Lyon looke so grim.

11   Such fearefull fit assaid her trembling hart,
      Ne word to speake, ne joynt to move she had:
      The salvage nation feele her secret smart,
      And read her sorrow in her count'nance sad;
      Their frowning forheads with rough hornes yclad,
      And rusticke horror all a side doe lay,
      And gently grenning, shew a semblance glad
      To comfort her, and feare to put away,
    Their backward bent knees teach her humbly to obay.

9. (6) **uncouth:** strange; (7) **gin:** begin.
10. (4) **seely:** harmless, helpless; (8) **quit:** saved.
11. (1) **fearefull fit:** paroxysm of terror; (3) **salvage nation:** band
    of wild folk; (3) **smart:** agony; (6) **horror:** roughness; (7)
    grenning: grinning; (7) **semblance:** expression; (9) **obay:** pay
    obeisance (to her).

12   The doubtfull Damzell dare not yet commit
         Her single person to their barbarous truth,
         But still twixt feare and hope amazd does sit,
         Late learnd what harme to hastie trust ensu'th:
         They in compassion of her tender youth,
         And wonder of her beautie soveraine,
         Are wonne with pitty and unwonted ruth,
         And all prostrate upon the lowly plaine,
     Do kisse her feete, and fawne on her with count'nance
         faine.

13   Their harts she ghesseth by their humble guise,
         And yieldes her to extremitie of time;
         So from the ground she fearelesse doth arise,
         And walketh forth without suspect of crime:
         They all as glad, as birdes of joyous Prime,
         Thence lead her forth, about her dauncing round,
         Shouting, and singing all a shepheards ryme,
         And with greene braunches strowing all the ground,
     Do worship her, as Queene, with olive girlond cround.

14   And all the way their merry pipes they sound,
         That all the woods with doubled Eccho ring,
         And with their horned feet do weare the ground,
         Leaping like wanton kids in pleasant Spring.
         So towards old *Sylvanus* they her bring;
         Who with the noyse awaked, commeth out,
         To weet the cause, his weake steps governing,
         And aged limbs on Cypresse stadle stout,
     And with an yvie twyne his wast is girt about.

12. (1) **doubtfull:** apprehensive; (4) **Late learnd:** having lately
      been taught; (4) **ensu'th:** follows; (9) **faine:** glad.
13. (1) **guise:** behaviour; (2) **extremitie of time:** the present
      emergency; (5) **Prime:** morning (from canonical hours, 6 to
      9 a.m.), (or perhaps) spring time.
14. (8) **stadle:** a prop, support.

15 Far off he wonders, what them makes so glad,
　　　Or *Bacchus* merry fruit they did invent,　　　§
　　　Or *Cybeles* franticke rites have made them mad;
　　　They drawing nigh, unto their God present
　　　That flowre of faith and beautie excellent.
　　　The God himselfe vewing that mirrhour rare,
　　　Stood long amazd, and burnt in his intent;
　　　His owne faire *Dryope* now he thinkes not faire,
And *Pholoe* fowle, when her to this he doth compaire.

16 The woodborne people fall before her flat,
　　　And worship her as Goddesse of the wood;
　　　And old *Sylvanus* selfe bethinkes not, what
　　　To thinke of wight so faire, but gazing stood,
　　　In doubt to deeme her borne of earthly brood;
　　　Sometimes Dame *Venus* selfe he seemes to see,
　　　But *Venus* never had so sober mood;
　　　Sometimes *Diana* he her takes to bee,　　　§
But misseth bow, and shaftes, and buskins to her knee.

15. (2) **invent:** discover; (7) **in his intent:** i.e., in the intensity of his gaze.
16. (3) **selfe:** himself; (5) **deeme:** consider; (5) **brood:** origin, parentage; (9) **buskins:** high boots.

§ *Bacchus*: Also called Dionysus, the son of Zeus and Semele, a god of vegetation but particularly of the grape-harvest and of wine. *Cybele*: An early Earth-mother figure, primarily a goddess of fertility but also of mountains and of nature in its wild states; worship of her was characterized by "franticke rites" and ecstatic states of prophetic rapture. *Dryope*: Daughter of King Dryops; her long-time companions were the Nymphs by whom she was finally carried off and turned into one of them. *Pholoe*: A mountain-nymph loved by Pan or, as Spenser here has him, Silvanus.
§ *Diana*: The virgin huntress-goddess, also known as Artemis.

17 By vew of her he ginneth to revive
     His ancient love, and dearest *Cyparisse*,
     And calles to mind his pourtraiture alive,
     How faire he was, and yet not faire to this,
     And how he slew with glauncing dart amisse
     A gentle Hynd, the which the lovely boy
     Did love as life, above all worldly blisse;
     For griefe whereof the lad n'ould after joy,
  But pynd away in anguish and selfe-wild annoy.

18 The wooddy Nymphes, faire *Hamadryades*   §
     Her to behold do thither runne apace,
     And all the troupe of light-foot *Naiades*,
     Flocke all about to see her lovely face:
     But when they vewed have her heavenly grace,
     They envie her in their malitious mind,
     And fly away for feare of fowle disgrace:
     But all the *Satyres* scorne their woody kind,
  And henceforth nothing faire, but her on earth they find.

19 Glad of such lucke, the luckelesse lucky maid,
     Did her content to please their feeble eyes,
     And long time with that salvage people staid,
     To gather breath in many miseries.
     During which time her gentle wit she plyes,
     To teach them truth, which worship her in vaine,
     And made her th'Image of Idolatryes;
     But when their bootlesse zeale she did restraine
  From her own worship, they her Asse would worship
       fayn.

17. (1) **ginneth:** begins; (3) **pourtraiture alive:** living image; (4) **to this:** as compared to this; (5) **amisse:** accidentally; (6) **Hynd:** doe; (8) **n'ould:** would not; (8) **joy:** take pleasure (in anything); (9) **selfe-wild annoy:** self-destructive grief.
18. (8) **woody kind:** woodland kin.
19. (2) **her content to please:** content herself with favouring; (2) **feeble:** i.e., ignorant; (5) **wit:** knowledge, intelligence; (5) **plyes:** applies; (9) **fayn:** gladly.

§ *Hamadryades*: Tree-nymphs – both the guardians and the indwelling spirits of trees. *Naiades*: Nymphs particularly associated with fresh-water streams, springs, and lakes.

20   It fortuned a noble warlike knight
      By just occasion to that forrest came,
      To seeke his kindred, and the lignage right,
      From whence he tooke his well deserved name:
      He had in armes abroad wonne muchell fame,
      And fild far landes with glorie of his might,
      Plaine, faithfull, true, and enimy of shame,
      And ever lov'd to fight for Ladies right,
But in vaine glorious frayes he litle did delight.

21   A Satyres sonne yborne in forrest wyld,
      By straunge adventure as it did betyde,
      And there begotten of a Lady myld,
      Faire *Thyamis* the daughter of *Labryde*,
      That was in sacred bands of wedlocke tyde
      To *Therion*, a loose unruly swayne;
      Who had more joy to raunge the forrest wyde,
      And chase the salvage beast with busie payne,
Then serve his Ladies love, and wast in pleasures vayne.

22   The forlorne mayd did with loves longing burne,
      And could not lacke her lovers company,
      But to the wood she goes, to serve her turne,
      And seeke her spouse, that from her still does fly,
      And followes other game and venery:
      A Satyre chaunst her wandring for to find,
      And kindling coles of lust in brutish eye,
      The loyall links of wedlocke did unbind,
And made her person thrall unto his beastly kind.

20. (1) **fortuned:** happened that; (1) **knight:** i.e., Sir Satyrane;
     (2) **By just occasion:** on worthy business; (3) **lignage:** lineage;
     (5) **muchell:** great; (9) **frayes:** battles, quarrels.
21. (2) **betyde:** happen; (6) **swayne:** youth; (8) **payne:** care; (9)
     Then: than; (9) **wast:** spend himself.
22. (2) **lacke:** do without; (5) **venery:** i.e., hunting; (9) **thrall:**
     slave.

23 So long in secret cabin there he held
      Her captive to his sensuall desire,
      Till that with timely fruit her belly sweld,
      And bore a boy unto that salvage sire:
      Then home he suffred her for to retire,
      For ransome leaving him the late borne childe;
      Whom till to ryper yeares he gan aspire,
      He noursled up in life and manners wilde,
    Emongst wild beasts and woods, from lawes of men
        exilde.

24 For all he taught the tender ymp, was but
      To banish cowardize and bastard feare;
      His trembling hand he would him force to put
      Upon the Lyon and the rugged Beare,
      And from the she Beares teats her whelps to teare;
      And eke wyld roring Buls he would him make
      To tame, and ryde their backes not made to beare;
      And the Robuckes in flight to overtake,
    That every beast for feare of him did fly and quake.

25 Thereby so fearelesse, and so fell he grew,
      That his owne sire and maister of his guise
      Did often tremble at his horrid vew,
      And oft for dread of hurt would him advise,
      The angry beasts not rashly to despise,
      Nor too much to provoke; for he would learne
      The Lyon stoup to him in lowly wise,
      (A lesson hard) and make the Libbard sterne
    Leave roaring, when in rage he for revenge did earne.

23. (5) **suffred:** permitted; (7) **aspire:** attain; (8) **noursled up:** reared, brought up.
24. (1) **ymp:** child; (7) **to beare:** i.e., to carry riders.
25. (1) **fell:** fierce; (2) **maister of his guise:** tutor in his manner of life; (3) **horrid vew:** rough appearance; (6) **learne:** teach, train; (7) **stoup:** to cringe, crouch; (7) **in lowly wise:** humbly; (8) **Libbard:** leopard; (9) **earne:** yearn, long.

26   And for to make his powre approved more,
        Wyld beasts in yron yokes he would compell;
        The spotted Panther, and the tusked Bore,
        The Pardale swift, and the Tigre cruell;
        The Antelope, and Wolfe both fierce and fell;
        And them constraine in equall teme to draw.
        Such joy he had, their stubborne harts to quell,
        And sturdie courage tame with dreadfull aw,
That his beheast they feared, as a tyrans law.

27   His loving mother came upon a day
        Unto the woods, to see her little sonne;
        And chaunst unwares to meet him in the way,
        After his sportes, and cruell pastime donne,
        When after him a Lyonesse did runne,
        That roaring all with rage, did lowd requere
        Her children deare, whom he away had wonne:
        The Lyon whelpes she saw how he did beare,
And lull in rugged armes, withouten childish feare.

28   The fearefull Dame all quaked at the sight,
        And turning backe, gan fast to fly away,
        Untill with love revokt from vaine affright,
        She hardly yet perswaded was to stay,
        And then to him these womanish words gan say;
        Ah *Satyrane*, my dearling, and my joy,
        For love of me leave off this dreadfull play;
        To dally thus with death, is no fit toy,
Go find some other play-fellowes, mine own sweet boy.

26. (4) **Pardale:** leopard; (6) **constraine:** force; (9) **beheast:** command.
27. (3) **unwares:** suddenly; (6) **requere:** demand.
28. (3) **revokt:** recalled.

29   In these and like delights of bloudy game
      He trayned was, till ryper yeares he raught,
      And there abode, whilst any beast of name
      Walkt in that forest, whom he had not taught
      To feare his force: and then his courage haught
      Desird of forreine foemen to be knowne,
      And far abroad for straunge adventures sought:
      In which his might was never overthrowne,
But through all Faery lond his famous worth was blown.

30   Yet evermore it was his manner faire,
      After long labours and adventures spent,
      Unto those native woods for to repaire,
      To see his sire and ofspring auncient.
      And now he thither came for like intent;
      Where he unwares the fairest *Una* found,
      Straunge Lady, in so straunge habiliment,
      Teaching the Satyres, which her sat around,
Trew sacred lore, which from her sweet lips did redound.

31   He wondred at her wisedome heavenly rare,
      Whose like in womens wit he never knew;
      And when her curteous deeds he did compare,   §
      Gan her admire, and her sad sorrowes rew,
      Blaming of Fortune, which such troubles threw,
      And joyd to make proofe of her crueltie
      On gentle Dame, so hurtlesse, and so trew:
      Thenceforth he kept her goodly company,
And learnd her discipline of faith and veritie.

---

29. (2) **raught:** reached; (5) **haught:** high, noble.
30. (3) **repaire:** come back to; (4) **ofspring:** source of being, (or) place of origin; (7) **habiliment:** dress; (9) **lore:** learning, doctrine; (9) **redound:** flow.
31. (2) **wit:** mind, intelligence; (3) **compare:** (probably) obtained some idea of.

§ *compare*: In Spenser this word can mean "to gather together", "to obtain or acquire" (as in Canto IV, stanza 28); hence the present phrase could mean something like "when he had obtained some idea (formed an impression) of her courteous deeds". Spenser also uses the word in its usual modern sense, and again in the sense of "to rival or vie with". Thus the phrase might mean "when he had compared her [Una's] deeds with those he knew of other women", or, just possibly, "when he had matched courtesies with her".

32 But she all vowd unto the *Redcrosse* knight,
　　　 His wandring perill closely did lament,
　　　 Ne in this new acquaintaunce could delight,
　　　 But her deare heart with anguish did torment,
　　　 And all her wit in secret counsels spent,
　　　 How to escape. At last in privie wise
　　　 To *Satyrane* she shewed her intent;
　　　 Who glad to gain such favour, gan devise,
　　How with that pensive Maid he best might thence arise.

33 So on a day when Satyres all were gone,
　　　 To do their service to *Sylvanus* old,
　　　 The gentle virgin left behind alone
　　　 He led away with courage stout and bold.
　　　 Too late it was, to Satyres to be told,
　　　 Or ever hope recover her againe:
　　　 In vaine he seekes that having cannot hold.
　　　 So fast he carried her with carefull paine,
　　That they the woods are past, and come now to
　　　　 the plaine.

34 The better part now of the lingring day,
　　　 They traveild had, when as they farre espide
　　　 A wearie wight forwandring by the way,
　　　 And towards him they gan in hast to ride,
　　　 To weet of newes, that did abroad betide,
　　　 Or tydings of her knight of the *Redcrosse*.
　　　 But he them spying, gan to turne aside,
　　　 For feare as seemd, or for some feigned losse;
　　More greedy they of newes, fast towards him do crosse.

32. (2) **closely:** secretly, inwardly; (6) **in privie wise:** in confidence;
(8) **devise:** consider.
33. (6) **Or ever hope:** or for them ever to hope to; (8) **carefull
paine:** wary skill.
34. (5) **betide:** take place; (8) **or for . . . losse:** or on pretence of
searching for something lost.

35 A silly man, in simple weedes forworne,
      And soild with dust of the long dried way;
      His sandales were with toilesome travell torne,
      And face all tand with scorching sunny ray,
      As he had traveild many a sommers day,
      Through boyling sands of *Arabie* and *Ynde*;
      And in his hand a *Jacobs* staffe, to stay
      His wearie limbes upon: and eke behind,
  His scrip did hang, in which his needments he did bind.

36 The knight approching nigh, of him inquerd
      Tydings of warre, and of adventures new;
      But warres, nor new adventures none he herd.
      Then *Una* gan to aske, if ought he knew,
      Or heard abroad of that her champion trew,
      That in his armour bare a croslet red.
      Aye me, Deare dame (quoth he) well may I rew
      To tell the sad sight, which mine eies have red:
  These eyes did see that knight both living and eke ded.

37 That cruell word her tender hart so thrild,
      That suddein cold did runne through every vaine,
      And stony horrour all her sences fild
      With dying fit, that downe she fell for paine.
      The knight her lightly reared up againe,
      And comforted with curteous kind reliefe:
      Then wonne from death, she bad him tellen plaine
      The further processe of her hidden griefe;
  The lesser pangs can beare, who hath endur'd the chiefe.

35. (1) **forworne:** threadbare; (7) **Jacobs staffe:** i.e., pilgrim's staff; (9) **scrip:** bag, large wallet.
36. (7) **rew:** lament; (8) **red:** seen.
37. (1) **thrild:** pierced; (4) **dying fit:** a deathly seizure; (8) **processe:** details, matters concerning (the Redcross knight's fate).

38 Then gan the Pilgrim thus, I chaunst this day,
  This fatall day, that shall I ever rew,
  To see two knights in travell on my way
  (A sory sight) arraung'd in battell new,
  Both breathing vengeaunce, both of wrathfull hew:
  My fearefull flesh did tremble at their strife,
  To see their blades so greedily imbrew,
  That drunke with bloud, yet thristed after life:
 What more? the *Redcrosse* knight was slaine with
   Paynim knife.

39 Ah dearest Lord (quoth she) how might that bee,
  And he the stoutest knight, that ever wonne?
  Ah dearest dame (quoth he) how might I see
  The thing, that might not be, and yet was donne?
  Where is (said *Satyrane*) that Paynims sonne,
  That him of life, and us of joy hath reft?
  Not far away (quoth he) he hence doth wonne
  Foreby a fountaine, where I late him left
 Washing his bloudy wounds, that through the steele
   were cleft.

40 Therewith the knight thence marched forth in hast,
  Whiles *Una* with huge heavinesse opprest,
  Could not for sorrow follow him so fast;
  And soone he came, as he the place had ghest,
  Whereas that *Pagan* proud him selfe did rest,
  In secret shadow by a fountaine side:
  Even he it was, that earst would have supprest
  Faire *Una*: whom when *Satyrane* espide,
 With fowle reprochfull words he boldly him defide.

38. (5) **hew:** looks, appearance; (7) **imbrew:** thrust, flesh themselves; (8) **thristed:** thirsted.
39. (2) **wonne:** won a victory; (7) **wonne:** live, dwell; (8) **Foreby:** close by.
40. (4) **ghest:** guessed; (5) **Whereas:** (to) where; (7) **he it was:** i.e., Sansloy; (7) **supprest:** crushed, overthrown.

41   And said, Arise thou cursed Miscreaunt,
        That hast with knightlesse guile and trecherous train
        Faire knighthood fowly shamed, and doest vaunt
        That good knight of the *Redcrosse* to have slain:
        Arise, and with like treason now maintain
        Thy guilty wrong, or else thee guilty yield.
        The Sarazin this hearing, rose amain,
        And catching up in hast his three square shield,
  And shining helmet, soone him buckled to the field.

42   And drawing nigh him said, Ah misborne Elfe,
        In evill houre thy foes thee hither sent,
        Anothers wrongs to wreake upon thy selfe:
        Yet ill thou blamest me, for having blent
        My name with guile and traiterous intent;
        That *Redcrosse* knight, perdie, I never slew,
        But had he beene, where earst his armes were lent,
        Th'enchaunter vaine his errour should not rew:
  But thou his errour shalt, I hope now proven trew.

43   Therewith they gan, both furious and fell,
        To thunder blowes, and fiersly to assaile
        Each other, bent his enimy to quell,
        That with their force they perst both plate and maile,
        And made wide furrowes in their fleshes fraile,
        That it would pitty any living eie.
        Large floods of bloud adowne their sides did raile;
        But floods of bloud could not them satisfie:
  Both hungred after death: both chose to win, or die.

41. (1) **Miscreaunt:** villain; (2) **knightlesse:** unknightly; (2) **train:** trickery; (3) **vaunt:** brag, boast; (7) **amain:** at once; (8) **three square:** with three equal sides.
42. (4) **ill:** unjustly; (4) **blent:** mixed, tainted; (6) **perdie:** truly; (7) **earst:** lately; (8) **vaine:** foolish.
43. (3) **bent . . . quell:** bent on killing; (7) **raile:** stream.

44   So long they fight, and fell revenge pursue,
          That fainting each, themselves to breathen let,
          And oft refreshed, battell oft renue:
          As when two Bores with rancling malice met,
          Their gory sides fresh bleeding fiercely fret,
          Til breathlesse both them selves aside retire,
          Where foming wrath, their cruell tuskes they whet,
          And trample th'earth, the whiles they may respire;
     Then backe to fight againe, new breathed and entire.

45   So fiersly, when these knights had breathed once,
          They gan to fight returne, increasing more
          Their puissant force, and cruell rage attonce,
          With heaped strokes more hugely, then before,
          That with their drerie wounds and bloudy gore
          They both deformed, scarsely could be known.
          By this sad *Una* fraught with anguish sore,
          Led with their noise, which through the aire was
               thrown,
     Arriv'd, where they in erth their fruitles bloud had sown.

46   Whom all so soone as that proud Sarazin
          Espide, he gan revive the memory
          Of his lewd lusts, and late attempted sin,
          And left the doubtfull battell hastily,
          To catch her, newly offred to his eie:
          But *Satyrane* with strokes him turning, staid,
          And sternely bad him other businesse plie,
          Then hunt the steps of pure unspotted Maid:
     Wherewith he all enrag'd, these bitter speaches said.

44. (2) **themselves . . . let:** they halt to catch their breath;
     (5) **fret:** aggravate, go on worrying; (8) **respire:** take a breath;
     (9) **entire:** fresh.
45. (1) **when . . . once:** when once . . . had recovered their wind;
     (3) **attonce:** at the same time; (5) **drerie:** dreadful; (9)
     fruitles . . . sown: i.e., the bloodshed so far has been
     inconclusive.
46. (4) **doubtfull:** undecided; (7) **plie:** apply himself to.

47   O foolish faeries sonne, what furie mad
          Hath thee incenst, to hast thy dolefull fate?
          Were it not better, I that Lady had,
          Then that thou hadst repented it too late?
          Most sencelesse man he, that himselfe doth hate,
          To love another. Lo then for thine ayd
          Here take thy lovers token on thy pate.
          So they to fight; the whiles the royall Mayd
    Fled farre away, of that proud Paynim sore afrayd.

48   But that false *Pilgrim*, which that leasing told,
          Being in deed old *Archimage*, did stay
          In secret shadow, all this to behold,
          And much rejoyced in their bloudy fray:
          But when he saw the Damsell passe away
          He left his stond, and her pursewd apace,
          In hope to bring her to her last decay.
          But for to tell her lamentable cace,
    And eke this battels end, will need another place.

47. (4) **repented it:** thought better of it; (5) **himselfe . . . hate:**
     invites his own harm; (8) **the whiles:** meanwhile.
48. (1) **leasing:** lie (i.e., about the Redcross knight's death);
     (7) **last decay:** final destruction.

Canto VII

The Redcrosse knight is captive made
By Gyaunt proud opprest,
Prince Arthur meets with Una great-
ly with those newes distrest.

1 What man so wise, what earthly wit so ware,
   As to descry the crafty cunning traine,
  By which deceipt doth maske in visour faire,
  And cast her colours dyed deepe in graine,
  To seeme like Truth, whose shape she well can faine,
  And fitting gestures to her purpose frame,
  The guiltlesse man with guile to entertaine?
  Great maistresse of her art was that false Dame,
The false *Duessa*, cloked with *Fidessaes* name.

2   Who when returning from the drery *Night*,
  She fownd not in that perilous house of *Pryde*,
  Where she had left, the noble *Redcrosse* knight,
  Her hoped pray; she would no lenger bide,
  But forth she went, to seeke him far and wide.
  Ere long she fownd, whereas he wearie sate,
  To rest him selfe, foreby a fountaine side,
  Disarmed all of yron-coted Plate,
And by his side his steed the grassy forage ate.

opprest: overcome.
1. (1) **ware:** alert; (3) **maske:** disguise (itself); (3) **visour:** mask;
(4) **dyed . . . graine:** stained in a fast dye; (6) **frame:** form,
adapt, plan.
2. (7) **foreby:** close by.

3   He feedes upon the cooling shade, and bayes
      His sweatie forehead in the breathing wind,
      Which through the trembling leaves full gently playes
      Wherein the cherefull birds of sundry kind
      Do chaunt sweet musick, to delight his mind:
      The Witch approching gan him fairely greet,
      And with reproch of carelesnesse unkind
      Upbrayd, for leaving her in place unmeet,
    With fowle words tempring faire, soure gall with hony
        sweet.

4   Unkindnesse past, they gan of solace treat,
      And bathe in pleasaunce of the joyous shade,
      Which shielded them against the boyling heat,
      And with greene boughes decking a gloomy glade,
      About the fountaine like a girlond made;
      Whose bubbling wave did ever freshly well,
      Ne ever would through fervent sommer fade:
      The sacred Nymph, which therein wont to dwell,
    Was out of *Dianes* favour, as it then befell.   §

5   The cause was this: one day when *Phœbe* fayre
      With all her band was following the chace,
      This Nymph, quite tyr'd with heat of scorching ayre
      Sat downe to rest in middest of the race:
      The goddesse wroth gan fowly her disgrace,
      And bad the waters, which from her did flow,
      Be such as she her selfe was then in place.
      Thenceforth her waters waxed dull and slow,
    And all that drunke thereof, did faint and feeble grow.

3. (1) **bayes**: bathes; (7) **carelesnesse**: indifference, thought-lessness; (8) **place unmeet**: an undignified situation.
4. (1) **treat**: (to) talk of; (7) **fervent**: hot.
5. (5) **gan**: did; (7) **in place**: on the spot.

§ *Dianes*: Diana (Artemis), the virgin huntress-goddess and leader of the Nymphs, who was relentlessly jealous of her privacy. She is also the moon-goddess as shown in another of her names, *Phoebe* (Luna, Cynthia), which is given in the next stanza. Notice that her attendants are not only Nymphs of streams but the personifications of the streams themselves.

6   Hereof this gentle knight unweeting was,
       And lying downe upon the sandie graile,
       Drunke of the streame, as cleare as cristall glas;
       Eftsoones his manly forces gan to faile,
       And mightie strong was turnd to feeble fraile.
       His chaunged powres at first them selves not felt,
       Till crudled cold his corage gan assaile,
       And chearefull bloud in faintnesse chill did melt,
    Which like a fever fit through all his body swelt.

7   Yet goodly court he made still to his Dame,
       Pourd out in loosnesse on the grassy grownd,
       Both carelesse of his health, and of his fame:
       Till at the last he heard a dreadfull sownd,
       Which through the wood loud bellowing, did rebownd,
       That all the earth for terrour seemd to shake,
       And trees did tremble. Th'Elfe therewith astownd,
       Upstarted lightly from his looser make,
    And his unready weapons gan in hand to take.

8   But ere he could his armour on him dight,
       Or get his shield, his monstrous enimy
       With sturdie steps came stalking in his sight,
       An hideous Geant horrible and hye,
       That with his talnesse seemd to threat the skye,
       The ground eke groned under him for dreed;
       His living like saw never living eye,
       Ne durst behold: his stature did exceed
    The hight of three the tallest sonnes of mortall seed.

6. (1) **unweeting:** ignorant; (2) **graile:** gravel; (6) **not felt:** did not feel (the change); (7) **crudled:** curdling, congealing; (9) **swelt:** swelled.

7. (2) **Pourd . . . loosnesse:** stretched out slackly; (7) **astownd:** stunned, amazed; (8) **make:** companion.

8. (1) **dight:** put.

9 The greatest Earth his uncouth mother was,   §
  And blustring *Æolus* his boasted sire,
  Who with his breath, which through the world doth
    pas,
  Her hollow womb did secretly inspire,
  And fild her hidden caves with stormie yre,
  That she conceiv'd; and trebling the dew time,
  In which the wombes of women do expire,
  Brought forth this monstrous masse of earthly slime,
Puft up with emptie wind, and fild with sinfull crime.

10 So growen great through arrogant delight
  Of th'high descent, whereof he was yborne,
  And through presumption of his matchlesse might, ·
  All other powres and knighthood he did scorne.
  Such now he marcheth to this man forlorne,
  And left to losse: his stalking steps are stayde
  Upon a snaggy Oke, which he had torne
  Out of his mothers bowelles, and it made
His mortall mace, wherewith his foemen he dismayde.

11 That when the knight he spide, he gan advance
  With huge force and insupportable mayne,
  And towardes him with dreadfull fury praunce;
  Who haplesse, and eke hopelesse, all in vaine
  Did to him pace, sad battaile to darrayne,
  Disarmd, disgrast, and inwardly dismayde,
  And eke so faint in every joynt and vaine,
  Through that fraile fountaine, which him feeble made,
That scarsely could he weeld his bootlesse single blade.

 9. (1) **uncouth:** strange, unusual; (7) **expire:** complete the term
  of gestation.
10. (6) **losse:** disgrace; (6) **stayde:** supported; (9) **mortall:** deadly.
11. (2) **mayne:** power; (3) **praunce:** strut, swagger; (4) **haplesse:**
  unlucky; (5) **darrayne:** offer; (8) **fraile:** i.e., enervating; (9)
  bootlesse: useless; (9) **single:** (probably) own, special (or)
  single-edged; (possibly) unique or single-forged.

§ *Æolus*: A mortal, or a minor god, who rules the winds; he lives on
 the floating island of Aeolia with his six sons who are married to his
 six daughters. Here Spenser makes him the wind itself.

12   The Geaunt strooke so maynly mercilesse,
      That could have overthrowne a stony towre,
      And were not heavenly grace, that him did blesse,
      He had beene pouldred all, as thin as flowre:
      But he was wary of that deadly stowre,
      And lightly lept from underneath the blow:
      Yet so exceeding was the villeins powre,
      That with the wind it did him overthrow,
And all his sences stound, that still he lay full low.

13   As when that divelish yron Engin wrought
      In deepest Hell, and framd by *Furies* skill,
      With windy Nitre and quick Sulphur fraught,
      And ramd with bullet round, ordaind to kill,
      Conceiveth fire, the heavens it doth fill
      With thundring noyse, and all the ayre doth choke,
      That none can breath, nor see, nor heare at will,
      Through smouldry cloud of duskish stincking smoke,
That th'onely breath him daunts, who hath escapt the
        stroke.

14   So daunted when the Geaunt saw the knight,
      His heavie hand he heaved up on hye,
      And him to dust thought to have battred quight,
      Untill *Duessa* loud to him gan crye;
      O great *Orgoglio*, greatest under skye,
      O hold thy mortall hand for Ladies sake,
      Hold for my sake, and do him not to dye,
      But vanquisht thine eternall bondslave make,
And me thy worthy meed unto thy Leman take.

12. (1) **maynly:** mightily; (3) **were not:** were it not for; (4) **pouldred:** pulverized; (4) **thin:** fine; (4) **flowre:** flour; (5) **stowre:** attack; (9) **stound:** bewildered.
13. (3) **fraught:** filled, charged; (8) **duskish:** dark; (9) **That th'onely breath:** so that the blast alone.
14. (6) **mortall:** killing, deadly; (7) **do . . . dye:** do not kill him; (9) **Leman:** paramour.

15 He hearkned, and did stay from further harmes,
  To gayne so goodly guerdon, as she spake:
  So willingly she came into his armes,
  Who her as willingly to grace did take,
  And was possessed of his new found make.
  Then up he tooke the slombred sencelesse corse,
  And ere he could out of his swowne awake,
  Him to his castle brought with hastie forse,
And in a Dongeon deepe him threw without remorse.

16 From that day forth *Duessa* was his deare,
  And highly honourd in his haughtie eye,
  He gave her gold and purple pall to weare,
  And triple crowne set on her head full hye,
  And her endowd with royall majestye:
  Then for to make her dreaded more of men,
  And peoples harts with awfull terrour tye,
  A monstrous beast ybred in filthy fen
He chose, which he had kept long time in darksome den.

17 Such one it was, as that renowmed Snake   §
  Which great *Alcides* in *Stremona* slew,
  Long fostred in the filth of *Lerna* lake,
  Whose many heads out budding ever new,
  Did breed him endlesse labour to subdew:
  But this same Monster much more ugly was;
  For seven great heads out of his body grew,
  An yron brest, and backe of scaly bras,
And all embrewd in bloud, his eyes did shine as glas.

15. (1) **stay:** refrain; (2) **guerdon:** reward; (4) **to grace:** into his favour; (5) **make:** companion, mate; (6) **slombred:** unconscious.
16. (1) **deare:** darling; (3) **pall:** robe.
17. (5) **breed:** cause; (9) **embrewd:** stained.

§ *renowmed Snake*: The nine-headed snake-monster, or Hydra, another of the pernicious offspring of the monsters Typhon and Echidna. Snakes never had any luck with Herakles (*great Alcides*, Hercules), who killed this one as the second of his twelve famous labours. *Stremona*: Strymon, the name of an ancient town in Thrace, and by extension the general region of Thrace.

18   His tayle was stretched out in wondrous length,
      That to the house of heavenly gods it raught,
      And with extorted powre, and borrow'd strength,
      The ever-burning lamps from thence it brought,
      And prowdly threw to ground, as things of nought;
      And underneath his filthy feet did tread
      The sacred things, and holy heasts foretaught.
    Upon this dreadfull Beast with sevenfold head
He set the false *Duessa*, for more aw and dread.

19   The wofull Dwarfe, which saw his maisters fall,
      Whiles he had keeping of his grasing steed,
      And valiant knight become a caytive thrall,
      When all was past, tooke up his forlorne weed,
      His mightie armour, missing most at need;
      His silver shield, now idle maisterlesse;
      His poynant speare, that many made to bleed,
      The ruefull moniments of heavinesse,
    And with them all departes, to tell his great distresse.

20   He had not travaild long, when on the way
      He wofull Ladie, wofull *Una* met,
      Fast flying from the Paynims greedy pray,
      Whilest *Satyrane* him from pursuit did let:
      Who when her eyes she on the Dwarfe had set,
      And saw the signes, that deadly tydings spake,
      She fell to ground for sorrowfull regret,
      And lively breath her sad brest did forsake,
    Yet might her pitteous hart be seene to pant and quake.

18. (2) **raught:** reached; (7) **heasts:** commandments; (7) **foretaught:** previously taught.
19. (4) **weed:** clothing; (5) **most at need:** when most needed; (7) **poynant:** sharp; (8) **moniments:** reminders, marks; (8) **heavinesse:** sorrow.
20. (3) **pray:** attempts to prey upon her; (4) **let:** hinder; (8) **lively:** life-giving.

21   The messenger of so unhappie newes,
      Would faine have dyde: dead was his hart within,
      Yet outwardly some little comfort shewes:
      At last recovering hart, he does begin
      To rub her temples, and to chaufe her chin,
      And every tender part does tosse and turne:
      So hardly he the flitted life does win,
      Unto her native prison to retourne:
  Then gins her grieved ghost thus to lament and mourne.

22   Ye dreary instruments of dolefull sight,
      That doe this deadly spectacle behold,
      Why do ye lenger feed on loathed light,
      Or liking find to gaze on earthly mould,
      Sith cruell fates the carefull threeds unfould,
      The which my life and love together tyde?
      Now let the stony dart of senselesse cold
      Perce to my hart, and pas through every side,
  And let eternall night so sad sight fro me hide.

23   O lightsome day, the lampe of highest *Jove*,
      First made by him, mens wandring wayes to guyde,
      When darkenesse he in deepest dongeon drove,
      Henceforth thy hated face for ever hyde,
      And shut up heavens windowes shyning wyde:
      For earthly sight can nought but sorrow breed,
      And late repentance, which shall long abyde.
      Mine eyes no more on vanitie shall feed,
  But seeled up with death, shall have their deadly meed.

21. (2) **faine:** gladly; (7) **hardly:** with great difficulty; (9) **ghost:** spirit.
22. (4) **liking . . . gaze:** find pleasure in gazing.
23. (6) **breed:** cause, bring forth; (9) **deadly meed:** hoped-for reward of death.

24   Then downe againe she fell unto the ground;
        But he her quickly reared up againe:
        Thrise did she sinke adowne in deadly swownd,
        And thrise he her reviv'd with busie paine:
        At last when life recover'd had the raine,
        And over-wrestled his strong enemie,
        With foltring tong, and trembling every vaine,
        Tell on (quoth she) the wofull Tragedie,
    The which these reliques sad present unto mine eie.

25   Tempestuous fortune hath spent all her spight,
        And thrilling sorrow throwne his utmost dart;
        Thy sad tongue cannot tell more heavy plight,
        Then that I feele, and harbour in mine hart:
        Who hath endur'd the whole, can beare each part.
        If death it be, it is not the first wound,
        That launched hath my brest with bleeding smart.
        Begin, and end the bitter balefull stound;
    If lesse, then that I feare, more favour I have found.

26   Then gan the Dwarfe the whole discourse declare,
        The subtill traines of *Archimago* old;
        The wanton loves of false *Fidessa* faire,
        Bought with the bloud of vanquisht Paynim bold:
        The wretched payre transform'd to treen mould;
        The house of Pride, and perils round about;
        The combat, which he with *Sansjoy* did hould;
        The lucklesse conflict with the Gyant stout,
    Wherein captiv'd, of life or death he stood in doubt.

24. (4) **paine:** care.
25. (2) **utmost:** last and worst; (7) **launched:** pierced; (8) **stound:**
    trouble, affliction; (9) **lesse, then that:** less than what.
26. (1) **discourse:** story, course of events; (5) **treen mould:** tree-
    like shape.

27   She heard with patience all unto the end,
         And strove to maister sorrowfull assay,
         Which greater grew, the more she did contend,
         And almost rent her tender hart in tway;
         And love fresh coles unto her fire did lay:
         For greater love, the greater is the losse.
         Was never Ladie loved dearer day,
         Then she did love the knight of the *Redcrosse*;
For whose deare sake so many troubles her did tosse.

28   At last when fervent sorrow slaked was,
         She up arose, resolving him to find
         A live or dead: and forward forth doth pas,
         All as the Dwarfe the way to her assynd:
         And evermore in constant carefull mind
         She fed her wound with fresh renewed bale;
         Long tost with stormes, and bet with bitter wind,
         High over hils, and low adowne the dale,
She wandred many a wood, and measurd many a vale.

29   At last she chaunced by good hap to meet
         A goodly knight, faire marching by the way
         Together with his Squire, arayed meet:
         His glitterand armour shined farre away,
         Like glauncing light of *Phœbus* brightest ray;
         From top to toe no place appeared bare,
         That deadly dint of steele endanger may:
         Athwart his brest a bauldrick brave he ware,
That shynd, like twinkling stars, with stons most
            pretious rare.

27. (2) **assay:** tribulation; (7) **loved . . . day:** loved the day more
dearly.
28. (4) **assynd:** pointed out; (6) **bale:** grief; (7) **bet:** buffeted.
29. (3) **meet:** properly, suitably; (7) **dint:** blow; (8) **bauldrick:**
baldric (i.e., belt to support sword or horn).

30   And in the midst thereof one pretious stone
      Of wondrous worth, and eke of wondrous mights,
      Shapt like a Ladies head, exceeding shone,
      Like *Hesperus* emongst the lesser lights,
      And strove for to amaze the weaker sights;
      Thereby his mortall blade full comely hong
      In yvory sheath, ycarv'd with curious slights;
      Whose hilts were burnisht gold, and handle strong
  Of mother pearle, and buckled with a golden tong.

31   His haughtie helmet, horrid all with gold,
      Both glorious brightnesse, and great terrour bred;
      For all the crest a Dragon did enfold
      With greedie pawes, and over all did spred
      His golden wings: his dreadfull hideous hed
      Close couched on the bever, seem'd to throw
      From flaming mouth bright sparkles fierie red,
      That suddeine horror to faint harts did show;
  And scaly tayle was stretcht adowne his backe full low.

32   Upon the top of all his loftie crest,
      A bunch of haires discolourd diversly,
      With sprincled pearle, and gold full richly drest,
      Did shake, and seem'd to daunce for jollity,
      Like to an Almond tree ymounted hye
      On top of greene *Selinis* all alone,
      With blossomes brave bedecked daintily;
      Whose tender locks do tremble every one
  At every little breath, that under heaven is blowne.

30. (5) **amaze . . . sights:** blind the gaze of eyes too weak to endure it; (7) **curious slights:** ingenious designs.
31. (1) **horrid:** bristling; (2) **bred:** caused; (6) **bever:** beaver (i.e., part of headpiece that covers face and can be raised and lowered).
32. (2) **discolourd diversly:** of various colours; (3) **drest:** arranged; (6) **Selinis:** (probably) mountain in Sicily; (7) **brave:** beautiful, gay.

33 His warlike shield all closely cover'd was,
  Ne might of mortall eye be ever seene;
  Not made of steele, nor of enduring bras,
  Such earthly mettals soone consumed bene:
  But all of Diamond perfect pure and cleene
  It framed was, one massie entire mould,
  Hewen out of Adamant rocke with engines keene,
  That point of speare it never percen could,
 Ne dint of direfull sword divide the substance would.

34 The same to wight he never wont disclose,
  But when as monsters huge he would dismay,
  Or daunt unequall armies of his foes,
  Or when the flying heavens he would affray;
  For so exceeding shone his glistring ray,
  That *Phœbus* golden face it did attaint,
  As when a cloud his beames doth over-lay;
  And silver *Cynthia* wexed pale and faint,
 As when her face is staynd with magicke arts constraint.

35 No magicke arts hereof had any might,
  Nor bloudie wordes of bold Enchaunters call,   §
  But all that was not such, as seemd in sight,
  Before that shield did fade, and suddeine fall:
  And when him list the raskall routes appall,
  Men into stones therewith he could transmew,
  And stones to dust, and dust to nought at all;
  And when him list the prouder lookes subdew,
 He would them gazing blind, or turne to other hew.

33. (6) **massie:** solid; (6) **entire mould:** single artifact.
34. (1) **disclose:** reveal, display; (2) **But:** except; (5) **his glistring:** its (i.e., the uncovered shield's) glittering; (6) **attaint:** sully; (9) **constraint:** force (of).
35. (1) **hereof:** over it (i.e., the shield); (5) **him list:** it pleased him to; (5) **routes:** crowds, hordes; (6) **transmew:** transform.

§ *call*: Probably a variant of the word "caul", a netted cap or head-dress, and hence a sorcerer's cap. But it could possibly mean "call" in the usual sense of an utterance and hence "spell" or "incantation".

36   Ne let it seeme, that credence this exceedes,
     For he that made the same, was knowne right well
     To have done much more admirable deedes.
     It *Merlin* was, which whylome did excell
     All living wightes in might of magicke spell:
     Both shield, and sword, and armour all he wrought
     For this young Prince, when first to armes he fell;
     But when he dyde, the Faerie Queene it brought
  To Faerie lond, where yet it may be seene, if sought.

37   A gentle youth, his dearely loved Squire
     His speare of heben wood behind him bare,
     Whose harmefull head, thrice heated in the fire,
     Had riven many a brest with pikehead square;
     A goodly person, and could menage faire
     His stubborne steed with curbed canon bit,
     Who under him did trample as the aire,
     And chauft, that any on his backe should sit;
  The yron rowels into frothy fome he bit.

38   When as this knight nigh to the Ladie drew,
     With lovely court he gan her entertaine;
     But when he heard her answeres loth, he knew
     Some secret sorrow did her heart distraine:
     Which to allay, and calme her storming paine,
     Faire feeling words he wisely gan display,
     And for her humour fitting purpose faine,
     To tempt the cause it selfe for to bewray;
  Wherewith emmov'd, these bleeding words she
       gan to say.

36. (3) **admirable:** wonderful, wonder-provoking; (4) **whylome:** once, at one time; (7) **to armes he fell:** became a knight.
37. (2) **heben:** ebony; (5) **menage:** manage, handle; (6) **canon bit:** smooth round bit; (9) **rowels:** rings of the bit.
38. (2) **lovely court:** friendly courtliness; (2) **entertaine:** to treat; (4) **distraine:** oppress; (7) **And for her . . . faine:** and improvise conversation appropriate to her troubled state.

39   What worlds delight, or joy of living speach
  Can heart, so plung'd in sea of sorrowes deepe,
  And heaped with so huge misfortunes, reach?
  The carefull cold beginneth for to creepe,
  And in my heart his yron arrow steepe,
  Soone as I thinke upon my bitter bale:
  Such helplesse harmes yts better hidden keepe,
  Then rip up griefe, where it may not availe,
My last left comfort is, my woes to weepe and waile.

40   Ah Ladie deare, quoth then the gentle knight,
  Well may I weene, your griefe is wondrous great;
  For wondrous great griefe groneth in my spright,
  Whiles thus I heare you of your sorrowes treat.
  But wofull Ladie let me you intrete,
  For to unfold the anguish of your hart:
  Mishaps are maistred by advice discrete,
  And counsell mittigates the greatest smart;
Found never helpe, who never would his hurts impart.

41   O but (quoth she) great griefe will not be tould,
  And can more easily be thought, then said.
  Right so; (quoth he) but he, that never would,
  Could never: will to might gives greatest aid.
  But griefe (quoth she) does greater grow displaid,
  If then it find not helpe, and breedes despaire.
  Despaire breedes not (quoth he) where faith is staid.
  No faith so fast (quoth she) but flesh does paire.
Flesh may empaire (quoth he) but reason can repaire.

39. (4) **carefull:** sad, grievous; (5) **steepe:** stain; (6) **bale:** sorrow,
grief; (7) **helplesse:** remediless; (8) **availe:** be of any help.
40. (3) **spright:** spirit; (4) **treat:** speak.
41. (4) **might:** ability, capacity; (7) **staid:** constant, steady; (8)
so fast: (is) so firm; (8) **paire:** weaken (it); (9) **empaire:**
impair.

42 His goodly reason, and well guided speach
   So deepe did settle in her gratious thought,
   That her perswaded to disclose the breach,
   Which love and fortune in her heart had wrought,
   And said; Faire Sir, I hope good hap hath brought
   You to inquire the secrets of my griefe,
   Or that your wisedome will direct my thought,
   Or that your prowesse can me yield reliefe:
  Then heare the storie sad, which I shall tell you briefe.

43 The forlorne Maiden, whom your eyes have seene
   The laughing stocke of fortunes mockeries,
   Am th'only daughter of a King and Queene,
   Whose parents deare, whilest equall destinies
   Did runne about, and their felicities
   The favourable heavens did not envy,
   Did spread their rule through all the territories,
   Which *Phison* and *Euphrates* floweth by,   §
  And *Gehons* golden waves doe wash continually.

44 Till that their cruell cursed enemy,
   An huge great Dragon horrible in sight,
   Bred in the loathly lakes of *Tartary*,
   With murdrous ravine, and devouring might
   Their kingdome spoild, and countrey wasted quight:
   Themselves, for feare into his jawes to fall,
   He forst to castle strong to take their flight,
   Where fast embard in mightie brasen wall,
  He has them now foure yeres besiegd to make
    them thrall.

42. (3) **her perswaded:** he persuaded her.
43. (4-5) **whilest . . . Did runne about:** whilst their presiding planets revolved undislocated in their orbits; (or perhaps) whilst the Fates circled impartially over them.
44. (3) **Tartary:** hell, place of punishment; (5) **spoild:** ravaged (or) deprived them of (their kingdom); (5) **wasted:** laid waste to; (8) **fast embard:** closely confined.

§ *Phison*: The Phison, *Euphrates*, and *Gehon* (Gihon) are three of the four branch rivers into which the river of Eden divided. (See Genesis 2:10-14.)

45 Full many knights adventurous and stout
       Have enterprizd that Monster to subdew;
       From every coast that heaven walks about,
       Have thither come the noble Martiall crew,
       That famous hard atchievements still pursew,
       Yet never any could that girlond win,
       But all still shronke, and still he greater grew:
       All they for want of faith, or guilt of sin,
    The pitteous pray of his fierce crueltie have bin.

46 At last yledd with farre reported praise,
       Which flying fame throughout the world had spred,
       Of doughtie knights, whom Faery land did raise,
       That noble order hight of Maidenhed,   §
       Forthwith to court of *Gloriane* I sped,
       Of *Gloriane* great Queene of glory bright,
       Whose kingdomes seat *Cleopolis* is red,
       There to obtaine some such redoubted knight,
    That Parents deare from tyrants powre deliver might.

47 It was my chance (my chance was faire and good)
       There for to find a fresh unproved knight,
       Whose manly hands imbrew'd in guiltie blood
       Had never bene, ne ever by his might
       Had throwne to ground the unregarded right:
       Yet of his prowesse proofe he since hath made
       (I witnesse am) in many a cruell fight;
       The groning ghosts of many one dismaide
    Have felt the bitter dint of his avenging blade.

45. (2) **enterprizd**: undertaken; (4) **Martiall**: warlike; (6) **girlond**:
      glory (of overcoming the dragon); (9) **pitteous**: pitiful.
46. (1) **yledd with**: drawn by; (4) **hight of**: named for (or)
      designated by (the Maiden Queen); (5) **Gloriane**: Gloriana;
      (7) **Cleopolis**: London; (7) **red**: named.
47. (3) **imbrew'd**: stained.

§ *That noble order hight of Maidenhed*: A compliment to Elizabeth,
naming her the patron of an Order pledged to her as Maiden Queen.
Perhaps there is also an allusion to the order of the Garter (founded
by Edward III *c.* 1347) in compliment to Elizabeth who, as the reign-
ing monarch, was the head of the Order.

48   And ye the forlorne reliques of his powre,
      His byting sword, and his devouring speare,
      Which have endured many a dreadfull stowre,
      Can speake his prowesse, that did earst you beare,
      And well could rule: now he hath left you heare,
      To be the record of his ruefull losse,
      And of my dolefull disaventurous deare:
      O heavie record of the good *Redcrosse*,
  Where have you left your Lord, that could so well
      you tosse?

49   Well hoped I, and faire beginnings had,
      That he my captive langour should redeeme,
      Till all unweeting, an Enchaunter bad
      His sence abusd, and made him to misdeeme
      My loyalty, not such as it did seeme;
      That rather death desire, then such despight.
      Be judge ye heavens, that all things right esteeme,
      How I him lov'd, and love with all my might,
  So thought I eke of him, and thinke I thought aright.

50   Thenceforth me desolate he quite forsooke,
      To wander, where wilde fortune would me lead,
      And other bywaies he himselfe betooke,
      Where never foot of living wight did tread,
      That brought not back the balefull body dead;
      In which him chaunced false *Duessa* meete,
      Mine onely foe, mine onely deadly dread,
      Who with her witchcraft and misseeming sweete,
  Inveigled him to follow her desires unmeete.

48. (4) **earst:** lately; (5) **rule:** manage, handle; (7) **disaventurous deare:** unlucky affliction; (8) **record:** reminders; (9) **tosse:** wield.
49. (2) **captive langour:** unshakeable oppression; (3) **all unweeting:** he (the knight) all unsuspecting; (4) **misdeeme:** think evil of; (6) **then such despight:** than (that I should do) such a wrong.
50. (7) **onely:** (also implies) special; (8) **misseeming:** dissimulation; (9) **unmeete:** unworthy.

51 At last by subtill sleights she him betraid
　　　Unto his foe, a Gyant huge and tall,
　　　Who him disarmed, dissolute, dismaid,
　　　Unwares surprised, and with mightie mall
　　　The monster mercilesse him made to fall,
　　　Whose fall did never foe before behold;
　　　And now in darkesome dungeon, wretched thrall,
　　　Remedilesse, for aie he doth him hold;
　　This is my cause of griefe, more great, then may be
　　　　told.

52 Ere she had ended all, she gan to faint:
　　　But he her comforted and faire bespake,
　　　Certes, Madame, ye have great cause of plaint,
　　　That stoutest heart, I weene, could cause to quake.
　　　But be of cheare, and comfort to you take:
　　　For till I have acquit your captive knight,
　　　Assure your selfe, I will you not forsake.
　　　His chearefull words reviv'd her chearelesse spright,
　　So forth they went, the Dwarfe them guiding ever right.

51. (1) **sleights:** stratagems; (3) **him disarmed:** him, being disarmed; (3) **dissolute:** enervated, enfeebled; (4) **mall:** club; (8) **aie:** ever.
52. (2) **faire:** gently; (2) **bespake:** addressed; (3) **Certes:** certainly, truly; (6) **acquit:** delivered.

Canto VIII

Faire virgin to redeeme her deare
brings Arthur to the fight:
Who slayes the Gyant, wounds the beast,
and strips Duessa quight.

1   A y me, how many perils doe enfold
    The righteous man, to make him daily fall?
    Were not, that heavenly grace doth him uphold,
    And stedfast truth acquite him out of all.
    Her love is firme, her care continuall,
    So oft as he through his owne foolish pride,
    Or weaknesse is to sinfull bands made thrall:
    Else should this *Redcrosse* knight in bands have dyde,
For whose deliverance she this Prince doth thither guide.

2   They sadly traveild thus, untill they came
    Nigh to a castle builded strong and hie:
    Then cryde the Dwarfe, lo yonder is the same,
    In which my Lord my liege doth lucklesse lie,
    Thrall to that Gyants hatefull tyrannie:
    Therefore, deare Sir, your mightie powres assay.
    The noble knight alighted by and by
    From loftie steede, and bad the Ladie stay,
To see what end of fight should him befall that day.

1. (3) **Were not:** were it not; (4) **acquite:** release, save; (5) **Her love:** i.e., Truth's love.
2. (6) **assay:** try; (7) **by and by:** immediately; (9) **end:** result.

3   So with the Squire, th'admirer of his might,
         He marched forth towards that castle wall;
         Whose gates he found fast shut, ne living wight
         To ward the same, nor answere commers call.
         Then tooke that Squire an horne of bugle small,
         Which hong adowne his side in twisted gold,
         And tassels gay. Wyde wonders over all
         Of that same hornes great vertues weren told,
     Which had approved bene in uses manifold.

4   Was never wight, that heard that shrilling sound,
         But trembling feare did feele in every vaine;
         Three miles it might be easie heard around,
         And Ecchoes three answerd it selfe againe:
         No false enchauntment, nor deceiptfull traine
         Might once abide the terror of that blast,
         But presently was voide and wholly vaine:
         No gate so strong, no locke so firme and fast,
     But with that percing noise flew open quite, or brast.

5   The same before the Geants gate he blew,
         That all the castle quaked from the ground,
         And every dore of freewill open flew.   §
         The Gyant selfe dismaied with that sownd,
         Where he with his *Duessa* dalliance fownd,
         In hast came rushing forth from inner bowre,
         With staring countenance sterne, as one astownd,
         And staggering steps, to weet, what suddein stowre,
     Had wrought that horror strange, and dar'd his
                 dreaded powre.

3. (4) **ward:** guard; (5) **bugle:** wild ox; (7) **over all:** everywhere;
   (9) **approved:** tested, demonstrated.
4. (7) **vaine:** powerless, futile; (9) **brast:** fractured, burst.
5. (3) **of freewill:** of its own accord; (6) **bowre:** chamber, apart-
   ment; (7) **astownd:** thunderstruck.

§ *And every dore . . . open flew*: Presumably every main entrance-way.
Doors to inner rooms remained locked (see stanza 34).

6   And after him the proud *Duessa* came,
      High mounted on her manyheaded beast,
      And every head with fyrie tongue did flame,
      And every head was crowned on his creast,
      And bloudie mouthed with late cruell feast.
      That when the knight beheld, his mightie shild
      Upon his manly arme he soone addrest,
      And at him fiercely flew, with courage fild,
    And eger greedinesse through every member thrild.

7   Therewith the Gyant buckled him to fight,
      Inflam'd with scornefull wrath and high disdaine,
      And lifting up his dreadfull club on hight,
      All arm'd with ragged snubbes and knottie graine,
      Him thought at first encounter to have slaine.
      But wise and warie was that noble Pere,
      And lightly leaping from so monstrous maine,
      Did faire avoide the violence him nere;
    It booted nought, to thinke, such thunderbolts to beare.

8   Ne shame he thought to shunne so hideous might:
      The idle stroke, enforcing furious way,
      Missing the marke of his misaymed sight
      Did fall to ground, and with his heavie sway
      So deepely dinted in the driven clay,
      That three yardes deepe a furrow up did throw:
      The sad earth wounded with so sore assay,
      Did grone full grievous underneath the blow,
    And trembling with strange feare, did like an
        earthquake show.

6. (5) **late:** recent; (7) **addrest:** set, adjusted.
7. (4) **snubbes:** knobs, stumps; (6) **Pere:** peer; (7) **maine:** strength; (8) **faire:** deftly, cleverly; (9) **It booted nought:** it was pointless.
8. (2) **idle:** useless; (4) **sway:** swing, stroke; (5) **dinted:** struck; (7) **assay:** assault.

9   As when almightie *Jove* in wrathfull mood,
      To wreake the guilt of mortall sins is bent,
      Hurles forth his thundring dart with deadly food,
      Enrold in flames, and smouldring dreriment,
      Through riven cloudes and molten firmament;
      The fierce threeforked engin making way,
      Both loftie towres and highest trees hath rent,
      And all that might his angrie passage stay,
  And shooting in the earth, casts up a mount of clay.

10   His boystrous club, so buried in the ground,
      He could not rearen up againe so light,
      But that the knight him at avantage found,
      And whiles he strove his combred clubbe to quight
      Out of the earth, with blade all burning bright
      He smote off his left arme, which like a blocke
      Did fall to ground, depriv'd of native might;
      Large streames of bloud out of the truncked stocke
  Forth gushed, like fresh water streame from riven rocke.

11   Dismaied with so desperate deadly wound,
      And eke impatient of unwonted paine,
      He loudly brayd with beastly yelling sound,
      That all the fields rebellowed againe;
      As great a noyse, as when in Cymbrian plaine
      An heard of Bulles, whom kindly rage doth sting,
      Do for the milkie mothers want complaine,
      And fill the fields with troublous bellowing,
  The neighbour woods around with hollow murmur ring.

9. (2) **bent:** determined; (3) **food:** anger, hostility; (4) **Enrold:** enveloped; (4) **smouldring:** suffocating; (4) **dreriment:** sorrow; (6) **engin:** instrument (or) agent; (8) **stay:** hinder, resist.
10. (1) **boystrous:** rough; (2) **light:** quickly, easily; (4) **quight:** work free, release.
11. (2) **unwonted:** unaccustomed; (5) **Cymbrian plaine:** either what is now known as Crimea, or Jutland; (6) **kindly rage:** natural rage of desire; (7) **want:** lack of, absence of.

12 That when his deare *Duessa* heard, and saw
    The evill stownd, that daungerd her estate,
    Unto his aide she hastily did draw
    Her dreadfull beast, who swolne with bloud of late
    Came ramping forth with proud presumpteous gate,
    And threatned all his heads like flaming brands.
    But him the Squire made quickly to retrate,
    Encountring fierce with single sword in hand,
And twixt him and his Lord did like a bulwarke stand.

13 The proud *Duessa* full of wrathfull spight,
    And fierce disdaine, to be affronted so,
    Enforst her purple beast with all her might
    That stop out of the way to overthroe,
    Scorning the let of so unequall foe:
    But nathemore would that courageous swayne
    To her yeeld passage, gainst his Lord to goe,
    But with outrageous strokes did him restraine,
And with his bodie bard the way atwixt them twaine.

14 Then tooke the angrie witch her golden cup,
    Which still she bore, replete with magick artes;
    Death and despeyre did many thereof sup,
    And secret poyson through their inner parts,
    Th'eternall bale of heavie wounded harts;
    Which after charmes and some enchauntments said,
    She lightly sprinkled on his weaker parts;
    Therewith his sturdie courage soone was quayd,
And all his senses were with suddeine dread dismayd.

12. (2) **stownd:** blow; (2) **estate:** state, position; (5) **gate:** gait, step; (6) **threatned:** threateningly reared; (8) **single:** single-edged (or) single-forged.
13. (2) **affronted:** confronted, stood up to (and so) affronted; (4) **stop:** obstacle; (5) **let of:** hindrance offered by; (6) **nathemore:** all the less; (8) **outrageous:** violent.
14. (5) **bale:** grief; (8) **quayd:** quelled.

15   So downe he fell before the cruell beast,
    Who on his necke his bloudie clawes did seize,
    That life nigh crusht out of his panting brest:
    No powre he had to stirre, nor will to rize.
    That when the carefull knight gan well avise,
    He lightly left the foe, with whom he fought,
    And to the beast gan turne his enterprise;
    For wondrous anguish in his hart it wrought,
To see his loved Squire into such thraldome brought.

16   And high advancing his bloud-thirstie blade,
    Stroke one of those deformed heads so sore,
    That of his puissance proud ensample made;
    His monstrous scalpe downe to his teeth it tore,
    And that misformed shape mis-shaped more:
    A sea of bloud gusht from the gaping wound,
    That her gay garments staynd with filthy gore,
    And overflowed all the field around;
That over shoes in bloud he waded on the ground.

17   Thereat he roared for exceeding paine,
    That to have heard, great horror would have bred,
    And scourging th'emptie ayre with his long traine,
    Through great impatience of his grieved hed
    His gorgeous ryder from her loftie sted
    Would have cast downe, and trod in durtie myre,
    Had not the Gyant soone her succoured;
    Who all enrag'd with smart and franticke yre,
Came hurtling in full fierce, and forst the knight retyre.

15. (2) **seize:** fix; (5) **avise:** notice, perceive; (6) **lightly:** nimbly;
    (9) **thraldome:** subjection.
16. (3) **ensample:** demonstration.
17. (3) **traine:** tail; (5) **sted:** place, seat.

18   The force, which wont in two to be disperst,
     In one alone left hand he now unites,
     Which is through rage more strong then both
        were erst;
     With which his hideous club aloft he dites,
     And at his foe with furious rigour smites,
     That strongest Oake might seeme to overthrow:
     The stroke upon his shield so heavie lites,
     That to the ground it doubleth him full low:
  What mortall wight could ever beare so monstrous
     blow?

19   And in his fall his shield, that covered was,
     Did loose his vele by chaunce, and open flew:
     The light whereof, that heavens light did pas,
     Such blazing brightnesse through the aier threw,
     That eye mote not the same endure to vew.
     Which when the Gyaunt spyde with staring eye,
     He downe let fall his arme, and soft withdrew
     His weapon huge, that heaved was on hye
  For to have slaine the man, that on the ground did lye.

20   And eke the fruitfull-headed beast, amaz'd
     At flashing beames of that sunshiny shield,
     Became starke blind, and all his senses daz'd,
     That downe he tumbled on the durtie field,
     And seem'd himselfe as conquered to yield.
     Whom when his maistresse proud perceiv'd to fall,
     Whiles yet his feeble feet for faintnesse reeld,
     Unto the Gyant loudly she gan call,
  O helpe *Orgoglio*, helpe, or else we perish all.

18. (1) **disperst:** divided; (2) **alone left:** single remaining; (3) **erst:** before; (4) **dites:** raises; (7) **lites:** falls.
19. (2) **his vele:** its covering; (5) **mote:** could.
20. (1) **fruitfull-headed:** many headed.

21 At her so pitteous cry was much amoov'd,
    Her champion stout, and for to ayde his frend,
    Againe his wonted angry weapon proov'd:
    But all in vaine: for he has read his end
    In that bright shield, and all their forces spend
    Themselves in vaine: for since that glauncing sight,
    He hath no powre to hurt, nor to defend;
    As where th'Almighties lightning brond does light,
It dimmes the dazed eyen, and daunts the senses quight.

22 Whom when the Prince, to battell new addrest,
    And threatning high his dreadfull stroke did see,
    His sparkling blade about his head he blest,
    And smote off quite his right leg by the knee,
    That downe he tombled; as an aged tree,
    High growing on the top of rocky clift,
    Whose hartstrings with keene steele nigh hewen be,
    The mightie trunck halfe rent, with ragged rift
Doth roll adowne the rocks, and fall with fearefull drift.

23 Or as a Castle reared high and round,
    By subtile engins and malitious slight
    Is undermined from the lowest ground,
    And her foundation forst, and feebled quight,
    At last downe falles, and with her heaped hight
    Her hastie ruine does more heavie make,
    And yields it selfe unto the victours might;
    Such was this Gyaunts fall, that seemd to shake
The stedfast globe of earth, as it for feare did quake.

21. (1) **amoov'd**: aroused; (3) **proov'd**: tried to bring into play;
(8) **brond**: brand, bolt; (8) **light**: flash, light up, (also) fall,
strike.
22. (1) **addrest**: set, prepared; (3) **blest**: brandished; (7) **nigh
hewen**: nearly cut through; (8) **rift**: split, tear; (9) **drift**:
impetus.
23. (2) **slight**: ingenuity, artifice.

24   The knight then lightly leaping to the pray,
        With mortall steele him smot againe so sore,
        That headlesse his unweldy bodie lay,
        All wallowd in his owne fowle bloudy gore,
        Which flowed from his wounds in wondrous store.
        But soone as breath out of his breast did pas,
        That huge great body, which the Gyaunt bore,
        Was vanisht quite, and of that monstrous mas
    Was nothing left, but like an emptie bladder was.

25   Whose grievous fall, when false *Duessa* spide,
        Her golden cup she cast unto the ground,
        And crowned mitre rudely threw aside;
        Such percing griefe her stubborne hart did wound,
        That she could not endure that dolefull stound,
        But leaving all behind her, fled away:
        The light-foot Squire her quickly turnd around,
        And by hard meanes enforcing her to stay,
    So brought unto his Lord, as his deserved pray.

26   The royall Virgin, which beheld from farre,
        In pensive plight, and sad perplexitie,
        The whole atchievement of this doubtfull warre,
        Came running fast to greet his victorie,
        With sober gladnesse, and myld modestie,
        And with sweet joyous cheare him thus bespake;
        Faire braunch of noblesse, flowre of chevalrie,
        That with your worth the world amazed make,
    How shall I quite the paines, ye suffer for my sake?

24. (3) **unweldy:** unwieldy.
26. (3) **atchievement:** accomplishment; (3) **doubtfull:** fearful,
    awful; (9) **quite:** repay.

27   And you fresh bud of vertue springing fast,
         Whom these sad eyes saw nigh unto deaths dore,
         What hath poore Virgin for such perill past,
         Wherewith you to reward? Accept therefore
         My simple selfe, and service evermore;
         And he that high does sit, and all things see
         With equall eyes, their merites to restore,
         Behold what ye this day have done for mee,
    And what I cannot quite, requite with usuree.

28   But sith the heavens, and your faire handeling
         Have made you maister of the field this day,
         Your fortune maister eke with governing,
         And well begun end all so well, I pray,
         Ne let that wicked woman scape away;
         For she it is, that did my Lord bethrall,
         My dearest Lord, and deepe in dongeon lay,
         Where he his better dayes hath wasted all.
    O heare, how piteous he to you for ayd does call.

29   Forthwith he gave in charge unto his Squire,
         That scarlot whore to keepen carefully;
         Whiles he himselfe with greedie great desire
         Into the Castle entred forcibly,
         Where living creature none he did espye;
         Then gan he lowdly through the house to call:
         But no man car'd to answere to his crye.
         There raignd a solemne silence over all,
    Nor voice was heard, nor wight was seene in bowre
            or hall.

27. (7) **equall:** impartial; (9) **usuree:** interest.
28. (1) **sith:** since; (3) **maister:** control and complete; (3) **governing:** considered conduct; (6) **bethrall:** bring to captivity.

30   At last with creeping crooked pace forth came
          An old old man, with beard as white as snow,
        That on a staffe his feeble steps did frame,
        And guide his wearie gate both too and fro:
        For his eye sight him failed long ygo,
        And on his arme a bounch of keyes he bore,
        The which unused rust did overgrow:
        Those were the keyes of every inner dore,
     But he could not them use, but kept them still in store.

31   But very uncouth sight was to behold,
          How he did fashion his untoward pace,
        For as he forward moov'd his footing old,
        So backward still was turnd his wrincled face,
        Unlike to men, who ever as they trace,
        Both feet and face one way are wont to lead.
        This was the auncient keeper of that place,
        And foster father of the Gyant dead;
     His name *Ignaro* did his nature right aread.

32   His reverend haires and holy gravitie
          The knight much honord, as beseemed well,
        And gently askt, where all the people bee,
        Which in that stately building wont to dwell.
        Who answerd him full soft, he could not tell.
        Againe he askt, where that same knight was layd,
        Whom great *Orgoglio* with his puissaunce fell
        Had made his caytive thrall; againe he sayde,
     He could not tell: ne ever other answere made.

30. (3) **frame:** support; (4) **gate:** walking.
31. (1) **uncouth:** strange; (2) **untoward:** awkward, ungainly; (5) **trace:** walk; (9) **Ignaro:** Ignorance; (9) **aread:** indicate, make known.
32. (2) **beseemed:** befitted; (8) **caytive:** captive.

33   Then asked he, which way he in might pas:
        He could not tell, againe he answered.
        Thereat the curteous knight displeased was,
        And said, Old sire, it seemes thou hast not red
        How ill it sits with that same silver hed
        In vaine to mócke, or mockt in vaine to bee:
        But if thou be, as thou art pourtrahed
        With natures pen, in ages grave degree,
    Aread in graver wise, what I demaund of thee.

34   His answere likewise was, he could not tell.
        Whose sencelesse speach, and doted ignorance
        When as the noble Prince had marked well,
        He ghest his nature by his countenance,
        And calmd his wrath with goodly temperance.
        Then to him stepping, from his arme did reach
        Those keyes, and made himselfe free enterance.
        Each dore he opened without any breach;
    There was no barre to stop, nor foe him to empeach.

35   There all within full rich arayd he found,
        With royall arras and resplendent gold,
        And did with store of every thing abound,
        That greatest Princes presence might behold.
        But all the floore (too filthy to be told)
        With bloud of guiltlesse babes, and innocents trew,
        Which there were slaine, as sheepe out of the fold,
        Defiled was, that dreadfull was to vew,
    And sacred ashes over it was strowed new.

33. (4) **red:** perceived; (8) **ages . . . degree:** the sober stage of
life; (9) **Aread:** tell, answer.
34. (2) **doted:** senile, dotard; (4) **countenance:** demeanour; (8)
without any breach: without having to break his way in; (9)
empeach: hinder.
35. (2) **arras:** tapestry; (4) **That greatest . . . behold:** that might
see (be worthy of) the greatest princes; (9) **sacred:** accursed.

36   And there beside of marble stone was built
        An Altare, carv'd with cunning imagery,
        On which true Christians bloud was often spilt,
        And holy Martyrs often doen to dye,
        With cruell malice and strong tyranny:
        Whose blessed sprites from underneath the stone
        To God for vengeance cryde continually,
        And with great griefe were often heard to grone,
    That hardest heart would bleede, to heare their
            piteous mone.

37   Through every rowme he sought, and every bowr,
        But no where could he find that wofull thrall:
        At last he came unto an yron doore,
        That fast was lockt, but key found not at all
        Emongst that bounch, to open it withall;
        But in the same a little grate was pight,
        Through which he sent his voyce, and lowd did call
        With all his powre, to weet, if living wight
    Were housed therewithin, whom he enlargen might.

38   Therewith an hollow, dreary, murmuring voyce
        These piteous plaints and dolours did resound;
        O who is that, which brings me happy choyce
        Of death, that here lye dying every stound,
        Yet live perforce in balefull darkenesse bound?
        For now three Moones have changed thrice their hew,
        And have beene thrice hid underneath the ground,
        Since I the heavens chearefull face did vew:
    O welcome thou, that doest of death bring tydings trew.

36. (2) **imagery:** figures, images; (4) **doen to die:** put to death.
37. (2) **that wofull thrall:** i.e., the Redcross knight; (6) **pight:** set;
    (9) **enlargen:** set free.
38. (1) **Therewith:** then in; (4) **stound:** moment; (6) **hew:** shape.

39   Which when that Champion heard, with percing point
       Of pitty deare his hart was thrilled sore,
       And trembling horrour ran through every joynt,
       For ruth of gentle knight so fowle forlore:
       Which shaking off, he rent that yron dore,
       With furious force, and indignation fell;
       Where entred in, his foot could find no flore,
       But all a deepe descent, as darke as hell,
    That breathed ever forth a filthie banefull smell.

40   But neither darkenesse fowle, nor filthy bands,
       Nor noyous smell his purpose could withhold,
       (Entire affection hateth nicer hands)
       But that with constant zeale, and courage bold,
       After long paines and labours manifold,
       He found the meanes that Prisoner up to reare;
       Whose feeble thighes, unhable to uphold
       His pined corse, him scarse to light could beare,
    A ruefull spectacle of death and ghastly drere.

41   His sad dull eyes deepe sunck in hollow pits,
       Could not endure th'unwonted sunne to view;
       His bare thin cheekes for want of better bits,
       And empty sides deceived of their dew,
       Could make a stony hart his hap to rew;
       His rawbone armes, whose mighty brawned bowrs
       Were wont to rive steele plates, and helmets hew,
       Were cleane consum'd, and all his vitall powres
    Decayd, and all his flesh shronk up like withered
         flowres.

39. (2) **deare:** grievous, sorrowful; (2) **thrilled:** pierced.
40. (1) **bands:** bonds; (2) **noyous:** poisonous; (3) **nicer:** over-nice, finicky; (8) **pined corse:** wasted body; (9) **ruefull:** pitiful; (9) **drere:** dreariness.
41. (3) **better bits:** nourishing food; (4) **deceived . . . dew:** cheated of what they needed; (5) **hap:** fate; (6) **brawned bowrs:** brawny muscles; (7) **rive:** split open.

42   Whom when his Lady saw, to him she ran
      With hasty joy: to see him made her glad,
      And sad to view his visage pale and wan,
      Who earst in flowres of freshest youth was clad.
      Tho when her well of teares she wasted had,
      She said, Ah dearest Lord, what evill starre
      On you hath frownd, and pourd his influence bad,
      That of your selfe ye thus berobbed arre,   §
  And this misseeming hew your manly looks doth marre?

43   But welcome now my Lord, in wele or woe,
      Whose presence I have lackt too long a day;
      And fie on Fortune mine avowed foe,
      Whose wrathfull wreakes them selves do now alay.
      And for these wrongs shall treble penaunce pay
      Of treble good: good growes of evils priefe.
      The chearelesse man, whom sorrow did dismay,
      Had no delight to treaten of his griefe;
  His long endured famine needed more reliefe.

44   Faire Lady, then said that victorious knight,
      The things, that grievous were to do, or beare,
      Them to renew, I wote, breeds no delight;
      Best musicke breeds delight in loathing eare: §
      But th'onely good, that growes of passed feare,
      Is to be wise, and ware of like agein.
      This dayes ensample hath this lesson deare
      Deepe written in my heart with yron pen,
  That blisse may not abide in state of mortall men.

42. (9) **misseeming hew:** unseemly condition.
43. (4) **wreakes:** punishments; (6) **good . . . priefe:** good grows
    out of the enduring of evil; (8) **treaten of:** talk about.
44. (3) **wote:** know; (6) **ware:** (to) beware, be wary.

§ *That of your selfe . . . berobbed arre*: Perhaps merely a comment on
  the knight's starved condition: "that your body has had to consume
  itself in this way in order to survive". Or perhaps a comment with
  moral overtones: "that you have done yourself this kind of damage".
§ *delight*: (line 4): Repetition of the word "delight" in this stanza
  makes Spenser's meaning difficult. It could easily be a printing error,
  the compositor's eye having tripped on the "delight" in line 3. But
  even as they stand Arthur's words could be taken to mean, "To go
  over these ugly events would, I know, be very disagreeable considering that it takes nothing less than the most beautiful music to please
  an unwilling ear."

45   Henceforth sir knight, take to you wonted strength,
      And maister these mishaps with patient might;
      Loe where your foe lyes stretcht in monstrous length,
      And loe that wicked woman in your sight,
      The roote of all your care, and wretched plight,
      Now in your powre, to let her live, or dye.
      To do her dye (quoth *Una*) were despight,
      And shame t'avenge so weake an enimy;
   But spoile her of her scarlot robe, and let her fly.

46   So as she bad, that witch they disaraid,
      And robd of royall robes, and purple pall,
      And ornaments that richly were displaid;
      Ne spared they to strip her naked all.
      Then when they had despoild her tire and call,
      Such as she was, their eyes might her behold,
      That her misshaped parts did them appall,
      A loathly, wrinckled hag, ill favoured, old,
   Whose secret filth good manners biddeth not be told.

47   Her craftie head was altogether bald,
      And as in hate of honorable eld,
      Was overgrowne with scurfe and filthy scald;
      Her teeth out of her rotten gummes were feld,
      And her sowre breath abhominably smeld;
      Her dried dugs, like bladders lacking wind,
      Hong downe, and filthy matter from them weld;
      Her wrizled skin as rough, as maple rind,
   So scabby was, that would have loathd all womankind.

45. (5) **care:** trouble; (7) **do her dye:** put her to death; (9) **spoile:** deprive, strip.
46. (2) **pall:** cloak; (5) **tire:** attire; (5) **call:** headdress; (8) **ill favoured:** repulsive.
47. (2) **eld:** old age; (3) **scald:** scabbiness; (4) **feld:** broken, chipped; (7) **weld:** welled, oozed.

48   Her neather parts, the shame of all her kind,
      My chaster Muse for shame doth blush to write;
      But at her rompe she growing had behind
      A foxes taile, with dong all fowly dight;
      And eke her feete most monstrous were in sight;
      For one of them was like an Eagles claw,
      With griping talaunts armd to greedy fight,
      The other like a Beares uneven paw:
  More ugly shape yet never living creature saw.

49   Which when the knights beheld, amazd they were,
      And wondred at so fowle deformed wight.
      Such then (said *Una*) as she seemeth here,
      Such is the face of falshood, such the sight
      Of fowle *Duessa*, when her borrowed light
      Is laid away, and counterfesaunce knowne.
      Thus when they had the witch disrobed quight,
      And all her filthy feature open showne,
  They let her goe at will, and wander wayes unknowne.

50   She flying fast from heavens hated face,
      And from the world that her discovered wide,
      Fled to the wastfull wildernesse apace,
      From living eyes her open shame to hide,
      And lurkt in rocks and caves long unespide.
      But that faire crew of knights, and *Una* faire
      Did in that castle afterwards abide,
      To rest them selves, and weary powres repaire,
  Where store they found of all, that dainty was and rare.

48. (4) **dight:** bedaubed, smirched; (7) **talaunts:** talons.
49. (6) **counterfesaunce:** deception, counterfeiting; (8) **feature:** form, person.
50. (2) **discovered wide:** fully displayed; (3) **wastfull:** desolate; (9) **store:** supply.

Canto IX

His loves and lignage Arthur tells:
The knights knit friendly bands:
Sir Trevisan flies from Despayre,
Whom Redcrosse knight withstands.

1   O Goodly golden chaine, wherewith yfere
        The vertues linked are in lovely wize:
      And noble minds of yore allyed were,
      In brave poursuit of chevalrous emprize,
      That none did others safety despize,
      Nor aid envy to him, in need that stands,
      But friendly each did others prayse devize,
      How to advaunce with favourable hands,
   As this good Prince redeemd the *Redcrosse* knight
        from bands.

2   Who when their powres empaird through labour long,
        With dew repast they had recured well,
      And that weake captive wight now wexed strong,
      Them list no lenger there at leasure dwell,
      But forward fare, as their adventures fell,
      But ere they parted, *Una* faire besought
      That straunger knight his name and nation tell;
      Least so great good, as he for her had wrought,
   Should die unknown, and buried be in thanklesse thought.

   lignage: lineage.
1. (1) **yfere:** together, in harmony; (4) **emprize:** undertaking;
   (6) **envy to:** begrudge; (7) **devize:** contrive, work for; (8)
   advaunce: further (a career).
2. (2) **repast:** refreshment; (2) **recured:** restored; (4) **Them list:**
   they wished; (5) **as their . . . fell:** wherever their adventures
   should lead them; (8) **Least:** lest.

3   Faire virgin (said the Prince) ye me require
      A thing without the compas of my wit:
      For both the lignage and the certain Sire,
      From which I sprong, from me are hidden yit.
      For all so soone as life did me admit
      Into this world, and shewed heavens light,
      From mothers pap I taken was unfit;
      And streight delivered to a Faery knight,
    To be upbrought in gentle thewes and martiall might.

4   Unto old *Timon* he me brought bylive,
      Old *Timon*, who in youthly yeares hath beene
      In warlike feates th'expertest man alive,
      And is the wisest now on earth I weene;
      His dwelling is low in a valley greene,
      Under the foot of *Rauran* mossy hore,
      From whence the river *Dee* as silver cleene
      His tombling billowes rolls with gentle rore:
    There all my dayes he traind me up in vertuous lore.

5   Thither the great Magicien *Merlin* came,
      As was his use, ofttimes to visit me:
      For he had charge my discipline to frame,
      And Tutours nouriture to oversee.
      Him oft and oft I askt in privitie,
      Of what loines and what lignage I did spring:
      Whose aunswere bad me still assured bee,
      That I was sonne and heire unto a king,
    As time in her just terme the truth to light would bring.

3. (2) **without:** outside, beyond; (7) **unfit:** immature, unfashioned;
  (9) **gentle thewes:** (the) manners of nobility.
4. (1) **bylive:** immediately; (6) **Rauran:** hill in Wales; (6) **mossy
  hore:** white with moss.
5. (2) **his use:** his custom, habit; (3) **frame:** plan and direct;
  (4) **nouriture:** rearing (of Arthur).

6   Well worthy impe, said then the Lady gent,
       And Pupill fit for such a Tutours hand.
       But what adventure, or what high intent
       Hath brought you hither into Faery land,
       Aread Prince *Arthur*, crowne of Martiall band?
       Full hard it is (quoth he) to read aright
       The course of heavenly cause, or understand
       The secret meaning of th'eternall might,
    That rules mens wayes, and rules the thoughts of
          living wight.

7   For whither he through fatall deepe foresight
       Me hither sent, for cause to me unghest,
       Or that fresh bleeding wound, which day and night
       Whilome doth rancle in my riven brest,
       With forced fury following his behest,   §
       Me hither brought by wayes yet never found,
       You to have helpt I hold my selfe yet blest.
       Ah curteous knight (quoth she) what secret wound
    Could ever find, to grieve the gentlest hart on ground?

8   Deare Dame (quoth he) you sleeping sparkes awake,
       Which troubled once, into huge flames will grow,
       Ne ever will their fervent fury slake,
       Till living moysture into smoke do flow,
       And wasted life do lye in ashes low.
       Yet sithens silence lesseneth not my fire,
       But told it flames, and hidden it does glow,
       I will revele, what ye so much desire:
    Ah Love, lay downe thy bow, the whiles I may respire.

6. (1) **impe:** scion.
7. (1) **whither:** whether; (1) **fatall:** fateful, destined; (3) **wound:** i.e., wound of love; (4) **Whilome:** continuously; (5) **his behest:** its (i.e., love's) own drives.
8. (6) **sithens:** since; (9) **respire:** rest.

§ *forced fury*: "Furious compulsion" is one editor's nice rendering of this phrase (*The Faerie Queene*, Bk. I., ed. G. W. Kitchin, Oxford, 1867).

9   It was in freshest flowre of youthly yeares,
      When courage first does creepe in manly chest,
      Then first the coale of kindly heat appeares
      To kindle love in every living brest;
      But me had warnd old *Timons* wise behest,
      Those creeping flames by reason to subdew,
      Before their rage grew to so great unrest,
      As miserable lovers use to rew,
    Which still wex old in woe, whiles woe still wexeth new.

10   That idle name of love, and lovers life,
      As losse of time, and vertues enimy
      I ever scornd, and joyd to stirre up strife,
      In middest of their mournfull Tragedy,
      Ay wont to laugh, when them I heard to cry,
      And blow the fire, which them to ashes brent:
      Their God himselfe, griev'd at my libertie,
      Shot many a dart at me with fiers intent,
    But I them warded all with wary government.

11   But all in vaine: no fort can be so strong,
      Ne fleshly brest can armed be so sound,
      But will at last be wonne with battrie long,
      Or unawares at disavantage found;
      Nothing is sure, that growes on earthly ground:
      And who most trustes in arme of fleshly might,
      And boasts, in beauties chaine not to be bound,
      Doth soonest fall in disaventrous fight,
    And yeeldes his caytive neck to victours most despight.

9. (3) **kindly heat:** natural desire; (5) **behest:** instruction; (8) **use to rew:** are always complaining about; (9) **Which:** who.
10. (5) **Ay wont:** always accustomed; (6) **brent:** burnt; (9) **government:** management, conduct.
11. (3) **battrie:** bombardment, assault; (8) **disaventrous:** disastrous; (9) **most despight:** fullest malice.

12 Ensample make of him your haplesse joy,
    And of my selfe now mated, as ye see;
    Whose prouder vaunt that proud avenging boy
    Did soone pluck downe, and curbd my libertie.
    For on a day prickt forth with jollitie
    Of looser life, and heat of hardiment,
    Raunging the forest wide on courser free,
    The fields, the floods, the heavens with one consent
Did seeme to laugh on me, and favour mine intent.

13 For-wearied with my sports, I did alight
    From loftie steed, and downe to sleepe me layd;
    The verdant gras my couch did goodly dight,
    And pillow was my helmet faire displayd:
    Whiles every sence the humour sweet embayd,
    And slombring soft my hart did steale away,
    Me seemed, by my side a royall Mayd
    Her daintie limbes full softly down did lay:
So faire a creature yet saw never sunny day.

14 Most goodly glee and lovely blandishment
    She to me made, and bad me love her deare,
    For dearely sure her love was to me bent,
    As when just time expired should appeare.
    But whether dreames delude, or true it were,
    Was never hart so ravisht with delight,
    Ne living man like words did ever heare,
    As she to me delivered all that night;
And at her parting said, She Queene of Faeries hight.

12. (1) **Ensample . . . joy:** learn from your unlucky lover's (i.e.,
the Redcross knight's) example; (2) **mated:** overthrown;
(3) **proud . . . boy:** i.e., Cupid; (5) **prickt forth:** decked out;
(6) **looser:** uncommitted, carefree; (9) **favour:** be propitious to.
13. (3) **dight:** furnish; (4) **faire displayd:** carefully placed; (5)
humour sweet: sweetness of sleep; (5) **embayd:** bathed, per-
vaded.
14. (1) **glee:** joy, mirth; (1) **blandishment:** allurement; (4) **just:**
appropriate, due; (9) **hight:** was called.

15 When I awoke, and found her place devoyd,
     And nought but pressed gras, where she had lyen,
     I sorrowed all so much, as earst I joyd,
     And washed all her place with watry eyen.
     From that day forth I lov'd that face divine;
     From that day forth I cast in carefull mind,
     To seeke her out with labour, and long tyne,
     And never vow to rest, till her I find,
  Nine monethes I seeke in vaine yet ni'll that vow
     unbind.

16 Thus as he spake, his visage wexed pale,
     And chaunge of hew great passion did bewray;
     Yet still he strove to cloke his inward bale,
     And hide the smoke, that did his fire display,
     Till gentle *Una* thus to him gan say;
     O happy Queene of Faeries, that hast found
     Mongst many, one that with his prowesse may
     Defend thine honour, and thy foes confound:
  True Loves are often sown, but seldom grow on ground.

17 Thine, O then, said the gentle *Redcrosse* knight,
     Next to that Ladies love, shalbe the place,
     O fairest virgin, full of heavenly light,
     Whose wondrous faith, exceeding earthly race,
     Was firmest fixt in mine extremest case.
     And you, my Lord, the Patrone of my life,
     Of that great Queene may well gaine worthy grace:
     For only worthy you through prowes priefe
  Yf living man mote worthy be, to be her liefe.

15. (1) **devoyd:** empty; (6) **cast:** resolved; (7) **tyne:** affliction;
(9) **ni'll:** will not.
16. (3) **bale:** distress.
17. (4) **faith:** fidelity; (7) **Of that:** from that; (8) **onely worthy
you:** you only are worthy; (8) **prowes priefe:** proof of valour;
(9) **liefe:** beloved.

18 So diversly discoursing of their loves,
  The golden Sunne his glistring head gan shew,
  And sad remembraunce now the Prince amoves,
  With fresh desire his voyage to pursew:
  Als *Una* earnd her traveill to renew.
  Then those two knights, fast friendship for to bynd,
  And love establish each to other trew,
  Gave goodly gifts, the signes of gratefull mynd,
And eke as pledges firme, right hands together joynd.

19 Prince *Arthur* gave a boxe of Diamond sure,
  Embowd with gold and gorgeous ornament,
  Wherein were closd few drops of liquor pure,
  Of wondrous worth, and vertue excellent,
  That any wound could heale incontinent:
  Which to requite, the *Redcrosse* knight him gave
  A booke, wherein his Saveours testament
  Was writ with golden letters rich and brave;
A worke of wondrous grace, and able soules to save.

20 Thus beene they parted, *Arthur* on his way
  To seeke his love, and th'other for to fight
  With *Unaes* foe, that all her realme did pray.
  But she now weighing the decayed plight,
  And shrunken synewes of her chosen knight,
  Would not a while her forward course pursew,
  Ne bring him forth in face of dreadfull fight,
  Till he recovered had his former hew:
For him to be yet weake and wearie well she knew.

18. (3) **amoves:** moves, inspires; (5) **Als:** also; (5) **earnd:** longed.
19. (2) **Embowd:** covered; (5) **incontinent:** immediately; (6) **Which to requite:** in return for which; (8) **brave:** handsome.
20. (3) **pray:** pillage, prey upon; (4) **decayed plight:** weakened condition; (8) **hew:** state, condition.

21 So as they traveild, lo they gan espy
    An armed knight towards them gallop fast,
    That seemed from some feared foe to fly,
    Or other griesly thing, that him agast.
    Still as he fled, his eye was backward cast,
    As if his feare still followed him behind;
    Als flew his steed, as he his bands had brast,
    And with his winged heeles did tread the wind,
As he had been a fole of *Pegasus* his kind.

22 Nigh as he drew, they might perceive his head
    To be unarmd, and curld uncombed heares
    Upstaring stiffe, dismayd with uncouth dread;
    Nor drop of bloud in all his face appeares
    Nor life in limbe: and to increase his feares,
    In fowle reproch of knighthoods faire degree,
    About his neck an hempen rope he weares,
    That with his glistring armes does ill agree;
But he of rope or armes has now no memoree.

23 The *Redcrosse* knight toward him crossed fast,
    To weet, what mister wight was so dismayd:
    There him he finds all sencelesse and aghast,
    That of him selfe he seemd to be afrayd;
    Whom hardly he from flying forward stayd,
    Till he these wordes to him deliver might;
    Sir knight, aread who hath ye thus arayd,
    And eke from whom make ye this hasty flight:
For never knight I saw in such misseeming plight.

21. (4) **agast:** terrified; (7) **Als:** also; (9) **a fole . . . kind:** a foal of the breed of, or kin to, Pegasus (i.e., the winged horse of Greek mythology).
22. (2) **heares:** hairs; (3) **Upstaring:** standing up.
23. (2) **what mister:** what manner of; (5) **hardly:** with difficulty; (5) **stayd:** prevented; (7) **aread:** tell, say; (9) **misseeming:** unseemly.

24   He answerd nought at all, but adding new
      Feare to his first amazment, staring wide
      With stony eyes, and hartlesse hollow hew,
      Astonisht stood, as one that had aspide
      Infernall furies, with their chaines untide.
      Him yet againe, and yet againe bespake
      The gentle knight; who nought to him replide,
      But trembling every joynt did inly quake,
   And foltring tongue at last these words seemd
        forth to shake.

25   For Gods deare love, Sir knight, do me not stay;
      For loe he comes, he comes fast after mee.
      Eft looking backe would faine have runne away;
      But he him forst to stay, and tellen free
      The secret cause of his perplexitie:
      Yet nathemore by his bold hartie speach,
      Could his bloud-frosen hart emboldned bee,
      But through his boldnesse rather feare did reach,
   Yet forst, at last he made through silence suddein
        breach.

26   And am I now in safetie sure (quoth he)
      From him, that would have forced me to dye?
      And is the point of death now turnd fro mee,
      That I may tell this haplesse history?
      Feare nought: (quoth he) no daunger now is nye.
      Then shall I you recount a ruefull cace,
      (Said he) the which with this unlucky eye
      I late beheld, and had not greater grace
   Me reft from it, had bene partaker of the place.

25. (1) **stay:** detain; (3) **Eft:** then; (6) **nathemore:** none the more.
26. (4) **haplesse:** unlucky; (9) **partaker:** fellow-victim (in the disaster of . . .).

27 I lately chaunst (Would I had never chaunst)
  With a faire knight to keepen companee,
  Sir *Terwin* hight, that well himselfe advaunst
  In all affaires, and was both bold and free,
  But not so happie as mote happie bee:
  He lov'd, as was his lot, a Ladie gent,
  That him againe lov'd in the least degree:
  For she was proud, and of too high intent,
 And joyd to see her lover languish and lament.

28 From whom returning sad and comfortlesse,
  As on the way together we did fare,
  We met that villen (God from him me blesse)
  That cursed wight, from whom I scapt whyleare,
  A man of hell, that cals himselfe *Despaire*:
  Who first us greets, and after faire areedes
  Of tydings strange, and of adventures rare:
  So creeping close, as Snake in hidden weedes,
 Inquireth of our states, and of our knightly deedes.

29 Which when he knew, and felt our feeble harts
  Embost with bale, and bitter byting griefe,
  Which love had launched with his deadly darts,
  With wounding words and termes of foule repriefe,
  He pluckt from us all hope of due reliefe,
  That earst us held in love of lingring life;
  Then hopelesse hartlesse, gan the cunning thiefe
  Perswade us die, to stint all further strife:
 To me he lent this rope, to him a rustie knife.

27. (5) **as mote . . . bee:** as he might have been; (6) **lot:** fate;
(7) **That him . . . degree:** who did not return his love in the
least; (8) **intent:** aspiration.
28. (3) **blesse:** deliver, save; (4) **whyleare:** a moment ago; (8)
hidden: concealing.
29. (2) **Embost with:** sunk in; (2) **bale:** grief; (4) **repriefe:**
reproach; (6) **earst:** till then; (8) **stint:** put a stop to, preclude.

30 With which sad instrument of hastie death,
  That wofull lover, loathing lenger light,
  A wide way made to let forth living breath.
  But I more fearefull, or more luckie wight,
  Dismayd with that deformed dismall sight,
  Fled fast away, halfe dead with dying feare:
  Ne yet assur'd of life by you, Sir knight,
  Whose like infirmitie like chaunce may beare:
  But God you never let his charmed speeches heare.

31 How may a man (said he) with idle speach
  Be wonne, to spoyle the Castle of his health?
  I wote (quoth he) whom triall late did teach,
  That like would not for all this worldes wealth:
  His subtill tongue, like dropping honny, mealt'h
  Into the hart, and searcheth every vaine,
  That ere one be aware, by secret stealth
  His powre is reft, and weaknesse doth remaine.
  O never Sir desire to try his guilefull traine.

32 Certes (said he) hence shall I never rest,
  Till I that treachours art have heard and tride;
  And you Sir knight, whose name mote I request,
  Of grace do me unto his cabin guide.
  I that hight *Trevisan* (quoth he) will ride
  Against my liking backe, to doe you grace:
  But nor for gold nor glee will I abide
  By you, when ye arrive in that same place;
  For lever had I die, then see his deadly face.

30. (5) **deformed:** hideous, hateful; (7) **Ne yet:** nor (am I) yet.
31. (2) **wonne:** persuaded; (4) **That like . . . not:** who would not go through that again; (5) **mealt'h:** melts.
32. (1) **hence:** from now on; (2) **treachours:** traitor's; (6) **to doe you grace:** as a favour to you; (7) **glee:** (?) anything that glitters; (9) **lever:** rather.

33 Ere long they come, where that same wicked wight
     His dwelling has, low in an hollow cave,
     Farre underneath a craggie clift ypight,
     Darke, dolefull, drearie, like a greedie grave,
     That still for carrion carcases doth crave:
     On top whereof aye dwelt the ghastly Owle,
     Shrieking his balefull note, which ever drave
     Farre from that haunt all other chearefull fowle;
And all about it wandring ghostes did waile and howle.

34 And all about old stockes and stubs of trees,
     Whereon nor fruit, nor leafe was ever seene,
     Did hang upon the ragged rocky knees;
     On which had many wretches hanged beene,
     Whose carcases were scattered on the greene,
     And throwne about the cliffs. Arrived there,
     That bare-head knight for dread and dolefull teene,
     Would faine have fled, ne durst approchen neare,
But th'other forst him stay, and comforted in feare.

35 That darkesome cave they enter, where they find
     That cursed man, low sitting on the ground,
     Musing full sadly in his sullein mind;
     His griesie lockes, long growen, and unbound,
     Disordred hong about his shoulders round,
     And hid his face; through which his hollow eyne
     Lookt deadly dull, and stared as astound;
     His raw-bone cheekes through penurie and pine,
Were shronke into his jawes, as he did never dine.

33. (3) **ypight:** situated.
34. (3) **knees:** crags, outcroppings.
35. (6) **eyne:** eyes; (8) **pine:** privation.

36 His garment nought but many ragged clouts,
　　　With thornes together pind and patched was,
　　　The which his naked sides he wrapt abouts;
　　　And him beside there lay upon the gras
　　　A drearie corse, whose life away did pas,
　　　All wallowd in his owne yet luke-warme blood,
　　　That from his wound yet welled fresh alas;
　　　In which a rustie knife fast fixed stood,
　　And made an open passage for the gushing flood.

37 Which piteous spectacle, approving trew
　　　The wofull tale that *Trevisan* had told,
　　　When as the gentle *Redcrosse* knight did vew,
　　　With firie zeale he burnt in courage bold,
　　　Him to avenge, before his bloud were cold,
　　　And to the villein said, Thou damned wight,
　　　The author of this fact, we here behold,
　　　What justice can but judge against thee right,
　　With thine owne bloud to price his bloud, here shed in
　　　　sight.

38 What franticke fit (quoth he) hath thus distraught
　　　Thee, foolish man, so rash a doome to give?
　　　What justice ever other judgement taught,
　　　But he should die, who merites not to live?
　　　None else to death this man despayring drive,
　　　But his owne guiltie mind deserving death.
　　　Is then unjust to each his due to give?
　　　Or let him die, that loatheth living breath?
　　Or let him die at ease, that liveth here uneath?

36. (2) **pind:** pinned.
37. (1) **approving trew:** substantiating; (8) **right:** rightly; (9) **price:** pay the price of.
38. (2) **doome:** judgment; (5) **None else . . . drive:** nothing drives this despairing man to death; (6) **deserving:** which deserves; (9) **uneath:** uneasily.

39   Who travels by the wearie wandring way,
       To come unto his wished home in haste,
       And meetes a flood, that doth his passage stay,
       Is not great grace to helpe him over past,
       Or free his feet, that in the myre sticke fast?
       Most envious man, that grieves at neighbours good,
       And fond, that joyest in the woe thou hast,
       Why wilt not let him passe, that long hath stood
  Upon the banke, yet wilt thy selfe not passe the flood?

40   He there does now enjoy eternall rest
       And happie ease, which thou doest want and crave,
       And further from it daily wanderest:
       What if some litle paine the passage have,
       That makes fraile flesh to feare the bitter wave?
       Is not short paine well borne, that brings long ease,
       And layes the soule to sleepe in quiet grave?
       Sleepe after toyle, port after stormie seas,
  Ease after warre, death after life does greatly please.

41   The knight much wondred at his suddeine wit,
       And said, The terme of life is limited,
       Ne may a man prolong, nor shorten it;
       The souldier may not move from watchfull sted,
       Nor leave his stand, untill his Captaine bed.
       Who life did limit by almightie doome,
       (Quoth he) knowes best the termes established;
       And he, that points the Centonell his roome,
  Doth license him depart at sound of morning droome.

39. (7) **fond:** deluded; (9) **yet wilt . . . passe:** just because you
yourself do not want to cross.
40. (2) **want:** lack; (6) **well borne:** well worth bearing.
41. (4) **sted:** position, post; (5) **bed:** bids; (6) **doome:** decree; (8)
points: appoints; (8) **roome:** post; (9) **droome:** drum.

42   Is not his deed, what ever thing is donne,
        In heaven and earth? did not he all create
        To die againe? all ends that was begonne.
        Their times in his eternall booke of fate
        Are written sure, and have their certaine date.
        Who then can strive with strong necessitie,
        That holds the world in his still chaunging state,
        Or shunne the death ordaynd by destinie?
  When houre of death is come, let none aske whence,
        nor why.

43   The lenger life, I wote the greater sin,
        The greater sin, the greater punishment:
        All those great battels, which thou boasts to win,
        Through strife, and bloud-shed, and avengement,
        Now praysd, hereafter deare thou shalt repent:
        For life must life, and bloud must bloud repay.
        Is not enough thy evill life forespent?   §
        For he, that once hath missed the right way,
  The further he doth goe, the further he doth stray.

44   Then do no further goe, no further stray,
        But here lie downe, and to thy rest betake,
        Th'ill to prevent, that life ensewen may.
        For what hath life, that may it loved make,
        And gives not rather cause it to forsake?
        Feare, sicknesse, age, losse, labour, sorrow, strife,
        Paine, hunger, cold, that makes the hart to quake;
        And ever fickle fortune rageth rife,
  All which, and thousands mo do make a loathsome life.

43. (5) **deare:** sorely.
44. (3) **ensewen may:** may yet result in.

§ *Is not . . . forespent?*: Has not your evil life dragged itself out long enough?

45   Thou wretched man, of death hast greatest need,
     If in true ballance thou wilt weigh thy state:
     For never knight, that dared warlike deede,
     More lucklesse disaventures did amate:
     Witnesse the dongeon deepe, wherein of late
     Thy life shut up, for death so oft did call;
     And though good lucke prolonged hath thy date,
     Yet death then, would the like mishaps forestall,
  Into the which hereafter thou maiest happen fall.

46   Why then doest thou, O man of sin, desire
     To draw thy dayes forth to their last degree?
     Is not the measure of thy sinfull hire
     High heaped up with huge iniquitie,
     Against the day of wrath, to burden thee?
     Is not enough, that to this Ladie milde
     Thou falsed hast thy faith with perjurie,
     And sold thy selfe to serve *Duessa* vilde,
  With whom in all abuse thou hast thy selfe defilde?

47   Is not he just, that all this doth behold
     From highest heaven, and beares an equall eye?
     Shall he thy sins up in his knowledge fold,
     And guiltie be of thine impietie?
     Is not his law, Let every sinner die:
     Die shall all flesh? what then must needs be donne,
     Is it not better to doe willinglie,
     Then linger, till the glasse be all out ronne?
  Death is the end of woes: die soone, O faeries sonne.

45. (2) **ballance:** scales; (4) **disaventures:** disasters; (4) **amate:** haunt, plague; (7) **date:** term of life.
46. (3) **hire:** service.
47. (2) **equall:** impartial; (8) **glasse:** hour-glass.

48 The knight was much enmoved with his speach,
      That as a swords point through his hart did perse,
      And in his conscience made a secret breach,
      Well knowing true all, that he did reherse,
      And to his fresh remembrance did reverse
      The ugly vew of his deformed crimes,
      That all his manly powres it did disperse,
      As he were charmed with inchaunted rimes,
That oftentimes he quakt, and fainted oftentimes.

49 In which amazement, when the Miscreant
      Perceived him to waver weake and fraile,
      Whiles trembling horror did his conscience dant,
      And hellish anguish did his soule assaile,
      To drive him to despaire, and quite to quaile,
      He shew'd him painted in a table plaine,
      The damned ghosts, that doe in torments waile,
      And thousand feends that doe them endlesse paine
With fire and brimstone, which for ever shall remaine.

50 The sight whereof so throughly him dismaid,
      That nought but death before his eyes he saw,
      And ever burning wrath before him laid,
      By righteous sentence of th'Almighties law:
      Then gan the villein him to overcraw,
      And brought unto him swords, ropes, poison, fire,
      And all that might him to perdition draw;
      And bad him choose, what death he would desire:
For death was due to him, that had provokt Gods ire.

48. (5) **reverse**: recall.
49. (3) **dant**: daunt; (5) **quite to quaile**: i.e., to complete dismay;
    (6) **table**: picture.
50. (5) **overcraw**: exult over.

51   But when as none of them he saw him take,
     He to him raught a daggèr sharpe and keene,
     And gave it him in hand: his hand did quake,
     And tremble like a leafe of Aspin greene,
     And troubled bloud through his pale face was seene
     To come, and goe with tydings from the hart,
     As it a running messenger had beene.
     At last resolv'd to worke his finall smart,
  He lifted up his hand, that backe againe did start.

52   Which when as *Una* saw, through every vaine
     The crudled cold ran to her well of life,
     As in a swowne: but soone reliv'd againe,
     Out of his hand she snatcht the cursed knife,
     And threw it to the ground, enraged rife,
     And to him said, Fie, fie, faint harted knight,
     What meanest thou by this reprochfull strife?
     Is this the battell, which thou vauntst to fight
  With that fire-mouthed Dragon, horrible and bright?

53   Come, come away, fraile, feeble, fleshly wight,
     Ne let vaine words bewitch thy manly hart,
     Ne divelish thoughts dismay thy constant spright.
     In heavenly mercies hast thou not a part?
     Why shouldst thou then despeire, that chosen art?
     Where justice growes, there grows eke greater grace,
     The which doth quench the brond of hellish smart,
     And that accurst hand-writing doth deface.   §
  Arise, Sir knight arise, and leave this cursed place.

51. (2) **raught:** handed; (8) **smart:** hurt.
52. (2) **well of life:** i.e., heart; (3) **reliv'd:** revived; (5) **rife:** deeply.
53. (6) **eke:** even; (7) **brond:** firebrand, flame.

§ *that accurst hand-writing*: The legal writ of divine judgment against
sinners (see Colossians 2:13-14).

54 So up he rose, and thence amounted streight.
　　Which when the carle beheld, and saw his guest
　　Would safe depart, for all his subtill sleight,
　　He chose an halter from among the rest,
　　And with it hung himselfe, unbid unblest.
　　But death he could not worke himselfe thereby;
　　For thousand times he so himselfe had drest,
　　Yet nathelesse it could not doe him die,
　Till he should die his last, that is eternally.

54. (1) **amounted streight:** mounted straightway; (2) **carle:** churl;
(3) **sleight:** wiles; (5) **unbid:** without a prayer; (7) **drest:**
disposed, arranged; (8) **doe him die:** kill him.

Canto X

> *Her faithfull knight faire Una brings*
> *to house of Holinesse,*
> *Where he is taught repentance, and*
> *the way to heavenly blesse.*

1 WHat man is he, that boasts of fleshly might,
       And vaine assurance of mortality,
    Which all so soone, as it doth come to fight,
    Against spirituall foes, yeelds by and by,
    Or from the field most cowardly doth fly?
    Ne let the man ascribe it to his skill,
    That thorough grace hath gained victory.
    If any strength we have, it is to ill,
But all the good is Gods, both power and eke will.

2 By that, which lately hapned, *Una* saw,
       That this her knight was feeble, and too faint;
    And all his sinews woxen weake and raw,
    Through long enprisonment, and hard constraint,
    Which he endured in his late restraint,
    That yet he was unfit for bloudie fight:
    Therefore to cherish him with diets daint,
    She cast to bring him, where he chearen might,
Till he recovered had his late decayed plight.

blesse: bliss.
1. (4) **by and by:** immediately.
2. (3) **raw:** unpractised, rusty; (4) **hard constraint:** severe
   distress; (5) **restraint:** confinement; (7) **daint:** choice (adj.);
   (8) **chearen:** regain his cheerfulness.

3 There was an auntient house not farre away,
  Renowmd throughout the world for sacred lore,
  And pure unspotted life: so well they say
  It governd was, and guided evermore,
  Through wisedome of a matrone grave and hore;
  Whose onely joy was to relieve the needes
  Of wretched soules, and helpe the helpelesse pore:
  All night she spent in bidding of her bedes,
And all the day in doing good and godly deedes.

4 Dame *Cælia* men did her call, as thought
  From heaven to come, or thither to arise,
  The mother of three daughters, well upbrought
  In goodly thewes, and godly exercise:
  The eldest two most sober, chast, and wise,
  Fidelia and *Speranza* virgins were,
  Though spousd, yet wanting wedlocks solemnize;
  But faire *Charissa* to a lovely fere
Was lincked, and by him had many pledges dere.

5 Arrived there, the dore they find fast lockt;
  For it was warely watched night and day,
  For feare of many foes: but when they knockt,
  The Porter opened unto them streight way:
  He was an aged syre, all hory gray,
  With lookes full lowly cast, and gate full slow,
  Wont on a staffe his feeble steps to stay,
  Hight *Humiltâ*. They passe in stouping low;
For streight and narrow was the way, which he did show.

3. (2) **lore:** learning, doctrine; (5) **hore:** venerable; (8) **bidding
. . . bedes:** saying her prayers.
4. (4) **thewes:** manners; (8) **fere:** mate.
5. (2) **warely:** alertly; (8) **Hight:** called.

6 Each goodly thing is hardest to begin,
  But entred in a spacious court they see,
  Both plaine, and pleasant to be walked in,
  Where them does meete a francklin faire and free, §
  And entertaines with comely courteous glee,
  His name was *Zele*, that him right well became,
  For in his speeches and behaviour hee
  Did labour lively to expresse the same,
 And gladly did them guide, till to the Hall they came.

7 There fairely them receives a gentle Squire,
  Of milde demeanure, and rare courtesie,
  Right cleanly clad in comely sad attire;
  In word and deede that shew'd great modestie,
  And knew his good to all of each degree,
  Hight *Reverence*. He them with speeches meet
  Does faire entreat; no courting nicetie,
  But simple true, and eke unfained sweet,
 As might become a Squire so great persons to greet.

8 And afterwards them to his Dame he leades,
  That aged Dame, the Ladie of the place:
  Who all this while was busie at her beades:
  Which doen, she up arose with seemely grace,
  And toward them full matronely did pace.
  Where when that fairest *Una* she beheld,
  Whom well she knew to spring from heavenly race,
  Her hart with joy unwonted inly sweld,
 As feeling wondrous comfort in her weaker eld.

6. (2) **entred in:** having entered; (5) **glee:** gladness.
7. (1) **fairely:** amiably; (3) **sad:** dark-toned, quiet; (5) **knew his good:** i.e., knew how to conduct himself properly; (7) **entreat:** treat; (7) **courting:** courtier-like; (7) **nicetie:** preciosity.
8. (9) **eld:** old age.

§ *francklin*: A franklin or freeholder, i.e., a man of free but not noble birth; somewhat like a country squire in rank and status.

9   And her embracing said, O happie earth,
      Whereon thy innocent feet doe ever tread,
      Most vertuous virgin borne of heavenly berth,
      That to redeeme thy woefull parents head,
      From tyrans rage, and ever-dying dread,
      Hast wandred through the world now long a day;
      Yet ceasest not thy wearie soles to lead,
      What grace hath thee now hither brought this way?
    Or doen thy feeble feet unweeting hither stray?

10   Strange thing it is an errant knight to see
      Here in this place, or any other wight,
      That hither turnes his steps. So few there bee,
      That chose the narrow path, or seeke the right:
      All keepe the broad high way, and take delight
      With many rather for to go astray,
      And be partakers of their evill plight,
      Then with a few to walke the rightest way;
    O foolish men, why haste ye to your owne decay?

11   Thy selfe to see, and tyred limbs to rest,
      O matrone sage (quoth she) I hither came,
      And this good knight his way with me addrest,
      Led with thy prayses and broad-blazed fame,
      That up to heaven is blowne. The auncient Dame,
      Him goodly greeted in her modest guise,
      And entertaynd them both, as best became,
      With all the court'sies, that she could devise,
    Ne wanted ought, to shew her bounteous or wise.

  9. (5) **ever-dying dread:** ever-present fear, or threat, of death;
     (9) **feeble:** tired.
10. (9) **decay:** destruction.
11. (6) **guise:** fashion; (9) **Ne wanted ought:** nor failed in any-
    thing.

12   Thus as they gan of sundry things devise,
    Loe two most goodly virgins came in place,
    Ylinked arme in arme in lovely wise,
    With countenance demure, and modest grace,
    They numbred even steps and equall pace:
    Of which the eldest, that *Fidelia* hight,
    Like sunny beames threw from her Christall face,
    That could have dazd the rash beholders sight,
And round about her head did shine like heavens light.

13   She was araied all in lilly white,
    And in her right hand bore a cup of gold,
    With wine and water fild up to the hight,
    In which a Serpent did himselfe enfold,   §
    That horrour made to all, that did behold;
    But she no whit did chaunge her constant mood:
    And in her other hand she fast did hold
    A booke, that was both signd and seald with blood,
Wherein darke things were writ, hard to be understood.

14   Her younger sister, that *Speranza* hight,
    Was clad in blew, that her beseemed well;
    Not all so chearefull seemed she of sight,
    As was her sister; whether dread did dwell,
    Or anguish in her hart, is hard to tell:
    Upon her arme a silver anchor lay,   §
    Whereon she leaned ever, as befell:
    And ever up to heaven, as she did pray,
Her stedfast eyes were bent, ne swarved other way.

12. (1) **devise:** converse.
13. (3) **to the hight:** i.e., to the brim.
14. (7) **befell:** it happened; (9) **swarved:** swerved, turned.

§ *a Serpent*: The serpent is not only an image of temptation, poison, and death; it can also be an image of health, healing, and life. Cf. the serpent in the wilderness (Numbers 21:4-9), or the emblem of the medical profession, Asclepius' staff entwined by a snake.
§ *a silver anchor*: See Hebrews 6:19; the same emblem is used on the original title-page of *The Faerie Queene*.

15   They seeing *Una*, towards her gan wend,
    Who them encounters with like courtesie;
    Many kind speeches they betwene them spend,
    And greatly joy each other well to see:
    Then to the knight with shamefast modestie
    They turne themselves, at *Unaes* meeke request,
    And him salute with well beseeming glee;
    Who faire them quites, as him beseemed best,
And goodly gan discourse of many a noble gest.

16   Then *Una* thus; But she your sister deare,
    The deare *Charissa* where is she become?
    Or wants she health, or busie is elsewhere?
    Ah no, said they, but forth she may not come:
    For she of late is lightned of her wombe,
    And hath encreast the world with one sonne more,
    That her to see should be but troublesome.
    Indeede (quoth she) that should her trouble sore,
But thankt be God, and her encrease so evermore.

17   Then said the aged *Cælia*, Deare dame,
    And you good Sir, I wote that of your toyle,
    And labours long, through which ye hither came,
    Ye both forwearied be: therefore a whyle
    I read you rest, and to your bowres recoyle.
    Then called she a Groome, that forth him led
    Into a goodly lodge, and gan despoile
    Of puissant armes, and laid in easie bed;
His name was meeke *Obedience* rightfully ared.

15. (1) **wend:** move; (5) **shamefast:** bashful; (7) **beseeming:** becoming; (9) **gest:** exploit.
16. (2) **where . . . become:** where has she gone? (or) what has become of her?; (3) **wants she health:** is she sick?; (9) **her encrease so:** may he (God) so increase her, (or) may she increase so.
17. (5) **read:** advise; (5) **recoyle:** retire; (7) **despoile:** unburden, disencumber; (9) **ared:** understood.

18   Now when their wearie limbes with kindly rest,
     And bodies were refresht with due repast,
     Faire *Una* gan *Fidelia* faire request,
     To have her knight into her schoolehouse plaste,
     That of her heavenly learning he might taste,
     And heare the wisedome of her words divine.
     She graunted, and that knight so much agraste,
     That she him taught celestiall discipline,
And opened his dull eyes, that light mote in them shine.

19   And that her sacred Booke, with bloud ywrit,
     That none could read, except she did them teach,
     She unto him disclosed every whit,
     And heavenly documents thereout did preach,
     That weaker wit of man could never reach,
     Of God, of grace, of justice, of free will,
     That wonder was to heare her goodly speach:
     For she was able, with her words to kill,
And raise againe to life the hart, that she did thrill.

20   And when she list poure out her larger spright,
     She would commaund the hastie Sunne to stay,
     Or backward turne his course from heavens hight;
     Sometimes great hostes of men she could dismay;
     Dry-shod to passe, she parts the flouds in tway;
     And eke huge mountaines from their native seat
     She would commaund, themselves to beare away,
     And throw in raging sea with roaring threat.
Almightie God her gave such powre, and puissance
     great.

18. (4) **plaste:** placed, enrolled; (7) **agraste:** favoured.
19. (4) **documents:** teachings; (9) **thrill:** penetrate.
20. (1) **list:** chose to; (5) **tway:** two, twain.

21 The faithfull knight now grew in litle space,
  By hearing her, and by her sisters lore,
  To such perfection of all heavenly grace,
  That wretched world he gan for to abhore,
  And mortall life gan loath, as thing forlore,
  Greev'd with remembrance of his wicked wayes,
  And prickt with anguish of his sinnes so sore,
  That he desirde to end his wretched dayes:
So much the dart of sinfull guilt the soule dismayes.

22 But wise *Speranza* gave him comfort sweet,
  And taught him how to take assured hold
  Upon her silver anchor, as was meet;
  Else had his sinnes so great, and manifold
  Made him forget all that *Fidelia* told.
  In this distressed doubtfull agonie,
  When him his dearest *Una* did behold,
  Disdeining life, desiring leave to die,
She found her selfe assayld with great perplexitie.

23 And came to *Cælia* to declare her smart,
  Who well acquainted with that commune plight,
  Which sinfull horror workes in wounded hart,
  Her wisely comforted all that she might,
  With goodly counsell and advisement right;
  And streightway sent with carefull diligence,
  To fetch a Leach, the which had great insight
  In that disease of grieved conscience,
And well could cure the same; His name was *Patience*.

21. (1) **in litle space:** within a short time; (2) **lore:** teaching, doctrine; (5) **forlore:** depraved.
23. (1) **smart:** trouble; (7) **Leach:** doctor.

24   Who comming to that soule-diseased knight,
        Could hardly him intreat, to tell his griefe:
        Which knowne, and all that noyd his heavie spright
        Well searcht, eftsoones he gan apply reliefe
        Of salves and med'cines, which had passing priefe,
        And thereto added words of wondrous might:
        By which to ease he him recured briefe,
        And much asswag'd the passion of his plight,
    That he his paine endur'd, as seeming now more light.

25   But yet the cause and root of all his ill,
        Inward corruption, and infected sin,
        Not purg'd nor heald, behind remained still,
        And festring sore did rankle yet within,
        Close creeping twixt the marrow and the skin.
        Which to extirpe, he laid him privily
        Downe in a darkesome lowly place farre in,
        Whereas he meant his corrosives to apply,
    And with streight diet tame his stubborne malady.

26   In ashes and sackcloth he did array
        His daintie corse, proud humors to abate,
        And dieted with fasting every day,
        The swelling of his wounds to mitigate,
        And made him pray both early and eke late:
        And ever as superfluous flesh did rot
        Amendment readie still at hand did wayt,
        To pluck it out with pincers firie whot,
    That soone in him was left no one corrupted jot.

24. (2) **hardly:** scarcely; (2) **intreat:** persuade; (3) **noyd:** troubled;
    (5) **passing priefe:** extraordinary efficacy; (7) **to ease . . .
    briefe:** he quickly (or, perhaps, temporarily) restored some
    comfort to him.
25. (6) **extirpe:** extirpate, root out; (9) **streight:** strict.
26. (2) **daintie:** fastidious; (2) **humors:** traits; (8) **whot:** hot.

27 And bitter *Penance* with an yron whip,
    Was wont him once to disple every day:
    And sharpe *Remorse* his hart did pricke and nip,
    That drops of bloud thence like a well did play;
    And sad *Repentance* used to embay,
    His bodie in salt water smarting sore,
    The filthy blots of sinne to wash away.
    So in short space they did to health restore
The man that would not live, but earst lay at deathes
      dore.

28 In which his torment often was so great,
    That like a Lyon he would cry and rore,
    And rend his flesh, and his owne synewes eat.
    His owne deare *Una* hearing evermore
    His ruefull shriekes and gronings, often tore
    Her guiltlesse garments, and her golden heare,
    For pitty of his paine and anguish sore;
    Yet all with patience wisely she did beare;
For well she wist, his crime could else be never cleare.

29 Whom thus recover'd by wise Patience,
    And trew *Repentance* they to *Una* brought:
    Who joyous of his cured conscience,
    Him dearely kist, and fairely eke besought
    Himselfe to chearish, and consuming thought
    To put away out of his carefull brest.
    By this *Charissa*, late in child-bed brought,
    Was woxen strong, and left her fruitfull nest;
To her faire *Una* brought this unacquainted guest.

27. (2) **disple:** discipline; (5) **embay:** bathe; (9) **would not:** did
not want to.
28. (9) **crime:** sense of guilt.
29. (5) **consuming:** self-destructive, corrosive.

30   She was a woman in her freshest age,
        Of wondrous beauty, and of bountie rare,
        With goodly grace and comely personage,
        That was on earth not easie to compare;
        Full of great love, but *Cupids* wanton snare
        As hell she hated, chast in worke and will;
        Her necke and breasts were ever open bare,
        That ay thereof her babes might sucke their fill;
    The rest was all in yellow robes arayed still.

31   A multitude of babes about her hong,
        Playing their sports, that joyd her to behold,
        Whom still she fed, whiles they were weake and
            young,
        But thrust them forth still, as they wexed old:
        And on her head she wore a tyre of gold,
        Adornd with gemmes and owches wondrous faire,
        Whose passing price uneath was to be told;
        And by her side there sate a gentle paire
    Of turtle doves, she sitting in an yvorie chaire.

32   The knight and *Una* entring, faire her greet,
        And bid her joy of that her happie brood;
        Who them requites with court'sies seeming meet,
        And entertaines with friendly chearefull mood.
        Then *Una* her besought, to be so good,
        As in her vertuous rules to schoole her knight,
        Now after all his torment well withstood,
        In that sad house of *Penaunce*, where his spright
    Had past the paines of hell, and long enduring night.

30. (4) **compare:** match; (9) **still:** always.
31. (2) **that joyd her:** whom it delighted her; (5) **tyre:** headdress;
    (6) **owches:** ornamental brooches; (7) **passing:** surpassing; (7)
    uneath: scarcely.
32. (3) **requites:** repays; (3) **meet:** suitable, proper.

33   She was right joyous of her just request,
            And taking by the hand that Faeries sonne,
            Gan him instruct in every good behest,
            Of love, and righteousnesse, and well to donne,
            And wrath, and hatred warely to shonne,
            That drew on men Gods hatred, and his wrath,
            And many soules in dolours had fordonne:
            In which when him she well instructed hath,
From thence to heaven she teacheth him the ready path.

34   Wherein his weaker wandring steps to guide,
            An auncient matrone she to her does call,
            Whose sober lookes her wisedome well descride:
            Her name was *Mercie*, well knowne over all,
            To be both gratious, and eke liberall:
            To whom the carefull charge of him she gave,
            To lead aright, that he should never fall
            In all his wayes through this wide worldes wave,
That Mercy in the end his righteous soule might save.

35   The godly Matrone by the hand him beares
            Forth from her presence, by a narrow way,
            Scattred with bushy thornes, and ragged breares,
            Which still before him she remov'd away,
            That nothing might his ready passage stay:
            And ever when his feet encombred were,
            Or gan to shrinke, or from the right to stray,
            She held him fast, and firmely did upbeare,
As carefull Nourse her child from falling oft does reare.

33. (1) **was right joyous:** rejoiced in; (4) **well to donne:** to do good; (5) **warely to shonne:** carefully to shun; (7) **fordonne:** destroyed.
34. (3) **descride:** revealed; (4) **over all:** everywhere.
35. (2) **her presence:** i.e., Charissa's presence; (3) **breares:** briars; (9) **reare:** raise.

36   Eftsoones unto an holy Hospitall,
          That was fore by the way, she did him bring,
          In which seven Bead-men that had vowed all
          Their life to service of high heavens king
          Did spend their dayes in doing godly thing:
          Their gates to all were open evermore,
          That by the wearie way were traveiling,
          And one sate wayting ever them before,
     To call in commers-by, that needy were and pore.

37   The first of them that eldest was, and best,
          Of all the house had charge and governement,
          As Guardian and Steward of the rest:
          His office was to give entertainement
          And lodging, unto all that came, and went:
          Not unto such, as could him feast againe,
          And double quite, for that he on them spent,
          But such, as want of harbour did constraine:
     Those for Gods sake his dewty was to entertaine.

38   The second was as Almner of the place,
          His office was, the hungry for to feed,
          And thristy give to drinke, a worke of grace:
          He feard not once him selfe to be in need,
          Ne car'd to hoord for those, whom he did breede:
          The grace of God he layd up still in store,
          Which as a stocke he left unto his seede;   §
          He had enough, what need him care for more?
     And had he lesse, yet some he would give to the pore.

36. (2) **fore by:** close by; (3) **Bead-men:** men devoted to prayer.
37. (1) **best:** the Superior, first in seniority; (6) **feast againe:** feast
him in return; (7) **double quite:** repay double; (8) **constraine:**
oblige (to accept hospitality).
38. (1) **Almner:** official distributor of alms; (5) **hoord . . . breede:**
accumulate a secret reserve of what he produced.

§ *Which as a stocke . . . unto his seede*: "Which he left as one lets a
stalk go to seed" (and so continue to propagate and increase itself).

39 The third had of their wardrobe custodie,
  In which were not rich tyres, nor garments gay,
  The plumes of pride, and wings of vanitie,
  But clothes meet to keepe keene could away,
  And naked nature seemely to aray;
  With which bare wretched wights he dayly clad,
  The images of God in earthly clay;
  And if that no spare cloths to give he had,
 His owne coate he would cut, and it distribute glad.

40 The fourth appointed by his office was,
  Poore prisoners to relieve with gratious ayd,
  And captives to redeeme with price of bras,
  From Turkes and Sarazins, which them had stayd;
  And though they faultie were, yet well he wayd,
  That God to us forgiveth every howre
  Much more then that, why they in bands were layd,
  And he that harrowd hell with heavie stowre, §
 The faultie soules from thence brought to his heavenly
   bowre.

41 The fift had charge sicke persons to attend,
  And comfort those, in point of death which lay;
  For them most needeth comfort in the end,
  When sin, and hell, and death do most dismay
  The feeble soule departing hence away.
  All is but lost, that living we bestow,
  If not well ended at our dying day.
  O man have mind of that last bitter throw;
 For as the tree does fall, so lyes it ever low.

39. (2) **tyres:** clothes; (4) **could:** cold; (5) **seemely:** decently.
40. (3) **redeeme:** ransom; (3) **price:** payment; (4) **stayd:** enslaved;
  (5) **wayd:** considered; (7) **then that, why:** than that for which;
  (8) **with . . . stowre:** in a dire encounter.
41. (8) **throw:** pang, throe.

§ *he that harrowd hell*: The Harrowing of Hell names the tradition
according to which Christ descended into Limbo, or the first circle of
hell, to deliver the waiting, imperfect souls of the righteous who had
died before his advent. Christ's descent not only robbed Satan of
many semi-victims but also his very approach, according to Dante's
Divine Comedy ("Inferno", Canto XII), left the topography of hell
badly damaged.

42   The sixt had charge of them now being dead,
     In seemely sort their corses to engrave,
     And deck with dainty flowres their bridall bed,
     That to their heavenly spouse both sweet and brave
     They might appeare, when he their soules shall save.
     The wondrous workemanship of Gods owne mould,
     Whose face he made, all beasts to feare, and gave
     All in his hand, even dead we honour should.
  Ah dearest God me graunt, I dead be not defould.

43   The seventh now after death and buriall done,
     Had charge the tender Orphans of the dead
     And widowes ayd, least they should be undone:
     In face of judgement he their right would plead,
     Ne ought the powre of mighty men did dread
     In their defence, nor would for gold or fee
     Be wonne their rightfull causes downe to tread:
     And when they stood in most necessitee,
  He did supply their want, and gave them ever free.

44   There when the Elfin knight arrived was,
     The first and chiefest of the seven, whose care
     Was guests to welcome, towardes him did pas:
     Where seeing *Mercie*, that his steps up bare,
     And always led, to her with reverence rare
     He humbly louted in meeke lowlinesse,
     And seemely welcome for her did prepare:
     For of their order she was Patronesse,
  Albe *Charissa* were their chiefest founderesse.

42. (2) **engrave:** bury; (7-8) **gave/All . . . hand:** gave him charge over everything.
43. (7) **wonne:** persuaded, bribed.
44. (6) **louted:** bowed; (9) **Albe:** although.

45 There she awhile him stayes, him selfe to rest,
    That to the rest more able he might bee:
    During which time, in every good behest
    And godly worke of Almes and charitee
    She him instructed with great industree;
    Shortly therein so perfect he became,
    That from the first unto the last degree,
    His mortall life he learned had to frame
In holy righteousnesse, without rebuke or blame.

46 Thence forward by that painfull way they pas,
    Forth to an hill, that was both steepe and hy;
    On top whereof a sacred chappell was,
    And eke a litle Hermitage thereby,
    Wherein an aged holy man did lye,
    That day and night said his devotion,
    Ne other worldly busines did apply;
    His name was heavenly *Contemplation*;
Of God and goodnesse was his meditation.

47 Great grace that old man to him given had;
    For God he often saw from heavens hight,
    All were his earthly eyen both blunt and bad,
    And through great age had lost their kindly sight,
    Yet wondrous quick and persant was his spright,
    As Eagles eye, that can behold the Sunne:
    That hill they scale with all their powre and might,
    That his frayle thighes nigh wearie and fordonne
Gan faile, but by her helpe the top at last he wonne.

45. (1) **stayes:** detains; (2) **to the rest:** for what was still to follow.
47. (1) **given had:** had had given; (3) **All:** although; (4) **kindly:** natural, physical; (5) **persant:** sharp, discerning; (8) **fordonne:** exhausted.

48   There they do finde that godly aged Sire,
     With snowy lockes adowne his shoulders shed,
     As hoarie frost with spangles doth attire
     The mossy braunches of an Oke halfe ded.
     Each bone might through his body well be red,
     And every sinew seene through his long fast:
     For nought he car'd his carcas long unfed;
     His mind was full of spirituall repast,
And pyn'd his flesh, to keepe his body low and chast.

49   Who when these two approching he aspide,
     At their first presence grew agrieved sore,
     That forst him lay his heavenly thoughts aside;
     And had he not that Dame respected more,
     Whom highly he did reverence and adore,
     He would not once have moved for the knight.
     They him saluted standing far afore;
     Who well them greeting, humbly did requight,
And asked, to what end they clomb that tedious height.

50   What end (quoth she) should cause us take such paine,
     But that same end, which every living wight
     Should make his marke, high heaven to attaine?
     Is not from hence the way, that leadeth right
     To that most glorious house, that glistreth bright
     With burning starres, and everliving fire,
     Whereof the keyes are to thy hand behight
     By wise *Fidelia*? she doth thee require,
To shew it to this knight, according his desire.

48. (5) **well be red:** clearly seen; (6) **through:** as a result of; (9) **pyn'd:** starved; (9) **low:** in submission.
49. (4) **more:** (?) greatly (or) more than he resented the intrusion; (7) **far afore:** at some distance before him; (8) **requight:** return their salutation.
50. (7) **behight:** consigned, entrusted.

51   Thrise happy man, said then the father grave,
      Whose staggering steps thy steady hand doth lead,
      And shewes the way, his sinfull soule to save.
      Who better can the way to heaven aread,
      Then thou thy selfe, that was both borne and bred
      In heavenly throne, where thousand Angels shine?
      Thou doest the prayers of the righteous sead
      Present before the majestie divine,
   And his avenging wrath to clemencie incline.

52   Yet since thou bidst, thy pleasure shalbe donne.
      Then come thou man of earth, and see the way,
      That never yet was seene of Faeries sonne,
      That never leads the traveiler astray,
      But after labours long, and sad delay,
      Brings them to joyous rest and endlesse blis.
      But first thou must a season fast and pray,
      Till from her bands the spright assoiled is,
   And have her strength recur'd from fraile infirmitis.

53   That done, he leads him to the highest Mount;
      Such one, as that same mighty man of God,
      That bloud-red billowes like a walled front
      On either side disparted with his rod,
      Till that his army dry-foot through them yod,
      Dwelt fortie dayes upon; where writ in stone
      With bloudy letters by the hand of God,
      The bitter doome of death and balefull mone
   He did receive, whiles flashing fire about him shone.

51. (7) **righteous sead**: i.e., sons of righteousness, the chosen seed.
52. (2) **man of earth**: (both) ordinary mortal (and) ploughman, farmer (see Stanza 66); (8) **assoiled**: released, saved; (9) **recur'd**: restored.
53. (2) **man of God**: Moses; (5) **yod**: went; (8) **doome**: law; (8-9) **balefull . . . receive**: lamentable penalties of evil were delivered to him.

54   Or like that sacred hill, whose head full hie,
     Adornd with fruitfull Olives all arownd,
     Is, as it were for endlesse memory
     Of that deare Lord, who oft thereon was fownd,
     For ever with a flowring girlond crownd:
     Or like that pleasaunt Mount, that is for ay
     Through famous Poets verse each where renownd,
     On which the thrise three learned Ladies play
   Their heavenly notes, and make full many a lovely lay.

55   From thence, far off he unto him did shew
     A litle path, that was both steepe and long,
     Which to a goodly Citie led his vew;
     Whose wals and towres were builded high and strong
     Of perle and precious stone, that earthly tong
     Cannot describe, nor wit of man can tell;
     Too high a ditty for my simple song;
     The Citie of the great king hight it well,
   Wherein eternall peace and happinesse doth dwell.

56   As he thereon stood gazing, he might see
     The blessed Angels to and fro descend
     From highest heaven, in gladsome companee,
     And with great joy into that Citie wend,
     As commonly as friend does with his frend.
     Whereat he wondred much, and gan enquere,
     What stately building durst so high extend
     Her loftie towres unto the starry sphere,
   And what unknowen nation there empeopled were.

54. (1) **sacred hill:** Mount of Olives; (6) **Mount:** Parnassus; (7) **each where:** everywhere; (8) **thrise . . . Ladies:** the nine Muses; (9) **lay:** song.
55. (8) **hight it well:** it is well named.
56. (4) **wend:** go.

57   Faire knight (quoth he) *Hierusalem* that is,
     The new *Hierusalem*, that God has built
     For those to dwell in, that are chosen his,
     His chosen people purg'd from sinfull guilt,
     With pretious bloud, which cruelly was spilt
     On cursed tree, of that unspotted lam,
     That for the sinnes of all the world was kilt:
     Now are they Saints all in that Citie sam,
  More deare unto their God, then younglings to their
      dam.

58   Till now, said then the knight, I weened well,
     That great *Cleopolis*, where I have beene,   §
     In which that fairest *Faerie Queene* doth dwell,
     The fairest Citie was, that might be seene;
     And that bright towre all built of christall cleene,
     Panthea, seemd the brightest thing, that was:
     But now by proofe all otherwise I weene;
     For this great Citie that does far surpas,
  And this bright Angels towre quite dims that towre of
      glas.

59   Most trew, then said the holy aged man;
     Yet is *Cleopolis* for earthly frame,
     The fairest peece, that eye beholden can:
     And well beseemes all knights of noble name,
     That covet in th'immortall booke of fame
     To be eternized, that same to haunt,
     And doen their service to that soveraigne Dame,
     That glorie does to them for guerdon graunt:
  For she is heavenly borne, and heaven may justly vaunt.

57. (1) **Hierusalem:** Jerusalem; (8) **sam:** together; (9) **dam:**
mother.
58. (1) **weened well:** truly supposed.
59. (2) **for earthly frame:** as far as earthly constructions go;
(6) **haunt:** frequent; (9) **heaven . . . vaunt:** may justly boast
of being heavenly.

§ *Cleopolis*: As far as this is a compliment to the historical Queen
Elizabeth and her capital city, Cleopolis is London. *Panthea* has been
editorially linked to several possible structures including Westminster
Abbey, Greenwich Palace, Windsor Castle, and Richmond Castle.

60   And thou faire ymp, sprong out from English race,
      How ever now accompted Elfins sonne,
      Well worthy doest thy service for her grace,
      To aide a virgin desolate foredonne.
      But when thou famous victorie hast wonne,
      And high emongst all knights hast hong thy shield,
      Thenceforth the suit of earthly conquest shonne,
      And wash thy hands from guilt of bloudy field:
  For bloud can nought but sin, and wars but sorrowes
      yield.

61   Then seeke this path, that I to thee presage,
      Which after all to heaven shall thee send;
      Then peaceably thy painefull pilgrimage
      To yonder same *Hierusalem* do bend,
      Where is for thee ordaind a blessed end:
      For thou emongst those Saints, whom thou doest see,
      Shalt be a Saint, and thine owne nations frend
      And Patrone: thou Saint *George* shalt called bee,
  Saint *George* of mery England, the signe of victoree.

62   Unworthy wretch (quoth he) of so great grace,
      How dare I thinke such glory to attaine?
      These that have it attaind, were in like cace
      (Quoth he) as wretched, and liv'd in like paine.
      But deeds of armes must I at last be faine,
      And Ladies love to leave so dearely bought?
      What need of armes, where peace doth ay remaine,
      (Said he) and battailes none are to be fought?
  As for loose loves are vaine, and vanish into nought.

60. (2) **accompted:** considered to be; (4) **foredonne:** in extremity;
     (7) **suit:** pursuit; (7) **shonne:** avoid, abandon.
61. (1) **presage:** point out.
62. (5) **faine . . . to leave:** obliged (or) content to relinquish
     (deeds of arms) and my lady's love.

63   O let me not (quoth he) then turne againe
  Backe to the world, whose joyes so fruitlesse are;
  But let me here for aye in peace remaine,
  Or streight way on that last long voyage fare,
  That nothing may my present hope empare.
  That may not be (said he) ne maist thou yit
  Forgo that royall maides bequeathed care,
  Who did her cause into thy hand commit,
Till from her cursed foe thou have her freely quit.

64   Then shall I soone, (quoth he) so God me grace,
  Abet that virgins cause disconsolate,
  And shortly backe returne unto this place,
  To walke this way in Pilgrims poore estate.
  But now aread, old father, why of late
  Didst thou behight me borne of English blood,
  Whom all a Faeries sonne doen nominate?
  That word shall I (said he) avouchen good,
Sith to thee is unknowne the cradle of thy brood.

65   For well I wote, thou springst from ancient race
  Of *Saxon* kings, that have with mightie hand
  And many bloudie battailes fought in place
  High reard their royall throne in *Britane* land,
  And vanquisht them, unable to withstand:
  From thence a Faerie thee unweeting reft,
  There as thou slepst in tender swadling band,
  And her base Elfin brood there for thee left.
Such men do Chaungelings call, so chaungd by Faeries
   theft.

63. (5) **empare:** spoil; (7) **care:** charge, commission; (9) **quit:** released.
64. (4) **poore estate:** humble condition; (6) **behight:** pronounce; (7) **nominate:** call; (8) **avouchen good:** make good.
65. (5) **vanquisht them:** i.e., the Britons; (6) **thee unweeting:** you all unaware; (8) **brood:** offspring; (9) **chaungd:** exchanged.

66 Thence she thee brought into this Faerie lond,
  And in an heaped furrow did thee hyde,
  Where thee a Ploughman all unweeting fond,
  As he his toylesome teme that way did guyde,
  And brought thee up in ploughmans state to byde,
  Whereof *Georgos* he thee gave to name;
  Till prickt with courage, and thy forces pryde,
  To Faery court thou cam'st to seeke for fame,
 And prove thy puissaunt armes, as seemes thee best
   became.

67 O holy Sire (quoth he) how shall I quight
  The many favours I with thee have found,
  That hast my name and nation red aright,
  And taught the way that does to heaven bound?
  This said, adowne he looked to the ground,
  To have returnd, but dazed were his eyne,
  Through passing brightnesse, which did quite confound
  His feeble sence, and too exceeding shyne.
 So darke are earthly things compard to things divine.

68 At last whenas himselfe he gan to find,
  To *Una* back he cast him to retire;
  Who him awaited still with pensive mind.
  Great thankes and goodly meed to that good syre,
  He thence departing gave for his paines hyre.
  So came to *Una*, who him joyd to see,
  And after litle rest, gan him desire,
  Of her adventure mindfull for to bee.
 So leave they take of *Cælia*, and her daughters three.

66. (3) **fond:** came across; (6) **thee . . . name:** named you; (7) **prickt with:** spurred by; (7) **forces pryde:** pride of strength; (9) **as seemes . . . became:** as, it now seems, was the most fitting course for you to have taken.
67. (3) **red:** named, identified; (7) **passing:** surpassing.
68. (1) **himselfe . . . find:** began to come to himself; (2) **cast . . . retire:** resolved to turn; (4) **meed:** reward; (5) **for . . . hyre:** as recompense for the trouble he had taken.

Canto XI

> The knight with that old Dragon fights
>   two dayes incessantly:
> The third him overthrowes, and gayns
>   most glorious victory.

1   High time now gan it wex for *Una* faire,
      To thinke of those her captive Parents deare,
    And their forwasted kingdome to repaire:
    Whereto whenas they now approched neare,
    With hartie words her knight she gan to cheare,
    And in her modest manner thus bespake;
    Deare knight, as deare, as ever knight was deare,
    That all these sorrowes suffer for my sake,
  High heaven behold the tedious toyle, ye for me take.

2   Now are we come unto my native soyle,
      And to the place, where all our perils dwell;
    Here haunts that feend, and does his dayly spoyle,
    Therefore henceforth be at your keeping well,
    And ever ready for your foeman fell.
    The sparke of noble courage now awake,
    And strive your excellent selfe to excell;
    That shall ye evermore renowmed make,
  Above all knights on earth, that batteill undertake.

1. (3) **forwasted:** desolated; (5) **cheare:** encourage; (9) **High . . . behold:** may high heaven watch and note.
2. (3) **does his . . . spoyle:** wreaks his daily ravage; (4) **be at . . . well:** be very much on your guard.

3   And pointing forth, lo yonder is (said she)
      The brasen towre in which my parents deare
      For dread of that huge feend emprisond be,
      Whom I from far see on the walles appeare,
      Whose sight my feeble soule doth greatly cheare:
      And on the top of all I do espye
      The watchman wayting tydings glad to heare,
      That O my parents might I happily
Unto you bring, to ease you of your misery.

4   With that they heard a roaring hideous sound,
      That all the ayre with terrour filled wide,
      And seemd uneath to shake the stedfast ground.
      Eftsoones that dreadfull Dragon they espide,
      Where stretcht he lay upon the sunny side
      Of a great hill, himselfe like a great hill.
      But all so soone, as he from far descride
      Those glistring armes, that heaven with light did fill,
He rousd himselfe full blith, and hastned them untill.

5   Then bad the knight his Lady yede aloofe,
      And to an hill her selfe with draw aside,
      From whence she might behold that battailles proof
      And eke be safe from daunger far descryde:
      She him obayd, and turnd a little wyde.
      Now O thou sacred Muse, most learned Dame,   §
      Faire ympe of *Phœbus*, and his aged bride,
      The Nourse of time, and everlasting fame,
That warlike hands ennoblest with immortall name;

3. (8) **That:** i.e., which (tidings).
4. (3) **uneath:** uneasily (i.e., into uneasy tremors); (7) **But all so:** but as; (7) **descride:** spotted; (9) **blith:** gladly; (9) **untill:** towards.
5. (1) **yede aloofe:** move some way off; (5) **wyde:** aside, away.

§ *O thou sacred Muse*: Probably Calliope, Muse of epic poetry, but perhaps Clio, Muse of history. Calliope and Clio seem to be co-presidents over *The Faerie Queene*, though the case has been strongly put both for the one and for the other as Spenser's senior, presiding Muse throughout the poem. (See vol. I, pp. 506-15, of the Variorum edition of Spenser's works.) *his aged bride*: Mnemosyne (Memory); Spenser more than once gives Phoebus Apollo as the father of the Muses, though in classical mythology Zeus (Jove) is given as their father and Apollo as their leader.

6   O gently come into my feeble brest,
      Come gently, but not with that mighty rage,
      Wherewith the martiall troupes thou doest infest,
      And harts of great Heroës doest enrage,
      That nought their kindled courage may aswage,
      Soone as thy dreadfull trompe begins to sownd:
      The God of warre with his fiers equipage
      Thou doest awake, sleepe never he so sownd,
  And scared nations doest with horrour sterne astownd.

7   Faire Goddesse lay that furious fit aside,
      Till I of warres and bloudy *Mars* do sing,
      And Briton fields with Sarazin bloud bedyde,
      Twixt that great faery Queene and Paynim king,
      That with their horrour heaven and earth did ring,
      A worke of labour long, and endlesse prayse:
      But now a while let downe that haughtie string,
      And to my tunes thy second tenor rayse,
  That I this man of God his godly armes may blaze.

8   By this the dreadfull Beast drew nigh to hand,
      Halfe flying, and halfe footing in his hast,
      That with his largenesse measured much land,
      And made wide shadow under his huge wast;
      As mountaine doth the valley overcast.
      Approching nigh, he reared high afore
      His body monstrous, horrible, and vast,
      Which to increase his wondrous greatnesse more,
  Was swolne with wrath, and poyson, and with bloudy
        gore.

6. (2) **rage:** frenzy, fury of inspiration; (3) **infest:** seize, assail;
    (5) **aswage:** cool, dampen; (7) **equipage:** retinue.
7. (7) **haughtie string:** high strain (of song); (8) **second tenor:**
    i.e., secondary strain; (9) **armes:** feats of arms; (9) **blaze:**
    celebrate.
8. (4) **wast:** bulk (literally, waist); (6) **afore:** in front.

9   And over, all with brasen scales was armd,
        Like plated coate of steele, so couched neare,
        That nought mote perce, ne might his corse be harmd
        With dint of sword, nor push of pointed speare;
        Which as an Eagle, seeing pray appeare,
        His aery plumes doth rouze, full rudely dight,
        So shaked he, that horrour was to heare,
        For as the clashing of an Armour bright,
    Such noyse his rouzed scales did send unto the knight.

10   His flaggy wings when forth he did display,
        Were like two sayles, in which the hollow wynd
        Is gathered full, and worketh speedy way:
        And eke the pennes, that did his pineons bynd,
        Were like mayne-yards, with flying canvas lynd,
        With which whenas him list the ayre to beat,
        And there by force unwonted passage find,
        The cloudes before him fled for terrour great,
    And all the heavens stood still amazed with his threat.

11   His huge long tayle wound up in hundred foldes,
        Does overspred his long bras-scaly backe,
        Whose wreathed boughts when ever he unfoldes,
        And thicke entangled knots adown does slacke,
        Bespotted as with shields of red and blacke,
        It sweepeth all the land behind him farre,
        And of three furlongs does but litle lacke;
        And at the point two stings in-fixed arre,
    Both deadly sharpe, that sharpest steele exceeden farre.

9. (2) **so couched neare:** so closely articulated; (6) **rouze:** ruffle;
    (6) **full . . . dight:** angrily arrayed; (9) **rouzed:** bristled.
10. (1) **flaggy:** folded, tucked; (4) **pennes:** long-feathers, main or
    pinion feathers.
11. (3) **boughts:** coils.

12   But stings and sharpest steele did far exceed
      The sharpnesse of his cruell rending clawes;
      Dead was it sure, as sure as death in deed,
      What ever thing does touch his ravenous pawes,
      Or what within his reach he ever drawes.
      But his most hideous head my toung to tell,
      Does tremble: for his deepe devouring jawes
      Wide gaped, like the griesly mouth of hell,
  Through which into his darke abisse all ravin fell.

13   And that more wondrous was, in either jaw
      Threeranckes of yron teeth enraunged were,
      In which yet trickling bloud and gobbets raw
      Of late devoured bodies did appeare,
      That sight thereof bred cold congealed feare:
      Which to increase, and all atonce to kill,
      A cloud of smoothering smoke and sulphur seare
      Out of his stinking gorge forth steemed still,
  That all the ayre about with smoke and stench did fill.

14   His blazing eyes, like two bright shining shields,
      Did burne with wrath, and sparkled living fyre;
      As two broad Beacons, set in open fields,
      Send forth their flames farre off to every shyre,
      And warning give, that enemies conspyre,
      With fire and sword the region to invade;
      So flam'd his eyne with rage and rancorous yre:
      But farre within, as in a hollow glade,
  Those glaring lampes were set, that made a dreadfull
      shade.

12. (1-2) **did far exceed . . . clawes:** i.e., But the sharpness of
his . . . claws far exceeded; (9) **ravin:** prey.
13. (7) **seare:** searing.

15   So dreadfully he towards him did pas,
  Forelifting up aloft his speckled brest,
  And often bounding on the brused gras,
  As for great joyance of his newcome guest.
  Eftsoones he gan advance his haughtie crest,
  As chauffed Bore his bristles doth upreare,
  And shoke his scales to battell readie drest;
  That made the *Redcrosse* knight nigh quake for feare,
As bidding bold defiance to his foeman neare.

16   The knight gan fairely couch his steadie speare,
  And fiercely ran at him with rigorous might:
  The pointed steele arriving rudely theare,
  His harder hide would neither perce, nor bight,
  But glauncing by forth passed forward right;
  Yet sore amoved with so puissant push,
  The wrathfull beast about him turned light,
  And him so rudely passing by, did brush
With his long tayle, that horse and man to ground did
  rush.

17   Both horse and man up lightly rose againe,
  And fresh encounter towards him addrest:
  But th'idle stroke yet backe recoyld in vaine,
  And found no place his deadly point to rest.
  Exceeding rage enflam'd the furious beast,
  To be avenged of so great despight;
  For never felt his imperceable brest
  So wondrous force, from hand of living wight;
Yet had he prov'd the powre of many a puissant knight.

15. (6) **chauffed:** enraged, harried; (7) **drest:** disposed.
16. (1) **gan:** did; (7) **light:** quickly.
17. (1) **lightly:** nimbly; (3) **th'idle:** the useless; (9) **prov'd:** tested, experienced.

18 Then with his waving wings displayed wyde,
        Himselfe up high he lifted from the ground,
        And with strong flight did forcibly divide
        The yielding aire, which nigh too feeble found
        Her flitting partes, and element unsound,
        To beare so great a weight: he cutting way
        With his broad sayles, about him soared round:
        At last low stouping with unweldie sway,
    Snatcht up both horse and man, to beare them quite
        away.

19 Long he them bore above the subject plaine,
        So farre as Ewghen bow a shaft may send,
        Till struggling strong did him at last constraine,
        To let them downe before his flightes end:
        As hagard hauke presuming to contend
        With hardie fowle, above his hable might,
        His wearie pounces all in vaine doth spend,
        To trusse the pray too heavie for his flight;
    Which comming downe to ground, does free it selfe by
        fight.

20 He so disseized of his gryping grosse,
        The knight his thrillant speare againe assayd
        In his bras-plated body to embosse,
        And three mens strength unto the stroke he layd;
        Wherewith the stiffe beame quaked, as affrayd,
        And glauncing from his scaly necke, did glyde
        Close under his left wing, then broad displayd.
        The percing steele there wrought a wound full wyde,
    That with the uncouth smart the Monster lowdly cryde.

18. (5) **partes**: qualities; (5) **unsound**: yielding; (8) **stouping**: swooping (as of falcons); (8) **sway**: pass, attack.
19. (1) **subject plaine**: the plain below; (2) **Ewghen**: of yew; (5) **hagard**: wild, untrained; (6) **above . . . might**: (that is) more than he can manage; (7) **pounces**: talons; (8) **trusse**: pierce and grip into a manageable bundle.
20. (1) **He so . . . grosse**: He (i.e., the dragon) having thus lost his formidable grip; (3) **embosse**: plunge; (5) **beame**: spear-shaft; (9) **uncouth smart**: unaccustomed pain.

21   He cryde, as raging seas are wont to rore,
     When wintry storme his wrathfull wreck does threat,
     The rolling billowes beat the ragged shore,
     As they the earth would shoulder from her seat,
     And greedie gulfe does gape, as he would eat
     His neighbour element in his revenge:
     Then gin the blustring brethren boldly threat,
     To move the world from off his stedfast henge,
   And boystrous battell make, each other to avenge.

22   The steely head stucke fast still in his flesh,
     Till with his cruell clawes he snatcht the wood,
     And quite a sunder broke. Forth flowed fresh
     A gushing river of blacke goarie blood,
     That drowned all the land, whereon he stood;
     The streame thereof would drive a water-mill.
     Trebly augmented was his furious mood
     With bitter sense of his deepe rooted ill,
   That flames of fire he threw forth from his large
         nosethrill.

23   His hideous tayle then hurled he about,
     And therewith all enwrapt the nimble thyes
     Of his froth-fomy steed, whose courage stout
     Striving to loose the knot, that fast him tyes,
     Himselfe in streighter bandes too rash implyes,
     That to the ground he is perforce constraynd
     To throw his rider: who can quickly ryse
     From off the earth, with durty bloud distaynd,
   For that reprochfull fall right fowly he disdaynd.

21. (4) **shoulder:** dislodge; (6) **neighbour element:** i.e., the land;
(7) **brethren:** i.e., the winds; (8) **henge:** axis.
22. (8) **deepe rooted ill:** i.e., the deeply embedded spearhead; (9)
nosethrill: nostril.
23. (5) **rash implyes:** rashly entangles; (7) **can:** did; (8) **distaynd:**
stained.

24 And fiercely tooke his trenchand blade in hand,
  With which he stroke so furious and so fell,
  That nothing seemd the puissance could withstand:
  Upon his crest the hardned yron fell,
  But his more hardned crest was armd so well,
  That deeper dint therein it would not make;
  Yet so extremely did the buffe him quell;
  That from thenceforth he shund the like to take,
But when he saw them come, he did them still forsake.

25 The knight was wrath to see his stroke beguyld,
  And smote againe with more outrageous might;
  But backe againe the sparckling steele recoyld,
  And left not any marke, where it did light;
  As if in Adamant rocke it had bene pight.
  The beast impatient of his smarting wound,
  And of so fierce and forcible despight,
  Thought with his wings to stye above the ground;
But his late wounded wing unserviceable found.

26 Then full of griefe and anguish vehement,
  He lowdly brayd, that like was never heard,
  And from his wide devouring oven sent
  A flake of fire, that flashing in his beard,
  Him all amazd, and almost made affeard:
  The scorching flame sore swinged all his face,
  And through his armour all his bodie seard,
  That he could not endure so cruell cace,
But thought his armes to leave, and helmet to unlace.

25. (1) **beguyld:** foiled; (5) **pight:** set (or) struck (against); (8) **stye:** mount.
26. (3) **oven:** i.e., throat; (4) **flake:** flame; (6) **swinged:** singed.

27   Not that great Champion of the antique world,   §
     Whom famous Poetes verse so much doth vaunt,
     And hath for twelve huge labours high extold,
     So many furies and sharpe fits did haunt,
     When him the poysoned garment did enchaunt
     With *Centaures* bloud, and bloudie verses charm'd,
     As did this knight twelve thousand dolours daunt,
     Whom fyrie steele now burnt, that earst him arm'd,
That erst him goodly arm'd, now most of all him harm'd.

28   Faint, wearie, sore, emboyled, grieved, brent
     With heat, toyle, wounds, armes, smart, and inward
        fire
     That never man such mischiefes did torment;
     Death better were, death did he oft desire,
     But death will never come, when needes require.
     Whom so dismayd when that his foe beheld,
     He cast to suffer him no more respire,
     But gan his sturdie sterne about to weld,
And him so strongly stroke, that to the ground him feld.

29   It fortuned (as faire it then befell)
     Behind his backe unweeting, where he stood,
     Of auncient time there was a springing well,
     From which fast trickled forth a silver flood,
     Full of great vertues, and for med'cine good.
     Whylome, before that cursed Dragon got
     That happie land, and all with innocent blood
     Defyld those sacred waves, it rightly hot
The well of life, ne yet his vertues had forgot.

27. (1) **Champion**: Herakles (Hercules).
28. (1) **emboyled**: perturbed; (1) **brent**: burnt; (7) **cast to suffer him**: determined to allow him; (8) **weld**: swing, flail.
29. (1) **faire**: happily; (6) **Whylome**: formerly; (8) **rightly hot**: was rightly called; (9) **ne yet his**: nor yet its.

§ *great Champion*: Herakles (Hercules) killed the centaur Nessus for trying to run off with Herakles' new bride Deianeira. Just before he died Nessus told Deianeira to keep some of his blood as a love-charm; should Herakles' affection for her cool, she was to smear one of his garments with it and thus win his affection back. But some years later, when she did so smear a shirt and send it to

30   For unto life the dead it could restore,
      And guilt of sinfull crimes cleane wash away,
      Those that with sicknesse were infected sore,
      It could recure, and aged long decay
      Renew, as one were borne that very day.
      Both *Silo* this, and *Jordan* did excell,   §
      And th'English *Bath*, and eke the german *Spau*,
      Ne can *Cephise*, nor *Hebrus* match this well:
  Into the same the knight backe overthrown, fell.

31   Now gan the golden *Phœbus* for to steepe
      His fierie face in billowes of the west,
      And his faint steedes watred in Ocean deepe,
      Whiles from their journall labours they did rest,
      When that infernall Monster, having kest
      His wearie foe into that living well,
      Can high advance his broad discoloured brest,
      Above his wonted pitch, with countenance fell,
  And clapt his yron wings, as victor he did dwell.

32   Which when his pensive Ladie saw from farre,
      Great woe and sorrow did her soule assay,
      As weening that the sad end of the warre,
      And gan to highest God entirely pray,
      That feared chance from her to turne away;
      With folded hands and knees full lowly bent
      All night she watcht, ne once adowne would lay
      Her daintie limbs in her sad dreriment,
  But praying still did wake, and waking did lament.

31. (4) **journall:** daily; (5) **kest:** flung; (7) **discoloured:** many-coloured; (9) **as:** as if.
32. (4) **entirely:** whole-heartedly; (8) **dreriment:** dismay.

Herakles, the blood of Nessus turned out to be a fiery poison and once Herakles had put on the poisoned shirt he could not tear it off. Being half divine, he could not be killed outright by the poison, and so ended his agony by jumping onto a funeral pyre from where his immortal part was taken to live among the gods of Olympus.
§ *Silo*: The pool of Siloam (see John 9:7). *Jordon*: The river Jordan, in whose waters the leper Naaman was cleansed (see II King 5:1-14). *Cephise*: The river Cephissus in Boeotia and the *Hebrus* in Thrace were both famous for their beautiful and beneficial, if not actually healing, waters.

33 The morrow next gan early to appeare,
     That *Titan* rose to runne his daily race;   §
     But early ere the morrow next gan reare
     Out of the sea faire *Titans* deawy face,
     Up rose the gentle virgin from her place,
     And looked all about, if she might spy
     Her loved knight to move his manly pace:
     For she had great doubt of his safety,
  Since late she saw him fall before his enemy.

34 At last she saw, where he upstarted brave
     Out of the well, wherein he drenched lay;
     As Eagle fresh out of the Ocean wave,   §
     Where he hath left his plumes all hoary gray,
     And deckt himselfe with feathers youthly gay,
     Like Eyas hauke up mounts unto the skies,
     His newly budded pineons to assay,
     And marveiles at himselfe, still as he flies:
  So new this new-borne knight to battell new did rise.

35 Whom when the damned feend so fresh did spy,
     No wonder if he wondred at the sight,
     And doubted, whether his late enemy
     It were, or other new supplied knight.
     He, now to prove his late renewed might,
     High brandishing his bright deaw-burning blade,
     Upon his crested scalpe so sore did smite,
     That to the scull a yawning wound it made:
  The deadly dint his dulled senses all dismaid.

34. (6) **Eyas hauke:** newly fledged hawk.
35. (6) **deaw-burning:** dew-bright.

§ *Titan*: One of Spenser's names for the sun. Usually Titan is a family
name; i.e., there are twelve Titans, six brothers and six sisters, the
children of Uranus and Gaia. One pair of Titans, Hyperion and Thea,
are anciently given as the parents of Helios, the sun.
§ *As Eagle fresh*: "And it is a true fact that when the eagle grows old
and his wings become heavy and his eyes become darkened with a
mist, then he goes in search of a fountain, and, over against it, he
flies up to the heights of heaven, even unto the circle of the sun;
and there he singes his wings and at the same time evaporates the
fog of his eyes, in a ray of the sun. Then, at length, taking a header

36 I wote not, whether the revenging steele
  Were hardned with that holy water dew,
  Wherein he fell, or sharper edge did feele,
  Or his baptized hands now greater grew;
  Or other secret vertue did ensew;
  Else never could the force of fleshly arme,
  Ne molten mettall in his bloud embrew:
  For till that stownd could never wight him harme,
 By subtilty, nor slight, nor might, nor mighty charme.

37 The cruell wound enraged him so sore,
  That loud he yelded for exceeding paine;
  As hundred ramping Lyons seem'd to rore,
  Whom ravenous hunger did thereto constraine:
  Then gan he tosse aloft his stretched traine,
  And therewith scourge the buxome aire so sore,
  That to his force to yeelden it was faine;
  Ne ought his sturdie strokes might stand afore,
 That high trees overthrew, and rocks in peeces tore.

38 The same advauncing high above his head,
  With sharpe intended sting so rude him smot,
  That to the earth him drove, as stricken dead,
  Ne living wight would have him life behot:
  The mortall sting his angry needle shot
  Quite through his shield, and in his shoulder seasd,
  Where fast it stucke, ne would there out be got:
  The griefe thereof him wondrous sore diseasd,
 Ne might his ranckling paine with patience be appeasd.

36. (2) **dew**: true, fitting (in function and effect); (7) **embrew**: dip, plunge.
37. (2) **yelded**: yelled; (6) **buxome**: yielding.
38. (1) **The same**: i.e., his tail; (2) **intended**: extended; (4) **him life behot**: given anything for his chances; (6) **seasd**: lodged; (8) **diseasd**: afflicted.

down into the fountain, he dips himself three times in it, and instantly he is renewed with a great vigour of plumage and splendour of vision." (From T. H. White's translation of *The Bestiary*).

39 But yet more mindfull of his honour deare,
  Then of the grievous smart, which him did wring,
  From loathed soile he can him lightly reare,
  And strove to loose the farre infixed sting:
  Which when in vaine he tryde with struggeling,
  Inflam'd with wrath, his raging blade he heft,
  And strooke so strongly, that the knotty string
  Of his huge taile he quite a sunder cleft,
 Five joynts thereof he hewd, and but the stump him left.

40 Hart cannot thinke, what outrage, and what cryes,
  With foule enfouldred smoake and flashing fire,
  The hell-bred beast threw forth unto the skyes,
  That all was covered with darknesse dire:
  Then fraught with rancour, and engorged ire,
  He cast at once him to avenge for all,
  And gathering up himselfe out of the mire,
  With his uneven wings did fiercely fall,
 Upon his sunne-bright shield, and gript it fast withall.

41 Much was the man encombred with his hold,
  In feare to lose his weapon in his paw,
  Ne wist yet, how his talants to unfold;
  Nor harder was from *Cerberus* greedie jaw §
  To plucke a bone, then from his cruell claw
  To reave by strength the griped gage away:
  Thrise he assayd it from his foot to draw,
  And thrise in vaine to draw it did assay,
 It booted nought to thinke, to robbe him of his pray.

39. (3) **lightly:** nimbly.
40. (2) **enfouldred:** black as a thundercloud.
41. (3) **talants:** talons; (3) **unfold:** break the grip of; (6) **reave:**
take; (6) **griped:** fast-gripped; (6) **gage:** pledge (i.e., the
shield).

§ *Cerberus*: The three-headed hell-hound who guards the entrance ways
to the underworld.

42   Tho when he saw no power might prevaile,
          His trustie sword he cald to his last aid,
          Wherewith he fiercely did his foe assaile,
          And double blowes about him stoutly laid,
          That glauncing fire out of the yron plaid;
          As sparckles from the Andvile use to fly,
          When heavie hammers on the wedge are swaid;
          Therewith at last he forst him to unty
      One of his grasping feete, him to defend thereby.

43   The other foot, fast fixed on his shield,
          Whenas no strength, nor stroks mote him constraine
          To loose, ne yet the warlike pledge to yield,
          He smot thereat with all his might and maine,
          That nought so wondrous puissance might sustaine;
          Upon the joynt the lucky steele did light,
          And made such way, that hewd it quite in twaine;
          The paw yet missed not his minisht might,
      But hong still on the shield, as it at first was pight.

44   For griefe thereof, and divelish despight,
          From his infernall fournace forth he threw
          Huge flames, that dimmed all the heavens light,
          Enrold in duskish smoke and brimstone blew;
          As burning *Aetna* from his boyling stew
          Doth belch out flames, and rockes in peeces broke,
          And ragged ribs of mountaines molten new,
          Enwrapt in coleblacke clouds and filthy smoke,
      That all the land with stench, and heaven with horror
          choke.

42. (7) **swaid:** struck; (9) **him to defend:** to defend himself.
43. (8) **minisht:** diminished; (8-9) **missed not . . . on the shield:**
      i.e., the talon still gripped the shield as if unaware it had been
      severed.
44. (4) **Enrold:** enveloped.

45   The heate whereof, and harmefull pestilence
         So sore him noyd, that forst him to retire
         A little backward for his best defence,
         To save his bodie from the scorching fire,
         Which he from hellish entrailes did expire.
         It chaunst (eternall God that chaunce did guide)
         As he recoyled backward, in the mire
         His nigh forwearied feeble feet did slide,
      And downe he fell, with dread of shame sore terrifide.

46   There grew a goodly tree him faire beside,
         Loaden with fruit and apples rosie red,
         As they in pure vermilion had beene dide,
         Whereof great vertues over all were red:
         For happie life to all, which thereon fed,
         And life eke everlasting did befall:
         Great God it planted in that blessed sted
         With his almightie hand, and did it call
      The tree of life, the crime of our first fathers fall.   §

47   In all the world like was not to be found,
         Save in that soile, where all good things did grow,
         And freely sprong out of the fruitfull ground,
         As incorrupted Nature did them sow,
         Till that dread Dragon all did overthrow.
         Another like faire tree eke grew thereby,
         Whereof who so did eat, eftsoones did know
         Both good and ill: O mornefull memory:
      That tree through one mans fault hath doen us all to dy.

45. (5) **expire:** exhale; (8) **forwearied:** exhausted.
46. (4) **over all:** everywhere; (4) **red:** declared; (7) **sted:** spot.
47. (9) **doen:** caused.

§ *the crime of our first fathers fall*: Here *the crime* means "the cause
at issue" in a legal sense. There were two special trees in Eden (see the
next stanza and also Genesis 2:9). After Adam and Eve had exercised
their power of choice in disobedience and had eaten of the tree of
the knowledge of good and evil, the cause at issue became whether
or not they should be allowed to remain in Eden to eat of the second
tree – the tree of life – and so live forever. In this sense the second
tree became the cause which issued in their expulsion from Eden.

48 From that first tree forth flowd, as from a well,
  A trickling streame of Balme, most soveraine
  And daintie deare, which on the ground still fell,
  And overflowed all the fertill plaine,
  As it had deawed bene with timely raine:
  Life and long health that gratious ointment gave,
  And deadly woundes could heale, and reare again
  The senselesse corse appointed for the grave.
Into that same he fell: which did from death him save.

49 For nigh thereto the ever damned beast
  Durst not approch, for he was deadly made,
  And all that life preserved, did detest:
  Yet he it oft adventur'd to invade.
  By this the drouping day-light gan to fade,
  And yeeld his roome to sad succeeding night,
  Who with her sable mantle gan to shade
  The face of earth, and wayes of living wight,
And high her burning torch set up in heaven bright.

50 When gentle *Una* saw the second fall
  Of her deare knight, who wearie of long fight,
  And faint through losse of bloud, mov'd not at all,
  But lay as in a dreame of deepe delight,
  Besmeard with pretious Balme, whose vertuous might
  Did heale his wounds, and scorching heat alay,
  Againe she stricken was with sore affright,
  And for his safetie gan devoutly pray;
And watch the noyous night, and wait for joyous day.

48. (3) **daintie deare:** choicely precious.
49. (2) **deadly:** for death; (4) **invade:** attack.
50. (9) **noyous:** harmful, troublesome.

51 The joyous day gan early to appeare,
  And faire *Aurora* from the deawy bed   §
  Of aged *Tithone* gan her selfe to reare,
  With rosie cheekes, for shame as blushing red;
  Her golden lockes for haste were loosely shed
  About her eares, when *Una* her did marke
  Clymbe to her charet, all with flowers spred,
  From heaven high to chase the chearelesse darke;
With merry note her loud salutes the mounting larke.

52 Then freshly up arose the doughtie knight,
  All healed of his hurts and woundes wide,
  And did himselfe to battell readie dight;
  Whose early foe awaiting him beside
  To have devourd, so soone as day he spyde,
  When now he saw himselfe so freshly reare,
  As if late fight had nought him damnifyde,
  He woxe dismayd, and gan his fate to feare;
Nathlesse with wonted rage he him advaunced neare.

53 And in his first encounter, gaping wide,
  He thought attonce him to have swallowd quight,
  And rusht upon him with outragious pride;
  Who him r'encountring fierce, as hauke in flight,
  Perforce rebutted backe. The weapon bright
  Taking advantage of his open jaw,
  Ran through his mouth with so importune might,
  That deepe emperst his darksome hollow maw,
And back retyrd, his life bloud forth with all did draw.

51. (7) **charet:** chariot.
52. (3) **dight:** make; (6) **himselfe:** i.e., the knight; (7) **damnifyde:** damaged, hurt; (9) **wonted:** (his) usual.
53. (4) **r'encountring:** engaging, counter-attacking; (5) **Perforce:** brusquely, forcefully; (7) **so importune:** such irresistible; (9) **back retyrd:** being drawn back out.

§ *Aurora*: Eos, the dawn-goddess, mother of the Morning Star, the Evening Star, the Planets, and the Four Winds, who fell in love with the Trojan prince *Tithone* (Tithonus). At her request her uncle Zeus granted Tithonus immortality. But since she had forgotten also to request eternal youth for Tithonus, he declined into old age and just went on getting older and older – hence the stock epithet "*aged*".

54   So downe he fell, and forth his life did breath,
     That vanisht into smoke and cloudes swift;
     So downe he fell, that th'earth him underneath
     Did grone, as feeble so great load to lift;
     So downe he fell, as an huge rockie clift,
     Whose false foundation waves have washt away,
     With dreadfull poyse is from the mayneland rift,
     And rolling downe, great *Neptune* doth dismay;
  So downe he fell, and like an heaped mountaine lay.

55   The knight himselfe even trembled at his fall,
     So huge and horrible a masse it seem'd;
     And his deare Ladie, that beheld it all,
     Durst not approch for dread, which she misdeem'd,
     But yet at last, when as the direfull feend
     She saw not stirre, off-shaking vaine affright,
     She nigher drew, and saw that joyous end:
     Then God she praysd, and thankt her faithfull knight,
  That had atchiev'd so great a conquest by his might.

54. (7) **poyse:** pull of force.
55. (4) **which she misdeem'd:** in which dread she made a misjudgment (i.e., was afraid that the dragon might not be really
dead).

Canto XII

Faire Una to the Redcrosse knight
betrouthed is with joy:
Though false Duessa it to barre
her false sleights doe imploy.

1 Behold I see the haven nigh at hand,
      To which I meane my wearie course to bend;
      Vere the maine shete, and beare up with the land,
      The which afore is fairely to be kend,
      And seemeth safe from stormes, that may offend;
      There this faire virgin wearie of her way
      Must landed be, now at her journeyes end:
      There eke my feeble barke a while may stay,
   Till merry wind and weather call her thence away.

2 Scarsely had *Phœbus* in the glooming East
      Yet harnessed his firie-footed teeme,
      Ne reard above the earth his flaming creast,
      When the last deadly smoke aloft did steeme,
      That signe of last outbreathed life did seeme,
      Unto the watchman on the castle wall;
      Who thereby dead that balefull Beast did deeme,
      And to his Lord and Ladie lowd gan call,
   To tell, how he had seene the Dragons fatall fall.

1. (3) **Vere . . . shete:** adjust the mainsail; (4) **to be kend:** in view; (8) **barke:** ship.
2. (7) **dead . . . deeme:** took . . . to be dead.

3 Uprose with hastie joy, and feeble speed
  That aged Sire, the Lord of all that land,
  And looked forth, to weet, if true indeede
  Those tydings were, as he did understand,
  Which whenas true by tryall he out fond,
  He bad to open wyde his brazen gate,
  Which long time had bene shut, and out of hond
  Proclaymed joy and peace through all his state;
For dead now was their foe, which them forrayed late.

4 Then gan triumphant Trompets sound on hie,
  That sent to heaven the ecchoed report
  Of their new joy, and happie victorie
  Gainst him, that had them long opprest with tort,
  And fast imprisoned in sieged fort.
  Then all the people, as in solemne feast,
  To him assembled with one full consort,
  Rejoycing at the fall of that great beast,
From whose eternall bondage now they were releast.

5 Forth came that auncient Lord and aged Queene,
  Arayd in antique robes downe to the ground,
  And sad habiliments right well beseene;
  A noble crew about them waited round
  Of sage and sober Peres, all gravely gownd;
  Whom farre before did march a goodly band
  Of tall young men, all hable armes to sownd,
  But now they laurell braunches bore in hand;
Glad signe of victorie and peace in all their land.

3. (3) **weet:** ascertain (for himself); (7) **out of hond:** at once;
(9) **forrayed:** preyed upon.
4. (4) **tort:** injury; (7) **consort:** accord.
5. (2) **antique:** ancient, venerable with tradition; (3) **sad . . .
beseene:** dark-coloured clothes of very handsome appearance;
(5) **Peres:** peers; (7) **all hable . . . sownd:** all proper men-at-
arms.

6   Unto that doughtie Conquerour they came,
      And him before themselves prostrating low,
      Their Lord and Patrone loud did him proclame,
      And at his feet their laurell boughes did throw.
      Soone after them all dauncing on a row
      The comely virgins came, with girlands dight,
      As fresh as flowres in medow greene do grow,
      When morning deaw upon their leaves doth light:
    And in their hands sweet Timbrels all upheld on hight.

7   And them before, the fry of children young
      Their wanton sports and childish mirth did play,
      And to the Maydens sounding tymbrels sung
      In well attuned notes, a joyous lay,
      And made delightfull musicke all the way,
      Untill they came, where that faire virgin stood;
      As faire *Diana* in fresh sommers day,
      Beholds her Nymphes, enraung'd in shadie wood,
    Some wrestle, some do run, some bathe in christall flood.

8   So she beheld those maydens meriment
      With chearefull vew; who when to her they came,
      Themselves to ground with gratious humblesse bent,
      And her ador'd by honorable name,
      Lifting to heaven her everlasting fame:
      Then on her head they set a girland greene,
      And crowned her twixt earnest and twixt game;
      Who in her selfe-resemblance well beseene,
    Did seeme such, as she was, a goodly maiden Queene.

7. (1) **fry:** swarm; (4) **lay:** song; (8) **Beholds:** watching; (8) **enraung'd:** disposed, deployed at ease.
8. (3) **humblesse:** humility; (7) **twixt . . . game:** half in earnest half in play; (8) **selfe-resemblance:** appearance.

9   And after, all the raskall many ran,
      Heaped together in rude rablement,
      To see the face of that victorious man:
      Whom all admired, as from heaven sent,
      And gazd upon with gaping wonderment.
      But when they came, where that dead Dragon lay,
      Stretcht on the ground in monstrous large extent,
      The sight with idle feare did them dismay,
  Ne durst approch him nigh, to touch, or once assay.

10   Some feard, and fled; some feard and well it faynd;
      One that would wiser seeme, then all the rest,
      Warnd him not touch, for yet perhaps remaynd
      Some lingring life within his hollow brest,
      Or in his wombe might lurke some hidden nest
      Of many Dragonets, his fruitfull seed;
      Another said, that in his eyes did rest
      Yet sparckling fire, and bad thereof take heed;
  Another said, he saw him move his eyes indeed.

11   One mother, when as her foolehardie chyld
      Did come too neare, and with his talants play,
      Halfe dead through feare, her litle babe revyld,
      And to her gossips gan in counsell say;
      How can I tell, but that his talants may
      Yet scratch my sonne, or rend his tender hand?
      So diversly themselves in vaine they fray;
      Whiles some more bold, to measure him nigh stand,
  To prove how many acres he did spread of land.

  9. (1) **after**: next behind; (1) **raskall many**: common folk; (2) **rablement**: crowd, rabble; (8) **idle**: groundless.
10. (1) **faynd**: disguised.
11. (3) **revyld**: scolded; (4) **gossips**: cronies, neighbours; (7) **in vaine**: needlessly; (7) **fray**: frighten, alarm; (8) **nigh**: close by.

12   Thus flocked all the folke him round about,
      The whiles that hoarie king, with all his traine,
      Being arrived, where that champion stout
      After his foes defeasance did remaine,
      Him goodly greetes, and faire does entertaine,
      With princely gifts of yvorie and gold,
      And thousand thankes him yeelds for all his paine.
      Then when his daughter deare he does behold,
 Her dearely doth imbrace, and kisseth manifold.

13   And after to his Pallace he them brings,
      With shaumes, and trompets, and with Clarions sweet;
      And all the way the joyous people sings,
      And with their garments strowes the paved street:
      Whence mounting up, they find purveyance meet
      Of all, that royall Princes court became,
      And all the floore was underneath their feet
      Bespred with costly scarlot of great name,
 On which they lowly sit, and fitting purpose frame.

14   What needs me tell their feast and goodly guize,
      In which was nothing riotous nor vaine?
      What needs of daintie dishes to devize,
      Of comely services, or courtly trayne?
      My narrow leaves cannot in them containe
      The large discourse of royall Princes state.
      Yet was their manner then but bare and plaine:
      For th'antique world excesse and pride did hate;
 Such proud luxurious pompe is swollen up but late.

12. (4) **defeasance:** defeat; (5) **goodly:** courteously; (7) **paine:** trouble; (9) **manifold:** many times.
13. (2) **shaumes:** shawms (a shawm is an oboe-like instrument); (5) **purveyance meet:** suitable provision; (6) **became:** was appropriate to; (8) **name:** quality; (9) **purpose:** conversation; (9) **frame:** engage in.
14. (1) **guize:** behaviour; (3) **devize:** tell, recount; (6) **large discourse:** ample account.

15   Then when with meates and drinkes of every kinde
      Their fervent appetites they quenched had,
      That auncient Lord gan fit occasion finde,
      Of straunge adventures, and of perils sad,
      Which in his travell him befallen had,
      For to demaund of his renowmed guest:
      Who then with utt'rance grave, and count'nance sad,
      From point to point, as is before exprest,
  Discourst his voyage long, according his request.

16   Great pleasure mixt with pittifull regard,
      That godly King and Queene did passionate,
      Whiles they his pittifull adventures heard,
      That oft they did lament his lucklesse state,
      And often blame the too importune fate,
      That heapd on him so many wrathfull wreakes:
      For never gentle knight, as he of late,
      So tossed was in fortunes cruell freakes;
  And all the while salt teares bedeawd the hearers cheaks.

17   Then said the royall Pere in sober wise;
      Deare Sonne, great beene the evils, which ye bore
      From first to last in your late enterprise,
      That I note, whether prayse, or pitty more:
      For never living man, I weene, so sore
      In sea of deadly daungers was distrest;
      But since now safe ye seised have the shore,
      And well arrived are, (high God be blest)
  Let us devize of ease and everlasting rest.

15. (4) **sad:** grievous; (7) **sad:** sober, modest; (9) **Discourst:** described.
16. (2) **passionate:** express feelingly; (5) **importune:** severe; (6) **wreakes:** blows, punishments; (8) **freakes:** whims.
17. (1) **Pere:** peer; (4) **note:** do not know; (4) **whether prayse:** whether to praise; (9) **devize:** talk of.

18   Ah dearest Lord, said then that doughty knight,
      Of ease or rest I may not yet devize;
      For by the faith, which I to armes have plight,
      I bounden am streight after this emprize,
      As that your daughter can ye well advize,
      Backe to returne to that great Faerie Queene,
      And her to serve six years in warlike wize,
      Gainst that proud Paynim king, that workes her teene:
  Therefore I ought crave pardon, till I there have beene.

19   Unhappie falles that hard necessitie,
      (Quoth he) the troubler of my happie peace,
      And vowed foe of my felicitie;
      Ne I against the same can justly preace:
      But since that band ye cannot now release,
      Nor doen undo; (for vowes may not be vaine)
      Soone as the terme of those six yeares shall cease,
      Ye then shall hither backe returne againe,
  The marriage to accomplish vowd betwixt you twain.

20   Which for my part I covet to performe,
      In sort as through the world I did proclame,
      That who so kild that monster most deforme,
      And him in hardy battaile overcame,
      Should have mine onely daughter to his Dame,
      And of my kingdome heire apparaunt bee:
      Therefore since now to thee perteines the same,
      By dew desert of noble chevalree,
  Both daughter and eke kingdome, lo I yield to thee.

18. (4) **emprize:** undertaking; (8) **workes her teene:** plots her harm.
19. (4) **preace:** dispute, contend; (6) **doen undo:** repudiate a commitment.
20. (1) **covet:** long; (2) **In sort as:** even as.

21 Then forth he called that his daughter faire,
  The fairest *Un'* his onely daughter deare,
  His onely daughter, and his onely heyre;
  Who forth proceeding with sad sober cheare,
  As bright as doth the morning starre appeare
  Out of the East, with flaming lockes bedight,
  To tell that dawning day is drawing neare,
  And to the world does bring long wished light;
So faire and fresh that Lady shewd her selfe in sight.

22 So faire and fresh, as freshest flowre in May;
  For she had layd her mournefull stole aside,
  And widow-like sad wimple throwne away,
  Wherewith her heavenly beautie she did hide,
  Whiles on her wearie journey she did ride;
  And on her now a garment she did weare,
  All lilly white, withoutten spot, or pride,
  That seemd like silke and silver woven neare,
But neither silke nor silver therein did appeare.

23 The blazing brightnesse of her beauties beame,
  And glorious light of her sunshyny face
  To tell, were as to strive against the streame.
  My ragged rimes are all too rude and bace,
  Her heavenly lineaments for to enchace.
  Ne wonder; for her owne deare loved knight,
  All were she dayly with himselfe in place,
  Did wonder much at her celestiall sight:
Oft had he seene her faire, but never so faire dight.

21. (3) **heyre:** heir; (4) **sad:** serious, solemn; (4) **cheare:** expression; (6) **bedight:** adorned.
22. (7) **pride:** ostentation; (8) **neare:** finely, closely.
23. (4) **bace:** lowly; (5) **enchace:** i.e., enhance, set off; (7) **All were . . . place:** though she had been daily in his company.

24   So fairely dight, when she in presence came,
       She to her Sire made humble reverence,
       And bowed low, that her right well became,
       And added grace unto her excellence:
       Who with great wisedome, and grave eloquence
       Thus gan to say. But eare he thus had said,
       With flying speede, and seeming great pretence,
       Came running in, much like a man dismaid,
   A Messenger with letters, which his message said.

25   All in the open hall amazed stood,
       At suddeinnesse of that unwarie sight,
       And wondred at his breathlesse hastie mood.
       But he for nought would stay his passage right,
       Till fast before the king he did alight;
       Where falling flat, great humblesse he did make,
       And kist the ground, whereon his foot was pight;
       Then to his hands that writ he did betake,
   Which he disclosing, red thus, as the paper spake.

26   To thee, most mighty king of *Eden* faire,
       Her greeting sends in these sad lines addrest,
       The wofull daughter, and forsaken heire
       Of that great Emperour of all the West;
       And bids thee be advized for the best,
       Ere thou thy daughter linck in holy band
       Of wedlocke to that new unknowen guest:
       For he already plighted his right hand
   Unto another love, and to another land.

24. (6) **eare:** before; (7) **seeming . . . pretence:** apparently about some vital business.
25. (2) **unwarie:** unexpected; (4) **right:** straight ahead; (5) **fast before:** right in front of; (5) **did alight:** came to a halt; (6) **did make:** made a display of; (7) **pight:** placed; (8) **writ:** document; (8) **betake:** deliver; (9) **disclosing:** unfolding.
26. (2) **addrest:** drawn up, prepared.

27   To me sad mayd, or rather widow sad,
        He was affiaunced long time before,
        And sacred pledges he both gave, and had,
        False erraunt knight, infamous, and forswore:
        Witnesse the burning Altars, which he swore,   §
        And guiltie heavens of his bold perjury,
        Which though he hath polluted oft of yore,
        Yet I to them for judgement just do fly,
     And them conjure t'avenge this shamefull injury.

28   Therefore since mine he is, or free or bond,
        Or false or trew, or living or else dead,
        Withhold, O soveraine Prince, your hasty hond
        From knitting league with him, I you aread;
        Ne weene my right with strength adowne to tread,
        Through weakenesse of my widowhed, or woe:
        For truth is strong, her rightfull cause to plead,
        And shall find friends, if need requireth soe.
     So bids thee well to fare, Thy neither friend, nor foe,
           Fidessa.

29   When he these bitter byting words had red,
        The tydings straunge did him abashed make,
        That still he sate long time astonished
        As in great muse, ne word to creature spake.
        At last his solemne silence thus he brake,
        With doubtfull eyes fast fixed on his guest;
        Redoubted knight, that for mine onely sake
        Thy life and honour late adventurest,
     Let nought be hid from me, that ought to be exprest.

27. (7) **Which:** i.e., the altars and the heavens; (9) **conjure:** make
    a solemn appeal to.
28. (1) **or . . . or:** whether . . . or; (4) **league:** i.e., marriage
    alliance; (4) **aread:** advise; (5) **Ne weene:** nor think; (6)
    widowhed: widowed state.
29. (4) **in great muse:** in a deep study; (7) **mine onely sake:** my
    sake alone; (8) **late adventurest:** recently hazarded.

§ *Witnesse the burning Altars . . . bold perjury*: i.e., "Witness the burning altars by which he swore and witness the heavens, now obligated
  to avenge themselves on his bold perjury."

30 What meane these bloudy vowes, and idle threats,
  Throwne out from womanish impatient mind?
  What heavens? what altars? what enraged heates
  Here heaped up with termes of love unkind,
  My conscience cleare with guilty bands would bind?
  High God be witnesse, that I guiltlesse ame.
  But if your selfe, Sir knight, ye faultie find,
  Or wrapped be in loves of former Dame,
With crime do not it cover, but disclose the same.

31 To whom the *Redcrosse* knight this answere sent,
  My Lord, my King, be nought hereat dismayd,
  Till well ye wote by grave intendiment,
  What woman, and wherefore doth me upbrayd
  With breach of love, and loyalty betrayd.
  It was in my mishaps, as hitherward
  I lately traveild, that unwares I strayd
  Out of my way, through perils straunge and hard;
That day should faile me, ere I had them all declard.

32 There did I find, or rather I was found
  Of this false woman, that *Fidessa* hight,
  Fidessa hight the falsest Dame on ground,
  Most false *Duessa*, royall richly dight,
  That easie was t'invegle weaker sight:
  Who by her wicked arts, and wylie skill,
  Too false and strong for earthly skill or might,
  Unwares me wrought unto her wicked will,
And to my foe betrayd, when least I feared ill.

30. (6) **ame:** am.
31. (3) **intendiment:** consideration.
32. (4-5) **royall . . . t'invegle:** so got up in the riches of royalty
that it was easy for her to hoodwink; (8) **Unwares:** without
my knowing it; (8) **me wrought:** bent me.

33 Then stepped forth the goodly royall Mayd,
    And on the ground her selfe prostrating low,
    With sober countenaunce thus to him sayd;
    O pardon me, my soveraigne Lord, to show
    The secret treasons, which of late I know
    To have bene wroght by that false sorceresse.
    She onely she it is, that earst did throw
    This gentle knight into so great distresse,
That death him did awaite in dayly wretchednesse.

34 And now it seemes, that she suborned hath
    This craftie messenger with letters vaine,
    To worke new woe and improvided scath,
    By breaking of the band betwixt us twaine;
    Wherein she used hath the practicke paine
    Of this false footman, clokt with simplenesse,
    Whom if ye please for to discover plaine,
    Ye shall him *Archimago* find, I ghesse,
The falsest man alive; who tries shall find no lesse.

35 The king was greatly moved at her speach,
    And all with suddein indignation fraight,
    Bad on that Messenger rude hands to reach.
    Eftsoones the Gard, which on his state did wait,
    Attacht that faitor false, and bound him strait:
    Who seeming sorely chauffed at his band,
    As chained Beare, whom cruell dogs do bait,
    With idle force did faine them to withstand,
And often semblaunce made to scape out of their hand.

34. (3) **improvided scath:** unforeseen harm; (5) **practicke paine:** artful efforts; (7) **discover:** reveal, expose.
35. (2) **fraight:** filled; (3) **Bad on . . . reach:** ordered that messenger to be taken and held by force; (5) **Attacht:** arrested; (5) **faitor:** scoundrel; (8) **idle:** wasted, useless; (8) **faine:** pretend; (9) **semblaunce made:** made as if.

36 But they him layd full low in dungeon deepe,
        And bound him hand and foote with yron chains.
        And with continuall watch did warely keepe;
        Who then would thinke, that by his subtile trains
        He could escape fowle death or deadly paines?
        Thus when that Princes wrath was pacifide,
        He gan renew the late forbidden banes,
        And to the knight his daughter deare he tyde,
    With sacred rites and vowes for ever to abyde.

37 His owne two hands the holy knots did knit,
        That none but death for ever can devide;
        His owne two hands, for such a turne most fit,
        The housling fire did kindle and provide,
        And holy water thereon sprinckled wide;
        At which the bushy Teade a groome did light,
        And sacred lampe in secret chamber hide,
        Where it should not be quenched day nor night,
    For feare of evill fates, but burnen ever bright.

38 Then gan they sprinckle all the posts with wine,
        And made great feast to solemnize that day;
        They all perfumde with frankencense divine,
        And precious odours fetcht from far away,
        That all the house did sweat with great aray: §
        And all the while sweete Musicke did apply
        Her curious skill, the warbling notes to play,
        To drive away the dull Melancholy;
    The whiles one sung a song of love and jollity.

36. (3) **warely:** carefully; (4) **trains:** wiles; (7) **banes:** banns of
    marriage.
37. (3) **turne:** (ceremonial) act; (4) **housling:** i.e., sacramental;
    (4) **provide:** plenish, furnish; (5) **wide:** liberally; (6) **Teade:**
    torch; (6) **groome:** attendant.
38. (3) **They all perfumde:** they perfumed everything; (7) **curious:**
    ingenious.

§ *all the house did sweat with great aray*: "The whole household
exerted itself over great festive preparations"; or, "The whole household exuded the costly, bustling atmosphere of great festive preparations".

39   During the which there was an heavenly noise
        Heard sound through all the Pallace pleasantly,
        Like as it had bene many an Angels voice,
        Singing before th'eternall majesty,
        In their trinall triplicities on hye;   §
        Yet wist no creature, whence that heavenly sweet
        Proceeded, yet eachone felt secretly
        Himselfe thereby reft of his sences meet,
     And ravished with rare impression in his sprite.

40   Great joy was made that day of young and old,
        And solemne feast proclaimd throughout the land,
        That their exceeding merth may not be told:
        Suffice it heare by signes to understand
        The usuall joyes at knitting of loves band.
        Thrise happy man the knight himselfe did hold,
        Possessed of his Ladies hart and hand,
        And ever, when his eye did her behold,
     His heart did seeme to melt in pleasures manifold.

41   Her joyous presence and sweet company
        In full content he there did long enjoy,
        Ne wicked envie, ne vile gealosy
        His deare delights were able to annoy:
        Yet swimming in that sea of blisfull joy,
        He nought forgot, how he whilome had sworne,
        In case he could that monstrous beast destroy,
        Unto his Farie Queene backe to returne:
     The which he shortly did, and *Una* left to mourne.

39. (5) **trinall triplicities:** i.e., threefold trinities; (6) **sweet:** sweetness; (8) **meet:** proper, i.e., own (and/or) normal.
40. (6) **himselfe did hold:** considered himself.
41. (6) **whilome:** formerly.

§ *trinall triplicities*: In angelology there were nine orders of angels, usually given in three groups of three. One common grouping was:

1ST TRINE:	(1) Seraphim	(2) Cherubim	(3) Thrones
2ND TRINE:	(4) Dominations	(5) Virtues	(6) Powers
3RD TRINE:	(7) { Princedoms / Principalities	(8) Archangels	(9) Angels

42   Now strike your sailes ye jolly Mariners,
     For we be come unto a quiet rode,
     Where we must land some of our passengers,
     And light this wearie vessell of her lode.
     Here she a while may make her safe abode,
     Till she repaired have her tackles spent,
     And wants supplide. And then againe abroad
     On the long voyage whereto she is bent:
Well may she speede and fairely finish her intent.

42. (2) **rode:** roadstead, anchorage; (6) **spent:** worn-out.

TWO CANTOS
OF
MUTABILITIE:

Which, both for Forme and Matter, appeare
to be parcell of some following Booke of the
FAERIE QUEENE,
(∴)
UNDER THE LEGEND
OF
Constancie.

Never before imprinted.

[1609]

Canto VI

> *Proud* Change (*not pleasd, in mortall things,*
> *beneath the Moone, to raigne*)
> *Pretends, as well of Gods, as Men,*
> *to be the Soveraine.*

1 What man that sees the ever-whirling wheele
    Of *Change,* the which all mortall things doth sway,
    But that therby doth find, and plainly feele,
    How MUTABILITY in them doth play
    Her cruell sports, to many mens decay?
    Which that to all may better yet appeare,
    I will rehearse that whylome I heard say,
    How she at first her selfe began to reare,
  Gainst all the Gods, and th'empire sought from them to
        beare.

Pretends: claims.
1. (2) **sway:** rule; (3) **But that therby:** who does not find
   from that; (5) **to many mens decay:** to the destruction of
   many men; (6) **Which that . . . appeare:** the which, so that
   it may become clearer to everybody; (7) **that whylome:** what
   once; (9) **to beare:** to bear away, carry off.

2 But first, here falleth fittest to unfold
      Her antique race and linage ancient,
      As I have found it registred of old,
      In *Faery* Land mongst records permanent:
      She was, to weet, a daughter by descent
      Of those old *Titans*, that did whylome strive   §
      With *Saturnes* sonne for heavens regiment.
      Whom, though high *Jove* of kingdome did deprive,
   Yet many of their stemme long after did survive.

3 And many of them, afterwards obtain'd
      Great power of *Jove*, and high authority;
      As *Hecaté*, in whose almighty hand,
      He plac't all rule and principality,
      To be by her disposed diversly,
      To Gods, and men, as she them list divide:
      And drad *Bellona*, that doth sound on hie   §
      Warres and allarums unto Nations wide,
   That makes both heaven and earth to tremble at her
         pride.

2. (1) **here falleth . . . unfold**: i.e., this is the best place to
   explain; (2) **race**: family; (5) **to weet**: to wit; (7) **regiment**:
   rule; (9) **stemme**: stock.
3. (2) **power of Jove**: power from Jove; (3) **As Hecaté**: such as
   Hecate; (5) **diversly**: variously; (6) **as she . . . divide**: as she
   chose to divide them; (7) **And drad**: and such as the dreaded.

§ *Titans*: The twelve children of Coelus (Uranus, Sky-father) and
  Tellus (Gaia, Earth-mother). The youngest Titan, Cronus (Saturn),
  maimed his father Coelus and displaced him as ruler of the world.
  In turn, Saturn and his brother Titans were defeated and displaced
  by Saturn's children, the younger race of gods called the Olympians,
  who were led by *Saturnes sonne*, that is, Jove (Zeus).
§ *Bellona*: The Roman war-goddess, counterpart of the Greek war-
  goddess Enyo. Enyo, and to some extent Bellona, are subsidiary off-
  shoots of Ares (Mars), the god of war.

4   So likewise did this *Titanesse* aspire,
         Rule and dominion to her selfe to gaine;
         That as a Goddesse, men might her admire,
         And heavenly honours yield, as to them twaine.
         And first, on earth she sought it to obtaine;
         Where she such proofe and sad examples shewed
         Of her great power, to many ones great paine,
         That not men onely (whom she soone subdewed)
    But eke all other creatures, her bad dooings rewed.

5   For, she the face of earthly things so changed,
         That all which Nature had establisht first
         In good estate, and in meet order ranged,
         She did pervert, and all their statutes burst:
         And all the worlds faire frame (which none yet durst
         Of Gods or men to alter or misguide)
         She alter'd quite, and made them all accurst
         That God had blest; and did at first provide
    In that still happy state for ever to abide.

6   Ne shee the lawes of Nature onely brake,
         But eke of Justice, and of Policie;
         And wrong of right, and bad of good did make,
         And death for life exchanged foolishlie:
         Since which, all living wights have learn'd to die,
         And all this world is woxen daily worse.
         O pittious worke of MUTABILITIE!
         By which, we all are subject to that curse,
    And death in stead of life have sucked from our Nurse.

4. (3) **admire:** wonder at; (4) **them twaine:** those two (i.e.,
   Hecate and Bellona); (6) **sad examples:** weighty examples;
   (7) **to many ones:** to many a one's; (9) **But eke:** but also;
   (9) **rewed:** lamented.
5. (3) **estate:** condition; (8) **provide:** establish.
6. (1) **Ne shee . . . brake:** she not only broke; (2) **Policie:** statecraft, government; (5) **wights:** people; (6) **is woxen:** has
   become.

7   And now, when all the earth she thus had brought
         To her behest, and thralled to her might,
     She gan to cast in her ambitious thought,
     T'attempt th'empire of the heavens hight,
     And *Jove* himselfe to shoulder from his right.
     And first, she past the region of the ayre,
     And of the fire, whose substance thin and slight,
     Made no resistance, ne could her contraire,
         But ready passage to her pleasure did prepaire.

8   Thence, to the Circle of the Moone she clambe,
         Where *Cynthia* raignes in everlasting glory,   §
     To whose bright shining palace straight she came,
     All fairely deckt with heavens goodly story;   §
     Whose silver gates (by which there sate an hory
     Old aged Sire, with hower-glasse in hand,
     Hight *Tyme*) she entred, were he liefe or sory:
     Ne staide till she the highest stage had scand,
         Where *Cynthia* did sit, that never still did stand.

7. (2) **To her behest:** under her control; (2) **thralled:** enslaved;
    (3) **She gan to cast:** she resolved; (8) **ne . . . contraire:** nor
    could hinder her.
8. (1) **clambe:** climbed; (3) **straight:** straightway; (5) **sate an
    hory:** sat a grey; (7) **Hight Tyme:** called Time; (7) **were
    he liefe:** were he glad; (8) **Ne staide:** nor halted; (8) **scand:**
    scanned (or) ascended.

§ *Cynthia*: One of the names of the moon-goddess and hence of the
   moon itself; she is also called Artemis or Diana. The name Cynthia
   comes from the version of her story in which the Titaness Leto gave
   birth to her while resting against Mount Cynthus.
§ *deckt with heavens goodly story*: i.e., "laid out in the pleasant archi-
   tecture of heaven" (if *story* is taken to mean a row of columns or
   windows); or perhaps "embellished with beautiful paintings of
   heaven" (if *story* is taken in the sense of the verb meaning to decorate with, or represent in, painting or sculpture).

9   Her sitting on an Ivory throne shee found,
      Drawne of two steeds, th'one black, the other white,
      Environd with tenne thousand starres around,
      That duly her attended day and night;
      And by her side, there ran her Page, that hight
      Vesper, whom we the Evening-starre intend:
      That with his Torche, still twinkling like twylight,
      Her lightened all the way where she should wend,
    And joy to weary wandring travailers did lend:

10   That when the hardy *Titanesse* beheld
      The goodly building of her Palace bright,
      Made of the heavens substance, and up-held
      With thousand Crystall pillors of huge hight,
      Shee gan to burne in her ambitious spright,
      And t'envie her that in such glorie raigned.
      Eftsoones she cast by force and tortious might,
      Her to displace; and to her selfe to have gained
    The kingdome of the Night, and waters by her wained.

11   Boldly she bid the Goddesse downe descend,
      And let her selfe into that Ivory throne;
      For, shee her selfe more worthy thereof wend,
      And better able it to guide alone:
      Whether to men, whose fall she did bemone,   §
      Or unto Gods, whose state she did maligne,
      Or to th'infernall Powers, her need give lone
      Of her faire light, and bounty most benigne,
    Her selfe of all that rule shee deemed most condigne.

  9. (5) **that hight:** named; (6) **intend:** call; (9) **lend:** grant.
10. (5) **spright:** spirit; (7) **Eftsoones:** at once; (7) **tortious:** wicked;
     (9) **wained:** move (i.e., tidally).
11. (3) **shee her selfe . . . wend:** she considered herself; (7) **her
     need give lone:** to whom she must make a loan; (9) **condigne:**
     worthy.

§ *whose fall she did bemone*: i.e., Cynthia did bemoan? It seems as if
all the feminine pronouns in this stanza should refer to Mutabilitie
who is, indeed, relentlessly self-centred; but it is very unlike her to
bemoan the fall of any of her victims. Perhaps, then, the "she" in
line 5 refers to Cynthia, the Moon herself.

12 But shee that had to her that soveraigne seat
        By highest *Jove* assign'd, therein to beare
        Nights burning lamp, regarded not her threat,
        Ne yielded ought for favour or for feare;
        But with sterne countenaunce and disdainfull cheare,
        Bending her horned browes, did put her back:
        And boldly blaming her for comming there,
        Bade her attonce from heavens coast to pack,
    Or at her perill bide the wrathfull Thunders wrack.

13 Yet nathemore the *Giantesse* forbare:
        But boldly preacing-on, raught forth her hand
        To pluck her downe perforce from off her chaire;
        And there-with lifting up her golden wand,
        Threatned to strike her if she did with-stand.
        Where-at the starres, which round about her blazed,
        And eke the Moones bright wagon, still did stand,
        All beeing with so bold attempt amazed,
    And on her uncouth habit and sterne looke still gazed.

12. (4) **Ne yielded ought for:** nor gave way either for; (5) **cheare:**
    look; (6) **horned:** (from horn-shaped crescent of moon); (8)
    to pack: to make off.
13. (1) **nathemore:** never the more; (1) **forbare:** refrained; (2)
    preacing-on: pressing forward; (9) **uncouth habit:** strange
    dress.

14 Meane-while, the lower World, which nothing knew
   Of all that chaunced here, was darkned quite;
   And eke the heavens, and all the heavenly crew
   Of happy wights, now unpurvaide of light,
   Were much afraid, and wondred at that sight;
   Fearing least *Chaos* broken had his chaine,   §
   And brought againe on them eternall night:
   But chiefely *Mercury*, that next doth raigne,
  Ran forth in haste, unto the king of Gods to plaine.

15 All ran together with a great out-cry,
   To *Joves* faire Palace, fixt in heavens hight;
   And beating at his gates full earnestly,
   Gan call to him aloud with all their might,
   To know what meant that suddaine lack of light.
   The father of the Gods when this he heard,
   Was troubled much at their so strange affright,
   Doubting least *Typhon* were againe uprear'd,   §
  Or other his old foes, that once him sorely fear'd.

14. (2) **that chaunced:** i.e., that was going on; (4) **wights:** creatures; (4) **unpurvaide:** deprived; (9) **plaine:** complain.

15. (8) **Doubting least:** fearing lest; (9) **Or other his:** or some other of his; (9) **him sorely fear'd:** badly frightened him.

§ *Chaos*: The dark, formless void which contained the potentialities of all kinds of matter and from which arose, first, Night and her brother the Depth, then Love – Eros in his creative aspect as bringer of life and form out of chaotic matter. *Mercury*: The Olympian god here thought of in his aspect as the planet whose sphere is next beyond the moon's.

§ *Typhon*: The monster with a hundred dragon-shaped heads who fought with Jove (Zeus) and was struck down by his thunderbolts and buried under Mt. Aetna. In overwhelming Typhon, Jove's thunderbolts set fire to Aetna, which has been a volcano ever since.

16   Eftsoones the sonne of *Maia* forth he sent   §
        Downe to the Circle of the Moone, to knowe
        The cause of this so strange astonishment,
        And why shee did her wonted course forslowe;
        And if that any were on earth belowe
        That did with charmes or Magick her molest,
        Him to attache, and downe to hell to throwe:
        But, if from heaven it were, then to arrest
    The Author, and him bring before his presence prest.

17   The wingd-foot God, so fast his plumes did beat,
        That soone he came where-as the *Titanesse*
        Was striving with faire *Cynthia* for her seat:
        At whose strange sight, and haughty hardinesse,
        He wondred much, and feared her no lesse.
        Yet laying feare aside to doe his charge,
        At last, he bade her (with bold stedfastnesse)
        Ceasse to molest the Moone to walke at large,
    Or come before high *Jove*, her dooings to discharge.

18   And there-with-all, he on her shoulder laid
        His snaky-wreathed Mace, whose awfull power
        Doth make both Gods and hellish fiends affraid:
        Where-at the *Titanesse* did sternely lower,
        And stoutly answer'd, that in evill hower
        He from his *Jove* such message to her brought,
        To bid her leave faire *Cynthias* silver bower;
        Sith shee his *Jove* and him esteemed nought,
    No more then *Cynthia's* selfe; but all their kingdoms
        sought.

16. (4) **wonted:** usual, accustomed; (4) **forslowe:** retard; (7)
    attache: arrest; (9) **prest:** immediately.
17. (4) **hardinesse:** audacity; (8) **Ceasse to . . . at large:** to stop
    interfering with Moon's free progress; (9) **discharge:** give an
    account of.
18. (1) **And there-with-all:** and with that; (2) **snaky-wreathed
    Mace:** i.e., caduceus; (4) **lower:** scowl; (8) **Sith:** since.

§ *sonne of Maia*: Hermes (Mercury), here seen in his aspect as messenger or herald of the gods. To bear his messages or summonses all
the faster Hermes wears winged sandals; hence the epithet *wingd-foot
God* in the next stanza.

19   The Heavens Herald staid not to reply,
         But past away, his doings to relate
       Unto his Lord; who now in th'highest sky,
       Was placed in his principall Estate,
       With all the Gods about him congregate:
       To whom when *Hermes* had his message told,
       It did them all exceedingly amate,
       Save *Jove*; who, changing nought his count'nance
             bold,
    Did unto them at length these speeches wise unfold;

20   Harken to mee awhile yee heavenly Powers;
         Ye may remember since th'Earths cursed seed   §
       Sought to assaile the heavens eternall towers,
       And to us all exceeding feare did breed:
       But how we then defeated all their deed,
       Yee all doe knowe, and them destroied quite;
       Yet not so quite, but that there did succeed
       An off-spring of their bloud, which did alite
    Upon the fruitfull earth, which doth us yet despite.

19. (4) **principall Estate:** i.e., highest council; (5) **congregate:**
     gathered; (7) **amate:** dismay; (8) **Save Jove:** except Jove.
20. (7) **Yet not so quite:** yet not so completely; (8) **alite:** alight,
     land; (9) **which doth . . . despite:** who still bears a grudge.

§ *th'Earths cursed seed*: The Titans. When Zeus and his brothers and
sisters rose against their Titan father Cronus, the other Titans – except
for Prometheus – came to the aid of Cronus. The younger gods
defeated the Titans only after a desperate, drawn-out struggle in
which they were helped by some of Earth's other, pre-Titanic children such as the fearsome Cyclopes.

21 Of that bad seed is this bold woman bred,
       That now with bold presumption doth aspire
       To thrust faire *Phœbe* from her silver bed,   §
       And eke our selves from heavens high Empire,
       If that her might were match to her desire:
       Wherefore, it now behoves us to advise
       What way is best to drive her to retire;
       Whether by open force, or counsell wise,
    Areed ye sonnes of God, as best ye can devise.

22 So having said, he ceast; and with his brow
       (His black eye-brow, whose doomefull dreaded beck
       Is wont to wield the world unto his vow,
       And even the highest Powers of heaven to check)
       Made signe to them in their degrees to speake:
       Who straight gan cast their counsell grave and wise.
       Meane-while, th'Earths daughter, thogh she nought
               did reck
    Of *Hermes* message; yet gan now advise,
    What course were best to take in this hot bold emprize.

23 Eftsoones she thus resolv'd; that whil'st the Gods
       (After returne of *Hermes* Embassie)
       Were troubled, and amongst themselves at ods,
       Before they could new counsels re-allie,
       To set upon them in that extasie;
       And take what fortune time and place would lend:
       So, forth she rose, and through the purest sky
       To *Joves* high Palace straight cast to ascend,
    To prosecute her plot: Good on-set boads good end.

21. (4) **And eke our selves:** and even us; (6) **to advise:** to con-
    sider; (9) **Areed:** advise, give counsel.
22. (2) **doomefull:** fateful; (3) **Is wont to wield:** is accustomed to
    sway; (3) **vow:** will; (6) **Who straight gan cast:** who im-
    mediately formulated; (7) **nought did reck/Of:** could not
    have cared less about.
23. (4) **re-allie:** reformulate; (5) **extasie:** frenzy of astonished
    confusion; (8) **straight . . . ascend:** resolved to ascend im-
    mediately; (9) **Good on-set boads:** a good beginning bodes.

§ *Phœbe*: Another name for Cynthia (Diana, Artemis), the Moon.
  This name recalls her aspect as the sister and feminine counterpart
  of Phoebus Apollo.

24   Shee there arriving, boldly in did pass;
      Where all the Gods she found in counsell close,
      All quite unarm'd, as then their manner was.
      At sight of her they suddaine all arose,
      In great amaze, ne wist what way to chose.
      But *Jove*, all fearelesse, forc't them to aby;
      And in his soveraine throne, gan straight dispose
      Himselfe more full of grace and Majestie,
  That mote encheare his friends, and foes mote terrifie.

25   That, when the haughty *Titanesse* beheld,
      All were she fraught with pride and impudence,
      Yet with the sight thereof was almost queld;
      And inly quaking, seem'd as reft of sense,
      And voyd of speech in that drad audience;
      Untill that *Jove* himselfe, her selfe bespake:
      Speake thou fraile woman, speake with confidence,
      Whence art thou, and what doost thou here now
          make?
  What idle errand hast thou, earths mansion to forsake?

26   Shee, halfe confused with his great commaund,
      Yet gathering spirit of her natures pride,
      Him boldly answer'd thus to his demaund:
      I am a daughter, by the mothers side,
      Of her that is Grand-mother magnifide
      Of all the Gods, great *Earth*, great *Chaos* child:
      But by the fathers (be it not envide)
      I greater am in bloud (whereon I build)
  Then all the Gods, though wrongfully from heaven exil'd.

24. (5) **ne wist . . . to chose:** i.e., not knowing quite what course
to follow; (6) **aby:** attend to him, await his action; (9) **That
mote encheare:** which could not but hearten.
25. (2) **All were she:** though she was; (4) **as reft:** as if bereft; (6)
her selfe bespake: addressed her; (8) **what doost . . . make:**
what are you doing here now?
26. (5) **magnifide:** exalted.

27   For, *Titan* (as ye all acknowledge must)   §
        Was *Saturnes* elder brother by birth-right;
        Both, sonnes of *Uranus*: but by unjust
        And guilefull meanes, through *Corybantes* slight,
        The younger thrust the elder from his right:
        Since which, thou *Jove*, injuriously hast held
        The Heavens rule from *Titans* sonnes by might;
        And them to hellish dungeons downe hast feld:
    Witnesse ye Heavens the truth of all that I have teld.

28   Whil'st she thus spake, the Gods that gave good eare
        To her bold words, and marked well her grace,
        Beeing of stature tall as any there
        Of all the Gods, and beautifull of face,
        As any of the Goddesses in place,
        Stood all astonied, like a sort of Steeres;
        Mongst whom, some beast of strange and forraine
            race,
        Unwares is chaunc't, far straying from his peeres:
    So did their ghastly gaze bewray their hidden feares.

27. (6) **injuriously:** wrongfully; (8) **feld:** thrown.
28. (5) **in place:** present; (6) **like a sort of Steeres:** like a huddle of oxen; (7) **race:** species; (8) **Unwares is chaunc't:** i.e., suddenly happens to appear; (9) **ghastly:** terror-stricken.

§ In classical mythology Titan is a generic rather than a personal name. In making it a personal name Spenser is following Natalis Comes (*c.* 1520-82), the Italian mythographer who is one of Spenser's chief immediate sources for mythological stories and their interpretations. Natalis Comes' version of heavenly power-politics has the effect of strengthening Mutabilitie's case, which is that Cronus (Saturn) and his descendants are usurping tyrants who achieved and maintained ascendancy over Titan and his issue by a mixture of trickery and force. *Corybantes slight*: Mutabilitie cites the Corybantes' trick as a typical example of the guile to be expected from the likes of Cronus (Saturn) and his son Zeus (Jove). To defeat a prophecy that one day a child of his would overthrow him, Cronus took the precaution of swallowing each successive infant presented to him by his wife Rhea (Ops). When about to give birth to her sixth child, Rhea hid herself on the island of Crete, and when delivered, she presented Cronus with a wrapped-up stone to swallow in place of the new child, Zeus. The Cybele-worshipping Corybantes, together with a band of Cretan warriors called the Curetes, set up a racket of yells and clashing of spears against shields to prevent the cries of the infant from giving him away to his father.

29   Till having pauz'd awhile, *Jove* thus bespake;
    Will never mortall thoughts ceasse to aspire,
    In this bold sort, to Heaven claime to make,
    And touch celestiall seates with earthly mire?
    I would have thought, that bold *Procrustes* hire,   §
    Or *Typhons* fall, or proud *Ixions* paine,
    Or great *Prometheus*, tasting of our ire,
    Would have suffiz'd, the rest for to restraine;
And warn'd all men by their example to refraine:

30   But now, this off-scum of that cursed fry,
    Dare to renew the like bold enterprize,
    And chalenge th'heritage of this our skie;
    Whom what should hinder, but that we likewise
    Should handle as the rest of her allies,
    And thunder-drive to hell? With that, he shooke
    His Nectar-deawed locks, with which the skyes
    And all the world beneath for terror quooke,
And eft his burning levin-brond in hand he tooke.

31   But, when he looked on her lovely face,
    In which, faire beames of beauty did appeare,
    That could the greatest wrath soone turne to grace
    (Such sway doth beauty even in Heaven beare)
    He staide his hand: and having chang'd his cheare,
    He thus againe in milder wise began;
    But ah! if Gods should strive with flesh yfere,
    Then shortly should the progeny of Man
Be rooted out, if *Jove* should doe still what he can:

29. (5) **hire:** wages, punishment.
30. (1) **fry:** swarm, brood; (4) **Whom:** i.e., Jove (whom=us=me; Jove is using the royal plural); (8) **quooke:** quaked; (9) **And eft:** and then; (9) **levin-brond:** lightning bolt.
31. (5) **cheare:** aspect, mood; (7) **yfere:** together; (9) **doe still . . . can:** always actually do what he is capable of.

§ *Procrustes hire*: Procrustes was a brigand who lured weary, unwary travellers to his house and into a bed to which he fitted them, with fatal results, by either trimming or stretching them. His punishment was to be eventually fitted to his own bed by the Greek hero Theseus. *Typhons fall* was the result of his attempt to overthrow Zeus. *Ixions paine* was to be stretched on an endlessly revolving wheel for attempting to seduce Hera (Juno), consort of Zeus. The Titan *Prometheus*

32   But thee faire *Titans* child, I rather weene,
      Through some vaine errour or inducement light,
      To see that mortall eyes have never seene;
      Or through ensample of thy sisters might,
      Bellona; whose great glory thou doost spight,
      Since thou hast seene her dreadfull power belowe,
      Mongst wretched men (dismaide with her affright)
      To bandie Crownes, and Kingdomes to bestowe:
    And sure thy worth, no lesse then hers doth seem to
        showe.

33   But wote thou this, thou hardy *Titanesse*,
      That not the worth of any living wight
      May challenge ought in Heavens interesse;
      Much lesse the Title of old *Titans* Right:
      For, we by Conquest of our soveraine might,
      And by eternall doome of Fates decree,
      Have wonne the Empire of the Heavens bright;
      Which to our selves we hold, and to whom wee
    Shall worthy deeme partakers of our blisse to bee.

34   Then ceasse thy idle claime thou foolish gerle,
      And seeke by grace and goodnesse to obtaine
      That place from which by folly *Titan* fell;
      There-to thou maist perhaps, if so thou faine
      Have *Jove* thy gratious Lord and Soveraigne.
      So, having said, she thus to him replide;
      Ceasse *Saturnes* sonne, to seeke by proffers vaine
      Of idle hopes t'allure mee to thy side,
    For to betray my Right, before I have it tride.

32. (1) **weene:** think; (2) **light:** frivolous; (3) **To see that:** to see
what; (5) **spight:** envy.
33. (1) **But wote thou this:** but be assured of this; (3) **in . . .
interesse:** which concerns heaven; (6) **doome:** pronounce-
ment, judgment.
34. (4) **if so thou faine:** if you so wish; (9) **tride:** tried, tested in
court.

tasted Zeus' ire for outwitting him and bringing men the gift of
fire against his orders; as punishment Zeus chained Prometheus to a
mountain crag where every day his liver, having been renewed over-
night, was torn out by an eagle.

35   But thee, O *Jove*, no equall Judge I deeme
        Of my desert, or of my dewfull Right;
        That in thine owne behalfe maist partiall seeme:
        But to the highest him, that is behight
        Father of Gods and men by equall might;
        To weet, the God of Nature, I appeale.
        There-at *Jove* wexed wroth, and in his spright
        Did inly grudge, yet did it well conceale;
   And bade *Dan Phœbus* Scribe her Appellation seale.

36   Eftsoones the time and place appointed were,
        Where all, both heavenly Powers, and earthly wights,
        Before great Natures presence should appeare,
        For triall of their Titles and best Rights:
        That was, to weet, upon the highest hights
        Of *Arlo-hill* (Who knowes not *Arlo-hill*?)   §
        That is the highest head (in all mens sights)
        Of my old father *Mole*, whom Shepheards quill
   Renowmed hath with hymnes fit for a rurall skill.

35. (1) **equall:** impartial; (1) **deeme:** consider; (4) **the highest him:** the highest one; (4) **behight:** called; (9) **Dan Phœbus Scribe:** Master (Lord) Apollo's clerk; (9) **seale:** affix his seal (to her Appeal).
36. (2) **earthly wights:** mortals.

§ *Arlo-hill*: Galtymore, highest peak on *father Mole*, Spenser's name for the Irish range which includes the Ballyhoura Hills and the Galtees.

37   And, were it not ill fitting for this file,
            To sing of hilles and woods, mongst warres and
                Knights,
            I would abate the sternenesse of my stile,
            Mongst these sterne stounds to mingle soft delights;
            And tell how *Arlo* through *Dianaes* spights
            (Beeing of old the best and fairest Hill
            That was in all this holy-Islands hights)
            Was made the most unpleasant, and most ill.
        Meane while, O *Clio*, lend *Calliope* thy quill.   §

38   Whylome, when IRELAND florished in fame
            Of wealths and goodnesse, far above the rest
            Of all that beare the *British* Islands name,
            The Gods then us'd (for pleasure and for rest)
            Oft to resort there-to, when seem'd them best:
            But none of all there-in more pleasure found,
            Then *Cynthia*; that is soveraine Queene profest
            Of woods and forrests, which therein abound,
        Sprinkled with wholsom waters, more then most on
            ground.

37. (1) **file**: recital, account; (5) **spights**: grudges, ill-will.
38. (1) **Whylome**: once; (9) **more then most on ground**: more
    than most (other places) on earth.

§ *O Clio, lend Calliope thy quill*: This could mean (1) that Clio (his-
    tory) has been the chief inspiration of the poem up to this point
    but is about to give way for a while to Calliope (epic poetry); or
    (2) that Calliope has been, and still is, the poem's chief inspiration
    but wishes for a moment to write with Clio's pen.

39 But mongst them all, as fittest for her game,
    Either for chace of beasts with hound or boawe,
    Or for to shroude in shade from *Phœbus* flame,
    Or bathe in fountaines that doe freshly flowe,
    Or from high hilles, or from the dales belowe,
    She chose this *Arlo*; where shee did resort
    With all her Nymphes enranged on a rowe,
    With whom the woody Gods did oft consort:
For, with the Nymphes, the Satyres love to play and
    sport.

40 Amongst the which, there was a Nymph that hight
    Molanna; daughter of old father *Mole*,   §
    And sister unto *Mulla*, faire and bright:
    Unto whose bed false *Bregog* whylome stole,
    That Shepheard *Colin* dearely did condole,
    And made her lucklesse loves well knowne to be.
    But this *Molanna*, were she not so shole,
    Were no lesse faire and beautifull then shee:
Yet as she is, a fairer flood may no man see.

39. (1) **game:** recreation, amusement; (2) **boawe:** bow (and arrows); (3) **shroude:** shelter; (5) **Or from . . . or from:** either from . . . or from; (7) **enranged on:** arranged in.
40. (5) **That Shepheard Colin:** with whom the shepherd Colin; (5) **dearely:** i.e., in sympathetic grief; (7) **shole:** shallow.

§ *Molanna*: The Behanagh stream; the *Mulla* is the Awbeg, which flowed through Spenser's own property of Kilcolman; the *Bregog* is the Bregoge stream. *Shepheard Colin* is Spenser's name for himself, and he is recalling a story of Mulla and Bregog that he had told in *Colin Clouts Come Home Againe.*

41   For, first, she springs out of two marble Rocks,
        On which, a grove of Oakes high mounted growes,
        That as a girlond seemes to deck the locks
        Of som faire Bride, brought forth with pompous
            showes
        Out of her bowre, that many flowers strowes:
        So, through the flowry Dales she tumbling downe,
        Through many woods, and shady coverts flowes
        (That on each side her silver channell crowne)
     Till to the Plaine she come, whose Valleyes shee doth
        drowne.

42   In her sweet streames, *Diana* used oft
        (After her sweatie chace and toilesome play)
        To bathe her selfe; and after, on the soft
        And downy grasse, her dainty limbes to lay
        In covert shade, where none behold her may:
        For, much she hated sight of living eye.
        Foolish God *Faunus*, though full many a day   §
        He saw her clad, yet longed foolishly
     To see her naked mongst her Nymphes in privity.

43   No way he found to compasse his desire,
        But to corrupt *Molanna*, this her maid,
        Her to discover for some secret hire:
        So, her with flattering words he first assaid;
        And after, pleasing gifts for her purvaid,
        Queene-apples, and red Cherries from the tree,
        With which he her allured and betraid,
        To tell what time he might her Lady see
     When she her selfe did bathe, that he might secret bee.

41. (4) **pompous**: ceremonious; (5) **bowre, that . . . strowes:**
    chamber strewn with many flowers, (or, referring back to
    Bride) who scatters many flowers.
42. (9) **in privity**: in secrecy.
43. (3) **Her to discover**: to reveal her; (3) **hire**: payment, reward;
    (4) **assaid**: sounded (her) out, tried; (5) **purvaid**: provided.

§ *Faunus*: A Roman god, often identified with Pan, the goat-footed
god of forests and herdsmen.

44 There-to hee promist, if shee would him pleasure
        With this small boone, to quit her with a better;
        To weet, that where-as shee had out of measure
        Long lov'd the *Fanchin*, who by nought did set her,
        That he would undertake, for this to get her
        To be his Love, and of him liked well:
        Besides all which, he vow'd to be her debter
        For many moe good turnes then he would tell;
The least of which, this little pleasure should excell.

45 The simple maid did yield to him anone;
        And eft him placed where he close might view
        That never any saw, save onely one;   §
        Who, for his hire to so foole-hardy dew,
        Was of his hounds devour'd in Hunters hew.
        Tho, as her manner was on sunny day,
        Diana, with her Nymphes about her, drew
        To this sweet spring; where, doffing her array,
She bath'd her lovely limbes, for *Jove* a likely pray.

46 There *Faunus* saw that pleased much his eye,
        And made his hart to tickle in his brest,
        That for great joy of some-what he did spy,
        He could him not containe in silent rest;
        But breaking forth in laughter, loud profest
        His foolish thought. A foolish *Faune* indeed,
        That couldst not hold thy selfe so hidden blest,
        But wouldest needs thine owne conceit areed.
Babblers unworthy been of so divine a meed.

44. (2) **to quit her:** to repay her; (3) **out of measure:** beyond
      measure; (4) **Fanchin:** river Funsheon; (4) **who by nought . . .
      her:** who cared nothing for her; (8) **then he would tell:** than
      he would tell.
45. (1) **anone:** anon, very soon; (2) **eft:** (soon) thereafter; (4)
      for his hire . . . dew: as due punishment for such foolhardi-
      ness; (5) **hew:** form, shape; (6) **Tho:** then.
46. (7) **couldst not hold . . . blest:** i.e., could not, being so for-
      tunately hidden, contain yourself; (8) **conceit:** thought(s); (8)
      areed: proclaim, give away; (9) **meed:** present, gift.

§ *save onely one . . . Hunters hew*: The reference is to the hunter
Actaeon who, in the story as told by Ovid, is actually turned into a

47 The Goddesse, all abashed with that noise,
         In haste forth started from the guilty brooke;
         And running straight where-as she heard his voice,
         Enclos'd the bush about, and there him tooke,
         Like darred Larke; not daring up to looke
         On her whose sight before so much he sought.
         Thence, forth they drew him by the hornes, and
              shooke
         Nigh all to peeces, that they left him nought;
     And then into the open light they forth him brought.

48 Like as an huswife, that with busie care
         Thinks of her Dairie to make wondrous gaine,
         Finding where-as some wicked beast unware
         That breakes into her Dayr'house, there doth draine
         Her creaming pannes, and frustrate all her paine;
         Hath in some snare or gin set close behind,
         Entrapped him, and caught into her traine,
         Then thinkes what punishment were best assign'd,
     And thousand deathes deviseth in her vengefull mind:

49 So did *Diana* and her maydens all
         Use silly *Faunus*, now within their baile:
         They mocke and scorne him, and him foule miscall;
         Some by the nose him pluckt, some by the taile,
         And by his goatish beard some did him haile:
         Yet he (poore soule) with patience all did beare;
         For, nought against their wils might countervaile:
         Ne ought he said what ever he did heare;
     But hanging downe his head, did like a Mome appeare.

47. (5) **darred:** i.e., mesmerized with terror.
48. (2) **Thinks of her:** thinks from her; (2) **gaine:** profit; (3)
unware: suddenly; (5) **paine:** labour, efforts; (6) **gin:** net;
(7) **traine:** trap.
49. (2) **baile:** custody; (3) **miscall:** revile; (5) **him haile:** drag
him, tug him; (9) **Mome:** lout, simpleton.

deer and torn to pieces by his own hounds in punishment for having
blundered upon Diana bathing.

50   At length, when they had flouted him their fill,
     They gan to cast what penaunce him to give.
     Some would have gelt him, but that same would spill
     The Wood-gods breed, which must for ever live:
     Others would through the river him have drive,
     And ducked deepe: but that seem'd penaunce light;
     But most agreed and did this sentence give,
     Him in Deares skin to clad; and in that plight,
To hunt him with their hounds, him selfe save how hee
     might.

51   But *Cynthia's* selfe, more angry then the rest,
     Thought not enough, to punish him in sport,
     And of her shame to make a gamesome jest;
     But gan examine him in straighter sort,
     Which of her Nymphes, or other close consort,
     Him thither brought, and her to him betraid?
     He, much affeard, to her confessed short,
     That 'twas *Molanna* which her so bewraid.
Then all attonce their hands upon *Molanna* laid.

52   But him (according as they had decreed)
     With a Deeres-skin they covered, and then chast
     With all their hounds that after him did speed;
     But he more speedy, from them fled more fast
     Then any Deere: so sore him dread aghast.
     They after follow'd all with shrill out-cry,
     Shouting as they the heavens would have brast:
     That all the woods and dales where he did flie,
Did ring againe, and loud reeccho to the skie.

50. (2) **They gan to cast:** they began to consider; (3) **gelt:** castrated; (3) **spill:** destroy; (4) **breed:** species (and/or) fertility.
51. (4) **in straighter sort:** more closely, strictly; (7) **short:** soon, quickly.
52. (5) **so sore him . . . aghast:** i.e., so terrible was his dread; (7) **brast:** burst.

53 So they him follow'd till they weary were;
  When, back returning to *Molann'* againe,
  They, by commaund'ment of *Diana*, there
  Her whelm'd with stones. Yet *Faunus* (for her paine)
  Of her beloved *Fanchin* did obtaine,
  That her he would receive unto his bed.
  So now her waves passe through a pleasant Plaine,
  Till with the *Fanchin* she her selfe doe wed,
And (both combin'd) themselves in one faire river spred.

54 Nath'lesse, *Diana*, full of indignation,
  Thence-forth abandond her delicious brooke;
  In whose sweet streame, before that bad occasion,
  So much delight to bathe her limbes she tooke:
  Ne onely her, but also quite forsooke
  All those faire forrests about *Arlo* hid,
  And all that Mountaine, which doth over-looke
  The richest champian that may else be rid,
And the faire *Shure*, in which are thousand Salmons
   bred.

55 Them all, and all that she so deare did way,
  Thence-forth she left; and parting from the place,
  There-on an heavy haplesse curse did lay,
  To weet, that Wolves, where she was wont to space,
  Should harbour'd be, and all those Woods deface,
  And Thieves should rob and spoile that Coast around.
  Since which, those Woods, and all the goodly Chase,
  Doth to this day with Wolves and Thieves abound:
Which too-too true that lands in-dwellers since have
   found.

53. (5) **Of her beloved:** from her beloved; (5) **did obtaine:** won agreement.
54. (8) **champian:** champaign, plain; (8) **that may else be rid:** that may be seen anywhere.
55. (1) **so deare did way:** held so dear; (3) **haplesse:** calamity-ridden; (4) **wont to space:** accustomed to range; (7) **Chase:** i.e., hunting-area, game-country.

Canto VII

*Pealing, from Jove, to Natur's Bar,
    bold Alteration pleades
Large Evidence: but Nature soone
    her righteous Doome areads.*

1   Ah! whither doost thou now thou greater Muse   §
        Me from these woods and pleasing forrests bring?
    And my fraile spirit (that dooth oft refuse
    This too high flight, unfit for her weake wing)
    Lift up aloft, to tell of heavens King
    (Thy soveraine Sire) his fortunate successe,
    And victory, in bigger noates to sing,
    Which he obtain'd against that *Titanesse*,
That him of heavens Empire sought to dispossesse.

2   Yet sith I needs must follow thy behest,
        Doe thou my weaker wit with skill inspire,
    Fit for this turne; and in my feeble brest
    Kindle fresh sparks of that immortall fire,
    Which learned minds inflameth with desire
    Of heavenly things: for, who but thou alone,
    That art yborne of heaven and heavenly Sire,
    Can tell things doen in heaven so long ygone;
So farre past memory of man that may be knowne.

Large: specious; **Doome areads:** judgment pronounces.
1. (4) **unfit for:** i.e., too much for; (7) **bigger noates:** louder notes.
2. (1) **Yet sith . . . behest:** Yet since I must obey your command; (3) **turne:** change, modulation (back to the main theme); (8) **doen:** done; (8) **ygone:** ago.

§ *thou greater Muse*: Calliope (epic poetry), or perhaps Clio (history). For part of the debate on which of the two Muses this is, see vol. I, pp. 506-15, of the Variorum edition of Spenser's works.

3   Now, at the time that was before agreed,
      The Gods assembled all on *Arlo* hill;
      As well those that are sprung of heavenly seed,
      As those that all the other world doe fill,
      And rule both sea and land unto their will:
      Onely th'infernall Powers might not appeare;
      Aswell for horror of their count'naunce ill,
      As for th'unruly fiends which they did feare;
    Yet *Pluto* and *Proserpina* were present there.   §

4   And thither also came all other creatures,
      What-ever life or motion doe retaine,
      According to their sundry kinds of features;
      That *Arlo* scarsly could them all containe;
      So full they filled every hill and Plaine:
      And had not *Natures* Sergeant (that is *Order*)
      Them well disposed by his busie paine,
      And raunged farre abroad in every border,
    They would have caused much confusion and disorder.

5   Then forth issewed (great goddesse) great dame *Nature*,
      With goodly port and gracious Majesty;
      Being far greater and more tall of stature
      Then any of the gods or Powers on hie:
      Yet certes by her face and physnomy,
      Whether she man or woman inly were,
      That could not any creature well descry:
      For, with a veile that wimpled every where,
    Her head and face was hid, that mote to none appeare.

3. (4) **the other world:** i.e., the earth; (7-8) **Aswell for . . . As for:** both because . . . and also because; (7) **ill:** forbidding, ugly.
4. (3) **features:** forms, characters; (7) **busie paine:** busy labour, efforts.
5. (2) **goodly port:** beautiful bearing; (5) **certes:** certainly; (5) **physnomy:** countenance; (7) **descry:** make out; (8) **that wimpled:** that lay folded; (9) **that mote to none:** so that to none it might.

§ *Pluto and Proserpina*: That is, the only representatives present from the underworld were its King and Queen.

6   That some doe say was so by skill devized,
      To hide the terror of her uncouth hew,
      From mortall eyes that should be sore agrized;
      For that her face did like a Lion shew,
      That eye of wight could not indure to view:
      But others tell that it so beautious was,
      And round about such beames of splendor threw,
      That it the Sunne a thousand times did pass,
  Ne could be seene, but like an image in a glass.

7   That well may seemen true: for, well I weene
      That this same day, when she on *Arlo* sat,
      Her garment was so bright and wondrous sheene,
      That my fraile wit cannot devize to what
      It to compare, nor finde like stuffe to that,
      As those three sacred *Saints*, though else most wise, §
      Yet on mount *Thabor* quite their wits forgat,
      When they their glorious Lord in strange disguise
  Transfigur'd sawe; his garments so did daze their eyes.

8   In a fayre Plaine upon an equall Hill,
      She placed was in a pavilion;
      Not such as Craftes-men by their idle skill
      Are wont for Princes states to fashion:
      But th'earth her self of her owne motion,
      Out of her fruitfull bosome made to growe
      Most dainty trees; that, shooting up anon,
      Did seeme to bow their bloosming heads full lowe,
  For homage unto her, and like a throne did shew.

6. (1) **That some doe say:** some say it (i.e., the veil); (2) **uncouth hew:** strange appearance; (3) **agrized:** horrified.
7. (1) **That well . . . true:** that seems very likely to be true; (3) **sheene:** brilliant; (6) **else:** elsewhere; (9) **daze:** dazzle.
8. (1) **equall:** symmetrical (or) central; (3) **idle:** empty; (5) **her self of her . . . motion:** i.e., spontaneously.

§ *three sacred Saints*: Peter, James, and John (see Matthew 17:1-8 and Mark 9:2-6). In the Geneva Bible (1560) *mount Thabor* (Tabor) is noted as the Mount of Transfiguration.

9   So hard it is for any living wight,
       All her array and vestiments to tell,
       That old *Dan Geffrey* (in whose gentle spright
       The pure well head of Poesie did dwell)
       In his *Foules parley* durst not with it mel,   §
       But it transferd to *Alane*, who he thought
       Had in his *Plaint of kindes* describ'd it well:
       Which who will read set forth so as it ought,
  Go seek he out that *Alane* where he may be sought.

10   And all the earth far underneath her feete
       Was dight with flowres, that voluntary grew
       Out of the ground, and sent forth odours sweet,
       Tenne thousand mores of sundry sent and hew,
       That might delight the smell, or please the view:
       The which, the Nymphes, from all the brooks thereby
       Had gathered, which they at her foot-stoole threw;
       That richer seem'd then any tapestry,
  That Princes bowres adorne with painted imagery.

11   And *Mole* himselfe, to honour her the more,
       Did deck himself in freshest faire attire,
       And his high head, that seemeth alwaies hore
       With hardned frosts of former winters ire,
       He with an Oaken girlond now did tire,
       As if the love of some new Nymph late seene,
       Had in him kindled youthfull fresh desire,
       And made him change his gray attire to greene;
  Ah gentle *Mole*! such joyance hath thee well beseene.

9. (3) **Dan Geffrey**: Master Geoffrey, i.e., Chaucer; (5) **mel**: meddle; (8) **set forth . . . ought**: set out properly.
10. (4) **mores**: plants; (4) **hew**: colour; (6) **The which**: i.e., which flowers and plants.
11. (1) **Mole**: mountain-range beneath which assembly is gathered; (5) **tire**: decorate; (9) **hath thee well beseene**: has enhanced you splendidly.

§ *Foules parley*: Spenser follows Chaucer's *Parlement of Foules* (*Foules parley*) both in his description of Nature as president of such an assembly and also in his referring the reader to Alanus de Insulis' *De Planctu Naturae* (*Plaint of kindes*).

12 Was never so great joyance since the day,
      That all the gods whylome assembled were,
      On *Hæmus* hill in their divine array,   §
      To celebrate the solemne bridall cheare,
      Twixt *Peleus*, and dame *Thetis* pointed there;
      Where *Phœbus* self, that god of Poets hight,
      They say did sing the spousall hymne full cleere,
      That all the gods were ravisht with delight
Of his celestiall song, and Musicks wondrous might.

13 This great Grandmother of all creatures bred
      Great *Nature*, ever young yet full of eld,
      Still mooving, yet unmoved from her sted;
      Unseene of any, yet of all beheld;
      Thus sitting in her throne as I have teld,
      Before her came dame *Mutabilitie*;
      And being lowe before her presence feld,
      With meek obaysance and humilitie,
Thus gan her plaintif Plea, with words to amplifie;

14 To thee O greatest goddesse, onely great,
      An humble suppliant loe, I lowely fly
      Seeking for Right, which I of thee entreat;
      Who Right to all dost deale indifferently,
      Damning all Wrong and tortious Injurie,
      Which any of thy creatures doe to other
      (Oppressing them with power, unequally)
      Sith of them all thou art the equall mother,
And knittest each to each, as brother unto brother.

12. (5) **pointed:** appointed; (6) **hight:** is called.
13. (2) **full of eld:** ancient of days (eld=age); (3) **sted:** place;
     (7) **feld:** prostrated; (9) **plaintif Plea:** plea as plaintiff.
14. (4) **indifferently:** impartially; (5) **tortious:** wrongful; (7) **un-
     equally:** unfairly.

§ *Hæmus* hill: A hill in Thessaly. Usually Mount Pelion (also in
Thessaly) is given as the site of this particular wedding. The offspring
of this marriage between the mortal King *Peleus* and the sea-goddess
Thetis was Achilles. Zeus (Jove) himself had had an eye on Thetis
but on second thought, in deference to a prophecy that Thetis was
to bear a son who should be greater than his father, let Peleus have
her.

15   To thee therefore of this same *Jove* I plaine,
          And of his fellow gods that faine to be,
          That challenge to themselves the whole worlds raign;
          Of which, the greatest part is due to me,
          And heaven it selfe by heritage in Fee:
          For, heaven and earth I both alike do deeme,
          Sith heaven and earth are both alike to thee;
          And, gods no more then men thou doest esteeme:
     For, even the gods to thee, as men to gods do seeme.

16   Then weigh, O soveraigne goddesse, by what right
          These gods do claime the worlds whole soverainty;
          And that is onely dew unto thy might
          Arrogate to themselves ambitiously:
          As for the gods owne principality,
          Which *Jove* usurpes unjustly; that to be
          My heritage, *Jove's* self cannot deny,
          From my great Grandsire *Titan*, unto mee,
     Deriv'd by dew descent; as is well knowen to thee.

17   Yet mauger *Jove*, and all his gods beside,
          I doe possesse the worlds most regiment;
          As, if ye please it into parts divide,
          And every parts inholders to convent,
          Shall to your eyes appeare incontinent.
          And first, the Earth (great mother of us all)
          That only seems unmov'd and permanent,
          And unto *Mutability* not thrall;
     Yet is she chang'd in part, and eeke in generall.

15. (2) **faine to be:** who pretend to be gods; (3) **That challenge to:** who claim for; (3) **raign:** sovereignty; (5) **in Fee:** as a hereditary right; (6) **deeme:** consider, take to be.
16. (4) **Arrogate:** usurp.
17. (1) **Yet mauger:** yet in spite of; (2) **worlds most regiment:** sovereignty over most of the world; (4) **inholders:** tenants, incumbents; (4) **convent:** summon together; (5) **incontinent:** right away; (9) **eeke:** also, even.

18   For, all that from her springs, and is ybredde,
    How-ever fayre it flourish for a time,
    Yet see we soone decay; and, being dead,
    To turne again unto their earthly slime:
    Yet, out of their decay and mortall crime,
    We daily see new creatures to arize;
    And of their Winter spring another Prime,
    Unlike in forme, and chang'd by strange disguise:
So turne they still about, and change in restlesse wise.

19   As for her tenants; that is, man and beasts,
    The beasts we daily see massacred dy,
    As thralls and vassalls unto mens beheasts:
    And men themselves doe change continually,
    From youth to eld, from wealth to poverty,
    From good to bad, from bad to worst of all.
    Ne doe their bodies only flit and fly:
    But eeke their minds (which they immortall call)
Still change and vary thoughts, as new occasions fall.

20   Ne is the water in more constant case;
    Whether those same on high, or these belowe.
    For, th'Ocean moveth stil, from place to place;
    And every River still doth ebbe and flowe:
    Ne any Lake, that seems most still and slowe,
    Ne Poole so small, that can his smoothnesse holde,
    When any winde doth under heaven blowe;
    With which, the clouds are also tost and roll'd;
Now like great Hills; and, streight, like sluces, them
      unfold.

18. (1) **ybredde:** nourished, brought up; (5) **mortall crime:** i.e., doom to which mortality is subject; (7) **Prime:** springtime.
19. (3) **beheasts:** commands; (5) **eld:** old age; (9) **fall:** take place, occur.
20. (1) **Ne is:** nor is; (9) **them unfold:** open themselves.

21 So likewise are all watry living wights
   Still tost, and turned, with continuall change,
   Never abyding in their stedfast plights.
   The fish, still floting, doe at randon range,
   And never rest; but evermore exchange
   Their dwelling places, as the streames them carrie:
   Ne have the watry foules a certaine grange,
   Wherein to rest, ne in one stead do tarry;
  But flitting still doe flie, and still their places vary.

22 Next is the Ayre: which who feeles not by sense
   (For, of all sense it is the middle meane)
   To flit still? and, with subtill influence
   Of his thin spirit, all creatures to maintaine,
   In state of life? O weake life! that does leane
   On thing so tickle as th'unsteady ayre;
   Which every howre is chang'd, and altred cleane
   With every blast that bloweth fowle or faire:
  The faire doth it prolong; the fowle doth it impaire.

23 Therein the changes infinite beholde,
   Which to her creatures every minute chaunce;
   Now, boyling hot: streight, friezing deadly cold:
   Now, faire sun-shine, that makes all skip and daunce:
   Streight, bitter storms and balefull countenance,
   That makes them all to shiver and to shake:
   Rayne, hayle, and snowe do pay them sad penance,
   And dreadfull thunder-claps (that make them quake)
  With flames and flashing lights that thousand changes
    make.

21. (1) **wights:** creatures; (3) **stedfast plights:** states of rest; (7)
grange: home; (8) **stead:** location.

22. (2) **middle meane:** universal carrier, conductor; (6) **tickle:**
mobile, unstable; (7) **altred cleane:** completely changed; (9)
impaire: worsen, (?) shorten.

23. (2) **chaunce:** happen; (3) **streight:** next instant; (7) **pay . . .**
penance: deal out heavy punishment.

24   Last is the fire: which, though it live for ever,
        Ne can be quenched quite; yet, every day,
        Wee see his parts, so soone as they do sever,
        To lose their heat, and shortly to decay;
        So, makes himself his owne consuming pray.
        Ne any living creatures doth he breed:
        But all, that are of others bredd, doth slay;
        And, with their death, his cruell life dooth feed;
    Nought leaving, but their barren ashes, without seede.

25   Thus, all these fower (the which the ground-work bee
        Of all the world, and of all living wights)
        To thousand sorts of *Change* we subject see:
        Yet are they chang'd (by other wondrous slights)
        Into themselves, and lose their native mights;
        The Fire to Aire, and th'Ayre to Water sheere,
        And Water into Earth: yet Water fights
        With Fire, and Aire with Earth approaching neere:
    Yet all are in one body, and as one appeare.

26   So, in them all raignes *Mutabilitie*;
        How-ever these, that Gods themselves do call,
        Of them doe claime the rule and soverainty:
        As, *Vesta*, of the fire æthereall;   §
        Vulcan, of this, with us so usuall;
        Ops, of the earth; and *Juno* of the Ayre;
        Neptune, of Seas; and Nymphes, of Rivers all.
        For, all those Rivers to me subject are:
    And all the rest, which they usurp, be all my share.

24. (3) **sever:** separate; (6) **breed:** produce, cause.
25. (1) **these fower:** these four (i.e., Earth, Water, Air, Fire);
    (3) **we subject see:** we see are subject; (4-5) **chang'd . . . Into
    themselves:** interchanged among themselves; (4) **slights:**
    processes; (6) **sheere:** clear, bright.
26. (5) **with us so usuall:** so familiar to us (as distinct from the
    ethereal fire).

§ *Vesta*: Vesta (Hestia) is the oldest child of Saturn (Cronus) and
Ops (Rhea); she is the goddess of pure celestial fire and of the con-
secrated hearth-fire; in Rome her sacred fire was tended by the
Vestal Virgins. *Vulcan*: Hephaestus, the artificer-god, associated with

27 Which to approven true, as I have told,
    Vouchsafe, O goddesse, to thy presence call
    The rest which doe the world in being hold:
    As, times and seasons of the yeare that fall:
    Of all the which, demand in generall,
    Or judge thy selfe, by verdit of thine eye,
    Whether to me they are not subject all.
    Nature did yeeld thereto; and by-and-by,
Bade *Order* call them all, before her Majesty.

28 So, forth issew'd the Seasons of the yeare;
    First, lusty *Spring*, all dight in leaves of flowres
    That freshly budded and new bloosmes did beare
    (In which a thousand birds had built their bowres
    That sweetly sung, to call forth Paramours):
    And in his hand a javelin he did beare,
    And on his head (as fit for warlike stoures)
    A guilt engraven morion he did weare;
That as some did him love, so others did him feare.

29 Then came the jolly *Sommer*, being dight
    In a thin silken cassock coloured greene,
    That was unlyned all, to be more light:
    And on his head a girlond well beseene
    He wore, from which as he had chauffed been
    The sweat did drop; and in his hand he bore
    A boawe and shaftes, as he in forrest greene
    Had hunted late the Libbard or the Bore,
And now would bathe his limbes, with labor heated sore.

27. (1) **Which to approven . . . told:** to prove conclusively that what I have said is true; (4) **that fall:** that occur; (6) **verdit:** verdict.
28. (2) **dight:** decked; (3) **bloosmes:** blossoms; (7) **stoures:** encounters; (8) **A guilt engraven morion:** a helmet engraved in gold.
29. (4) **well beseene:** beautiful; (5) **chauffed:** heated; (7) **boawe and shaftes:** bow and arrows; (8) **Libbard:** leopard.

fire in its more common, secular aspects and uses. *Ops*: A Roman divinity whom Spenser, following Boccaccio, thinks of as the earth-goddess; she is often identified with Rhea, wife of Cronus.

30   Then came the *Autumne* all in yellow clad,
        As though he joyed in his plentious store,
        Laden with fruits that made him laugh, full glad
        That he had banisht hunger, which to-fore
        Had by the belly oft him pinched sore.
        Upon his head a wreath that was enroll
        With eares of corne, of every sort he bore:
        And in his hand a sickle he did holde,
   To reape the ripened fruits the which the earth had yold.

31   Lastly, came *Winter* cloathed all in frize,
        Chattering his teeth for cold that did him chill,
        Whil'st on his hoary beard his breath did freese;
        And the dull drops that from his purpled bill
        As from a limbeck did adown distill.
        In his right hand a tipped staffe he held,
        With which his feeble steps he stayed still:
        For, he was faint with cold, and weak with eld;
   That scarse his loosed limbes he hable was to weld.

32   These, marching softly, thus in order went,
        And after them, the Monthes all riding came;
        First, sturdy *March* with brows full sternly bent,
        And armed strongly, rode upon a Ram,   §
        The same which over *Hellespontus* swam:
        Yet in his hand a spade he also hent,
        And in a bag all sorts of seeds ysame,
        Which on the earth he strowed as he went,
   And fild her womb with fruitfull hope of nourishment.

30. (4) **to-fore:** hitherto; (6) **enroll,** rolled, woven round; (7) **corne:** grain; (9) **yold:** yielded.

31. (1) **frize:** coarse woollen cloth; (3) **hoary:** frosty; (4) **bill:** nose; (5) **limbeck:** retort, distilling vessel; (7) **stayed still:** always steadied; (9) **hable was to weld:** was able to move.

32. (6) **hent:** grasped; (7) **ysame:** together.

§ *a Ram*: Phrixus and Helle, son and daughter of King Athamus of Boeotia, were on the point of being killed as sacrifices, in obedience to a false oracle arranged by their designing stepmother, when Zeus sent a great golden ram to carry them away. As the ram bore them eastward, Helle lost her grip on its back, fell off, and was drowned in the strait now called the Hellespont after her (*Hellespontus*,

33 Next came fresh *Aprill* full of lustyhed,
  And wanton as a Kid whose horne new buds:
  Upon a Bull he rode, the same which led
  Europa floting through th'*Argolick* fluds: §
  His hornes were gilden all with golden studs
  And garnished with garlonds goodly dight
  Of all the fairest flowres and freshest buds
  Which th'earth brings forth, and wet he seem'd in
    sight
 With waves, through which he waded for his loves
  delight.

34 Then came faire *May*, the fayrest mayd on ground,
  Deckt all with dainties of her seasons pryde,
  And throwing flowres out of her lap around:
  Upon two brethrens shoulders she did ride,
  The twinnes of *Leda*; which on eyther side §
  Supported her like to their soveraine Queene.
  Lord! how all creatures laught, when her they spide,
  And leapt and daunc't as they had ravisht beene!
 And *Cupid* selfe about her fluttred all in greene.

33. (1) **lustyhed:** lustiness, gusto; (4) **fluds:** seas; (8) **seem'd in sight:** seemed to the eye.
34. (8) **ravisht beene:** transported with delight.

"Helle's Sea"). Having been carried to safety on the far side of the
Euxine Sea, Phrixus sacrificed the ram to Zeus and hung its fleece
in a sacred grove to be guarded by a dragon. This wonderful golden
fleece became the object of Jason's quest.
§ *Europa*: The daughter of King Agenor of Tyre. Her beauty attracted
the attention of Zeus, who appeared to her in the form of a beautiful
white bull and swam out to sea with her on his back. Her child by
Zeus was Minos of Crete. Note in this passage that each month is
associated in some way with the appropriate zodiacal sign: Aries the
Ram, Taurus the Bull, Gemini the Twins, and so on.
§ *twinnes of Leda*: The Heavenly Twins, Castor and Polydeuces, fath-
ered upon Leda by Zeus, who ravished her in the form of a swan.

35   And after her, came jolly *June*, arrayd
      All in greene leaves, as he a Player were;
      Yet in his time, he wrought as well as playd,
      That by his plough-yrons mote right well appeare:
      Upon a Crab he rode, that him did beare
      With crooked crawling steps an uncouth pase,
      And backward yode, as Bargemen wont to fare   §
      Bending their force contrary to their face,
  Like that ungracious crew which faines demurest grace.

36   Then came hot *July* boyling like to fire,
      That all his garments he had cast away:
      Upon a Lyon raging yet with ire
      He boldly rode and made him to obay:
      It was the beast that whylome did forray
      The Nemæan forrest, till th'*Amphytrionide*   §
      Him slew, and with his hide did him array;
      Behinde his back a sithe, and by his side
  Under his belt he bore a sickle circling wide.

35. (3) **he wrought:** he worked; (4) **That by his . . . appeare:** which was very apparent from his plowshares; (6) **an uncouth pase:** a strange gait; (7) **yode:** went.
36. (5) **whylome:** once; (5) **forray:** ravage; (7) **did him array:** dressed himself; (8) **sithe:** scythe.

§ *As Bargemen . . . demurest grace:* Hypocrites – the "ungracious crew" who are not what they appear to be – are like bargemen who exert force on a bargepole in one direction in order to move the barge in another.
§ *th'Amphytrionide:* Hercules (Herakles), the first of whose labours was to destroy the Nemean lion.

37   The sixt was *August*, being rich arrayd
          In garment all of gold downe to the ground:
          Yet rode he not, but led a lovely Mayd
          Forth by the lilly hand, the which was cround
          With eares of corne, and full her hand was found;
          That was the righteous Virgin, which of old   §
          Liv'd here on earth, and plenty made abound;
          But, after Wrong was lov'd and Justice solde,
      She left th'unrighteous world and was to heaven extold.

38   Next him, *September* marched eeke on foote;
          Yet was he heavy laden with the spoyle
          Of harvests riches, which he made his boot,
          And him enricht with bounty of the soyle:
          In his one hand, as fit for harvests toyle,
          He held a knife-hook; and in th'other hand
          A paire of waights, with which he did assoyle
          Both more and lesse, where it in doubt did stand,
      And equall gave to each as justice duly scann'd.

37. (5) **full her hand was found:** her hand could be seen to be
    full (of produce); (9) **extold:** taken up.
38. (1) **eeke:** also; (3) **boot:** profit, booty; (7) **waights:** scales; (7)
    assoyle: i.e., determine; (9) **scann'd:** required upon scrutiny.

§ *the righteous Virgin*: Astraea, Justice herself, who is said to have left
the earth after the Golden Age of Saturn's rule.

39   Then came *October* full of merry glee:
        For, yet his noule was totty of the must,
        Which he was treading in the wine-fats see,
        And of the joyous oyle, whose gentle gust
        Made him so frollick and so full of lust:
        Upon a dreadfull Scorpion he did ride,
        The same which by *Dianaes* doom unjust   §
        Slew great *Orion*: and eeke by his side
    He had his ploughing share, and coulter ready tyde.

40   Next was *November*, he full grosse and fat,
        As fed with lard, and that right well might seeme;
        For, he had been a fatting hogs of late,
        That yet his browes with sweat, did reek and steem,
        And yet the season was full sharp and breem;
        In planting eeke he took no small delight:
        Whereon he rode, not easie was to deeme;   §
        For it a dreadfull *Centaure* was in sight,
    The seed of *Saturne*, and faire *Nais, Chiron* hight.

39. (2) **yet his noule . . . must:** his noggin was still giddy with
    new wine; (3) **the wine-fats see:** the sea of wine in the vats;
    (4) **gust:** taste; (5) **lust:** pleasure; (9) **coulter:** blade of a plow.
40. (2) **As fed:** as if fed; (2) **and that right . . . seeme:** and that
    might very well be the case; (5) **breem:** chilly; (7) **to deeme:**
    to imagine.

§ *Dianaes doom unjust*: The details of the story of Diana (Artemis)
and the great hunter *Orion* vary a good deal. Since he says that
Diana's judgment upon Orion was unjust, Spenser is probably thinking of the version in which Diana, in a fit of jealous anger over
Orion's prowess as a hunter, sent a scorpion whose sting killed him.
§ *Centaure*: The race of Centaurs, creatures part man, part horse, was
said to have descended from Centaurus, son of Ixion and Nephele,
who mated with wild mares on the slopes of Mount Pelion. Centaurs
tended to be a lustful, rough lot, but *Chiron* was a wise, gentle creature who had tutored such divine children and heroes as Achilles
and Jason. According to Boccaccio and Natalis Comes, *Chiron* was
set in the sky as the constellation Sagittarius.

41   And after him, came next the chill *December*:
      Yet he through merry feasting which he made,
      And great bonfires, did not the cold remember;
      His Saviours birth his mind so much did glad:
      Upon a shaggy-bearded Goat he rade,
      The same wherewith *Dan Jove* in tender yeares,   §
      They say, was nourisht by th'*Idæan* mayd;
      And in his hand a broad deepe boawle he beares;
Of which, he freely drinks an health to all his peeres.

42   Then came old *January*, wrapped well
      In many weeds to keep the cold away;
      Yet did he quake and quiver like to quell,
      And blowe his nayles to warme them if he may:
      For, they were numbd with holding all the day
      An hatchet keene, with which he felled wood,
      And from the trees did lop the needlesse spray:
      Upon an huge great Earth-pot steane he stood;
From whose wide mouth, there flowed forth the
        Romane floud.   §

41. (4) **did glad:** did gladden.
42. (2) **weeds:** clothes; (3) **like to quell:** as if about to perish;
    (7) **spray:** sprigs, small branches; (8) **Earth-pot steane:** (?)
    earthenware jar.

§ *Dan Jove*: As an infant the Lord Jove was reared on Crete in hiding
  from his father Saturn (Cronus). He was watched over by Amalthea,
  a nymph of Mount Ida (th'*Idæan mayd*), and suckled by a she-
  goat. In some versions of the story the name Amalthea is applied to
  the she-goat herself. Again, in some versions there is a second goat,
  reared along with Jove as his playfellow, which Jove eventually honoured by placing among the stars. Spenser mentions only the nursing
  she-goat and identifies her with Capricorn.
§ *the Romane floud*: The zodiacal reference in these lines is to
  Aquarius, represented as a figure pouring water (hence *floud*, or
  stream) from a large urn. The Roman flood is the river Tiber, and
  the point of Spenser's reference to this river in particular is that on
  the west bank of the Tiber at Rome there is a three-mile ridge, called
  the Janiculum, which was anciently associated with the god Janus;
  from Janus comes the name of the month January, and this is
  January's stanza.

43   And lastly, came cold *February*, sitting
   In an old wagon, for he could not ride;
   Drawne of two fishes for the season fitting,
   Which through the flood before did softly slyde
   And swim away: yet had he by his side
   His plough and harnesse fit to till the ground,
   And tooles to prune the trees, before the pride
   Of hasting Prime did make them burgein round:
  So past the twelve Months forth, and their dew places
    found.

44   And after these, there came the *Day*, and *Night*,
   Riding together both with equall pase,
   Th'one on a Palfrey blacke, the other white;
   But *Night* had covered her uncomely face
   With a blacke veile, and held in hand a mace,
   On top whereof the moon and stars were pight,
   And sleep and darknesse round about did trace:
   But *Day* did beare, upon his scepters hight,
  The goodly Sun, encompast all with beames bright.

45   Then came the *Howres*, faire daughters of high *Jove*, §
   And timely *Night*, the which were all endewed
   With wondrous beauty fit to kindle love;
   But they were Virgins all, and love eschewed,
   That might forslack the charge to them fore-shewed
   By mighty *Jove*; who did them Porters make
   Of heavens gate (whence all the gods issued)
   Which they did dayly watch, and nightly wake
  By even turnes, ne ever did their charge forsake.

43. (8) **burgein round:** burst into bud all over.
44. (2) **with equall pase:** with even gait, (or perhaps) in step; (6) **pight:** set; (7) **trace:** walk, pace.
45. (1) **Howres:** Hours; (5) **forslack;** neglect (i.e., tempt them to neglect); (5) **fore-shewed:** ordained.

§ *Howres*: The Hours (Horae) are usually given as the daughters of Themis (Order) and Jove. Besides being the Porters "of heavens gate" they are the goddesses of the fruitful seasons of the earth.

46   And after all came *Life*, and lastly *Death*;
        Death with most grim and griesly visage seene,
        Yet is he nought but parting of the breath;
        Ne ought to see, but like a shade to weene,
        Unbodied, unsoul'd, unheard, unseene.
        But *Life* was like a faire young lusty boy,
        Such as they faine *Dan Cupid* to have beene,
        Full of delightfull health and lively joy,
Deckt all with flowres, and wings of gold fit to employ.

47   When these were past, thus gan the *Titanesse*;
        Lo, mighty mother, now be judge and say,
        Whether in all thy creatures more or lesse
        CHANGE doth not raign and beare the greatest
             sway:
        For, who sees not, that *Time* on all doth pray?
        But *Times* do change and move continually.
        So nothing here long standeth in one stay:
        Wherefore, this lower world who can deny
But to be subject still to *Mutabilitie*?

48   Then thus gan *Jove*; Right true it is, that these
        And all things else that under heaven dwell
        Are chaung'd of *Time*, who doth them all disseise
        Of being: But, who is it (to me tell)
        That *Time* himselfe doth move and still compell
        To keepe his course? Is not that namely wee
        Which poure that vertue from our heavenly cell,
        That moves them all, and makes them changed be?
So them we gods doe rule, and in them also thee.

46. (4) **Ne ought to see . . . weene:** i.e., impossible to visualize
     except as a shadow; (7) **they faine:** they imagine.
47. (7) **standeth in one stay:** remains, rests in one state.
48. (3) **disseise:** dispossess; (5) **still compell:** continuously compel;
     (7) **cell:** dwelling.

49   To whom, thus *Mutability*: The things
  Which we see not how they are mov'd and swayd,
  Ye may attribute to your selves as Kings,
  And say they by your secret powre are made:
  But what we see not, who shall us perswade?
  But were they so, as ye them faine to be,
  Mov'd by your might, and ordred by your ayde;
  Yet what if I can prove, that even yee
 Your selves are likewise chang'd, and subject unto mee?

50   And first, concerning her that is the first,
  Even you faire *Cynthia*, whom so much ye make
  Joves dearest darling, she was bred and nurst
  On *Cynthus* hill, whence she her name did take:
  Then is she mortall borne, how-so ye crake;
  Besides, her face and countenance every day
  We changed see, and sundry forms partake,
  Now hornd, now round, now bright, now brown and
    gray:
 So that *as changefull as the Moone* men use to say.

51   Next, *Mercury*, who though he lesse appeare
  To change his hew, and alwayes seeme as one;
  Yet, he his course doth altar every yeare,
  And is of late far out of order gone:
  So *Venus* eeke, that goodly Paragone,
  Though faire all night, yet is she darke all day;
  And *Phœbus* self, who lightsome is alone,
  Yet is he oft eclipsed by the way,
 And fills the darkned world with terror and dismay.

49. (6) **them faine to be:** wrongly imagine them to be.
50. (2) **whom so much ye make:** whom you make so much of as;
  (5) **how-so ye crake:** however much you brag.
51. (7) **who lightsome is alone:** who is unique in radiance.

52 Now *Mars* that valiant man is changed most:
    For, he some times so far runs out of square,
    That he his way doth seem quite to have lost,
    And cleane without his usuall sphere to fare;
    That even these Star-gazers stonisht are
    At sight thereof, and damne their lying bookes:
    So likewise, grim Sir *Saturne* oft doth spare
    His sterne aspect, and calme his crabbed lookes:
So many turning cranks these have, so many crookes.

53 But you *Dan Jove*, that only constant are,
    And King of all the rest, as ye do clame,
    Are you not subject eeke to this misfare?
    Then let me aske you this withouten blame,
    Where were ye borne? some say in *Crete* by name,
    Others in *Thebes*, and others other-where;
    But wheresoever they comment the same,
    They all consent that ye begotten were,
And borne here in this world, ne other can appeare.

52. (2) **out of square:** out of true, off his course; (4) **cleane without:** clear outside; (4) **to fare:** to go; (7) **doth spare:** hold back, restrain; (8) **crabbed:** surly; (9) **turning cranks:** winding twists; (9) **crookes:** bends.
53. (1) **that only . . . are:** who alone is; (3) **misfare:** misfortune; (7) **comment the same:** imaginatively locate it (i.e., Jove's birthplace).

54　Then are ye mortall borne, and thrall to me,
　　　Unlesse the kingdome of the sky yee make
　　　Immortall, and unchangeable to be;
　　　Besides, that power and vertue which ye spake,　　§
　　　That ye here worke, doth may changes take,
　　　And your owne natures change: for, each of you
　　　That vertue have, or this, or that to make,
　　　Is checkt and changed from his nature trew,
　　By others opposition or obliquid view.

55　Besides, the sundry motions of your Spheares,
　　　So sundry waies and fashions as clerkes faine,
　　　Some in short space, and some in longer yeares;
　　　What is the same but alteration plaine?
　　　Onely the starrie skie doth still remaine:
　　　Yet do the Starres and Signes therein still move,
　　　And even it self is mov'd, as wizards saine.
　　　But all that moveth, doth mutation love:
　　Therefore both you and them to me I subject prove.

56　Then since within this wide great *Universe*
　　　Nothing doth firme and permanent appeare,
　　　But all things tost and turned by transverse:
　　　What then should let, but I aloft should reare
　　　My Trophee, and from all, the triumph beare?
　　　Now judge then (O thou greatest goddesse trew!)
　　　According as thy selfe doest see and heare,
　　　And unto me addoom that is my dew;
　　That is the rule of all, all being rul'd by you.

54. (4) **which ye spake:** which you were talking about; (7) **or this, or that to make:** to perform this or that; (9) **obliquid view:** i.e., obliquity of view.
55. (2) **as clerkes faine:** as scholars imagine (or, just possibly) delight in; (5) **still:** without motion; (6) **still:** continuously; (7) **wizards saine:** wise men say.
56. (3) **by transverse:** from side to side, back and forth; (4) **What then should . . . reare:** what's to prevent me, then, from raising; (5) **Trophee:** victory token or memorial; (8) **addoom:** adjudge; (8) **that is my dew:** what is my right.

§ *Besides, that power . . . or obliquid view:* Mutabilitie is arguing that Jove (the Sky) and all his planet-gods cannot possibly be con-

57   So having ended, silence long ensewed,
        Ne *Nature* to or fro spake for a space,
        But with firme eyes affixt, the ground still viewed.
        Meane while, all creatures, looking in her face,
        Expecting th'end of this so doubtfull case,
        Did hang in long suspence what would ensew,
        To whether side should fall the soveraigne place:
        At length, she looking up with chearefull view,
    The silence brake, and gave her doome in speeches few.

58   I well consider all that ye have sayd,
        And find that all things stedfastnes doe hate
        And changed be: yet being rightly wayd
        They are not changed from their first estate;
        But by their change their being doe dilate:
        And turning to themselves at length againe,
        Doe worke their owne perfection so by fate:
        Then over them Change doth not rule and raigne;
    But they raigne over change, and doe their states
            maintaine.

59   Cease therefore daughter further to aspire,
        And thee content thus to be rul'd by me:
        For thy decay thou seekst by thy desire;
        But time shall come that all shall changed bee,
        And from thenceforth, none no more change shall see.
        So was the *Titaness* put downe and whist,
        And *Jove* confirm'd in his imperiall see.
        Then was that whole assembly quite dismist,
    And *Natur's* selfe did vanish, whither no man wist.

57. (9) **doome:** judgment.
58. (3) **wayd:** weighed, considered; (4) **estate:** state of being; (7)
    Doe worke . . . so by fate: thus work, by necessity, towards.
59. (2) **thee content:** content yourself; (3) **decay:** destruction;
    (6) **whist:** silenced; (7) **see:** jurisdiction, seat of power; (9)
    wist: knew.

stant because of the effect that each of them has upon all the others.
In each's aspect as a heavenly body its path of orbit is affected by
its astronomical relation to all the others; in each's aspect as a heavenly power, or Intelligence, its astrological influence is continuously
modified by its own changing position, not to speak of the influence
of all the others.

The VIII Canto, unperfite

1   When I bethinke me on that speech whyleare,
    Of *Mutability*, and well it way:
      Me seemes, that though she all unworthy were
    Of the Heav'ns Rule; yet very sooth to say,
    In all things else she beares the greatest sway.
      Which makes me loath this state of life so tickle,
    And love of things so vaine to cast away;
      Whose flowring pride, so fading and so fickle,
  Short *Time* shall soon cut down with his consuming
      sickle.

2   Then gin I thinke on that which Nature sayd,
    Of that same time when no more *Change* shall be,
      But stedfast rest of all things firmely stayd
    Upon the pillours of Eternity,
    That is contrayr to *Mutalibitie*:
      For, all that moveth, doth in *Change* delight:
    But thence-forth all shall rest eternally
      With Him that is the God of Sabbaoth hight: §
  O! that great Sabbaoth God, grant me that Sabaoths
      sight.

---

unperfite: incomplete.
1. (1) **whyleare:** erstwhile; (2) **well it way:** think it over carefully; (3) **Me seemes:** it seems to me; (4) **yet very sooth to say:** yet to tell the honest truth; (6) **tickle:** precarious.
2. (3) **stayd:** fixed.

§ *Sabbaoth*: It is difficult to know how much to make of the distinction here between *Sabbaoth* and *Sabaoth*. Perhaps "Hosts" or "Armies" is intended by the first spelling and Sabbath, meaning "Day of Rest" or "Eternal Rest", by the second. But it seems quite likely that both spellings intend the same thing, with the notion of sabbath rest – in view of the context – being more probable than the notion of the Lord of Hosts. In the first collected edition of Spenser's works (1611), the word is spelled "Sabaoth" all three times.

A Letter of the Authors

EXPOUNDING HIS WHOLE INTENTION IN THE COURSE OF THIS WORKE:

WHICH FOR THAT IT GIVETH GREAT LIGHT TO THE READER, FOR THE BETTER UNDERSTANDING IS HEREUNTO ANNEXED

To the Right noble, and Valorous, Sir Walter Raleigh knight, Lo. Wardein of the Stanneryes, and her Majesties liefe-tenaunt of the County of Cornewayll.

Sir knowing how doubtfully all Allegories may be construed, and this booke of mine, which I have en-tituled the Faery Queene, being a continued Alle-gory, or darke conceit, I have thought good aswell for avoyding of gealous opinions and misconstruc-tions, as also for your better light in reading thereof, (being so by you commanded,) to discover unto you the general intention and meaning, which in the whole course therof I have fashioned, without ex-pressing of any particular purposes or by-accidents therein occasioned. The generall end therefore of all the booke is to fashion a gentleman or noble person in vertuous and gentle discipline: Which for that I conceived shoulde be most plausible and pleasing, be-ing coloured with an historicall fiction, the which the most part of men delight to read, rather for variety of matter, then for profite of the ensample: I chose the historye of king Arthure, as most fitte for the excellency of his person, being made famous by many mens former workes, and also furthest from

5

10

15

20

11. **end:** purpose.
13. **for that:** because.
17. **then:** than.

the daunger of envy, and suspition of present time.
In which I have followed all the antique Poets historicall, first Homere, who in the Persons of Agamemnon and Ulysses hath ensampled a good governour
and a vertuous man, the one in his Ilias, the other   *25*
in his Odysseis: then Virgil, whose like intention was
to doe in the person of Aeneas: after him Ariosto   §
comprised them both in his Orlando: and lately
Tasso dissevered them againe, and formed both parts
in two persons, namely that part which they in Philo-   *30*
sophy call Ethice, or vertues of a private man, coloured in his Rinaldo: The other named Politice in
his Godfredo. By ensample of which excellente Poets,
I labour to pourtraict in Arthure, before he was king,
the image of a brave knight, perfected in the twelve   *35*
private morall vertues, as Aristotle hath devised, the   §
which is the purpose of these first twelve bookes:
which if I finde to be well accepted, I may be perhaps encoraged, to frame the other part of politicke
vertues in his person, after that hee came to be king.   *40*
To some I know this Methode will seeme displea-
saunt, which had rather have good discipline delivered
plainly in way of precepts, or sermoned at large, as

24. **ensampled:** exemplified.
25. **the one . . . the other:** i.e.,
   Agamemnon and Ulysses
   respectively; **Ilias:** "Iliad".

26. **Odysseis:** "Odyssey".
33. **By ensample:** according to
   the example.

§ *Aeneas*: The hero of Virgil's epic poem *The Aeneid*, written during
   the years *c.* 29-19 B.C. *Orlando*: Hero of the Italian epic romance
   Orlando Furioso, written by Ludovico Ariosto (1474-1533) and published in its final form in 1532. *Rinaldo* and *Godfredo* (Goffredo):
   The chief figures in the epic poem *Gerusalemme Liberata*, brought
   out in the authorized edition in 1581 by the Italian poet Torquato
   Tasso (1544-95).
§ *Aristotle*: The Greek philosopher (384-322 B.C.). In a very general
   and unschematic way, Spenser's figure of Arthur and the original
   plan of *The Faerie Queene* are partly inspired by Aristotle's discussion of the "private" virtues (in his *Nicomachean Ethics*) and of the
   "public" virtues (in his *Politics*).

they use, then thus clowdily enwrapped in Allegori-
call devises. But such, me seeme, should be satisfide   45
with the use of these dayes, seeing all things accounted by their showes, and nothing esteemed of,
that is not delightfull and pleasing to commune sence.
For this cause is Xenophon preferred before Plato,   §
for that the one in the exquisite depth of his judge-   50
ment, formed a Commune welth such as it should
be, but the other in the person of Cyrus and the
Persians fashioned a governement such as might best
be: So much more profitable and gratious is doctrine by ensample, then by rule. So have I laboured   55
to doe in the person of Arthure: whome I conceive
after his long education by Timon, to whom he was
by Merlin delivered to be brought up, so soone as he
was borne of the Lady Igrayne, to have seene in a
dream or vision the Faery Queen, with whose excel-   60
lent beauty ravished, he awaking resolved to seeke
her out, and so being by Merlin armed, and by Timon throughly instructed, he went to seeke her forth
in Faerye land. In that Faery Queene I meane glory
in my generall intention, but in my particular I con-   65
ceive the most excellent and glorious person of our
soveraine the Queene, and her kingdome in Faery
land. And yet in some places els, I doe otherwise
shadow her. For considering she beareth two persons,
the one of a most royall Queene or Empresse, the   70
other of a most vertuous and beautifull Lady, this
latter part in some places I doe express in Belphœbe,

44. **then:** than.
46-7. **accounted by their showes:** considered, or judged, by their appearances.

48. **commune sence:** ordinary sensibilities.
68. **some places els:** some other places.

§ *Xenophon*: The Athenian soldier and author (*c.* 430 - *c.* 355 B.C.); Spenser's reference is to Xenophon's *Cyropaedia*. *Plato*: The Greek philosopher (*c.* 427-348 B.C.); the reference is to Plato's *Republic*.

fashioning her name according to your owne excellent conceipt of Cynthia, (Phœbe and Cynthia being both names of Diana.) So in the person of Prince 75 Arthure I sette forth magnificence in particular, which vertue for that (according to Aristotle and the rest) it is the perfection of all the rest, and conteineth in it them all, therefore in the whole course I mention the deedes of Arthure applyable to that vertue, 80 which I write of in that booke. But of the xii. other vertues, I make xii. other knights the patrones, for the more variety of the history: Of which these three bookes contayn three. The first of the knight of the Redcrosse, in whome I expresse Holynes: The se- 85 conde of Sir Guyon, in whome I sette forth Temperaunce: The third of Britomartis a Lady knight, in whome I picture Chastity. But because the beginning of the whole worke seemeth abrupte and as depending upon other antecedents, it needs that ye know the 90 occasion of these three knights severall adventures. For the Methode of a Poet historical is not such, as of an Historiographer. For an Historiographer discourseth of affayres orderly as they were donne, accounting as well the times as the actions, but a Poet 95 thrusteth into the middest, even where it most concerneth him, and there recoursing to the thinges forepaste, and divining of thinges to come, maketh a pleasing Analysis of all. The beginning therefore of my history, if it were to be told by an Historiogra- 100 pher, should be the twelfth booke, which is the last, where I devise that the Faery Queene kept her Annuall feaste xii. dayes, uppon which xii. severall dayes, the occasions of the xii. severall adventures happ- ned, which being undertaken by xii. severall knights, 105 are in these xii books severally handled and discoursed. The first was this. In the beginning of the

91. **severall:** respective.
98. **divining of:** portending, foretelling.

103. **severall:** separate (also, here, with the sense of) consecutive.
104. **hapned:** happened.

feast, there presented him selfe a tall clownishe younge man, who falling before the Queen of Faries desired a boone (as the manner then was) which during that feast she might not refuse: which was that hee might have the atchievement of any adventure, which during that feaste should happen, that being graunted, he rested him on the floore, unfitte through his rusticity for a better place. Soone after entred a faire Ladye in mourning weedes, riding on a white Asse, with a dwarfe behind her leading a warlike steed, that bore the Armes of a knight, and his speare in the dwarfes hand. Shee falling before the Queene of Faeries, complayned that her father and mother an ancient King and Queene, had bene by an huge dragon many years shut up in a brasen Castle, who thence suffred them not to yssew: and therefore besought the Faery Queene to assygne her some one of her knights to take on him that exployt. Presently that clownish person upstarting, desired that adventure: whereat the Queene much wondering, and the Lady much gainesaying, yet he earnestly importuned his desire. In the end the Lady told him that unlesse that armour which she brought, would serve him (that is the armour of a Christian man specified by Saint Paul v. Ephes.) that he could not succeed in that enterprise, which being forthwith put upon him with dewe furnitures thereunto, he seemed the goodliest man in al that company, and was well liked of the Lady. And eftesoones taking on him knighthood, and mounting on that straunge Courser, he went forth

110

115

120

125

130

§

135

112. **have the atchievement of:** be assigned to.
116. **weedes:** clothes.
123. **suffred:** permitted: **yssew:** come out.

128. **gainesaying:** objecting; **importuned:** begged for, pressed for.
134. **dewe furnitures:** suitable gear.

---

§ Spenser is referring the reader (v. = *vide* = see) to the Epistle to the Ephesians, particularly to chapter 6:10-17.

with her on that adventure: where beginneth the first
booke, vz.

A gentle knight was pricking on the playne. &c.   *140*

The second day ther came in a Palmer bearing an
Infant with bloody hands, whose Parents he complained to have bene slayn by an Enchaunteresse
called Acrasia: and therfore craved of the Faery
Queene, to appoint him some knight, to performe that   *145*
adventure, which being assigned to Sir Guyon, he
presently went forth with that same Palmer: which is
the beginning of the second booke and the whole subject thereof. The third day there came in, a Groome
who complained before the Faery Queene, that a vile   *150*
Enchaunter called Busirane had in hand a most faire
Lady called Amoretta, whom he kept in most grievous torment, because she would not yield him the
pleasure of her body. Whereupon Sir Scudamour the
lover of that Lady presently tooke on him that ad-   *155*
venture. But being unable to performe it by reason
of the hard Enchauntments, after long sorrow, in the
end met with Britomartis, who succoured him, and
reskewed his love.

But by occasion hereof, many other adventures   *160*
are intermedled, but rather as Accidents, then intend-
ments. As the love of Britomart, the overthrow of
Marinell, the misery of Florimell, the vertuousnes of
Belphœbe, the lasciviousnes of Hellenora, and many
the like.   *165*

Thus much Sir, I have briefly overronne to direct
your understanding to the wel-head of the History,
that from thence gathering the whole intention of the
conceit, ye may as in a handfull gripe al the dis-

139. **vz:** viz., i.e., namely.
140. **pricking:** riding, spurring.
161. **Accidents:** i.e., minor or
     subsidiary elements of the
plot; **then:** than; **intend-
ments:** main elements of
the plot.
166. **overronne:** gone over.

course, which otherwise may happily seeme tedious   *170*
and confused. So humbly craving the continuance of
your honorable favour towards me, and th' eternall
establishment of your happines, I humbly take leave.

23. January. 1589.

Yours most humbly affectionate.   *175*

Ed. Spenser.

170. **happily:** perchance, perhaps.

AMORETTI
AND
Epithalamion

Written not long since
by Edmunde
Spenser.

Printed for William
Ponsonby, 1595

1

Happy ye leaves when as those lilly hands,
  which hold my life in their dead doing might
  shall handle you and hold in loves soft bands,
  lyke captives trembling at the victors sight.
And happy lines, on which with starry light,
  those lamping eyes will deigne sometimes to look
  and reade the sorrowes of my dying spright,
  written with teares in harts close bleeding book.
And happy rymes bath'd in the sacred brooke,   §
  of *Helicon* whence she derived is,
  when ye behold that Angels blessed looke,
  my soules long lacked foode, my heavens blis.
Leaves, lines, and rymes, seeke her to please alone,
  whom if ye please, I care for other none.

2

Unquiet thought, whom at the first I bred,
  Of th'inward bale of my love pined hart:
  and sithens have with sighes and sorrowes fed,
  till greater then my wombe thou woxen art.
Breake forth at length out of the inner part,
  in which thou lurkest lyke to vipers brood:
  and seeke some succour both to ease my smart
  and also to sustayne thy selfe with food.
But if in presence of that fayrest proud
  thou chance to come, fall lowly at her feet:
  and with meeke humblesse and afflicted mood,
  pardon for thee, and grace for me intreat.
Which if she graunt, then live and my love cherish,
  if not, die soone, and I with thee will perish.

1. (2) **dead doing**: death dealing; (6) **lamping**: resplendent; (7)
   spright: spirit.
2. (3) **sithens**: since (then); (4) **thou woxen art**: you have grown;
   (7) **smart**: pain, grief.

§ *Helicon*: In classical sources Helicon is given as the name of a mountain sacred to the Muses. Here Spenser is following Chaucer and
   other medieval authors in making Helicon a sacred spring or stream
   rather than a mountain.

3

The soverayne beauty which I doo admyre,
   witnesse the world how worthy to be prayzed:
   the light wherof hath kindled heavenly fyre,
   in my fraile spirit by her from basenesse raysed.
That being now with her huge brightnesse dazed,
   base thing I can no more endure to view:
   but looking still on her I stand amazed,
   at wondrous sight of so celestiall hew.
So when my toung would speak her praises dew,
   it stopped is with thoughts astonishment:
   and when my pen would write her titles true,
   it ravisht is with fancies wonderment:
Yet in my hart I then both speake and write
   the wonder that my wit cannot endite.

4

New yeare forth looking out of Janus gate,   §
   Doth seeme to promise hope of new delight:
   and bidding th'old Adieu, his passed date
   bids all old thoughts to die in dumpish spright.
And calling forth out of sad Winters night,
   fresh love, that long hath slept in cheerlesse bower:
   wils him awake, and soone about him dight
   his wanton wings and darts of deadly power.
For lusty spring now in his timely howre,
   is ready to come forth him to receive:
   and warnes the Earth with divers colord flowre,
   to decke hir selfe, and her faire mantle weave.
Then you faire flowre, in whom fresh youth doth raine,
   prepare your selfe new love to entertaine.

3. (8) **hew:** form; (14) **endite:** set down on paper.
4. (4) **dumpish spright:** dispiritedness, dejection; (7) **dight:** put on, prepare; (10) **him:** i.e., Love.

§ *Janus*: The Roman god of beginnings and gateways; he is two-faced and can look backwards and forwards at the same time. He gives his name to the month called January.

5

Rudely thou wrongest my deare harts desire,
  In finding fault with her too portly pride:
  the thing which I doo most in her admire,
  is of the world unworthy most envide.
For in those lofty lookes is close implide,
  scorn of base things, and sdeigne of foule dishonor:
  thretning rash eies which gaze on her so wide,
  that loosely they ne dare to looke upon her.
Such pride is praise, such portlinesse is honor,
  that boldned innocence beares in hir eies:
  and her faire countenance like a goodly banner,
  spreds in defiaunce of all enemies.
Was never in this world ought worthy tride,
  without some spark of such self-pleasing pride.

6

Be nought dismayd that her unmoved mind
  doth still persist in her rebellious pride:
  such love not lyke to lusts of baser kynd,
  the harder wonne, the firmer will abide.
The durefull Oake, whose sap is not yet dride,
  is long ere it conceive the kindling fyre:
  but when it once doth burne, it doth divide
  great heat, and makes his flames to heaven aspire.
So hard it is to kindle new desire,
  in gentle brest that shall endure for ever:
  deepe is the wound, that dints the parts entire
  with chast affects, that naught but death can sever.
Then thinke not long in taking litle paine,
  to knit the knot, that ever shall remaine.

5. (2) **portly:** stately; (6) **sdeigne:** disdain; (8) **ne dare:** dare not;
(9) **portlinesse:** stateliness.
6. (5) **durefull:** enduring; (6) **conceive:** i.e., catches, takes to
itself; (7) **divide:** give off, radiate; (11) **parts:** endowments
(moral and intellectual as well as physical); (12) **affects:**
feelings, passions.

*　*　*　*　*

19

The merry Cuckow, messenger of Spring,
　　His trompet shrill hath thrise already sounded:
　　that wa᷁nes al lovers wayt upon their king,
　　who now is comming forth with girland crouned.
With noyse whereof the quyre of Byrds resounded
　　their anthemes sweet devized of loves prayse,
　　that all the woods theyr ecchoes back rebounded,
　　as if they knew the meaning of their layes.
But mongst them all, which did Loves honor rayse
　　no word was heard of her that most it ought,
　　but she his precept proudly disobayes,
　　and doth his ydle message set at nought.
Therefore O love, unlesse she turne to thee
　　ere Cuckow end, let her a rebell be.

20

In vaine I seeke and sew to her for grace,
　　and doe myne humble hart before her poure:
　　the whiles her foot she in my necke doth place,
　　and tread my life downe in the lowly floure.
And yet the Lyon that is Lord of power,
　　and reigneth over every beast in field:
　　in his most pride disdeigneth to devoure
　　the silly lambe that to his might doth yield.
But she more cruell and more salvage wylde,
　　then either Lyon or the Lyonesse:
　　shames not to be with guiltlesse bloud defylde,
　　but taketh glory in her cruelnesse.
Fayrer then fayrest let none ever say,
　　that ye were blooded in a yeelded pray.

19. (3) **wayt:** to wait; (4) **girland:** garland; (6) **devized of:** contrived of, drawn from (or perhaps) devised for; (8) **layes:** songs; (10) **it ought:** i.e., ought to raise Love's honour; (12) **ydle:** ineffective.
20. (1) **sew:** sue; (3) **the whiles:** while; (4) **floure:** ground, dust; (9) **salvage:** savage; (10) **then:** than.

21

Was it the worke of nature or of Art,
 which tempred so the feature of her face,
 that pride and meeknesse mixt by equall part,
 doe both appeare t'adorne her beauties grace?
For with mild pleasance, which doth pride displace,
 she to her love doth lookers eyes allure:
 and with sterne countenance back again doth chace
 their looser lookes that stir up lustes impure.
With such strange termes her eyes she doth inure,
 that with one looke she doth my life dismay:
 and with another doth it streight recure,
 her smile me drawes, her frowne me drives away.
Thus doth she traine and teach me with her lookes,
 such art of eyes I never read in bookes.

22

This holy season fit to fast and pray,
 Men to devotion ought to be inclynd:
 therefore, I lykewise on so holy day,
 for my sweet Saynt some service fit will find.
Her temple fayre is built within my mind,
 in which her glorious ymage placed is,
 on which my thoughts doo day and night attend
 lyke sacred priests that never thinke amisse.
There I to her as th'author of my blisse,
 will builde an altar to appease her yre:
 and on the same my hart will sacrifise,
 burning in flames of pure and chast desyre:
The which vouchsafe O goddesse to accept,
 amongst thy deerest relicks to be kept.

   * * * * *

21. (2) **tempred:** tempered; (5) **pleasance:** pleasantness; (9) **termes:** practices, i.e., ways of looking; (9) **inure:** employ; (11) **recure:** heal.

27

Faire proud now tell me why should faire be proud,
 Sith all worlds glorie is but drosse uncleane:
 and in the shade of death it selfe shall shroud,
 how ever now thereof ye little weene.
That goodly Idoll now so gay beseene,
 shall doffe her fleshes borowd fayre attyre:
 and be forgot as it had never beene,
 that many now much worship and admire.
Ne any then shall after it inquire,
 ne any mention shall thereof remaine:
 but what this verse, that never shall expyre,
 shall to you purchas with her thankles paine.
Faire be no lenger proud of that shall perish,
 but that which shal you make immortall, cherish.

* * * * *

30

My love is lyke to yse, and I to fyre;
 how comes it then that this her cold so great
 is not dissolv'd through my so hot desyre,
 but harder growes the more I her intreat?
Or how comes it that my exceeding heat
 is not delayd by her hart frosen cold:
 but that I burne much more in boyling sweat,
 and feele my flames augmented manifold?
What more miraculous thing may be told
 that fire which all thing melts, should harden yse:
 and yse which is congeald with sencelesse cold,
 should kindle fyre by wonderfull devyse?
Such is the powre of love in gentle mind,
 that it can alter all the course of kynd.

27. (1) **proud:** i.e., proud one; (2) **Sith:** since; (4) **weene:** consider, think; (9) **Ne any:** i.e., none; (10) **ne:** nor; (12) **her:** its; (13) **lenger:** longer; (13) **that:** what, that which.
30. (1) **yse:** ice; (6) **delayd:** weakened; (8) **manifold:** many times over; (12) **devyse:** process; (14) **kynd:** nature.

31

Ah why hath nature to so hard a hart,
   given so goodly giftes of beauties grace?
   whose pryde depraves each other better part,
   and all those pretious ornaments deface.
Sith to all other beastes of bloody race,
   a dreadfull countenaunce she given hath:
   that with theyr terrour al the rest may chace,
   and warne to shun the daunger of theyr wrath.
But my proud one doth worke the greater scath,
   through sweet allurement of her lovely hew:
   that she the better may in bloody bath
   of such poore thralls her cruell hands embrew.
But did she know how ill these two accord,
   such cruelty she would have soone abhord.

32

The paynefull smith with force of fervent heat,
   the hardest yron soone doth mollify:
   that with his heavy sledge he can it beat,
   and fashion to what he it list apply.
Yet cannot all these flames in which I fry,
   her hart more harde then yron soft awhit:
   ne all the playnts and prayers with which I
   doe beat on th'andvyle of her stubberne wit:
But still the more she fervent sees my fit,
   the more she frieseth in her wilfull pryde:
   and harder growes the harder she is smit,
   with all the playnts which to her be applyde.
What then remaines but I to ashes burne,
   and she to stones at length all frosen turne?

31. (3) **depraves:** perverts; (5) **beastes . . . race:** beasts of prey;
(9) **scath:** damage; (10) **hew:** countenance; (12) **embrew:**
plunge.
32. (1) **paynefull:** painstaking; (4) **he it list apply:** to what he wants
to use it for; (6) **soft awhit:** soften the least bit; (8) **th'andvyle:**
the anvil; (9) **the more . . . fit:** the more heated she sees is
my condition; (10) **frieseth:** freezes.

33

Great wrong I doe, I can it not deny,
 to that most sacred Empresse my dear dred,
 not finishing her Queene of faery,
 that mote enlarge her living prayses dead:
But lodwick, this of grace to me aread:
 doe ye not thinck th'accomplishment of it,
 sufficient worke for one mans simple head,
 all were it as the rest but rudely writ.
How then should I without another wit,
 thinck ever to endure so tædious toyle?
 sins that this one is tost with troublous fit,
 of a proud love that doth my spirite spoyle.
Ceasse then, till she vouchsafe to grawnt me rest,
 or lend you me another living brest.

* * * * *

37

What guyle is this, that those her golden tresses,
 She doth attyre under a net of gold:
 and with sly skill so cunningly them dresses,
 that which is gold or heare, may scarse be told?
Is it that mens frayle eyes, which gaze too bold,
 she may entangle in that golden snare:
 and being caught may craftily enfold
 theyr weaker harts, which are not wel aware?
Take heed therefore, myne eyes, how ye doe stare
 henceforth too rashly on that gui¹efull net,
 in which if ever ye entrapped are,
 out of her bands ye by no meanes shall get.
Fondnesse it were for any being free,
 to covet fetters, though they golden bee.

33. (2) **Empresse:** i.e., Queen Elizabeth; (3) **Queene of faery:** i.e.,
"The Faerie Queene"; (4) **mote:** must; (4) **dead:** (now) mori-
bund, i.e., going unsung; (5) **lodwick:** Spenser's friend
Ludovick Bryskett; (5) **this . . . aread:** tell me this of your
charity; (8) **all were it:** although it were; (11) **sins:** since; (13)
she: i.e., the proud lady-love.
37. (4) **heare:** hair; (13) **Fondnesse:** foolishness.

* * * * *

46

When my abodes prefixed time is spent,
  My cruell fayre streight bids me wend my way:
  but then from heaven most hideous stormes are sent
  as willing me against her will to stay.
Whom then shall I or heaven or her obay?
  the heavens know best what is the best for me:
  but as she will, whose will my life doth sway,
  my lower heaven, so it perforce must bee.
But ye high hevens, that all this sorowe see,
  sith all your tempests cannot hold me backe:
  aswage your stormes, or else both you and she
  will both together me too sorely wrack.
Enough it is for one man to sustaine
  the stormes, which she alone on me doth raine.

* * * * *

53

The Panther knowing that his spotted hyde
  Doth please all beasts but that his looks them fray:
  within a bush his dreadfull head doth hide,
  to let them gaze whylest he on them may pray.
Right so my cruell fayre with me doth play:
  for with the goodly semblant of her hew,
  she doth allure me to mine owne decay,
  and then no mercy will unto me shew.
Great shame it is, thing so divine in view,
  made for to be the worlds most ornament:
  to make the bayte her gazers to embrew,
  good shames to be to ill an instrument.
But mercy doth with beautie best agree,
  as in theyr maker ye them best may see.

46. (2) **streight:** promptly; (10) **sith:** since.
53. (2) **fray:** terrify; (6) **semblant:** appearance; (7) **decay:** destruction; (9) **in view:** to the eye; (10) **most:** greatest; (11) **embrew:** stain with blood.

54

Of this worlds Theatre in which we stay,
   My love lyke the Spectator ydly sits
   beholding me that all the pageants play,
   disguysing diversly my troubled wits.
Sometimes I joy when glad occasion fits,
   and mask in myrth lyke to a Comedy:
   soone after when my joy to sorrow flits,
   I waile and make my woes a Tragedy.
Yet she beholding me with constant eye,
   delights not in my merth nor rues my smart:
   but when I laugh she mocks, and when I cry
   she laughes, and hardens evermore her hart.
What then can move her? if nor merth nor mone,
   she is no woman, but a senceless stone.

55

So oft as I her beauty doe behold,
   And therewith doe her cruelty compare:
   I marvaile of what substance was the mould
   the which her made attonce so cruell faire.
Not earth; for her high thoghts more heavenly are,
   not water; for her love doth burne like fyre:
   not ayre; for she is not so light or rare,
   not fyre; for she doth friese with faint desire.
Then needs another Element inquire
   whereof she mote be made; that is the skye.
   for to the heaven her haughty lookes aspire:
   and eke her mind is pure immortall hye.
Then sith to heaven ye lykened are the best,
   be lyke in mercy as in all the rest.

54. (6) **mask:** perform masque-like (or) put on the mask (of comedy); (10) **rues:** pities; (10) **smart:** grief, pain; (13) **mone:** lamentation.
55. (3) **marvaile:** marvel; (4) **attonce . . . faire:** at the same time so cruel and so fair; (9) **needs . . . inquire:** there needs to be sought out; (10) **mote:** could.

56

Fayre ye be sure, but cruell and unkind,
   As is a Tygre that with greedinesse
   hunts after bloud, when he by chance doth find
   a feeble beast, doth felly him oppresse.
Fayre be ye sure, but proud and pittilesse,
   as in a storme, that all things doth prostrate:
   finding a tree alone all comfortlesse,
   beats on it strongly it to ruinate.
Fayre be ye sure, but hard and obstinate,
   as is a rocke amidst the raging floods:
   gaynst which a ship of succour desolate,
   doth suffer wreck both of her selfe and goods.
That ship, that tree, and that same beast am I,
   whom ye doe wreck, doe ruine, and destroy.

57

Sweet warriour when shall I have peace with you?
   High time it is, this warre now ended were:
   which I no lenger can endure to sue,
   ne your incessant battry more to beare:
So weake my powres, so sore my wounds appeare,
   that wonder is how I should live a jot,
   seeing my hart through launched every where
   with thousand arrowes, which your eies have shot:
Yet shoot ye sharpely still, and spare me not,
   but glory thinke to make these cruel stoures.
   ye cruell one, what glory can be got,
   in slaying him that would live gladly yours?
Make peace therefore, and graunt me timely grace,
   that al my wounds wil heale in little space.

56. (4) **felly:** fiercely; (11) **of succour desolate:** forlorn of help.
57. (4) **ne:** nor; (6) **a jot:** i.e., at all; (7) **launched:** pierced;
   (10) **glory thinke:** think it a glory; (10) **stoures:** attacks.

58

By her that is most assured to her selfe.

Weake is th'assurance that weake flesh reposeth
   In her owne powre, and scorneth others ayde:
   that soonest fals when as she most supposeth
   her selfe assurd, and is of nought affrayd.
All flesh is frayle, and all her strength unstayd,
   like a vaine bubble blowen up with ayre:
   devouring tyme and changeful chance have prayd
   her glories pride that none may it repayre.
Ne none so rich or wise, so strong or fayre,
   but fayleth trusting on his owne assurance:
   and he that standeth on the hyghest stayre
   fals lowest: for on earth nought hath enduraunce.
Why then doe ye proud fayre, misdeeme so farre,
   that to your selfe ye most assured arre?

59

Thrise happie she, that is so well assured
   Unto her selfe and setled so in hart:
   that nether will for better be allured,
   ne feard with worse to any chaunce to start,
But like a steddy ship doth strongly part
   the raging waves and keepes her course aright:
   ne ought for tempest doth from it depart,
   ne ought for fayrer weathers false delight.
Such selfe assurance need not feare the spight
   of grudging foes, ne favour seek of friends:
   but in the stay of her owne stedfast might,
   nether to one her selfe nor other bends.
Most happy she that most assured doth rest,
   but he most happy who such one loves best.

58. (5) **unstayd:** insecure; (7) **prayd:** preyed upon; (9-10) **Ne none
. . . but fayleth:** there is no one . . . who does not fail; (13)
misdeeme: misjudge.
59. (4) **ne feard . . . to start:** nor frightened with worse into
grabbing at any straw; (7-8) **ne ought for . . . ne ought for:**
neither for any . . . nor for any; (12) **nether . . . bends:**
bends herself neither to one nor the other.

60

They that in course of heavenly spheares are skild,
  To every planet point his sundry yeare:
  in which her circles voyage is fulfild,
  as Mars in three score yeares doth run his spheare.
So since the winged God his planet cleare,
  began in me to move, one yeare is spent:
  the which doth longer unto me appeare,
  then al those fourty which my life outwent.
Then by that count, which lovers books invent,
  the spheare of Cupid fourty yeares containes:
  which I have wasted in long languishment,
  that seemd the longer for my greater paines.
But let my loves fayre Planet short her wayes
  this yeare ensuing, or else short my dayes.

61

The glorious image of the makers beautie,
  My soverayne saynt, the Idoll of my thought,
  dare not henceforth above the bounds of dewtie,
  t'accuse of pride, or rashly blame for ought.
For being as she is divinely wrought,
  and of the brood of Angels hevenly borne:
  and with the crew of blessed Saynts upbrought,
  each of which did her with theyr guifts adorne;
The bud of joy, the blossome of the morne,
  the beame of light, whom mortal eyes admyre:
  what reason is it then but she should scorne
  base things that to her love too bold aspire?
Such heavenly formes ought rather worshipt be,
  then dare be lov'd by men of meane degree.

60. (2) **point:** assign; (2) **sundry:** particular; (8) **then:** than; (13)
short her wayes: shorten the path of its orbit.
61. (4) **ought:** anything; (6) **brood:** race.

62

The weary yeare his race now having run,
   The new begins his compast course anew:
     with shew of morning mylde he hath begun,
     betokening peace and plenty to ensew.
So let us, which this chaunge of weather vew,
   chaunge eeke our mynds and former lives amend,
     the old yeares sinnes forepast let us eschew,
     and fly the faults with which we did offend.
Then shall the new yeares joy forth freshly send,
   into the glooming world his gladsome ray:
     and all these stormes which now his beauty blend,
     shall turne to caulmes and tymely cleare away.
So likewise love cheare you your heavy spright,
   and chaunge old yeares annoy to new delight.

63

After long stormes and tempests sad assay,
   Which hardly I endured heretofore:
     in dread of death and daungerous dismay,
     with which my silly barke was tossed sore:
I doe at length descry the happy shore,
   in which I hope ere long for to arryve:
     fayre soyle it seemes from far and fraught with store
     of all that deare and daynty is alyve.
Most happy he that can at last atchyve
   the joyous safety of so sweet a rest:
     whose least delight sufficeth to deprive
     remembrance of all paines which him opprest.
All paines are nothing in respect of this,
   all sorrowes short that gaine eternall blisse.

62. (2) **compast:** circular; (4) **ensew:** follow; (5) **which:** who; (5) **vew:** view, look upon; (11) **blend:** blemish; (12) **caulmes:** calms; (12) **tymely:** early (and/or) opportunely; (13) **spright:** spirit; (14) **annoy:** grief.
63. (1) **sad assay:** grievous assault; (4) **silly:** helpless; (9) **atchyve:** achieve, win to.

64

Comming to kisse her lyps, (such grace I found)
    Me seemd I smelt a gardin of sweet flowres:
    that dainty odours from them threw around
    for damzels fit to decke their lovers bowres.
Her lips did smell lyke unto Gillyflowers,
    her ruddy cheekes lyke unto Roses red:
    her snowy browes lyke budded Bellamoures,
    her lovely eyes lyke Pincks but newly spred,
Her goodly bosome lyke a Strawberry bed,
    her neck lyke to a bounch of Cullambynes:
    her brest lyke lillyes, ere theyr leaves be shed,
    her nipples lyke yong blossomd Jessemynes:
Such fragrant flowres doe give most odorous smell,
    but her sweet odour did them all excell.

65

The doubt which ye misdeeme, fayre love, is vaine,
    That fondly feare to loose your liberty,
    when loosing one, two liberties ye gayne,
    and make him bond that bondage earst dyd fly.
Sweet be the bands, the which true love doth tye,
    without constraynt or dread of any ill:
    the gentle birde feeles no captivity
    within her cage, but singes and feeds her fill.
There pride dare not approch, nor discord spill
    the league twixt them, that loyal love hath bound:
    but simple truth and mutuall good will,
    seekes with sweet peace to salve each others wound:
There fayth doth fearlesse dwell in brasen towre,
    and spotlesse pleasure builds her sacred bowre.

64. (5) **Gillyflowers:** (e.g.) clove pinks.
65. (1) **misdeeme:** mistakenly entertain; (1) **vaine:** insubstantial;
    (4) **earst:** formerly; (9) **spill:** upset, spoil.

66

To all those happy blessings which ye have,
    with plenteous hand by heaven upon you thrown,
    this one disparagement they to you gave,
    that ye your love lent to so meane a one.
Yee whose high worths surpassing paragon,
    could not on earth have found one fit for mate,
    ne but in heaven matchable to none,
    why did ye stoup unto so lowly state?
But ye thereby much greater glory gate,
    then had ye sorted with a princes pere:
    for now your light doth more it selfe dilate,
    and in my darknesse greater doth appeare.
Yet since your light hath once enlumind me,
    with my reflex yours shall encreased be.

67

Lyke as a huntsman after weary chace,
    Seeing the game from him escapt away,
    sits downe to rest him in some shady place,
    with panting hounds beguiled of their pray:
So after long pursuit and vaine assay,
    when I all weary had the chace forsooke,
    the gentle deare returnd the selfe-same way,
    thinking to quench her thirst at the next brooke.
There she beholding me with mylder looke,
    sought not to fly, but fearelesse still did bide:
    till I in hand her yet halfe trembling tooke,
    and with her owne goodwill hir fyrmely tyde.
Strange thing me seemd to see a beast so wyld,
    so goodly wonne with her owne will beguyld.

66. (5) **Yee:** you; (5) **paragon:** (all) comparison; (7) **ne but . . . none:** i.e., unmatchable unless to someone in heaven; (9) **gate:** got; (10) **then:** than; (10) **sorted:** consorted; (10) **princes pere:** peer of princes; (11) **dilate:** augment; (13) **enlumind:** illumined, shined on; (14) **reflex:** reflection.

67. (4) **beguiled of:** foiled by, cheated of; (5) **assay:** trial, attempt; (14) **goodly:** well, happily; (14) **beguyld:** taken in, deprived (of the liberty of unattachment).

68

Most glorious Lord of lyfe that on this day,
  Didst make thy triumph over death and sin:
  and having harrowd hell didst bring away   §
  captivity thence captive us to win:
This joyous day, deare Lord, with joy begin,
  and grant that we for whom thou diddest dye
  being with thy deare blood clene washt from sin,
  may live for ever in felicity.
And that thy love we weighing worthily,
  may likewise love thee for the same againe:
  and for thy sake that all lyke deare didst buy,
  with love may one another entertayne.
So let us love, deare love, lyke as we ought,
  love is the lesson which the Lord us taught.

69

The famous warriors of the anticke world,
  Used Trophees to erect in stately wize:
  in which they would the records have enrold,
  of theyr great deeds and valarous emprize.
What trophee then shall I most fit devize,
  in which I may record the memory
  of my loves conquest, peerelesse beauties prise,
  adorn'd with honour, love, and chastity.
Even this verse vowd to eternity,
  shall be thereof immortall moniment:
  and tell her prayse to all posterity,
  that may admire such worlds rare wonderment.
The happy purchase of my glorious spoile,
  gotten at last with labour and long toyle.

68. (10) **the same:** i.e., "thy love"; (10) **againe:** in return.
69. (1) **anticke:** ancient; (4) **emprize:** enterprise(s); (7) **prise:** prize; (12) **that may . . . wonderment:** that it may admire such a wonder of the world; (13) **purchase:** winning; (13) **spoile:** war-prize, booty.

§ *having harrowd hell*: The Harrowing of Hell is the name of the tradition according to which Christ descended to the first circle of hell to deliver the waiting souls of the righteous who had died before his advent.

70

Fresh spring the herald of loves mighty king,
  In whose cote armour richly are displayd
  all sorts of flowers the which on earth do spring
  in goodly colours gloriously arrayd:
Goe to my love, where she is carelesse layd,
  yet in her winters bowre not well awake:
  tell her the joyous time wil not be staid
  unlesse she doe him by the forelock take.
Bid her therefore her selfe soone ready make,
  to wayt on love amongst his lovely crew:
  where every one that misseth then her make,
  shall be by him amearst with penance dew.
Make hast therefore sweet love, whilest it is prime,
  for none can call againe the passed time.

71

I joy to see how in your drawen work,   §
  Your selfe unto the Bee ye doe compare;
  and me unto the Spyder that doth lurke,
  in close away to catch her unaware.
Right so your selfe were caught in cunning snare
  of a deare foe, and thralled to his love:
  in whose streight bands ye now captived are
  so firmely, that ye never may remove.
But as your worke is woven all above,
  with woodbynd flowers and fragrant Eglantine:
  so sweet your prison you in time shall prove,
  with many deare delights bedecked fyne.
And all thensforth eternall peace shall see,
  betweene the Spyder and the gentle Bee.

70. (2) **cote armour:** coat of arms; (5) **carelesse:** carefree, i.e., still asleep; (7) **staid:** delayed; (11) **make:** mate; (12) **amearst:** punished; (13) **prime:** spring-time.

71. (4) **in close awayt:** in close watch; (5) **your selfe:** you yourself; (6) **thralled:** made captive; (7) **streight:** strict; (12) **fyne:** finely.

§ *drawen work*: Probably "drawn-work", a kind of ornamental weaving in which figures or patterns are formed by drawing out selected threads of the warp and woof. The term was current in print by 1595.

72

Oft when my spirit doth spred her bolder winges,
    In mind to mount up to the purest sky:
    it down is weighd with thoght of earthly things
    and clogd with burden of mortality,
Where when that soverayne beauty it doth spy,
    resembling heavens glory in her light:
    drawne with sweet pleasures bayt, it back doth fly,
    and unto heaven forgets her former flight.
There my fraile fancy fed with full delight,
    doth bath in blisse and mantleth most at ease:
    ne thinks of other heaven, but how it might
    her harts desire with most contentment please.
Hart need not wish none other happinesse,
    but here on earth to have such hevens blisse.

73

Being my selfe captyved here in care,
    My hart, whom none with servile bands can tye,
    but the fayre tresses of your golden hayre,
    breaking his prison forth to you doth fly.
Lyke as a byrd that in ones hand doth spy
    desired food, to it doth make his flight:
    even so my hart, that wont on your fayre eye
    to feed his fill, flyes backe unto your sight.
Doe you him take, and in your bosome bright,
    gently encage, that he may be your thrall:
    perhaps he there may learne with rare delight,
    to sing your name and prayses over all.
That it hereafter may you not repent,
    him lodging in your bosome to have lent.

72. (4) **clogd:** encumbered; (10) **mantleth:** spreads and preens (one wing then the other – like a bird at leisure).
73. (1) **care:** anxiety, troubles of this world; (7) **wont:** is accustomed; (12) **over:** above; (13) **repent:** regret; (14) **lent:** granted.

74

Most happy letters fram'd by skilfull trade,
   with which that happy name was first desynd:
   the which three times thrise happy hath me made,
   with guifts of body, fortune and of mind.
The first my being to me gave by kind,
   from mothers womb deriv'd by dew descent,
   the second is my sovereigne Queene most kind,
   that honour and large richesse to me lent.
The third my love, my lives last ornament,
   by whom my spirit out of dust was raysed:
   to speake her prayse and glory excellent,
   of all alive most worthy to be praysed.
Ye three Elizabeths for ever live,
   that three such graces did unto me give.

75

One day I wrote her name upon the strand,
   but came the waves and washed it away:
   agayne I wrote it with a second hand,
   but came the tyde, and made my paynes his pray.
Vayne man, sayd she, that doest in vaine assay,
   a mortall thing so to immortalize,
   for I my selve shall lyke to this decay,
   and eek my name bee wyped out lykewize.
Not so, (quod I) let baser things devize
   to dy in dust, but you shall live by fame:
   my verse your vertues rare shall eternize,
   and in the hevens wryte your glorious name.
Where whenas death shall all the world subdew,
   our love shall live, and later life renew.

74. (1) **trade:** craft; (5) **kind:** nature; (8) **richesse:** riches; (14) **graces:** unmerited gifts.
75. (4) **paynes:** efforts; (5) **assay:** try; (7) **shall . . . decay:** shall similarly suffer obliteration; (8) **eek:** also, even; (9) **quod:** quoth, said; (9) **devize/to dy:** i.e., submissively accept the prospect of dying.

76

Fayre bosome fraught with vertues richest tresure,
  The neast of love, the lodging of delight:
  the bowre of blisse, the paradice of pleasure,
  the sacred harbour of that hevenly spright:
How was I ravisht with your lovely sight,
  and my frayle thoughts too rashly led astray?
  whiles diving deepe through amorous insight,
  on the sweet spoyle of beautie they did pray.
And twixt her paps like early fruit in May,
  whose harvest seemd to hasten now apace:
  they loosely did theyr wanton winges display,
  and there to rest themselves did boldly place.
Sweet thoughts I envy your so happy rest,
  which oft I wisht, yet never was so blest.

77

Was it a dreame, or did I see it playne,
  a goodly table of pure yvory:
  all spred with juncats, fit to entertayne
  the greatest Prince with pompous roialty?
Mongst which there in a silver dish did ly
  twoo golden apples of unvalewd price:
  far passing those which Hercules came by,   §
  or those which Atalanta did entice.
Exceeding sweet, yet voyd of sinfull vice,
  That many sought yet none could ever taste,
  sweet fruit of pleasure brought from paradice
  by Love himselfe and in his garden plaste.
Her brest that table was so richly spredd,
  my thoughts the guests, which would thereon have
    fedd.

76. (8) **pray:** prey upon; (10) **apace:** quickly; (11) **they:** i.e., his "frayle thoughts".
77. (3) **juncats:** delicacies; (4) **pompous:** splendid; (6) **of unvalewd price:** priceless; (9) **voyd:** i.e., free; (12) **plaste:** placed.

§ *Hercules*: The twelfth and most difficult of the labours imposed upon Hercules (Herakles) was to go to the western end of the world and

78

Lackyng my love I go from place to place,
　　lyke a young fawne that late hath lost the hynd:
　　and seeke each where, where last I sawe her face,
　　whose ymage yet I carry fresh in mynd.
I seeke the fields with her late footing synd,
　　I seeke her bowre with her late presence deckt,
　　yet nor in field nor bowre I her can fynd:
　　yet field and bowre are full of her aspect.
But when myne eyes I thereunto direct,
　　they ydly back returne to me agayne,
　　and when I hope to see theyr trew object,
　　I fynd my selfe but fed with fancies vayne.
Ceasse then myne eyes, to seeke her selfe to see,
　　and let my thoughts behold her selfe in mee.

78. (2) **late hath lost:** has just lost; (5) **with her . . . synd:** signed with her recent footprints; (6) **deckt:** enhanced; (10) **ydly:** fruitlessly.

pluck the fruit from the golden apple-tree guarded by the sky-bearing Titan Atlas, a serpent, and three nymphs called the Hesperides. Hercules accomplished this labour with the reluctant and rather tricky help of Atlas. *Atalanta*: A beautiful athletic huntress who was averse to marriage and who announced that she would marry only the man who could beat her in a foot-race. She had many suitors but she invariably won these races and had all the losers killed except the few to whom fear lent an extraordinary burst of parting speed. Finally she was won by Hippomenes, who had been given three golden apples for the purpose by Venus Aphrodite; by dropping these apples – which Atalanta found irresistible – in her path on three occasions when she was about to overtake him, Hippomenes was just able to stay ahead of her and win his race and his bride.

79

Men call you fayre, and you doe credit it,
 For that your selfe ye dayly such doe see:
 but the trew fayre, that is the gentle wit,
 and vertuous mind, is much more praysd of me.
For all the rest, how ever fayre it be,
 shall turne to nought and loose that glorious hew:
 but onely that is permanent and free
 from frayle corruption, that doth flesh ensew.
That is true beautie: that doth argue you
 to be divine and borne of heavenly seed:
 deriv'd from that fayre Spirit, from whom al true
 and perfect beauty did at first proceed.
He onely fayre, and what he fayre hath made,
 all other fayre lyke flowres untymely fade.

80

After so long a race as I have run
 Through Faery land, which those six books compile,
 give leave to rest me being halfe fordonne,
 and gather to my selfe new breath awhile.
Then as a steed refreshed after toyle,
 out of my prison I will breake anew:
 and stoutly will that second worke assoyle,
 with strong endevour and attention dew.
Till then give leave to me in pleasant mew,
 to sport my muse and sing my loves sweet praise:
 the contemplation of whose heavenly hew,
 my spirit to an higher pitch will rayse.
But let her prayses yet be low and meane,
 fit for the handmayd of the Faery Queene.

---

79. (6) **hew:** hue; (8) **that doth . . . ensew:** which the flesh is a
result of, i.e., depends upon; (14) **untymely:** unfortunately.
80. (2) **compile:** comprise; (3) **give leave . . . me:** give me leave
to rest; (3) **fordonne:** exhausted; (7) **assoyle:** take on, dis-
charge; (9) **mew:** concealment; (11) **hew:** countenance.

81

Fayre is my love, when her fayre golden heares,
    with the loose wynd ye waving chance to marke:
    fayre when the rose in her red cheekes appeares,
    or in her eyes the fyre of love does sparke.
Fayre when her brest lyke a rich laden barke,
    with pretious merchandize she forth doth lay:
    fayre when that cloud of pryde, which oft doth dark
    her goodly light with smiles she drives away.
But fayrest she, when so she doth display
    the gate with pearles and rubyes richly dight:
    throgh which her words so wise do make their way
    to beare the message of her gentle spright.
The rest be works of natures wonderment,
    but this the worke of harts astonishment.

82

Joy of my life, full oft for loving you
    I blesse my lot, that was so lucky placed:
    but then the more your owne mishap I rew,
    that are so much by so meane love embased.
For had the equall hevens so much you graced
    in this as in the rest, ye mote invent
    som hevenly wit, whose verse could have enchased
    your glorious name in golden moniment.
But since ye deignd so goodly to relent
    to me your thrall, in whom is little worth,
    that little that I am, shall all be spent,
    in setting your immortall prayses forth.
Whose lofty argument uplifting me,
    shall lift you up unto an high degree.

81. (2) **chance:** happen; (7) **dark:** darken.
82. (3) **rew:** regret; (4) **embased:** debased; (5) **equall:** impartial;
(6) **mote:** i.e., would have to; (7) **enchased:** set, engraved; (13)
Whose . . . argument: which lofty theme.

83

My hungry eyes, through greedy covetize,
 Still to behold the object of theyr payne:
 with no contentment can themselves suffize,
 but having pine, and having not complayne.
For lacking it, they cannot lyfe sustayne,
 and seeing it, they gaze on it the more:
 in theyr amazement lyke Narcissus vayne   §
 whose eyes him starv'd: so plenty makes me pore.
Yet are myne eyes so filled with the store
 of that fayre sight, that nothing else they brooke:
 but loath the things which they did like before,
 and can no more endure on them to looke.
All this worlds glory seemeth vayne to me,
 and all theyr shewes but shadowes saving she.

84

Let not one sparke of filthy lustfull fyre
 breake out, that may her sacred peace molest:
 ne one light glance of sensuall desyre
 Attempt to work her gentle mindes unrest.
But pure affections bred in spotlesse brest,
 and modest thoughts breathd from wel tempred
  sprites,
 goe visit her in her chast bowre of rest,
 accompanyde with angelick delightes.
There fill your selfe with those most joyous sights, §
 the which my selfe could never yet attayne:
 but speake no word to her of these sad plights,
 which her too constant stiffenesse doth constrayn.
Onely behold her rare perfection,
 and blesse your fortunes fayre election.

83. (1) **covetize:** covetousness; (2) **payne:** care, concern; (10)
brooke: bear, put up with.
84. (4) **work:** bring about; (12) **stiffenesse:** formality; (12)
constrayn: incur; (14) **fayre election:** happy choice.

§ *Narcissus*: The beautiful, vain youth who, after spurning many offers
of love, fell in love with his own reflection in a pool. Mooning over

85

The world that cannot deeme of worthy things,
  when I doe praise her, say I doe but flatter:
so does the Cuckow, when the Mavis sings,
  begin his witlesse note apace to clatter.
But they that skill not of so heavenly matter,
  all that they know not, envy or admyre,
  rather then envy let them wonder at her,
  but not to deeme of her desert aspyre.
Deepe in the closet of my parts entyre,
  her worth is written with a golden quill:
  that me with heavenly fury doth inspire,
  and my glad mouth with her sweet prayses fill.
Which when as fame in her shrill trump shal thunder,
  let the world chose to envy or to wonder.

85. (1) **deeme of:** comprehend; (3) **Mavis:** thrush; (4) **apace:**
hurriedly; (5) **skill not:** know nothing about; (6) **admyre:**
wonder at; (7) **then:** than; (8) **but . . . aspyre:** but not think
to aspire to be deserving of her; (9) **parts entyre:** inner parts,
i.e., inner self; (11) **fury:** ecstatic inspiration.

his own image, he remained beside the pool until he had starved and
pined away of unrequitable self-love.
§ The phrase *your selfe* obscures the syntax of this sonnet since,
although singular, it has two plural antecedents: *pure affections* and
modest thoughts. It is quite possibly a compositor's error for "your
selves", since his eye could easily have been caught by the "selfe" in
the next line.

86

Venemous toung tipt with vile adders sting,
    Of that selfe kynd with which the Furies fell
    theyr snaky heads doe combe, from which a spring
    of poysoned words and spitefull speeches well.
Let all the plagues and horrid paines of hell,
    upon thee fall for thine accursed hyre:
    that with false forged lyes, which thou didst tel,
    in my true love did stirre up coles of yre,
The sparkes whereof let kindle thine own fyre,
    and catching hold on thine owne wicked hed
    consume thee quite, that didst with guile conspire
    in my sweet peace such breaches to have bred.
Shame be thy meed, and mischiefe thy reward,
    dew to thy selfe that it for me prepard.

87

Since I did leave the presence of my love,
    Many long weary dayes I have outworne:
    and many nights, that slowly seemd to move
    theyr sad protract from evening untill morne.
For when as day the heaven doth adorne,
    I wish that night the noyous day would end:
    and when as night hath us of light forlorne,
    I wish that day would shortly reascend.
Thus I the time with expectation spend,
    and faine my griefe with chaunges to beguile,
    that further seemes his terme still to extend,
    and maketh every minute seeme a myle.
So sorrow still doth seeme too long to last,
    but joyous houres doo fly away too fast.

---

86. (2) **selfe:** same; (2) **fell:** cruel, fierce; (6) **hyre:** wages; (12)
breaches: rents; (12) **bred:** caused; (13) **meed:** requital; (14)
dew: as owing.
87. (4) **protract:** length; (6) **noyous:** troublesome; (7) **forlorne:**
bereft; (10) **faine:** mistakenly imagine; (10) **beguile:** charm
away; (13) **still:** always.

88

Since I have lackt the comfort of that light,
    The which was wont to lead my thoughts astray:
    I wander as in darknesse of the night,
    affrayd of every dangers least dismay.
Ne ought I see, though in the clearest day,
    when others gaze upon theyr shadowes vayne:
    but th'onely image of that heavenly ray,
    whereof some glance doth in mine eie remayne.
Of which beholding the Idæa playne,   §
    through contemplation of my purest part:
    with light thereof I doe my selfe sustayne,
    and thereon feed my love-affamisht hart.
But with such brightnesse whylest I fill my mind,
    I starve my body and mine eyes doe blynd.

88. (2) **astray:** i.e., in wandering far; (4) **dismay:** dismaying effect; (5) **Ne ought I see:** nor do I see anything; (6) **vayne:** insubstantial; (7) **but th'onely:** except the single; (12) **love-affamisht:** love-starved.

§ *Idæa*: Here used in the Platonic sense in which Ideas are the highest realities – the eternal, changeless forms or patterns of which all created, transitory things in nature are but shadowy copies. The *purest part* is the highest "part" of the soul – the mind or intellect – which, in the Platonic scheme, is the only immortal part of man and the only part capable of apprehending the Ideas or Forms.

89

Lyke as the Culver on the bared bough,
    Sits mourning for the absence of her mate:
    and in her songs sends many a wishfull vow,
    for his returne that seemes to linger late.
So I alone now left disconsolate,
    mourne to my selfe the absence of my love:
    and wandring here and there all desolate,
    seek with my playnts to match that mournful dove:
Ne joy of ought that under heaven doth hove,
    can comfort me, but her owne joyous sight:
    whose sweet aspect both God and man can move,
    in her unspotted pleasauns to delight.
Dark is my day, whyles her fayre light I mis,
    and dead my life that wants such lively blis.

89. (1) **Culver:** dove; (8) **playnts:** plaints, griefs; (9) **hove:** rise,
flourish; (12) **pleasauns:** joy, pleasure; (14) **wants:** lacks, is
deprived of.

EPITHALAMION

Epithalamion

Ye learned sisters which have oftentimes   §
Beene to me ayding, others to adorne:
Whom ye thought worthy of your gracefull rymes,
That even the greatest did not greatly scorne
To heare theyr names sung in your simple layes,   5
But joyed in theyr prayse.
And when ye list your owne mishaps to mourne,
Which death, or love, or fortunes wreck did rayse,
Your string could soone to sadder tenor turne,
And teach the woods and waters to lament   10
Your dolefull dreriment.
Now lay those sorrowfull complaints aside,
And having all your heads with girland crownd,
Helpe me mine owne loves prayses to resound,
Ne let the same of any be envide: 15
So Orpheus did for his owne bride,   §
So I unto my selfe alone will sing,
The woods shall to me answer and my Eccho ring.

2. **Beene . . . adorne:** been of help to me in adorning others.
5. **layes:** songs.
6. **joyed:** rejoiced.
7. **list:** chose.
8. **rayse:** bring about.
9. **tenor:** tone.
11. **dreriment:** sorrow.
13. **girland:** garland.
15. **Ne:** nor.

§ *Ye learned sisters*: The nine Muses, daughters of Zeus (Jove) and Mnemosyne (Memory), and patron goddesses of the arts.
§ *Orpheus*: The son of the Muse Calliope and King Oeagrus of Thrace. Orpheus was a musician and poet of divine skill and power; beasts, trees, and the very rocks were moved by his song. His *owne bride* was the nymph Eurydice.

Early before the worlds light giving lampe,
His golden beame upon the hils doth spred,   20
Having disperst the nights unchearefull dampe,
Doe ye awake and with fresh lusty hed,
Go to the bowre of my beloved love,
My truest turtle dove,
Bid her awake; for Hymen is awake,   25 §
And long since ready forth his maske to move,
With his bright Tead that flames with many a flake,
And many a bachelor to waite on him,
In theyr fresh garments trim.
Bid her awake therefore and soone her dight,   30
For lo the wished day is come at last,
That shall for al the paynes and sorrowes past,
Pay to her usury of long delight:
And whylest she doth her dight,
Doe ye to her of joy and solace sing,   35
That all the woods may answer and your eccho ring.

22. **lusty hed**: jollity.	27. **Tead**: torch; **flake**: spark.
23. **bowre**: bedroom, bower.	30. **her dight**: dress herself.
26. **maske**: masque, (here) ritual procession with singing, costumes, dancing.	33. **usury**: interest.
	35. **solace**: delight.

§ *Hymen*: The Roman god of marriage. In Roman wedding processions he was celebrated and invoked with the ritual cry *io Hymen* (line 140).

Bring with you all the Nymphes that you can heare
Both of the rivers and the forrests greene:
And of the sea that neighbours to her neare,
Al with gay girlands goodly wel beseene.   *40*
And let them also with them bring in hand
Another gay girland
For my fayre love of lillyes and of roses,
Bound truelove wize with a blew silke riband.
And let them make great store of bridale poses,   *45*
And let them eeke bring store of other flowers
To deck the bridale bowers.
And let the ground whereas her foot shall tread,
For feare the stones her tender foot should wrong
Be strewed with fragrant flowers all along,   *50*
And diapred lyke the discolored mead.
Which done, doe at her chamber dore awayt,
For she will waken strayt,
The whiles doe ye this song unto her sing,
The woods shall to you answer and your Eccho ring. *55*

---

37. **can heare:** i.e., know of.
40. **goodly . . . beseene:** fetch-ingly pretty.
44. **truelove wize:** in a true-love-knot.
45. **poses:** posies.

46. **eeke:** also
51. **diapred:** i.e., carpeted; **dis-colored mead:** many-col-oured meadow.
53. **strayt:** immediately.

Ye Nymphes of Mulla which with carefull heed,   §
The silver scaly trouts doe tend full well,
And greedy pikes which use therein to feed,
(Those trouts and pikes all others doo excell)
And ye likewise which keepe the rushy lake,   60
Where none doo fishes take,
Bynd up the locks the which hang scatterd light,
And in his waters which your mirror make,
Behold your faces as the christall bright,
That when you come whereas my love doth lie,   65
No blemish she may spie.
And eke ye lightfoot mayds which keepe the deere,
That on the hoary mountayne use to towre,
And the wylde wolves which seeke them to devoure,
With your steele darts doo chace from comming neer,
Be also present heere,   71
To helpe to decke her and to help to sing,
That all the woods may answer and your eccho ring.

58. **use:** are accustomed, com-   68. **towre:** keep the heights
    monly.   (as of falcons).
62. **light:** lightly, loosely.   70. **chace:** chase.

§ *Mulla:* Spenser's special name for the Awbeg stream which flowed
through Kilcolman, his property in Ireland.

Wake, now my love, awake; for it is time,
The Rosy Morne long since left Tithones bed,   75 §
All ready to her silver coche to clyme,
And Phœbus gins to shew his glorious hed.   §
Hark how the cheerefull birds do chaunt theyr laies
And carroll of loves praise.
The merry Larke hir mattins sings aloft,   80
The thrush replyes, the Mavis descant playes,
The Ouzell shrills, the Ruddock warbles soft,
So goodly all agree with sweet consent,
To this dayes merriment.
Ah my deere love why doe ye sleepe thus long,   85
When meeter were that ye should now awake,
T'awayt the comming of your joyous make,
And hearken to the birds lovelearned song,
The deawy leaves among.
For they of joy and pleasance to you sing,   90
That all the woods them answer and theyr eccho ring.

76. **coche:** chariot.
80. **mattins:** i.e., morning song.
81. **Mavis:** song thrush; **descant:** counterpoint above the basic melody.
82. **Ouzell:** blackbird; **Ruddock:** robin redbreast.

86. **meeter were:** it would be more fitting.
87. **make:** mate.
88. **lovelearned song:** love-taught song (or) song skilled in the ways of love.

§ *Tithones*: The lover of Eos (Aurora), goddess of dawn or morning. Tithonus was a mortal who had been granted immortality by Zeus at the request of Eos. But since she had forgotten to include eternal youth in her request, Tithonus became impossibly old and eventually Eos turned him into a grasshopper.
§ *Phœbus*: Another name for Apollo, the sun-god, and hence the sun itself. Apollo is also the god of music, poetry, and prophecy.

My love is now awake out of her dreames,
And her fayre eyes like stars that dimmed were
With darksome cloud, now shew theyr goodly beames
More bright then Hesperus his head doth rere.   *95* §
Come now ye damzels, daughters of delight,
Helpe quickly her to dight,
But first come ye fayre houres which were begot   §
In Joves sweet paradice, of Day and Night,
Which doe the seasons of the yeare allot,   *100*
And al that ever in this world is fayre
Doe make and still repayre.
And ye three handmayds of the Cyprian Queene,   §
The which doe still adorne her beauties pride,
Helpe to addorne my beautifullest bride: *105*
And as ye her array, still throw betweene
Some graces to be seene,
And as ye use to Venus, to her sing,
The whiles the woods shal answer and your eccho ring.

95. **Hesperus:** evening star,   102. **still:** always, continuously.
     Venus' star.   107. **graces:** i.e., gifts, beauties.

§ *Hesperus*: The Evening Star, father of the Hesperides. Since he is the son of Eros, and since "evening star" is another name for the planet Venus, Hesperus has very close and poetically useful associations with Venus Aphrodite, the goddess of beauty and love.
§ *fayre houres*: The Hours (Horae) are usually given as the daughters of Jove (Zeus) and Themis (Order). They are often associated with festive, ceremonial occasions; when Venus Aphrodite rose new-born from the sea off the island of Cythera, it was the Hours who welcomed her, adorned her, and introduced her to the other Olympian gods.
§ *three handmayds*: The three Graces – Euphrosyne, Aglaia, and Thalia – who are ladies-in-waiting to Venus Aphrodite. Besides beauty, they are especially associated with such qualities as graciousness, liberality, and courtesy. *The Cyprian Queene*: Venus Aphrodite, so called because she came ashore at Cyprus after rising from the sea-foam off the shores of Cythera. Both islands are sacred to her.

Now is my love all ready forth to come,   *110*
Let all the virgins therefore well awayt,
And ye fresh boyes that tend upon her groome
Prepare your selves; for he is comming strayt.
Set all your things in seemely good aray
Fit for so joyfull day,   *115*
The joyfulst day that ever sunne did see.
Faire Sun, shew forth thy favourable ray,
And let thy lifull heat not fervent be
For feare of burning her sunshyny face,
Her beauty to disgrace.   *120*
O fayrest Phœbus, father of the Muse,
If ever I did honour thee aright,
Or sing the thing, that mote thy mind delight,
Doe not thy servants simple boone refuse,
But let this day let this one day be myne,   *125*
Let all the rest be thine.
Then I thy soverayne prayses loud wil sing,
That all the woods shal answer and theyr eccho ring.

112. **groome:** i.e., Spenser him-
    self.
113. **strayt:** now, immediately.
118. **lifull:** vital, life-giving.

120. **disgrace:** mar, disfigure.
123. **mote:** might.
124. **boone:** humble request,
    prayer.

Harke how the Minstrels gin to shrill aloud
Their merry Musick that resounds from far,   *130*
The pipe, the tabor, and the trembling Croud,
That well agree withouten breach or jar.
But most of all the Damzels doe delite,
When they their tymbrels smyte,
And thereunto doe daunce and carrol sweet,   *135*
That all the sences they doe ravish quite,
The whyles the boyes run up and downe the street,
Crying aloud with strong confused noyce,
As if it were one voyce.
Hymen io Hymen, Hymen they do shout,   *140*
That even to the heavens theyr shouting shrill
Doth reach, and all the firmament doth fill,
To which the people standing all about,
As in approvance doe thereto applaud
And loud advaunce her laud,   *145*
And evermore they Hymen Hymen sing,
That al the woods them answer and theyr eccho ring.

131. **tabor:** small drum; **Croud:** viol, fiddle.
132. **breach or jar:** pause or discord.
134. **tymbrels:** tambourines.
137. **The whyles:** whilst.
144. **approvance:** approval.
145. **advaunce her laud:** extol her praise(s).

Loe where she comes along with portly pace,
Lyke Phœbe from her chamber of the East,   §
Arysing forth to run her mighty race,   *150*
Clad all in white, that seemes a virgin best.
So well it her beseemes that ye would weene
Some angell she had beene.
Her long loose yellow locks lyke golden wyre,
Sprinckled with perle, and perling flowres a tweene,   §
Doe lyke a golden mantle her attyre,   *156*
And being crowned with a girland greene,
Seeme lyke some mayden Queene.
Her modest eyes abashed to behold
So many gazers, as on her do stare,   *160*
Upon the lowly ground affixed are.
Ne dare lift up her countenance too bold,
But blush to heare her prayses sung so loud,
So farre from being proud.
Nathlesse doe ye still loud her prayses sing,   *165*
That all the woods may answer and your eccho ring.

---

148. **portly:** stately. | 152. **beseemes:** becomes;
151. **seemes:** suits. | **weene:** think.
   | 165. **Nathlesse:** none the less.

§ *Phœbe*: The "bright one". One of the names for the moon-goddess,
seen here especially in her aspect as the feminine counterpart of
Phoebus Apollo, the sun.
§ *with perle, and perling flowres*: This might mean "with pearls and
flowers of pearl" but it is much more likely to mean "with fine-edged
lace-work and lacy flowers".

Tell me ye merchants daughters did ye see
So fayre a creature in your towne before?
So sweet, so lovely, and so mild as she,
Adornd with beautyes grace and vertues store,   *170*
Her goodly eyes lyke Saphyres shining bright,
Her forehead yvory white,
Her cheekes lyke apples which the sun hath rudded,
Her lips lyke cherryes charming men to byte,
Her brest like to a bowle of creame uncrudded,   *175*
Her paps lyke lyllies budded,
Her snowie necke lyke to a marble towre,
And all her body like a pallace fayre,
Ascending uppe with many a stately stayre,
To honors seat and chastities sweet bowre.   *180*
Why stand ye still ye virgins in amaze,
Upon her so to gaze,
Whiles ye forget your former lay to sing,
To which the woods did answer and your eccho ring?

173. **rudded:** reddened.
175. **uncrudded:** uncurdled, i.e.,
       smooth.

180. **To honors . . . bowre:**
       i.e., to the head — seat of
       the soul's higher faculties.

But if ye saw that which no eyes can see,   185
The inward beauty of her lively spright,
Garnisht with heavenly guifts of high degree,
Much more then would ye wonder at that sight,
And stand astonisht lyke to those which red
Medusaes mazeful hed.   190 §
There dwels sweet love and constant chastity,
Unspotted fayth and comely womanhed,
Regard of honour and mild modesty,
There Vertue raynes as Queene in royal throne,
And giveth lawes alone.   195
The which the base affections doe obay,
And yeeld theyr services unto her will,
Ne thought of thing uncomely ever may
Thereto approch to tempt her mind to ill.
Had ye once seene these her celestial threasures,   200
And unrevealed pleasures,
Then would ye wonder and her prayses sing,
That al the woods should answer and your echo ring.

186. **lively spright:** living spirit.   196. **base affections:** subordi-
189. **red:** looked at.   nate passions.
192. **womanhed:** womanliness.   200. **threasures:** treasures.

§ *Medusaes*: Medusa's. Medusa was one of three female monsters called
Gorgons. Mortals who met her gaze were turned to stone.

Open the temple gates unto my love,
Open them wide that she may enter in, *205*
And all the postes adorne as doth behove,
And all the pillours deck with girlands trim,
For to recyve this Saynt with honour dew,
That commeth in to you.
With trembling steps and humble reverence, *210*
She commeth in, before th'almighties vew:
Of her ye virgins learne obedience,
When so ye come into those holy places,
To humble your proud faces;
Bring her up to th'high altar that she may, *215*
The sacred ceremonies there partake,
The which do endlesse matrimony make,
And let the roring Organs loudly play
The praises of the Lord in lively notes,
The whiles with hollow throates *220*
The Choristers the joyous Antheme sing,
That al the woods may answere and their eccho ring.

206. **doth behove:** is fitting. 378. **Organs:** i.e., the pipes that
208. **recyve:** receive, welcome. make up one organ.

Behold whiles she before the altar stands
Hearing the holy priest that to her speakes
And blesseth her with his two happy hands,   *225*
How the red roses flush up in her cheekes,
And the pure snow with goodly vermill stayne,
Like crimsin dyde in grayne,
That even th'Angels which continually,
About the sacred Altare doe remaine,   *230*
Forget their service and about her fly,
Ofte peeping in her face that seemes more fayre,
The more they on it stare.
But her sad eyes still fastened on the ground,
Are governed with goodly modesty,   *235*
That suffers not one looke to glaunce awry,
Which may let in a little thought unsownd.
Why blush ye love to give to me your hand,
The pledge of all our band?
Sing ye sweet Angels, Alleluya sing,   *240*
That all the woods may answere and your eccho ring.

227. **vermill:** vermilion.   234. **sad:** serious, grave.
228. **dyde in grayne:** fast dyed   239. **band:** tie, bond.
     in cochineal.

Now al is done; bring home the bride againe,
Bring home the triumph of our victory,
Bring home with you the glory of her gaine,
With joyance bring her and with jollity.   *245*
Never had man more joyfull day then this,
Whom heaven would heape with blis.
Make feast therefore now all this live long day,
This day for ever to me holy is,
Poure out the wine without restraint or stay,   *250*
Poure not by cups, but by the belly full,
Poure out to all that wull,
And sprinkle all the postes and wals with wine,
That they may sweat, and drunken be withall.
Crowne ye God Bacchus with a coronall,   *255* §
And Hymen also crowne with wreathes of vine,
And let the Graces daunce unto the rest;
For they can doo it best:
The whiles the maydens doe theyr carroll sing,
To which the woods shal answer and theyr eccho ring.

244. **the glory . . . gaine:** the
glory of having won her.
250. **stay:** let-up.

252. **wull:** want (it).
255. **coronall:** wreath, circlet
of leaves and flowers.

§ *Bacchus*: Dionysus, the son of Zeus and Semele. He is the god of
the grape-harvest and of wine.

Ring ye the bels, ye yong men of the towne,   *261*
And leave your wonted labors for this day:
This day is holy; doe ye write it downe,
That ye for ever it remember may.
This day the sunne is in his chiefest hight,   *265*
With Barnaby the bright,   §
From whence declining daily by degrees,
He somewhat loseth of his heat and light,
When once the Crab behind his back he sees.
But for this time it ill ordained was,   *270*
To chose the longest day in all the yeare,
And shortest night, when longest fitter weare:
Yet never day so long, but late would passe.
Ring ye the bels, to make it weare away,
And bonefiers make all day,   *275*
And daunce about them, and about them sing:
That all the woods may answer, and your eccho ring.

262. **wonted:** usual.
270. **ill ordained:** poorly arranged.
272. **when longest . . . weare:** when the longest (night) would be more appropriate.
273. **late:** at last, eventually.
275. **bonefiers:** bonfires.

§ *Barnaby the bright*: St. Barnabas Day, now June 11, but June 22 (the summer solstice) according to the calendar of Spenser's day. By June 22 the sun has moved out of the zodiacal house of Cancer (*the Crab*) which he then sees "behind his back".

Ah when will this long weary day have end,
And lende me leave to come unto my love?
How slowly do the houres theyr numbers spend?   *280*
How slowly does sad Time his feathers move?
Hast thee O fayrest Planet to thy home
Within the Westerne fome:
Thy tyred steedes long since have need of rest.   §
Long though it be, at last I see it gloome,   *285*
And the bright evening star with golden creast
Appeare out of the East.
Fayre childe of beauty, glorious lampe of love
That all the host of heaven in rankes doost lead,
And guydest lovers through the nights dread,   *290*
How chearefully thou lookest from above,
And seemst to laugh atweene thy twinkling light
As joying in the sight
Of these glad many which for joy doe sing,
That all the woods them answer and their echo ring.

279. **lende:** grant.
281. **sad:** heavy, sedate.
282. **O fayrest Planet:** i.e., the
    sun.

289. **doost lead:** i.e., appears
    first.
292. **atweene:** amidst.
293. **As joying:** as if rejoicing.

§ *tyred steedes*: The chariot of the sun-god Helios, or Phoebus Apollo,
is drawn by immortal, fire-breathing horses controllable by him alone.
Phoebus is called *fayrest Planet* because the sun is one of the planets
in the Ptolemaic system.

Now ceasse ye damsels your delights forepast;　　296
Enough is it, that all the day was youres:
Now day is doen, and night is nighing fast:
Now bring the Bryde into the brydall boures.
Now night is come, now soone her disaray,　　300
And in her bed her lay;
Lay her in lillies and in violets,
And silken courteins over her display,
And odourd sheetes, and Arras coverlets.
Behold how goodly my faire love does ly　　305
In proud humility;
Like unto Maia, when as Jove her tooke,　　§
In Tempe, lying on the flowry gras,
Twixt sleepe and wake, after she weary was,
With bathing in the Acidalian brooke.　　310
Now it is night, ye damsels may be gon,
And leave my love alone,
And leave likewise your former lay to sing:
The woods no more shal answere, nor your echo ring.

296. **forepast:** (being now) ended.
298. **doen:** done; **nighing:** drawing near.
299. **boures:** chamber(s).
300. **disaray:** undress.
304. **odourd:** scented; **Arras:** of tapestry (Arras = an expensive tapestry).

§ *Maia*: One of the Pleiades, the seven daughters of the Titan Atlas. Upon her, Jove begot Mercury (Hermes), the herald and messenger of the gods. Spenser here shifts the scene of Jove's visit to Maia from Mount Cyllene in Arcadia to the Vale of Tempe in Thessaly. The *Acidalian brooke*, associated by some ancient authors with Venus, is in Boeotia. Spenser has therefore telescoped several locales into one and managed yet another suggestion of Venus.

Now welcome night, thou night so long expected,   *315*
That long daies labour doest at last defray,
And all my cares, which cruell love collected,
Hast sumd in one, and cancelled for aye:
Spread thy broad wing over my love and me,
That no man may us see,   *320*
And in thy sable mantle us enwrap,
From feare of perrill and foule horror free.
Let no false treason seeke us to entrap,
Nor any dread disquiet once annoy
The safety of our joy: *325*
But let the night be calme and quietsome,
Without tempestuous storms or sad afray:
Lyke as when Jove with fayre Alcmena lay,   §
When he begot the great Tirynthian groome:
Or lyke as when he with thy selfe did lie,   *330*
And begot Majesty.
And let the mayds and yongmen cease to sing:
Ne let the woods them answer, nor theyr eccho ring.

316. **defray:** make up for, pay   321. **sable:** black.
  for.   327. **sad afray:** grievous alarm.
318. **sumd in one:** gathered   330. **thy selfe:** i.e., Night.
  into a single total; **aye:**
  ever.

§ *Alcmena*: Wife of the Argive prince Amphitryon. In Amphitryon's
shape Zeus lay with Alcmena during a miraculously prolonged night
and begot Herakles (Hercules), the *great Tirynthian groome.* "Tirynthian" means from Tiryns (a city on the plain of Argos), sometimes
given as the birthplace of Herakles.

Let no lamenting cryes, nor dolefull teares,
Be heard all night within nor yet without: 335
Ne let false whispers breeding hidden feares,
Breake gentle sleepe with misconceived dout.
Let no deluding dreames, nor dreadful sights
Make sudden sad affrights;
Ne let housefyres, nor lightnings helpelesse harmes,   340
Ne let the Pouke, nor other evill sprights,   §
Ne let mischivous witches with theyr charmes,
Ne let hob Goblins, names whose sence we see not,
Fray us with things that be not.
Let not the shriech Oule, nor the Storke be heard: 345
Nor the night Raven that still deadly yels,
Nor damned ghosts cald up with mighty spels,
Nor griesly vultures make us once affeard:
Ne let th'unpleasant Quyre of Frogs still croking
Make us to wish theyr choking.   350
Let none of these theyr drery accents sing;
Ne let the woods them answer, nor theyr eccho ring.

336. Ne: nor.
337. **misconceived dout:** false
    fear, baseless doubt.
340. **helpelesse:** unavoidable.
341. **Pouke:** Puck.

342. **mischivous:** malevolent,
    malignant.
345. **shriech Oule:** screech owl.
348. **griesly:** grisly, ghastly.
349. **Quyre:** choir; **still:** con-
    tinuously.

§ *the Pouke*: Puck, also called Robin Goodfellow, is here thought of as
sinister, even satanic, rather than merely mischievous.

But let stil Silence trew night watches keepe,
That sacred peace may in assurance rayne,
And tymely sleep, when it is tyme to sleepe,   *355*
May poure his limbs forth on your pleasant playne,
The whiles an hundred little winged loves,
Like divers fethered doves,
Shall fly and flutter round about your bed,
And in the secret darke, that none reproves,   *360*
Their prety stealthes shal worke, and snares shal spread
To filch away sweet snatches of delight,
Conceald through covert night.
Ye sonnes of Venus, play your sports at will,
For greedy pleasure, carelesse of your toyes,   *365*
Thinks more upon her paradise of joyes,
Then what ye do, albe it good or ill.
All night therefore attend your merry play,
For it will soone be day:
Now none doth hinder you, that say or sing,   *370*
Ne will the woods now answer, nor your Eccho ring.

356. **your:** i.e., Night's.
358. **divers:** so many.
363. **covert:** covering.
365. **toyes:** pranks.

367. **albe it:** whether it be.
368. **attend:** go about, attend to.
370. **say:** talk, speak.

Who is the same, which at my window peepes?
Or whose is that faire face, that shines so bright?
Is it not Cinthia, she that never sleepes,   §
But walkes about high heaven al the night?   375
O fayrest goddesse, do thou not envy
My love with me to spy:
For thou likewise didst love, though now unthought,
And for a fleece of woll, which privily,
The Latmian shephard once unto thee brought,   380 §
His pleasures with thee wrought.
Therefore to us be favorable now;
And sith of wemens labours thou hast charge,
And generation goodly dost enlarge,
Encline thy will t'effect our wishfull vow,   385
And the chast wombe informe with timely seed,
That may our comfort breed:
Till which we cease our hopefull hap to sing,
Ne let the woods us answere, nor our Eccho ring.

378. **unthought:** (it is) forgotten, unsuspected.
379. **woll:** wool; **privily:** secretly.
383. **labours:** labour (of childbirth).
384. **enlarge:** increase (or) set free (in which case "generation" means the children set free by birth).
385. **wishfull vow:** ardent wish.
387. **breed:** bring about, increase.
388. **hopefull hap to sing:** to sing of the fortune we hope for.

§ *Cinthia*: Cynthia, the moon-goddess who aids fertility and presides over the conception of children and who, along with Juno (Hera), protects women in labour. The ancients sometimes distinguished between Cynthia and Juno, on the one hand, and on the other, Eileithyia, the birth-goddess who presides over parturition (the process of actually giving birth).

§ *The Latmian shephard*: Endymion, the shepherd of Mount Latmos, with whom the moon-goddess fell in love. Either Zeus or she herself cast Endymion into an eternal sleep so that she could enjoy him – perpetually young and beautiful – whenever she wished. According to Virgil it was the shepherd-god, Pan himself, who wooed the Moon with the gift of a fleece.

And thou great Juno, which with awful might   390 §
The lawes of wedlock still dost patronize,
And the religion of the faith first plight
With sacred rites hast taught to solemnize:
And eeke for comfort often called art
Of women in their smart,   395
Eternally bind thou this lovely band,
And all thy blessings unto us impart.
And thou glad Genius, in whose gentle hand,   §
The bridale bowre and geniall bed remaine,
Without blemish or staine,   400
And the sweet pleasures of theyr loves delight
With secret ayde doest succour and supply,
Till they bring forth the fruitfull progeny,
Send us the timely fruit of this same night.
And thou fayre Hebe, and thou Hymen free,   405 §
Grant that it may so be.
Til which we cease your further prayse to sing,
Ne any woods shal answer, nor your Eccho ring.

390. **awful:** august, venerable.
395. **smart:** pain, (perhaps)
    birth-pangs.
399. **geniall:** fruitful.

§ *Juno*: The consort of Jove (Zeus). She is the goddess of marriage
considered especially as a social institution and also, in Roman times,
under the name Lucina Juno, the patroness of women in labour.
§ *Genius*: "The begetter". Originally, Genius seems to have been a per-
sonification of the life-force of a clan, family, or individual; and
throughout its complicated history one persistent use of "Genius" was
to designate the god, or guardian, of the life-processes: generation,
procreation, birth. Hence a marriage is one of the most appropriate
occasions on which to invoke Genius. But from early Latin times a
Genius was also thought of as a personal attendant spirit whose chief
functions were to foster natural pleasures and desires and to promote
their gratification. Spenser is here using Genius as a major image of
both creativity and pleasure. Thus *geniall bed* means both the pro-
creative bed and also the bed in which the pleasures of sexual desire
are aroused and gratified.
§ *Hebe*: Wife of Herakles deified and sister of Eileithyia, the birth-
goddess. Hebe is the gods' cup-bearer and, as the goddess of youth
and youthful beauty, is able to renew youth in men.

And ye high heavens, the temple of the gods,
In which a thousand torches flaming bright   410
Doe burne, that to us wretched earthly clods,
In dreadful darknesse lend desired light;
And all ye powers which in the same remayne,
More then we men can fayne,
Poure out your blessing on us plentiously,   415
And happy influence upon us raine,
That we may raise a large posterity,
Which from the earth, which they may long possesse,
With lasting happinesse,
Up to your haughty pallaces may mount,   420
And for the guerdon of theyr glorious merit
May heavenly tabernacles there inherit,
Of blessed Saints for to increase the count.
So let us rest, sweet love, in hope of this,
And cease till then our tymely joyes to sing,   425
The woods no more us answer, nor our eccho ring.

409. **gods**: planetary and stellar
      Intelligences, or Powers.
413. **powers**: angelic ministers,
      (also, perhaps) stellar in-
      fluences; **in the same**: i.e.,
      in the "high heavens".
414. **fayne**: imagine.
421. **guerdon**: reward.

Song made in lieu of many ornaments,
With which my love should duly have bene dect,
Which cutting off through hasty accidents,
Ye would not stay your dew time to expect,   *430*
But promist both to recompens,
Be unto her a goodly ornament,
And for short time an endlesse moniment.

427. **in lieu:** instead.
428. **duly:** rightfully, properly;
    dect: decked, adorned.
433. **moniment:** memorial.

Prothalamion

Or

A Spousall Verse made by
Edm. Spenser.

IN HONOUR OF THE DOU-
ble mariage of the two Honorable & vertuous

Ladies, the Ladie Elizabeth *and the Ladie* Katherine
Somerset, Daughters to the Right Honourable the
Earle of *Worcester* and espoused to the two worthie
Gentlemen M. *Henry Gilford*, and
M. *William Peter* Esquyers.

AT LONDON
Printed for *William Ponsonby.*
1596.

Prothalamion

1

Calme was the day, and through the trembling ayre,
Sweete breathing *Zephyrus* did softly play   §
A gentle spirit, that lightly did delay
Hot *Titans* beames, which then did glyster fayre:
When I whom sullein care,   5
Through discontent of my long fruitlesse stay
In Princes Court, and expectation vayne
Of idle hopes, which still doe fly away,
Like empty shaddowes, did aflict my brayne,
Walkt forth to ease my payne   10
Along the shoare of silver streaming *Themmes*,
Whose rutty Bancke, the which his River hemmes,
Was paynted all with variable flowers,
And all the meades adornd with daintie gemmes,
Fit to decke maydens bowres,   15
And crowne their Paramours,
Against the Brydale day, which is not long:
    Sweete *Themmes* runne softly, till I end my Song.

3. **delay:** temper.   13. **variable:** various.
4. **glyster:** shine.   14. **meades:** meadows.
8. **idle:** impty.   17. **Against:** in preparation for.
11. **Themmes:** Thames.
12. **rutty:** rooty.

§ *Zephyrus*: Of the Four Winds, children of Aurora (Eos) the dawn-
goddess, Zephyrus is the one that blows from the west.

2

There, in a Meadow, by the Rivers side,
A Flocke of *Nymphes* I chaunced to espy,   *20 §*
All lovely Daughters of the Flood thereby,
With goodly greenish locks all loose untyde,
As each had bene a Bryde,
And each one had a little wicker basket,
Made of fine twigs entrayled curiously,   *25*
In which they gathered flowers to fill their flasket:
And with fine Fingers, cropt full feateously
The tender stalkes on hye.
Of every sort, which in that Meadow grew,
They gathered some; the Violet pallid blew,   *30*
The little Dazie, that at evening closes,
The virgin Lillie, and the Primrose trew,
With store of vermeil Roses,
To decke their Bridegromes posies,
Against the Brydale day, which was not long: *35*
 Sweete *Themmes* runne softly, till I end my Song.

21. **the Flood thereby:** the river
  (i.e., Thames) close by.
25. **entrayled curiously:** ingen-
  iously woven.

27. **fine:** neat; **full feateously:**
  very dexterously.
33. **vermeil:** vermilion.

§ *Nymphes*: Beautiful young women who are the guardian spirits or
resident divinities of woods, waters, and mountains. A nymph will
sometimes be used by a poet to personify a tree or class of trees, a
spring, a fountain, and so on. There are various classes of nymphs;
in the class of water-nymphs, the particular guardian spirits or personifications of rivers (such as the daughters of the Thames here
celebrated by Spenser) are called Naiades.

3

With that I saw two Swannes of goodly hewe,
Come softly swimming downe along the Lee;
Two fairer Birds I yet did never see:
The snow which doth the top of *Pindus* strew,   *40*
Did never whiter shew,
Nor *Jove* himselfe when he a Swan would be   §
For love of *Leda*, whiter did appeare:
Yet *Leda* was they say as white as he,
Yet not so white as these, nor nothing neare;   *45*
So purely white they were,
That even the gentle streame, the which them bare,
Seem'd foule to them, and bad his billowes spare
To wet their silken feathers, least they might
Soyle their fayre plumes with water not so fayre,   *50*
And marre their beauties bright,
That shone as heavens light,
Against their Brydale day, which was not long:
    Sweete *Themmes* runne softly, till I end my Song.

38. **Lee:** river that flows into   48. **spare/To wet:** to refrain
    the Thames.   from wetting.

§ *Jove . . . a Swan*: The children born as the result of this particular
conquest of Jove's were the twins Castor and Polydeuces.

4

Eftsoones the *Nymphes*, which now had Flowers their fill, 55
Ran all in haste, to see that silver brood,
As they came floating on the Christal Flood,
Whom when they sawe, they stood amazed still,
Their wondring eyes to fill.
Them seem'd they never saw a sight so fayre, 60
Of Fowles so lovely, that they sure did deeme
Them heavenly borne, or to be that same payre
Which through the Skie draw *Venus* silver Teeme, §
For sure they did not seeme
To be begot of any earthly Seede, 65
But rather Angels or of Angels breede:
Yet were they bred of *Somers-heat* they say,
In sweetest Season, when each Flower and weede
The earth did fresh aray,
So fresh they seem'd as day, 70
Even as their Brydale day, which was not long:
    Sweete *Themmes* runne softly, till I end my Song.

55. **Eftsoones:** at once; **had Flowers their fill:** had all the flowers they needed.
60. **Them seem'd:** it seemed to them.

67. **Somers-heat:** (play on) Somerset (maiden name of the two brides).
68. **weede:** plant.

§ *Venus silver Teeme*: The chariot of Venus is sometimes portrayed as being pulled by doves, the birds sacred to Venus, but more often (as here) by swans.

5

Then forth they all out of their baskets drew
Great store of Flowers, the honour of the field,
That to the sense did fragrant odours yield,   75
All which upon those goodly Birds they threw,
And all the Waves did strew,
That like old *Peneus* Waters they did seeme,   §
When downe along by pleasant *Tempes* shore
Scattred with Flowres, through *Thessaly* they streeme,   80
That they appeare through Lillies plenteous store,
Like a Brydes Chamber flore:
Two of those *Nymphes*, meane while, two Garlands bound,
Of freshest Flowres which in that Mead they found,
The which presenting all in trim Array,   85
Their snowie Foreheads therewithall they crownd,
Whil'st one did sing this Lay,
Prepar'd against that Day,
Against their Brydale day, which was not long:
   Sweete *Themmes* runne softly, till I end my Song.   90

74. **honour:** glory.
87. **this Lay:** this song (i.e.,
   the following stanza).

§ *old Peneus*: The river Peneus had been celebrated by earlier poets for
its verdant banks and beautiful water-flowers. Perhaps Spenser calls
Peneus "old" because he is given as the grandfather of Cyrene, one
of the nymphs beloved by Apollo.

6

Ye gentle Birdes, the worlds faire ornament,
And heavens glorie, whom this happie hower
Doth leade unto your lovers blisfull bower,
Joy may you have and gentle hearts content
Of your loves couplement: *95*
And let faire *Venus*, that is Queene of love,
With her heart-quelling Sonne upon you smile,
Whose smile they say, hath vertue to remove
All Loves dislike, and friendships faultie guile
For ever to assoile.   *100*
Let endlesse Peace your steadfast hearts accord,
And blessed Plentie wait upon your bord,
And let your bed with pleasures chast abound,
That fruitfull issue may to you afford,
Which may your foes confound,   *105*
And make your joyes redound,
Upon your Brydale day, which is not long:
  Sweet *Themmes* run softlie, till I end my Song.

92. **hower:** hour.
95. **couplement:** union.
97. **heart-quelling Sonne:**
  Eros (Cupid).

100. **assoile:** dispel.
101. **accord:** unite in accord.
104. **afford:** give.

7

So ended she; and all the rest around
To her redoubled that her undersong,   *110*
Which said, their bridale daye should not be long.
And gentle Eccho from the neighbour ground,   §
Their accents did resound.
So forth those joyous Birdes did passe along,
Adowne the Lee, that to them murmurde low,   *115*
As he would speake, but that he lackt a tong,
Yet did by signes his glad affection show,
Making his streame run slow.
And all the foule which in his flood did dwell
Gan flock about these twaine, that did excell   *120*
The rest, so far, as *Cynthia* doth shend   §
The lesser starres. So they enranged well,
Did on those two attend,
And their best service lend,
Against their wedding day, which was not long: *125*
    Sweete *Themmes* run softly, till I end my song.

110. **To her . . . undersong:**   119. **foule:** waterfowl.
    repeated her refrain.   121. **shend:** surpass.

§ *Eccho*: Echo was a nymph who, Juno felt, talked too much. By way
of punishment Juno deprived Echo of all uses of speech except the
ability to repeat the last words of other people's conversation. Echo
fell in love with the self-obsessed Narcissus and pined away in unrequited love until nothing was left of her except her curtailed voice.
§ *Cynthia*: The moon. Some of her other names are Luna, Diana,
Artemis, and Phoebe.

8

At length they all to mery *London* came,
To mery London, my most kyndly Nurse,
That to me gave his Lifes first native sourse:
Though from another place I take my name,   *130* §
An house of auncient fame.
There when they came, whereas those bricky towres,
The which on *Themmes* brode aged backe doe ryde,
Where now the studious Lawyers have their bowers,   §
There whylome wont the Templer Knights to byde,   *135*
Till they decayd through pride:
Next whereunto there standes a stately place,
Where oft I gayned giftes and goodly grace
Of that great Lord, which therein wont to dwell,
    Whose want too well, now feeles my freendles case: *140*
But Ah here fits not well
Olde woes but joyes to tell
Against the bridale daye, which is not long:
    Sweete *Themmes* runne softly, till I end my Song.

133. **brode:** broad.
135. **whylome:** once; **wont . . .
    to:** used to.

137. **stately place:** Earl of
    Leicester's palace.
140. **Whose want:** the lack of
    whom.

§ *Though from another place . . . my name*: Spenser is referring to
   Wormleighton or Althorp, seats of the Spencers, a noble family distantly related to him. The first five lines of stanza 8 mark one of the
   few passages in his work where Spenser gives us any autobiographical
   information.
§ *Where now the studious Lawyers*: The reference is to the Inner and
   Middle Temples, two of the four Inns of Court maintained by the
   legal profession. "Inns of Court" refers both to the legal society itself
   and to its four residences. *Templer Knights*: members of the military-
   religious order of Knights Templars, founded by crusaders in 1119 for
   the defence of the Latin Kingdom of Jerusalem. The order fell into
   disrepute and was suppressed in 1312.

9

Yet therein now doth lodge a noble Peer,   145
Great *Englands* glory and the Worlds wide wonder,
Whose dreadfull name, late through all *Spaine* did thunder,
And *Hercules* two pillors standing neere,   §
Did make to quake and feare:
Faire branch of Honor, flower of Chevalrie,   150
That fillest *England* with thy triumphes fame,
Joy have thou of thy noble victorie,   §
And endlesse happinesse of thine owne name
That promiseth the same:
That through thy prowesse and victorious armes,   155
Thy country may be freed from forraine harmes:
And great *Elisaes* glorious name may ring
Through al the world, fil'd with thy wide Alarmes,
Which some brave muse may sing
To ages following,   160
Upon the Brydale day, which is not long:
    Sweet *Themmes* runne softly, till I end my Song.

145. **noble Peer:** Earl of Essex.
147. **dreadfull:** awe-inspiring.
153. **happinesse . . . owne name:** (play between the Essex family name) Deve-
reux (and) "heureux", happy.
154. **the same:** i.e., happiness.
159. **muse:** i.e., poet.

§ *Hercules two pillors*: The Pillars of Hercules are two rocky promon-
tories, now called Gibraltar and Jebel Musa, on opposite sides of the
narrow western entrance to the Mediterranean. Hercules (Herakles)
set them up in the course of performing his tenth labour, which was
to find the cattle of King Geryon on their far western island pastures
and fetch them to Mycenae.
§ *thy noble victorie*: Essex was one of the leaders of the highly successful expedition against Cadiz in June 1596.

10

From those high Towers, this noble Lord issuing,
Like Radiant *Hesper* when his golden hayre
In th'*Ocean* billowes he hath Bathed fayre,   *165*
Descended to the Rivers open vewing,
With a great traine ensuing.
Above the rest were goodly to bee seene
Two gentle Knights of lovely face and feature
Beseeming well the bower of anie Queene,   *170*
With gifts of wit and ornaments of nature,
Fit for so goodly stature:
That like the twins of *Jove* they seem'd in sight,   §
Which decke the Bauldricke of the Heavens bright.
They two forth pacing to the Rivers side,   *175*
Received those two faire Brides, their Loves delight,
Which at th'appointed tyde,
Each one did make his Bryde,
Against their Brydale day, which is not long:
    Sweete *Themmes* runne softly, till I end my Song.   *180*

164. **Hesper:** Evening Star.
167. **traine ensuing:** retinue fol-
    lowing.

170. **Beseeming well:** fit to
    grace, well worthy of.
177. **tyde:** time.

§ *twins of Jove*: Castor and Polydeuces, who are also known as the
    Dioscuri (Sons of Jove) and, in their aspect as heavenly bodies, as
    the constellation Gemini.

Fowre Hymnes

MADE BY

EDM. SPENSER.

LONDON

Printed for William Ponsonby.

1596.

TO THE RIGHT HONORABLE AND MOST VERTUOUS LADIES,

the Ladie Margaret Countesse of Cumberland,

AND

the Ladie Marie Countesse of Warwicke

*Having in the greener times of my youth, composed these
former two Hymnes in the praise of Love and beautie, and
finding that the same too much pleased those of like age
and disposition, which being too vehemently caried with
that kind of affection, do rather sucke out poyson to their* 5
*strong passion, then hony to their honest delight, I was
moved by the one of you two most excellent Ladies, to call
in the same. But being unable so to doe, by reason that
many copies thereof were formerly scattered abroad, I resolved at least to amend, and by way of retractation to* 10
*reforme them, making in stead of those two Hymnes of
earthly or naturall love and beautie, two others of heavenly
and celestiall. The which I doe dedicate joyntly unto you
two honorable sisters, as to the most excellent and rare ornaments of all true love and beautie, both in the one and* 15
*the other kinde, humbly beseeching you to vouchsafe the
patronage of them, and to accept this my humble service,
in lieu of the great graces and honourable favours which ye
dayly shew unto me, untill such time as I may by better
meanes yeeld you some more notable testimonie of my* 20
thankfull mind and dutifull devotion.

And even so I pray for your happinesse.
Greenwich this first of September.
1596.

Your Honors most bounden ever 25
in all humble service.

Ed. Sp.

6. **then hony:** than honey.
7-8. **to call in:** i.e., suppress.
15-16. **both in the one . . .
    kinde:** i.e., both in earthly
    and heavenly love and also

in earthly and heavenly
beauty.
18. **in lieu of:** in return for.
20. **yeeld you:** make for you
    (or) offer you.
25. **bounden:** obligated.

AN HYMNE IN HONOUR OF

Love

L ove, that long since hast to thy mighty powre,   §
   Perforce subdude my poore captived hart,
And raging now therein with restlesse stowre,
Doest tyrannize in everie weaker part;
Faine would I seeke to ease my bitter smart,   5
By any service I might do to thee,
Or ought that else might to thee pleasing bee.

And now t'asswage the force of this new flame,
And make thee more propitious in my need,
I meane to sing the praises of thy name,   10
And thy victorious conquests to areed;
By which thou madest many harts to bleed
Of mighty Victors, with wyde wounds embrewed,
And by thy cruell darts to thee subdewed.

1. **Love:** Eros (Cupid).
3. **stowre:** commotion, turmoil.
7. **ought that else:** anything else that.

11. **areed:** proclaim, show forth.
13. **embrewed:** i.e., soaking, (or perhaps) perforated, covered (with).

§ *Love*: Cupid (Eros), usually given as the son of Venus Aphrodite (but see the note on page 405). In medieval and Renaissance love-literature the reign of Love in his younger or boyish aspect is often described by smarting lovers as an absolute tyranny since he can be, and often is, blind, ruthless, irresistible, and unpredictable.

Onely I feare my wits enfeebled late,   15
Through the sharpe sorrowes, which thou hast me bred,
Should faint, and words should faile me, to relate
The wondrous triumphs of thy great godhed.
But if thou wouldst vouchsafe to overspred
Me with the shadow of thy gentle wing,   20
I should enabled be thy actes to sing.

Come then, O come, thou mightie God of love,
Out of thy silver bowres and secret blisse,
Where thou doest sit in *Venus* lap above,
Bathing thy wings in her ambrosiall kisse,   25
That sweeter farre then any Nectar is;
Come softly, and my feeble breast inspire
With gentle furie, kindled of thy fire.

And ye sweet Muses, which have often proved   §
The piercing points of his avengefull darts,   30
And ye faire Nimphs, which oftentimes have loved   §
The cruell worker of your kindly smarts,
Prepare your selves, and open wide your harts,
For to receive the triumph of your glorie,
That made you merie oft, when ye were sorie.   35

16. **me bred:** brought upon,   28. **furie:** inspiration (fury
    caused me.   often translates as creative
25. **ambrosiall:** i.e., heavenly   ecstasy, divine madness).
    (ambrosia = food of the   32. **kindly smarts:** beneficial
    gods).   stings.

§ *Muses*: The nine patron goddesses of the Arts. They are the daughters
  of Zeus (Jove) and Mnemosyne (Memory).
§ *Nimphs*: The guardian spirits, personified as beautiful semi-divine
  young women, of such natural beauties as woods, springs, streams,
  and mountains.

And ye faire blossomes of youths wanton breed,
Which in the conquests of your beautie bost,
Wherewith your lovers feeble eyes you feed,
But sterve their harts, that needeth nourture most,
Prepare your selves, to march amongst his host,   40
And all the way this sacred hymne do sing,
Made in the honor of your Soveraigne king.

Great god of might, that reignest in the mynd,
  And all the bodie to thy hest doest frame,
Victor of gods, subduer of mankynd,   45
That doest the Lions and fell Tigers tame,
Making their cruell rage thy scornefull game,
And in their roring taking great delight;
Who can expresse the glorie of thy might?

Or who alive can perfectly declare,   50
The wondrous cradle of thine infancie?
When thy great mother *Venus* first thee bare,   §
Begot of Plentie and of Penurie,
Though elder then thine owne nativitie;
And yet a chyld, renewing still thy yeares;   55
And yet the eldest of the heavenly Peares.

36. **faire blossomes:** i.e., beau-
    tiful young women.
37. **Which in . . . bost:** who
    boast of.
39. **sterve:** starve.
44. **hest doest frame:** conforms

to your command.
46. **fell:** fierce.
47. **game:** sport.
56. **Peares:** peers (i.e., powers,
    lords).

§ *thy great mother Venus*: In the first sixty-odd lines of this poem
  Spenser cheerfully mixes three accounts of the origin and parentage
  of Love. According to one of the accounts of Love in Plato's *Symposium*, Penia (*Penurie*, Poverty) gate-crashed one of Zeus' parties
  and mated with Poros (*Plentie*) without his knowledge – he being the
  worse for nectar – and so conceived Love by him. This account makes
  Love one of the youngest gods. Another ancient Greek story makes
  him the first offspring of Night, herself the daughter of Chaos; from
  Love then descended all other gods and creatures. This account gives
  Love a prime role in all creation, making him the most powerful
  and, except for Night herself, the oldest of the gods.

For ere this worlds still moving mightie masse,
Out of great *Chaos* ugly prison crept,
In which his goodly face long hidden was
From heavens view, and in deepe darknesse kept,   60
Love, that had now long time securely slept
In *Venus* lap, unarmed then and naked,
Gan reare his head, by *Clotho* being waked.   §

And taking to him wings of his owne heate,
Kindled at first from heavens life-giving fyre,   65
He gan to move out of his idle seate,
Weakely at first, but after with desyre
Lifted aloft, he gan to mount up hyre,
And like fresh Eagle, make his hardie flight
Through all that great wide wast, yet wanting light.

Yet wanting light to guide his wandring way,   71
His owne faire mother, for all creatures sake,
Did lend him light from her owne goodly ray:
Then through the world his way he gan to take,
The world that was not till he did it make;   75
Whose sundrie parts he from them selves did sever,
The which before had lyen confused ever.

57. **still:** always, continually.
63. **Gan:** did.
68. **gan:** began.
70. **wast:** waste, wilderness (of chaos); **yet wanting:** still lacking.

76. **sever:** separate out, sort out.
77. **lyen confused ever:** always lain randomly mingled.

§ *Clotho*: One of the three Fates, the daughters of Nyx (Night). Clotho (Spinner) spins the thread of life, Lachesis (Apportioner) decides its length, and Atropos (Inflexible) cuts it. In mythology Zeus himself has to admit more than once that even he is subject to them.

The earth, the ayre, the water, and the fyre,
Then gan to raunge them selves in huge array,
And with contrary forces to conspyre   *80*
Each against other, by all meanes they may,
Threatning their owne confusion and decay:
Ayre hated earth, and water hated fyre,
Till Love relented their rebellious yre.

He then them tooke, and tempering goodly well   *85*
Their contrary dislikes with loved meanes,
Did place them all in order, and compell
To keepe them selves within their sundrie raines,
Together linkt with Adamantine chaines;   §
Yet so, as that in every living wight   *90*
They mixe themselves, and shew their kindly might.

So ever since they firmely have remained,
And duly well observed his beheast;
Through which now all these things that are contained
Within this goodly cope, both most and least   *95*
Their being have, and dayly are increast,
Through secret sparks of his infused fyre,
Which in the barraine cold he doth inspyre.

Thereby they all do live, and moved are
To multiply the likenesse of their kynd,   *100*
Whilest they seeke onely, without further care,
To quench the flame, which they in burning fynd:
But man, that breathes a more immortall mynd,
Not for lusts sake, but for eternitie,
Seekes to enlarge his lasting progenie.   *105*

80. **with contrary forces:** i.e.,
   in a tension of opposites.
88. **raines:** domains.
89. **Adamantine:** i.e., unyield-
   ing, unbreakable.
90. **wight:** creature.

93. **beheast:** command.
95. **cope:** i.e., framework.
101. **care:** concern(s).
102. **which they in . . . fynd:**
   in which they find themselves burning.

§ *Adamantine*: From "adamant", in legend the hardest of all stones and
later identified with diamond.

For having yet in his deducted spright,
Some sparks remaining of that heavenly fyre,
He is enlumind with that goodly light,
Unto like goodly semblant to aspyre:
Therefore in choice of love, he doth desyre   *110*
That seemes on earth most heavenly, to embrace,
That same is Beautie, borne of heavenly race.

For sure of all, that in this mortall frame
Contained is, nought more divine doth seeme,
Or that resembleth more th'immortall flame   *115*
Of heavenly light, then Beauties glorious beame.
What wonder then, if with such rage extreme
Fraile men, whose eyes seek heavenly things to see,
At sight thereof so much enravisht bee?

Which well perceiving, that imperious boy   *120*
Doth therwith tip his sharp empoisned darts;
Which glancing through the eyes with countenance coy,
Rest not, till they have pierst the trembling harts,
And kindled flame in all their inner parts,
Which suckes the blood, and drinketh up the lyfe *125*
Of carefull wretches with consuming griefe.

Thenceforth they playne, and make ful piteous mone
Unto the author of their balefull bane;
The daies they waste, the nights they grieve and grone,
Their lives they loath, and heavens light disdaine: *130*
No light but that, whose lampe doth yet remaine
Fresh burning in the image of their eye,
They deigne to see, and seeing it still dye.

106. **deducted:** blemished, diminished; **spright:** spirit.
108. **enlumind:** i.e., enlightened.
109. **like goodly semblant:** a beautiful likeness.
116. **then Beauties:** than Beauty's.
117. **rage:** passion.
122. **coy:** (perhaps usual meaning but can also mean) secret (and/or) modest.
126. **carefull:** anxious, careworn.
127. **playne:** complain.
128. **bane:** ruin, death.

The whylst thou tyrant Love doest laugh and scorne
At their complaints, making their paine thy play; *135*
Whylest they lye languishing like thrals forlorne,
The whyles thou doest triumph in their decay,
And otherwhyles, their dying to delay,
Thou doest emmarble the proud hart of her,
Whose love before their life they doe prefer.   *140*

So hast thou often done (ay me the more)
To me thy vassall, whose yet bleeding hart,
With thousand wounds thou mangled hast so sore
That whole remaines scarse any little part,
Yet to augment the anguish of my smart,   *145*
Thou hast enfrosen her disdainefull brest,
That no one drop of pitie there doth rest.

Why then do I this honor unto thee,
Thus to ennoble thy victorious name,
Since thou doest shew no favour unto mee,   *150*
Ne once move ruth in that rebellious Dame,
Somewhat to slacke the rigour of my flame?
Certes small glory doest thou winne hereby,
To let her live thus free, and me to dy.

But if thou be indeede, as men thee call,   *155*
The worlds great Parent, the most kind preserver
Of living wights, the soveraine Lord of all,
How falles it then, that with thy furious fervour,
Thou doest afflict as well the not deserver,
As him that doeth thy lovely heasts despize,   *160*
And on thy subjects most doest tyrannize?

134. **The whylst:** while.
136. **thrals:** slaves.
137. **The whyles . . . other-whyles:** at times . . . at times; **decay:** destruction.
139. **emmarble:** turn to marble.
141. **ay me the more:** all the worse for me!
144. **whole:** sound, unhurt.
149. **ennoble:** glorify.

151. **Ne:** nor; **move ruth:** inspire pity.
153. **Certes:** certainly, truly.
157. **wights:** creatures.
158. **How falles it:** how does it happen.
159. **the not deserver:** i.e., the one who does not deserve affliction.
160. **heasts:** demands.

Yet herein eke thy glory seemeth more,
By so hard handling those which best thee serve,
That ere thou doest them unto grace restore,
Thou mayest well trie if they will ever swerve,   *165*
And mayest them make it better to deserve,
And having got it, may it more esteeme,
For things hard gotten, men more dearely deeme.

So hard those heavenly beauties be enfyred,   §
As things divine, least passions doe impresse,   *170*
The more of stedfast mynds to be admyred,
The more they stayed be on stedfastnesse:
But baseborne mynds such lamps regard the lesse,
Which at first blowing take not hastie fyre,
Such fancies feele no love, but loose desyre.   *175*

For love is Lord of truth and loialtie,
Lifting himselfe out of the lowly dust,
On golden plumes up to the purest skie,
Above the reach of loathly sinfull lust,
Whose base affect through cowardly distrust   *180*
Of his weake wings, dare not to heaven fly,
But like a moldwarpe in the earth doth ly.

162. **eke:** also.
165. **trie:** test.
168. **deeme:** i.e., hold, esteem.
169. **enfyred:** tempered by fire.
174. **take not hastie fyre:** do
     not quickly catch fire.

175. **Such fancies:** i.e., the
     fancies of base-born
     minds.
180. **affect:** imitation (of real
     love).
182. **moldwarpe:** mole.

§ *So hard those . . . stedfastnesse*: Spenser perhaps means something
like this: "As divine entities those heavenly beauties are fire-forged
to such a hardness, first, lest the passions should mar them, and
second, because the more steadfast they are, the more will lovers of
steadfast mind be devoted to them."

His dunghill thoughts, which do themselves enure
To dirtie drosse, no higher dare aspyre,
Ne can his feeble earthly eyes endure   *185*
The flaming light of that celestiall fyre,
Which kindleth love in generous desyre,
And makes him mount above the native might
Of heavie earth, up to the heavens hight.

Such is the powre of that sweet passion,   *190*
That it all sordid basenesse doth expell,
And the refyned mynd doth newly fashion
Unto a fairer forme, which now doth dwell
In his high thought, that would it selfe excell;
Which he beholding still with constant sight,   *195*
Admires the mirrour of so heavenly light.

Whose image printing in his deepest wit,
He thereon feeds his hungrie fantasy,
Still full, yet never satisfyde with it,
Like *Tantale*, that in store doth sterved ly: *200 §*
So doth he pine in most satiety,
For nought may quench his infinite desyre,
Once kindled through that first conceived fyre.

183. **enure:** habituate.
188. **native might:** natural pull, drag.
195. **still:** always, continuously.
196. **of so heavenly:** of that so heavenly.

197. **printing:** stamping.
198. **fantasy:** fancy, (here probably) longing to apprehend.
200. **that in store . . . ly:** who lies starving in the midst of plenty.

§ *Tantale*: For making a mock of the gods and abusing their friendly hospitality, Tantalus is everlastingly punished by having to stand up to the chin in water with clusters of fruit hanging just above his head; whenever he bends to drink, the waters recede, and whenever he stretches to eat, the fruit wafts out of reach.

Thereon his mynd affixed wholly is,
Ne thinks on ought, but how it to attaine;   205
His care, his joy, his hope is all on this,
That seemes in it all blisses to containe,
In sight whereof, all other blisse seemes vaine.
Thrise happie man, might he the same possesse;
He faines himselfe, and doth his fortune blesse.   210

And though he do not win his wish to end,
Yet thus farre happie he him selfe doth weene,
That heavens such happie grace did to him lend,
As thing on earth so heavenly, to have seene,
His harts enshrined saint, his heavens queene,   215
Fairer then fairest, in his fayning eye,
Whose sole aspect he counts felicitye.

Then forth he casts in his unquiet thought,
What he may do, her favour to obtaine;
What brave exploit, what perill hardly wrought,   220
What puissant conquest, what adventurous paine,
May please her best, and grace unto him gaine:
He dreads no danger, nor misfortune feares,
His faith, his fortune, in his breast he beares.

Thou art his god, thou art his mightie guyde,   225
Thou being blind, letst him not see his feares,
But cariest him to that which he hath eyde,
Through seas, through flames, through thousand swords
          and speares:
Ne ought so strong that may his force withstand,
With which thou armest his resistlesse hand.   230

205. **on ought:** about anything.
210. **faines:** i.e., would imagine; **doth . . . blesse:** i.e., would bless.
211. **win his wish to end:** achieve the perfection of his wish.
212. **weene:** think.
213. **lend:** grant.

216. **fayning:** rejoicing.
217. **Whose sole aspect:** in the mere sight of whom.
218. **forth he casts:** he casts about; **unquiet:** restless.
220. **hardly:** with difficulty.
221. **paine:** effort, task.
229. **Ne ought:** nothing (is).

Witnesse *Leander*, in the Euxine waves,   §
And stout *Æneas* in the Trojane fyre,
Achilles preassing through the Phrygian glaives,
And *Orpheus* daring to provoke the yre
Of damned fiends, to get his love retyre: 235
For both through heaven and hell thou makest way,
To win them worship which to thee obay.

And if by all these perils and these paynes,
He may but purchase lyking in her eye,
What heavens of joy, then to himselfe he faynes,   240
Eftsoones he wypes quite out of memory,
What ever ill before he did aby:
Had it bene death, yet would he die againe,
To live thus happie as her grace to gaine.

Yet when he hath found favour to his will,   245
He nathemore can so contented rest,
But forceth further on, and striveth still
T'approch more neare, till in her inmost brest,
He may embosomd bee, and loved best;
And yet not best, but to be lov'd alone,   250
For love can not endure a Paragone.

232. **Trojane fyre**: fires (i.e., burning) of Troy.
233. **Phrygian glaives**: Trojan swords.
235. **to get his love retyre**: to accomplish the return (to life) of his beloved.
237. **them worship which**: honour for those who.
239. **purchase**: win.

240. **to himselfe he faynes**: he pictures to himself.
241. **Eftsoones**: immediately.
242. **aby**: endure.
244. **her grace**: her favour.
245. **to his will**: according to his desire.
246. **nathemore**: none the more.
251. **Paragone**: rival.

§ *Leander*: Leander swam the Hellespont to be with his beloved Hero. Out of filial love *Aeneas* fought through the fiery destruction of Troy to rescue his crippled old father, Anchises, and carry him to safety. *Achilles*: The Greek champion who loved the youth Patroclus and avenged his death by inflicting appalling havoc on the Trojan army, finally killing Prince Hector himself. The bride of *Orpheus*, for love of whom he dared a journey to the underworld, was Eurydice.

The feare whereof, O how doth it torment
His troubled mynd with more then hellish paine!
And to his fayning fansie represent
Sights never seene, and thousand shadowes vaine,
To breake his sleepe, and waste his ydle braine;　256
Thou that hast never lov'd canst not beleeve
Least part of th'evils which poore lovers greeve.

The gnawing envie, the hart-fretting feare,
The vaine surmizes, the distrustfull showes,　260
The false reports that flying tales doe beare,
The doubts, the daungers, the delayes, the woes,
The fayned friends, the unassured foes,
With thousands more then any tongue can tell,
Doe make a lovers life a wretches hell.　265

Yet is there one more cursed then they all,
That cancker worme, that monster Gelosie,
Which eates the hart, and feedes upon the gall,
Turning all loves delight to miserie,
Through feare of loosing his felicitie.　270
Ah Gods, that ever ye that monster placed
In gentle love, that all his joyes defaced.

By these, O Love, thou doest thy entrance make,
Unto thy heaven, and doest the more endeere
Thy pleasures unto those which them partake,　275
As after stormes when clouds begin to cleare,
The Sunne more bright and glorious doth appeare;
So thou thy folke, through paines of Purgatorie,
Dost beare unto thy blisse, and heavens glorie.

254. **fayning:** i.e., teeming with images, (fayning here = image-making); **fansie:** imagination.

255. **vaine:** frail, empty.

256. **ydle:** useless, i.e., in this case being unable to help.

260. **distrustfull showes:** untrustworthy appearances.

263. **fayned:** seeming; **unassured foes:** probable but unverified enemies.

272. **defaced:** marred.

273. **thy entrance:** i.e., the entranceway designed by Love.

274. **the more endeere:** make all the more valuable.

There thou them placest in a Paradize   *280*
Of all delight, and joyous happie rest,
Where they doe feede on Nectar heavenly wize,
With *Hercules* and *Hebe*, and the rest   §
Of *Venus* dearlings, through her bountie blest,
And lie like Gods in yvorie beds arayd,   *285*
With rose and lillies over them displayd.

There with thy daughter *Pleasure* they doe play   §
Their hurtlesse sports, without rebuke or blame,
And in her snowy bosome boldly lay
Their quiet heads, devoyd of guilty shame,   *290*
After full joyance of their gentle game,
Then her they crowne their Goddesse and their Queene,
And decke with floures thy altars well beseene.

Ay me, deare Lord, that ever I might hope,
For all the paines and woes that I endure,   *295*
To come at length unto the wished scope
Of my desire, or might my selfe assure,
That happie port for ever to recure.
Then would I thinke these paines no paines at all,
And all my woes to be but penance small.   *300*

Then would I sing of thine immortall praise
An heavenly Hymne, such as the Angels sing,
And thy triumphant name then would I raise
Bove all the gods, thee onely honoring,
My guide, my God, my victor, and my king;   *305*
Till then, dread Lord, vouchsafe to take of me
This simple song, thus fram'd in praise of thee.

284. **dearlings:** darlings, fav-
ourites.
286. **displayd:** spread.
288. **hurtlesse:** innocent.

291. **joyance:** enjoyment.
293. **well beseene:** beautiful.
298. **port:** haven; **recure:** regain.

§ *Hercules and Hebe*: Hebe, daughter of Hera (Juno) and cup-bearer
of the gods, was wedded to the demigod Herakles (Hercules) after
the immortal part of him had joined the gods on Olympus.
§ *Pleasure*: The daughter of Eros (Cupid, Love) and Psyche (Soul).

AN HYMNE IN HONOUR OF

Beautie

Ah whither, Love, wilt thou now carrie mee?
What wontlesse fury dost thou now inspire
Into my feeble breast, too full of thee?
Whylest seeking to aslake thy raging fyre,
Thou in me kindlest much more great desyre,   *5*
And up aloft above my strength doest rayse
The wondrous matter of my fyre to prayse.

That as I earst in praise of thine owne name,
So now in honour of thy Mother deare,
An honourable Hymne I eke should frame,   *10*
And with the brightnesse of her beautie cleare,
The ravisht harts of gazefull men might reare,
To admiration of that heavenly light,
From whence proceeds such soule enchaunting might.

Therto do thou great Goddesse, queene of Beauty,   *15*
Mother of love, and of all worlds delight,
Without whose soverayne grace and kindly dewty,
Nothing on earth seemes fayre to fleshly sight,
Doe thou vouchsafe with thy love-kindling light,
T'illuminate my dim and dulled eyne,   *20*
And beautifie this sacred hymne of thyne.

2. **wontlesse:** unaccustomed; **fury:** ecstasy of inspiration.

4. **aslake:** slake.

7. **matter of my fyre:** theme (or) cause of my desire for beauty.

8. **earst:** lately.

10. **eke should frame:** also should compose.

12. **gazeful:** gazing.

15. **queene of Beauty:** Venus.

17. **kindly dewty:** natural and beneficial function.

20. **eyne:** eyes.

That both to thee, to whom I meane it most,
And eke to her, whose faire immortall beame,　§
Hath darted fyre into my feeble ghost,
That now it wasted is with woes extreame,　*25*
It may so please that she at length will streame
Some deaw of grace, into my withered hart,
After long sorrow and consuming smart.

W hat time this worlds great workmaister did　§
　　　cast
To make al things, such as we now behold,　*30*
It seemes that he before his eyes had plast
A goodly Paterne to whose perfect mould,
He fashiond them as comely as he could,
That now so faire and seemely they appeare,
As nought may be amended any wheare.　*35*

That wondrous Paterne wheresoere it bee,
Whether in earth layd up in secret store,
Or else in heaven, that no man may it see
With sinfull eyes, for feare it to deflore,
Is perfect Beautie which all men adore,　*40*
Whose face and feature doth so much excell
All mortall sence, that none the same may tell.

24. **ghost**: spirit.
26. **streame**: let flow.
27. **deaw**: dew, balm.
28. **smart**: sorrow.

29. **What time**: when, at the
　　time; **did cast**: decided.
39. **deflore**: desecrate.

§ *to her*: The idealized, hard-to-win lady of the first two *Hymnes*. It
　may be that "her" also refers to an actual love of Spenser's; if so, the
　problem of her identity is a terribly difficult one, partly because these
　first two *Hymnes* were written anywhere from 1579 to 1591, and
　partly because they were just possibly revised before being pub-
　lished with the last two *Hymnes*.
§ *worlds great workmaister*: Probably a reference to Plato's Demiurge,
　an intermediary creator responsible for the creation of the material
　world on the model of the real, divine, eternal Forms or Ideas.

Thereof as every earthly thing partakes,
Or more or lesse by influence divine,
So it more faire accordingly it makes,   *45*
And the grosse matter of this earthly myne,
Which clotheth it, thereafter doth refyne,
Doing away the drosse which dims the light
Of that faire beame, which therein is empight.

For through infusion of celestiall powre,   *50*
The duller earth it quickneth with delight,
And life-full spirits privily doth powre
Through all the parts, that to the lookers sight
They seeme to please. That is thy soveraine might,
O *Cyprian* Queene, which flowing from the beame *55*
Of thy bright starre, thou into them doest streame.

That is the thing which giveth pleasant grace
To all things faire, that kindleth lively fyre,
Light of thy lampe, which shyning in the face,
Thence to the soule darts amorous desyre,   *60*
And robs the harts of those which it admyre,
Therewith thou pointest thy Sons poysned arrow,
That wounds the life, and wastes the inmost marrow.

46. **myne:** mine (i.e., lowly source of supply for the earthly material with which creative beauty works).

49. **empight:** embedded, implanted.

52. **privily:** secretly, inwardly; **powre:** pour.

55. **Cyprian Queene:** Venus.

61. **robs:** steals.

62. **pointest:** sharpen(eth) the tip.

How vainely then doe ydle wits invent,
That beautie is nought else, but mixture made   65
Of colours faire, and goodly temp'rament   §
Of pure complexions, that shall quickly fade
And passe away, like to a sommers shade,
Or that it is but comely composition
Of parts well measurd, with meet disposition.   70

Hath white and red in it such wondrous powre,
That it can pierce through th'eyes unto the hart,
And therein stirre such rage and restlesse stowre,
As nought but death can stint his dolours smart?
Or can proportion of the outward part,   75
Move such affection in the inward mynd,
That it can rob both sense and reason blynd?

Why doe not then the blossomes of the field,
Which are arayd with much more orient hew,
And to the sense most daintie odours yield,   80
Worke like impression in the lookers vew?
Or why doe not faire pictures like powre shew,
In which oftimes, we Nature see of Art
Exceld, in perfect limming every part.

66. **goodly temp'rament:** happy mixture and balance.
67. **complexions:** humours.
70. **parts:** qualities; **measurd:** proportioned; **meet:** suitable; **disposition:** arrangement.
73. **rage:** passion; **stowre:** turmoil.
74. **stint his dolours smart:** stop the pain of its grief.
76. **affection:** desire.
79. **orient hew:** brilliant colour.
83. **of Art:** by art.
84. **in perfect limming:** in the perfect painting of.

§ *temp'rament:* Temperament, *complexion*, and *disposition* are terms from the vocabulary of physiology, astrology, and what we would call psychology. All three terms have psychosomatic application and were used to a considerable degree interchangeably in accounting for the physical appearance, the state of bodily health, and the personality. One's appearance, bodily health, and personality were taken to be the interrelated effects of such causes as planetary influence, the mixture and balance of the four cardinal humours (or body-fluids) – blood, phlegm, yellow bile, black bile – and the mixture and balance of the four qualities – heat, cold, dry, and moist. In these lines *temp'rament* means "mixture and balance"; *complexions* means "humours"; *comely composition* means "pleasing accord"; and *disposition* means "arrangement".

But ah, beleeve me, there is more then so   85
That workes such wonders in the minds of men.
I that have often prov'd, too well it know;
And who so list the like assayes to ken,
Shall find by tryall, and confesse it then,
That Beautie is not, as fond men misdeeme,   90
An outward shew of things, that onely seeme.

For that same goodly hew of white and red,
With which the cheekes are sprinckled, shal decay,
And those sweete rosy leaves so fairely spred
Upon the lips, shall fade and fall away   95
To that they were, even to corrupted clay.
That golden wyre, those sparckling stars so bright
Shall turne to dust, and loose their goodly light.

But that faire lampe, from whose celestiall ray
That light proceedes, which kindleth lovers fire,   100
Shal never be extinguisht nor decay,
But when the vitall spirits doe expyre,   §
Unto her native planet shall retyre,
For it is heavenly borne and can not die,
Being a parcell of the purest skie.   105

85. **then so**: than that (i.e., mere colour and external proportion).
87. **prov'd**: tested by experience.
88. **who so list . . . to ken**: whoever chooses to embark upon similar tests (or) trials.
89. **by tryall**: by actual experience.
90. **fond**: foolish; **misdeeme**: mistakenly think.
97. **wyre**: i.e., hair; **stars**: i.e., eyes.
99. **faire lampe**: i.e., the rational (highest) part of the soul.
105. **parcell**: small portion; **purest skie**: highest heaven, empyrean.

§ *vitall spirits*: According to some Platonists, man is a tripartite creature made up of soul, spirit (or vital spirits), and body; it is the spirit which links soul to body and which mediates the powers of the soul throughout the body. Of the three parts, only the soul is immortal, and with the dissolution of the spirit and body, it returns to the planet of its origin, i.e., its *native planet*. Throughout this second *Hymne* Spenser is drawing heavily upon a famous commentary on Plato's *Symposium* by the Italian Platonist Marsilio Ficino (1433-99).

For when the soule, the which derived was
At first, out of that great immortall Spright,
By whom all live to love, whilome did pas
Downe from the top of purest heavens hight,
To be embodied here, it then tooke light   *110*
And lively spirits from that fayrest starre,
Which lights the world forth from his firie carre.

Which powre retayning still or more or lesse,
When she in fleshly seede is eft enraced,
Through every part she doth the same impresse,   *115*
According as the heavens have her graced,
And frames her house, in which she will be placed,
Fit for her selfe, adorning it with spoyle
Of th'heavenly riches, which she robd erewhyle.

Therof it comes, that these faire soules, which have
The most resemblance of that heavenly light,   *121*
Frame to themselves most beautifull and brave
Their fleshly bowre, most fit for their delight,
And the grosse matter by a soveraine might
Tempers so trim, that it may well be seene,   *125*
A pallace fit for such a virgin Queene.

107. **immortall Spright:** God, the One (who creates without division of, or loss to, himself).
111. **fayrest starre:** i.e., the sun (Spenser is using the Ptolemaic model of the universe).
112. **firie carre:** fiery chariot.
114. **eft enraced:** afterwards embodied.

115. **impresse:** i.e., carry the influence of.
119. **robd erewhyle:** recently brought with her (from her passage past the sun).
122. **Frame to:** form for.
123. **fleshly bowre:** i.e., body.
125. **trim:** pleasingly.
126. **virgin Queene:** i.e., rational soul.

So every spirit, as it is most pure,
And hath in it the more of heavenly light,
So it the fairer bodie doth procure
To habit in, and it more fairely dight   *130*
With chearefull grace and amiable sight.
For of the soule the bodie forme doth take:
For soule is forme, and doth the bodie make.

Therefore where ever that thou doest behold
A comely corpse, with beautie faire endewed,   *135*
Know this for certaine, that the same doth hold
A beauteous soule, with faire conditions thewed,
Fit to receive the seede of vertue strewed.
For all that faire is, is by nature good;
That is a signe to know the gentle blood.   *140*

Yet oft it falles, that many a gentle mynd
Dwels in deformed tabernacle drownd,
Either by chaunce, against the course of kynd,
Or through unaptnesse in the substance fownd,
Which it assumed of some stubborne grownd,   *145*
That will not yield unto her formes direction,
But is perform'd with some foule imperfection.

130. **dight**: adorns.
135. **corpse**: body.
137. **with faire . . . thewed**: schooled in beautiful qualities.
138. **strewed**: sown (in it).
141. **it falles**: it happens.
142. **tabernacle**: i.e., body (tabernacle = temporary shelter, also portable sanctuary); **drownd**: sunken.
143. **kynd**: nature.
144. **unaptnesse**: unadaptability, unworkability.
145. **grownd**: earth (or) earthy source.
146. **formes**: shaping power's.
147. **perform'd**: worked into shape.

And oft it falles (ay me the more to rew)
That goodly beautie, albe heavenly borne,
Is foule abusd, and that celestiall hew,   *150*
Which doth the world with her delight adorne,
Made but the bait of sinne, and sinners scorne;
Whilest every one doth seeke and sew to have it,
But every one doth seeke, but to deprave it.

Yet nathemore is that faire beauties blame,   *155*
But theirs that do abuse it unto ill:
Nothing so good, but that through guilty shame
May be corrupt, and wrested unto will.
Nathelesse the soule is faire and beauteous still,
How ever fleshes fault it filthy make: *160*
For things immortall no corruption take.

But ye faire Dames, the worlds deare ornaments,
And lively images of heavens light,
Let not your beames with such disparagements
Be dimd, and your bright glorie darkned quight,   *165*
But mindfull still of your first countries sight,
Doe still preserve your first informed grace,
Whose shadow yet shynes in your beauteous face.

Loath that foule blot, that hellish fierbrand,
Disloiall lust, faire beauties foulest blame,   *170*
That base affections, which your eares would bland,
Commend to you by loves abused name;
But is indeede the bondslave of defame,
Which will the garland of your glorie marre,
And quench the light of your bright shyning starre.

148. **ay me . . . rew:** the more's
the pity.
149. **albe:** although.
150. **hew:** aspect, appearance.
152. **sinners scorne:** i.e., the
object of cynical and con-
temptuous use by sinners.
153. **sew:** pursue.
154. **but to:** only in order to.
158. **will:** base desire.
159. **Nathelesse:** none the less.

166. **first countries sight:** i.e.,
the sights of heaven.
167. **first informed:** originally
infused.
170. **blame:** fault.
171. **bland:** flatteringly tempt.
172. **by loves . . . name:** under
the much-abused name of
love.
173. **defame:** dishonour.

But gentle Love, that loiall is and trew, *176*
Will more illumine your resplendent ray, *§*
And adde more brightnesse to your goodly hew,
From light of his pure fire, which by like way
Kindled of yours, your likenesse doth display, *180*
Like as two mirrours by opposd reflexion,
Doe both expresse the faces first impression.

Therefore to make your beautie more appeare,
It you behoves to love, and forth to lay
That heavenly riches, which in you ye beare, *185*
That men the more admyre their fountaine may,
For else what booteth that celestiall ray,
If it in darknesse be enshrined ever,
That it of loving eyes be vewed never?

But in your choice of Loves, this well advize, *190*
That likest to your selves ye them select,
The which your forms first sourse may sympathize,
And with like beauties parts be inly deckt:
For if you loosely love without respect,
It is no love, but a discordant warre, *195*
Whose unlike parts amongst themselves do jarre.

177. **more illumine:** i.e., intensify.

185. **That:** those.

186. **fountaine:** source.

187. **what booteth:** what is the use of.

190. **this well advize:** keep this well in mind.

192. **The which:** those with which.

193. **And with like . . . deckt:** and are inwardly adorned with similar qualities of beauty.

194. **respect:** careful choice, discrimination.

§ *Will more illumine*: In celebrating the action of Love Spenser here seems to have in mind a passage from Plato's *Phaedrus* where the lover is likened to a mirror in which the beloved can see himself – or, for Spenser's purposes, herself. The difficulty of this stanza is compounded by the confusing image of two facing mirrors. Perhaps Spenser is saying, "As the beauty of you faire Dames is something like a mirror which by reflection intensifies the beauty and attractiveness of true Love – now all the more attracted by such intensified beauty – are like mirrors in which you can see the true likeness of yourselves."

For Love is a celestiall harmonie,
Or likely harts composd of starres concent,
Which joyne together in sweete sympathie,
To worke ech others joy and true content,   *200*
Which they have harbourd since their first descent
Out of their heavenly bowres, where they did see
And know ech other here belov'd to bee.

Then wrong it were that any other twaine
Should in loves gentle band combyned bee,   *205*
But those whom heaven did at first ordaine,
And made out of one mould the more t'agree:
For all that like the beautie which they see,
Streight do not love: for love is not so light,
As streight to burne at first beholders sight.   *210*

But they which love indeede, looke otherwise,
With pure regard and spotlesse true intent,
Drawing out of the object of their eyes,
A more refyned forme, which they present
Unto their mind, voide of all blemishment;   *215*
Which it reducing to her first perfection,
Beholdeth free from fleshes frayle infection.

198. **starres concent:** i.e., the harmonious conjunction of the lovers' ruling stars or planets.
204. **twaine:** pair.
209. **Streight do not love:** do not straightway fall in love; **light:** superficial, frivolous.

213. **Drawing out of:** extrapolating, building up from; **eyes:** i.e., sight.
216. **Which it reducing . . . perfection:** which form, the mind, in further refining towards its original perfection.

And then conforming it unto the light,
Which in it selfe it hath remaining still
Of that first Sunne, yet sparckling in his sight,   *220*
Thereof he fashions in his higher skill,
An heavenly beautie to his fancies will,
And it embracing in his mind entyre,
The mirrour of his owne thought doth admyre.

Which seeing now so inly faire to be,   *225*
As outward it appeareth to the eye,
And with his spirits proportion to agree,
He thereon fixeth all his fantasie,
And fully setteth his felicitie,
Counting it fairer, then it is indeede,   *230*
And yet indeede her fairenesse doth exceed.

For lovers eyes more sharply sighted bee
Then other mens, and in deare loves delight
See more then any other eyes can see,
Through mutuall receipt of beames bright,   *235*
Which carrie privie message to the spright,
And to their eyes that inmost faire display,
As plaine as light discovers dawning day.

Therein they see through amorous eye-glaunces,
Armies of loves still flying too and fro,   *240*
Which dart at them their litle fierie launces,
Whom having wounded, backe againe they go,
Carrying compassion to their lovely foe;
Who seeing her faire eyes so sharpe effect,
Cures all their sorrowes with one sweete aspect.   *245*

222. **to his fancies will:** according to the desire of his imagination.
228. **thereon:** i.e., on the form of a heavenly beauty; **fantasie:** i.e., power of thought and imagination.
230. **then it is indeede:** than it actually is.
231. **doth exceede:** is surpassing, extraordinary.

236. **privie:** secret.
237. **faire:** beauty.
238. **discovers:** reveals, announces.
240. **loves:** charms, "cupids".
244. **seeing . . . so sharpe effect:** observing the so sharp effect of.
245. **aspect:** look.

In which how many wonders doe they reede
To their conceipt, that others never see,
Now of her smiles, with which their soules they feede,
Like Gods with Nectar in their bankets free,
Now of her lookes, which like to Cordials bee;   *250*
But when her words embassade forth she sends,
Lord how sweete musicke that unto them lends.

Sometimes upon her forhead they behold
A thousand Graces masking in delight,
Sometimes within her eye-lids they unfold   *255*
Ten thousand sweet belgards, which to their sight
Doe seeme like twinckling starres in frostie night:
But on her lips like rosy buds in May,
So many millions of chaste pleasures play.

All those, O *Cytherea*, and thousands more   *260 §*
Thy handmaides be, which do on thee attend
To decke thy beautie with their dainties store,
That may it more to mortall eyes commend,
And make it more admyr'd of foe and frend;
That in mens harts thou mayst thy throne enstall,
And spred thy lovely kingdome over all.   *266*

246. **reede:** pick out, name.
247. **To their conceipt:** in their thoughts.
249. **bankets free:** generous, lavish banquets.
251. **words embassade:** embassy of words.

252. **unto them lends:** gives, affords to them.
254. **masking:** i.e., dancing.
256. **belgards:** love-glances.
262. **dainties store:** repertory of delights.
266. **over all:** everywhere.

§ *Cytherea*: Venus Aphrodite, who was born from the sea-foam off the island of Cythera.

Then *Iö tryumph*, O great beauties Queene,   §
Advance the banner of thy conquest hie,
That all this world, the which thy vassals beene,
May draw to thee, and with dew fealtie,   270
Adore the powre of thy great Majestie,
Singing this Hymne in honour of thy name,
Compyld by me, which thy poore liegeman am.

In lieu whereof graunt, O great Soveraine,
That she whose conquering beautie doth captive   275
My trembling hart in her eternall chaine,
One drop of grace at length will to me give,
That I her bounden thrall by her may live,
And this same life, which first fro me she reaved,   §
May owe to her, of whom I it received.   280

And you faire *Venus* dearling, my deare dread,
Fresh flowre of grace, great Goddesse of my life,
When your faire eyes these fearefull lines shal read,
Deigne to let fall one drop of dew reliefe,
That may recure my harts long pyning griefe,   285
And shew what wondrous powre your beauty hath,
That can restore a damned wight from death.

269. **That all:** so that all creatures of; **beene:** are.
274. **In lieu whereof:** in return
for which.
275. **captive:** imprison.
278. **by her may live:** may live
in virtue of her.

281. **dread:** i.e., sovereign mistress (dread = one with
sovereign power and au-
thority).
283. **fearefull:** timid, hesitant.
284. **dew:** well-earned.
285. **recure:** heal.

§ *Iö tryumph*: A ritual cry appropriate to this celebration of the
triumph of Venus. Cf. "Io Hymen", the triumphant ritual cry to
Hymen, the marriage-god, in wedding processions (*Epithalamion*,
line 140).
§ *And this same life . . . received*: "And that she may give back (place
me in her debt for) that very life which she at first deprived me of
by force of her beauty".

AN HYMNE OF

Heavenly Love

L̲ove, life me up upon thy golden wings,
  From this base world unto thy heavens hight,
Where I may see those admirable things,
Which there thou workest by thy soveraine might,
Farre above feeble reach of earthly sight,   5
That I thereof an heavenly Hymne may sing
Unto the god of Love, high heavens king.

Many lewd layes (ah woe is me the more)
In praise of that mad fit, which fooles call love,
I have in th'heat of youth made heretofore,   10
That in light wits did loose affection move.
But all those follies now I do reprove,
And turned have the tenor of my string,
The heavenly prayses of true love to sing.

And ye that wont with greedy vaine desire   15
To reade my fault, and wondring at my flame,
To warme your selves at my wide sparckling fire,
Sith now that heat is quenched, quench my blame,
And in her ashes shrowd my dying shame:
For who my passed follies now pursewes,   20
Beginnes his owne, and my old fault renewes.

8. **lewd:** silly, stupid; **layes:** songs.
9. **fit:** seizure.
11. **light wits:** shallow minds; **affection:** desire(s); **move:** inspire, cause.
12. **reprove:** repudiate.
13. **turned . . . tenor:** have changed the tone.
15. **that wont:** who used to.
16. **my fault:** i.e., those morally flawed works of mine.
18. **Sith:** since.

Before this worlds great frame, in which al things
    Are now containd, found any being place,
Ere flitting Time could wag his eyas wings
About that mightie bound, which doth embrace   *25*
The rolling Spheres, and parts their houres by space,
    That high eternall powre, which now doth move
    In all these things, mov'd in it selfe by love.

It lov'd it selfe, because it selfe was faire;
    (For faire is lov'd;) and of it selfe begot   *30*
Like to it selfe his eldest sonne and heire,
Eternall, pure, and voide of sinfull blot,
The firstling of his joy, in whom no jot
    Of loves dislike, or pride was to be found,
    Whom he therefore with equall honour crownd.   *35*

With him he raignd, before all time prescribed,
In endlesse glorie and immortall might,
Together with that third from them derived,
Most wise, most holy, most almightie Spright,
Whose kingdomes throne no thought of earthly wight
    Can comprehend, much lesse my trembling verse   *41*
    With equall words can hope it to reherse.

Yet O most blessed Spirit, pure lampe of light,
Eternall spring of grace and wisedome trew,
Vouchsafe to shed into my barren spright,   *45*
Some little drop of thy celestiall dew,
That may my rymes with sweet infuse embrew,
    And give me words equall unto my thought,
    To tell the marveiles by thy mercie wrought.

24. **flitting:** fleeting; **eyas:** new-fledged.
25. **mightie bound:** Eighth Sphere, firmament of fixed stars.
26. **parts . . . space:** i.e., divides (or) measures their hours by its degrees.
34. **Of loves dislike:** of anything offensive to love.
42. **equall:** adequate.
47. **infuse:** infusion; **embrew:** imbue, pervade.
49. **marveiles:** marvels.

Yet being pregnant still with powrefull grace,   50
And full of fruitfull love, that loves to get
Things like himselfe, and to enlarge his race,
His second brood though not in powre so great,
Yet full of beautie, next he did beget
An infinite increase of Angels bright,   55
All glistring glorious in their Makers light.

To them the heavens illimitable hight,
Not this round heaven, which we from hence behold,
Adornd with thousand lamps of burning light,
And with ten thousand gemmes of shyning gold,   60
He gave as their inheritance to hold,
That they might serve him in eternall blis,
And be partakers of those joyes of his.

There they in their trinall triplicities   §
About him wait, and on his will depend,   65
Either with nimble wings to cut the skies,
When he them on his messages doth send,
Or on his owne dread presence to attend,
Where they behold the glorie of his light,
And caroll Hymnes of love both day and night.   70

51. **get:** beget.
52. **race:** family, progeny.
55. **increase:** i.e., number.

58. **round heaven:** firmament
of fixed stars.

§ *trinall triplicities*: In angelology the nine orders of angels were
usually arranged in groups of three. One such grouping was:

1ST TRINE	2ND TRINE	3RD TRINE
(1) Seraphim	(1) Cherubim	(1) Thrones
(2) Dominations	(2) Virtues	(2) Powers
(3) {Princedoms / Principalities}	(3) Archangels	(3) Angels

For another common but slightly different grouping see note on
page 277.

Both day and night is unto them all one,
For he his beames doth still to them extend,
That darknesse there appeareth never none,
Ne hath their day, ne hath their blisse an end,
But there their termelesse time in pleasure spend,   75
Ne ever should their happinesse decay,
Had not they dar'd their Lord to disobay.

But pride impatient of long resting peace,
Did puffe them up with greedy bold ambition,
That they gan cast their state how to increase,   80
Above the fortune of their first condition,
And sit in Gods owne seat without commission:
The brightest Angell, even the Child of light
Drew millions more against their God to fight.

Th'Almighty seeing their so bold assay,   85
Kindled the flame of his consuming yre,
And with his onely breath them blew away
From heavens hight, to which they did aspyre,
To deepest hell, and lake of damned fyre;
Where they in darknesse and dread horror dwell,   90
Hating the happie light from which they fell.

So that next off-spring of the Makers love,
Next to himselfe in glorious degree,
Degendering to hate fell from above
Through pride; (for pride and love may ill agree)   95
And now of sinne to all ensample bee:
How then can sinfull flesh it selfe assure,
Sith purest Angels fell to be impure?

73. **That darknesse . . . none:** so that no darkness ever appears there.
74. **Ne . . . ne:** neither . . . nor.
75. **termelesse time:** time without end.
76. **decay:** have been destroyed.
80. **gan cast:** considered, plotted.
82. **commission:** the rightful authority (to do so).
83. **brightest Angell:** Lucifer.
85. **assay:** attempt.
87. **his onely breath:** his breath alone.
94. **Degendering:** degenerating.
97. **it selfe assure:** be sure of itself.

But that eternall fount of love and grace,
Still flowing forth his goodnesse unto all,   *100*
Now seeing left a waste and emptie place
In his wyde Pallace, through those Angels fall,
Cast to supply the same, and to enstall
A new unknowen Colony therein,
Whose root from earths base groundworke shold begin.

Therefore of clay, base, vile, and next to nought,   *106*
Yet form'd by wondrous skill, and by his might:
According to an heavenly patterne wrought,
Which he had fashiond in his wise foresight,
He man did make, and breathd a living spright   *110*
Into his face most beautifull and fayre,
Endewd with wisedomes riches, heavenly, rare.

Such he him made, that he resemble might
Himselfe, as mortall thing immortall could;
Him to be Lord of every living wight,   *115*
He made by love out of his owne like mould,
In whom he might his mightie selfe behould:
For love doth love the thing belov'd to see,
That like it selfe in lovely shape may bee.

But man forgetfull of his makers grace,   *120*
No lesse then Angels, whom he did ensew,
Fell from the hope of promist heavenly place,
Into the mouth of death to sinners dew,
And all his off-spring into thraldome threw:
Where they for ever should in bonds remaine,   *125*
Of never dead, yet ever dying paine.

103. **Cast:** decided.
114. **as mortall . . . could:** as
     far as a mortal thing
     could resemble an im-
     mortal.
115. **living wight:** living crea-
     ture.

121. **then:** than; **whom . . .
     ensew:** whom he followed.
126. **Of never dead . . . paine:**
     i.e., of the never-ending
     pains of a living death.

Till that great Lord of Love, which him at first
Made of meere love, and after liked well,
Seeing him lie like creature long accurst,
In that deepe horror of despeyred hell,   *130*
Him wretch in doole would let no lenger dwell,
But cast out of that bondage to redeeme,
And pay the price, all were his debt extreeme.

Out of the bosome of eternall blisse,
In which he reigned with his glorious syre,   *135*
He downe descended, like a most demisse
And abject thrall, in fleshes fraile attyre,
That he for him might pay sinnes deadly hyre,
And him restore unto that happie state,
In which he stood before his haplesse fate.   *140*

In flesh at first the guilt committed was,
Therefore in flesh it must be satisfyde:
Nor spirit, nor Angell, though they man surpas,
Could make amends to God for mans misguyde,
But onely man himselfe, who selfe did slyde.   *145*
So taking flesh of sacred virgins wombe,
For mans deare sake he did a man become.

And that most blessed bodie, which was borne
Without all blemish or reprochfull blame,
He freely gave to be both rent and torne   *150*
Of cruell hands, who with despightfull shame
Revyling him, that them most vile became,
At length him nayled on a gallow tree,
And slew the just, by most unjust decree.

127. **him:** i.e., man.
128. **meere:** pure.
130. **despeyred:** hope-abandoned.
131. **Him wretch in doole:** him wretched in his grief.
132. **But cast . . . to redeeme:** but planned to redeem him.

133. **all were:** even though (his debt) were.
136. **demisse:** submissive.
138. **hyre:** wages.
144. **misguyde:** trespass.
145. **who selfe did slyde:** who himself did err.
151. **despightfull:** malicious.
152. **most vile:** most vilely.

O huge and most unspeakeable impression   *155*
Of loves deepe wound, that pierst the piteous hart
Of that deare Lord with so entyre affection,
And sharply launching every inner part,
Dolours of death into his soule did dart;
Doing him die, that never it deserved,   *160*
To free his foes, that from his heast had swerved.

What hart can feele least touch of so sore launch,
Or thought can think the depth of so deare wound?
Whose bleeding sourse their streames yet never staunch,
But stil do flow, and freshly still redound,   *165*
To heale the sores of sinfull soules unsound,
And clense the guilt of that infected cryme,
Which was enrooted in all fleshly slyme.

O blessed well of love, O floure of grace,
O glorious Morning starre, O lampe of light,   *170*
Most lively image of thy fathers face,
Eternall King of glorie, Lord of might,
Meeke lambe of God before all worlds behight,
How can we thee requite for all this good?
Or what can prize that thy most precious blood?   *175*

155. **impression:** imprint.
157. **so entyre:** such entire.
158. **launching:** penetrating.
160. **Doing him die:** putting him to death.
161. **heast:** command.
162. **launch:** a thrust.
163. **deare:** grievous and precious.

165. **redound:** well over, overflow.
173. **before all . . . behight:** ordained (to these titles and functions) before all worlds.
175. **what can prize:** what can adequately pay for.

Yet nought thou ask'st in lieu of all this love,
But love of us for guerdon of thy paine.
Ay me; what can us lesse then that behove?
Had he required life of us againe,
Had it beene wrong to aske his owne with gaine?   *180*
He gave us life, he it restored lost;
Then life were least, that us so litle cost.

But he our life hath left unto us free,
Free that was thrall, and blessed that was band;
Ne ought demaunds, but that we loving bee,   *185*
As he himselfe hath lov'd us afore hand,
And bound therto with an eternall band,
Him first to love, that us so dearely bought,
And next, our brethren to his image wrought.

Him first to love, great right and reason is,   *190*
Who first to us our life and being gave;
And after when we fared had amisse,
Us wretches from the second death did save;
And last the food of life, which now we have,
Even himselfe in his deare sacrament,   *195*
To feede our hungry soules unto us lent.

176. **in lieu of:** in return for.
177. **But love of us:** except our love; **guerdon:** reward.
178. **what can us . . . behove:** how can we fittingly return less than that.
179. **of us againe:** in return from us.
180. **his owne with gaine:** for the return, with interest, of what he had given.
181. **lost:** i.e., when it was lost.
182. **least:** i.e., the least we could offer in return.
184. **band:** bound.
187. **band:** bond.
192. **fared had amisse:** had gone astray.
196. **lent:** granted.

Then next to love our brethren, that were made
Of that selfe mould, and that selfe makers hand,
That we, and to the same againe shall fade,
Where they shall have like heritage of land,　　　　*200*
How ever here on higher steps we stand;
Which also were with selfe same price redeemed
That we, how ever of us light esteemed.

And were they not, yet since that loving Lord
Commaunded us to love them for his sake,　　　　*205*
Even for his sake, and for his sacred word,
Which in his last bequest he to us spake,
We should them love, and with their needs partake;
Knowing that whatsoere to them we give,
We give to him, by whom we all doe live.　　　　*210*

Such mercy he by his most holy reede
Unto us taught, and to approve it trew,
Ensampled it by his most righteous deede,
Shewing us mercie miserable crew,
That we the like should to the wretches shew,　　　　*215*
And love our brethren; thereby to approve,
How much himselfe that loved us, we love.

Then rouze thy selfe, O earth, out of thy soyle,
In which thou wallowest like to filthy swyne,
And doest thy mynd in durty pleasures moyle,　　　　*220*
Unmindfull of that dearest Lord of thyne;
Lift up to him thy heavie clouded eyne,
That thou his soveraine bountie mayst behold,
And read through love his mercies manifold.

198. **selfe:** same.
199. **That we:** as we were (also line 203).
200. **like heritage of land:** i.e., the grave.
202. **Which:** who.
203. **of us . . . esteemed:** lightly esteemed by us.
204. **And were they not:** and even if they weren't (so made and so redeemed).
208. **with . . . partake:** share in.
211. **reede:** counsel.
212. **approve:** prove.
213. **Ensampled it:** demonstrated it.
214. **Shewing . . . crew:** showing mercy on us – a miserable lot.
220. **moyle:** defile.
222. **eyne:** eyes.

Beginne from first, where he encradled was   *225*
In simple cratch, wrapt in a wad of hay,
Betweene the toylefull Oxe and humble Asse,
And in what rags, and in how base aray,
The glory of our heavenly riches lay,
When him the silly Shepheards came to see,   *230*
Whom greatest Princes sought on lowest knee.

From thence reade on the storie of his life,
His humble carriage, his unfaulty wayes,
His cancred foes, his fights, his toyle, his strife,
His paines, his povertie, his sharpe assayes,   *235*
Through which he past his miserable dayes,
Offending none, and doing good to all,
Yet being malist both of great and small.

And looke at last how of most wretched wights,
He taken was, betrayd, and false accused,   *240*
How with most scornefull taunts, and fell despights
He was revyld, disgrast, and foule abused,
How scourgd, how crownd, how buffeted, how brused;
And lastly how twixt robbers crucifyde,
With bitter wounds through hands, through feet and
     syde.   *245*

Then let thy flinty hart that feeles no paine,
Empierced be with pittifull remorse,
And let thy bowels bleede in every vaine,
At sight of his most sacred heavenly corse,
So torne and mangled with malicious forse,   *250*
And let thy soule, whose sins his sorrows wrought,
Melt into teares, and grone in grieved thought.

226. **cratch:** manger, hay-rack.
230. **silly:** innocent, simple.
233. **carriage:** demeanour.
234. **cancred:** bitter, venomous.
235. **assayes:** trials.
238. **malist:** viewed with malice.

239. **of most . . . wights:** by most miserable wretches.
241. **fell despights:** cruel injuries.
247. **pittifull remorse:** sharp feelings of pity.

With sence whereof whilest so thy softened spirit
Is inly toucht, and humbled with meeke zeale,
Through meditation of his endlesse merit,   *255*
Lift up thy mind to th'author of thy weale,
And to his soveraine mercie doe appeale;
Learne him to love, that loved thee so deare,
And in thy brest his blessed image beare.

With all thy hart, with all thy soule and mind,   *260*
Thou must him love, and his beheasts embrace:
All other loves, with which the world doth blind
Weake fancies, and stirre up affections base,
Thou must renounce, and utterly displace,
And give thy selfe unto him full and free,   *265*
That full and freely gave himselfe to thee.

Then shalt thou feele thy spirit so possest,
And ravisht with devouring great desire
Of his deare selfe, that shall thy feeble brest
Inflame with love, and set thee all on fire   *270*
With burning zeale, through every part entire,
That in no earthly thing thou shalt delight,
But in his sweet and amiable sight.

Thenceforth all worlds desire will in thee dye,
And all earthes glorie on which men do gaze,   *275*
Seeme durt and drosse in thy pure sighted eye,
Compar'd to that celestiall beauties blaze,
Whose glorious beames all fleshly sense doth daze
With admiration of their passing light,
Blinding the eyes and lumining the spright.   *280*

253. **With sence whereof:** in perceiving which.
256. **weale:** well-being.
263. **affections:** passions, desires.
279. **passing:** surpassing.
280. **lumining:** illumining.

Then shall thy ravisht soule inspired bee
With heavenly thoughts, farre above humane skil,
And thy bright radiant eyes shall plainely see
Th'Idee of his pure glorie, present still
Before thy face, that all thy spirits shall fill   *285*
With sweete enragement of celestiall love,
Kindled through sight of those faire things above.

284. **Th'Idee:** i.e., the eternal
essence; **still:** always.
286. **enragement:** ecstasy.

AN HYMNE OF

Heavenly Beautie

Rapt with the rage of mine own ravisht thought,
  Through contemplation of those goodly sights,
And glorious images in heaven wrought,
Whose wondrous beauty breathing sweet delights,
Do kindle love in high conceipted sprights: 5
I faine to tell the things that I behold,
But feele my wits to faile, and tongue to fold.

Vouchsafe then, O thou most almightie Spright,
From whom all guifts of wit and knowledge flow,
To shed into my breast some sparkling light   10
Of thine eternall Truth, that I may show
Some litle beames to mortall eyes below,
Of that immortall beautie, there with thee,
Which in my weake distraughted mynd I see.

That with the glorie of so goodly sight,   15
The hearts of men, which fondly here admyre
Faire seeming shewes, and feed on vaine delight,
Transported with celestiall desyre
Of those faire formes, may lift themselves up hyer,
And learne to love with zealous humble dewty   20
Th'eternall fountaine of that heavenly beauty.

1. **rage:** fervency.
5. **high conceipted:** exalted, high-minded; **sprights:** spirits.
6. **faine:** wish, long.
8. **almightie Spright:** Holy Spirit.
14. **distraughted:** distracted.
16. **fondly:** foolishly.
21. **fountaine:** source.

Beginning then below, with th'easie vew
  Of this base world, subject to fleshly eye,
From thence to mount aloft by order dew,
To contemplation of th'immortall sky,   25
Of the soare faulcon so I learne to fly,
That flags awhile her fluttering wings beneath,
Till she her selfe for stronger flight can breath.

Then looke who list, thy gazefull eyes to feed
With sight of that is faire, looke on the frame   30
Of this wyde *universe*, and therein reed
The endlesse kinds of creatures, which by name
Thou canst not count, much lesse their natures aime:
All which are made with wondrous wise respect,
And all with admirable beautie deckt.   35

First th'Earth, on adamantine pillers founded,
Amid the Sea engirt with brasen bands;
Then th'Aire still flitting, but yet firmely bounded
On everie side, with pyles of flaming brands,
Never consum'd nor quencht with mortall hands;   40
And last, that mightie shining christall wall,
Wherewith he hath encompassed this All.

26. **soare faulcon:** falcon in its
    first year.
27. **flags:** tries out, tentatively
    stretches.
28. **can breath:** can get her
    breath.
29. **list:** chooses, wants to;
    gazefull: gazing.
33. **much lesse . . . aime:**
    much less fathom their
    natures.
34. **respect:** care.

36. **adamantine:** i.e., unbreak-
    able.
37. **engirt:** encircled.
38. **still flitting:** continually
    moving.
39. **pyles:** banks, reaches; **flam-
    ing brands:** ethereal flames
    (sphere of ether = sphere
    of fire beyond the airy
    atmosphere).
41. **shining christall wall:**
    sphere of fixed stars.

By view whereof, it plainly may appeare,
That still as every thing doth upward tend,
And further is from earth, so still more cleare   45
And faire it growes, till to his perfect end
Of purest beautie, it at last ascend:
Ayre more then water, fire much more then ayre,
And heaven then fire appeares more pure and fayre.

Looke thou no further, but affixe thine eye   50
On that bright shynie round still moving Masse,
The house of blessed Gods, which men call *Skye*,
All sowd with glistring stars more thicke then grasse,
Whereof each other doth in brightnesse passe;
But those two most, which ruling night and day,   55
As King and Queene, the heavens Empire sway.

And tell me then, what hast thou ever seene,
That to their beautie may compared bee,
Or can the sight that is most sharpe and keene,
Endure their Captains flaming head to see?   60
How much lesse those, much higher in degree,
And so much fairer, and much more then these,
As these are fairer then the land and seas?

For farre above these heavens which here we see,
Be others farre exceeding these in light,   65
Not bounded, not corrupt, as these same bee,
But infinite in largenesse and in hight,
Unmoving, uncorrupt, and spotlesse bright,
That need no Sunne t'illuminate their spheres,
But their owne native light farre passing theirs.   70

51. **still:** always.
52. **Gods:** planets.
54. **Whereof each . . . passe:** among which each is brighter than the last.
56. **sway:** rule, govern.
60. **their Captains:** i.e., the sun's.
70. **theirs:** i.e., of the visible heavenly bodies.

And as these heavens still by degrees arize,
Untill they come to their first Movers bound,
That in his mightie compasse doth comprize,
And carrie all the rest with him around,
So those likewise doe by degrees redound,   75
And rise more faire, till they at last arive
To the most faire, whereto they all do strive.

Faire is the heaven, where happy soules have place,
In full enjoyment of felicitie,
Whence they doe still behold the glorious face   80
Of the divine eternall Majestie;
More faire is that, where those *Idees* on hie   §
Enraunged be, which *Plato* so admyred,
And pure *Intelligences* from God inspyred.

Yet fairer is that heaven, in which doe raine   85
The soveraine *Powres* and mightie *Potentates*,
Which in their high protections doe containe
All mortall Princes, and imperiall States;
And fayrer yet, whereas the royall Seates
And heavenly *Dominations* are set,   90
From whom all earthly governance is fet.

71. **these heavens:** i.e., the visible "lower" heavens.
72. **first Movers bound:** the Primum Mobile – Tenth Sphere.
75. **So those:** i.e., so the invisible "higher" heavens; **redound:** reach up and out.
83. **Enraunged:** ranked.
86. **Powres . . . Potentates:** members of the sixth and seventh angelic orders respectively.
89. **whereas:** is where; **Seates:** Thrones – members of the third angelic order.
90. **Dominations:** members of the fourth angelic order.
91. **fet:** derived.

§ *Idees*: In Plato's thought Ideas, or Forms, are the highest realities. They are the eternal, changeless patterns of all created things and they are sometimes spoken of as heavenly, incorporeal beings or *Intelligences*.

Yet farre more faire be those bright *Cherubins*,
Which all with golden wings are overdight,
Which from their faces dart out fierie light;
And those eternall burning *Seraphins*,   *95*
Yet fairer then they both, and much more bright
Be th'Angels and Archangels, which attend   §
On Gods owne person, without rest or end.

These thus in faire each other farre excelling,
As to the Highest they approch more neare,   *100*
Yet is that Highest farre beyond all telling,
Fairer then all the rest which there appeare,
Though all their beauties joynd together were:
How then can mortall tongue hope to expresse
The image of such endlesse perfectnesse?   *105*

Cease then my tongue, and lend unto my mynd
Leave to bethinke how great that beautie is,
Whose utmost parts so beautifull I fynd,
How much more those essentiall parts of his,
His truth, his love, his wisedome, and his blis, *110*
His grace, his doome, his mercy and his might,
By which he lends us of himselfe a sight.

92. **Cherubins:** angels of Con-
     templation — members of
     the second angelic order.
93. **overdight:** covered.
95. **Seraphins:** angels of Love

– members of the first and
highest angelic order.
106. **lend unto:** give.
111. **doome:** judgment.

§ *th'Angels and Archangels*: These are usually given as the two lowest
orders of angels, the ninth and eighth respectively. Spenser, moving
from the lower to the higher, has here made them the two highest
angelic orders. In the gloss the usual order of the angelic hierarchy
has been given.

Those unto all he daily doth display,
And shew himselfe in th'image of his grace,
As in a looking glasse, through which he may   *115*
Be seene, of all his creatures vile and base,
That are unable else to see his face,
His glorious face which glistereth else so bright,
That th'Angels selves can not endure his sight.

But we fraile wights, whose sight cannot sustaine   *120*
The Suns bright beames, when he on us doth shyne,
But that their points rebutted backe againe
Are duld, how can we see with feeble eyne,
The glory of that Majestie divine,
In sight of whom both Sun and Moone are darke,   *125*
Compared to his least resplendent sparke?

The meanes therefore which unto us is lent,
Him to behold, is on his workes to looke,
Which he hath made in beauty excellent,
And in the same, as in a brasen booke,   *130*
To reade enregistred in every nooke
His goodnesse, which his beautie doth declare,
For all thats good, is beautifull and faire.

116. **base:** lowly.
122. **But that . . . Are duld:**
i.e., unless the sunbeams
are dimmed by being
reflected.

127. **lent:** given.
130. **as in a brasen booke:** as
on a brass tablet (i.e.,
indelibly).
131. **enregistred:** recorded.

Thence gathering plumes of perfect speculation,
To impe the wings of thy high flying mynd,   *135*
Mount up aloft through heavenly contemplation,
From this darke world, whose damps the soule do
   blynd,
And like the native brood of Eagles kynd,   §
On that bright Sunne of glorie fixe thine eyes,
Clear'd from grosse mists of fraile infirmities.   *140*

Humbled with feare and awfull reverence,
Before the footestoole of his Majestie,
Throw thy selfe downe with trembling innocence,
Ne dare looke up with corruptible eye,
On the dred face of that great *Deity*,   *145*
For feare, lest if he chaunce to looke on thee,
Thou turne to nought, and quite confounded be.

But lowly fall before his mercie seate,   §
Close covered with the Lambes integrity,
From the just wrath of his avengefull threate,   *150*
That sits upon the righteous throne on hy:
His throne is built upon Eternity,
More firme and durable then steele or brasse,
Or the hard diamond, which them both doth passe.

135. **impe the wings:** fledge out the wings (and so increase power of wing-beat) by grafting in new feathers.
137. **damps:** vapours, fogs.
138. **kynd:** species.

149. **Lambes:** Christ's; **integrity:** perfect righteousness.
150. **his avengefull . . . That:** i.e., the threatening vengeance of him who.
154. **passe:** surpass (in durability).

§ *Eagles kynd*: True eagles were supposed to be able to look straight into the sun without blinking.
§ *mercie seate*: Originally the name of the golden seat or cover on top of the Ark of Israel. It was made of a piece with two golden cherubim who faced in on it and whose wings overshadowed it. From above the mercy seat God communed with his people. (See Exodus 25:17-22.)

His scepter is the rod of Righteousnesse,   *155*
With which he bruseth all his foes to dust,
And the great Dragon strongly doth represse,
Under the rigour of his judgement just;
His seate is Truth, to which the faithfull trust;
From whence proceed her beames so pure and bright,
That all about him sheddeth glorious light.   *161*

Light farre exceeding that bright blazing sparke,
Which darted is from *Titans* flaming head,
That with his beames enlumineth the darke
And dampish aire, wherby al things are red: *165*
Whose nature yet so much is marvelled
Of mortall wits, that it doth much amaze
The greatest wisards, which thereon do gaze.

But that immortall light which there doth shine,
Is many thousand times more bright, more cleare,
More excellent, more glorious, more divine,   *171*
Through which to God all mortall actions here,
And even the thoughts of men, do plaine appeare:
For from th'eternall Truth it doth proceed,
Through heavenly vertue, which her beames doe breed.

With the great glorie of that wondrous light,   *176*
His throne is all encompassed around,
And hid in his owne brightnesse from the sight
Of all that looke thereon with eyes unsound:
And underneath his feet are to be found   *180*
Thunder, and lightning, and tempestuous fyre,
The instruments of his avenging yre.

157. **Dragon:** Satan.
163. **Titans:** the sun's.
165. **red:** seen, discerned.

166. **marvelled/Of:** wondered
     at by.
168. **wisards:** sages, wise men.
175. **breed:** cause.

There in his bosome *Sapience* doth sit,   §
The soveraine dearling of the *Deity*,
Clad like a Queene in royall robes, most fit   *185*
For so great powre and peerelesse majesty.
And all with gemmes and jewels gorgeously
Adornd, that brighter then the starres appeare,
And make her native brightnes seem more cleare.

And on her head a crowne of purest gold   *190*
Is set, in signe of highest soveraignty,
And in her hand a scepter she doth hold,
With which she rules the house of God on hy,
And menageth the ever-moving sky,
And in the same these lower creatures all,   *195*
Subjected to her powre imperiall.

Both heaven and earth obey unto her will,
And all the creatures which they both containe:
For of her fulnesse which the world doth fill,
They all partake, and do in state remaine,   *200*
As their great Maker did at first ordaine,
Through observation of her high beheast,
By which they first were made, and still increast.

183. **Sapience:** Wisdom.
184. **soveraine dearling:** best beloved.
189. **native:** natural.
194. **menageth:** controls.
195. **the same:** i.e., the sky.

200. **in state:** in the condition of being.
202. **beheast:** command.
203. **still increast:** continuously multiplied.

§ *Sapience*: Cf. the figure of Wisdom or Sapience in Proverbs 3-9; and also Plato's description in the *Phaedrus* of Wisdom as the most beautiful of the Ideas, i.e., as Absolute Beauty. Spenser is perhaps also relying on St. Augustine's view that in the Scriptures Wisdom refers to the Son – the second person of the Trinity.

The fairenesse of her face no tongue can tell,
For she the daughters of all wemens race,   *205*
And Angels eke, in beautie doth excell,
Sparkled on her from Gods owne glorious face,
And more increast by her owne goodly grace,
That it doth farre exceed all humane thought,
Ne can on earth compared be to ought.   *210*

Ne could that Painter (had he lived yet)
Which pictured *Venus* with so curious quill,
That all posteritie admyred it,
Have purtrayd this, for all his maistring skill;
Ne she her selfe, had she remained still,   *215*
And were as faire, as fabling wits do fayne,
Could once come neare this beauty soverayne.

But had those wits the wonders of their dayes,
Or that sweete *Teian* Poet which did spend
His plenteous vaine in setting forth her prayse,   *220*
Seene but a glims of this, which I pretend,
How wondrously would he her face commend,
Above that Idole of his fayning thought,
That all the world shold with his rimes be fraught?

205. **wemens race:** womankind.
206. **eke:** also, even.
211. **Painter:** probably Apelles (4th century B.C.) who executed a very famous painting of Venus rising from the sea.
212. **so curious quill:** such an ingenious brush.
214. **maistring skill:** masterful skill.
215. **she her selfe:** Venus.
216. **fabling wits:** i.e., poets; **fayne:** depict (her).
219. **Teian Poet:** Anacreon (born *c.* 570 B.C.), most famous as writer of lyrics on love and pleasure.
220. **plenteous vaine:** fertile poetic vein.
221. **I pretend:** I am attempting to set forth.
223. **Idole of ... thought:** his merely fanciful idol (i.e., Venus).
224. **fraught:** filled.

How then dare I, the novice of his Art,   225
Presume to picture so divine a wight,
Or hope t'expresse her least perfections part,
Whose beautie filles the heavens with her light,
And darkes the earth with shadow of her sight?   §
Ah gentle Muse thou art too weake and faint,   230
The pourtraict of so heavenly hew to paint.

Let Angels which her goodly face behold
And see at will, her soveraigne praises sing,
And those most sacred mysteries unfold,
Of that faire love of mightie heavens king.   235
Enough is me t'admyre so heavenly thing,
And being thus with her huge love possest,
In th'only wonder of her selfe to rest.

But who so may, thrise happie man him hold,
Of all on earth, whom God so much doth grace,   240
And lets his owne Beloved to behold:
For in the view of her celestiall face,
All joy, all blisse, all happinesse have place,
Ne ought on earth can want unto the wight,
Who of her selfe can win the wishfull sight.   245

225. **the novice of his Art:** a novice in poetry, i.e., an unskilled poet.
227. **her least . . . part:** the least part of her perfection.
231. **hew:** form.
235. **faire love:** fair beloved, i.e., Sapience.

236. **t'admyre:** to wonder at.
238. **In th'only . . . rest:** to rest content in the wonder of her alone.
239. **him hold:** consider him.
244. **can want . . . wight:** can be lacking to the person.
245. **wishfull:** longed for.

§ *And darkes . . . her sight*: This seems to mean: "And the beauty of whose sight is so resplendent that its mere shadow is enough to make earth's reflected light dark by comparison".

For she out of her secret threasury,
Plentie of riches forth on him will powre,
Even heavenly riches, which there hidden ly
Within the closet of her chastest bowre,
Th'eternall portion of her precious dowre,   *250*
Which mighty God hath given to her free,
And to all those which thereof worthy bee.

None thereof worthy be, but those whom shee
Vouchsafeth to her presence to receave,
And letteth them her lovely face to see,   *255*
Wherof such wondrous pleasures they conceave,
And sweete contentment, that it doth bereave
Their soule of sense, through infinite delight,
And them transport from flesh into the spright.

In which they see such admirable things,   *260*
As carries them into an extasy,
And heare such heavenly notes, and carolings
Of Gods high praise, that filles the brasen sky,
And feele such joy and pleasure inwardly,
That maketh them all worldly cares forget,   *265*
And onely thinke on that before them set.

Ne from thenceforth doth any fleshly sense,
Or idle thought of earthly things remaine,
But all that earst seemd sweet, seemes now offense,
And all that pleased earst, now seemes to paine.   *270*
Their joy, their comfort, their desire, their gaine,
Is fixed all on that which now they see,
All other sights but fayned shadowes bee.

246. **threasury:** store of treasure.
250. **dowre:** dowry.
254. **to her presence:** into her presence.
256. **conceave:** take, apprehend.
257. **bereave:** deprive.
259. **spright:** spirit.
263. **brasen:** i.e., imperishable.
269. **earst:** formerly.
273. **fayned:** illusory.

And that faire lampe, which useth to enflame
The hearts of men with selfe consuming fyre,　*275*
Thenceforth seemes fowle, and full of sinfull blame;
And all that pompe, to which proud minds aspyre
By name of honor, and so much desyre,
Seemes to them basenesse, and all riches drosse,
And all mirth sadnesse, and all lucre losse.　*280*

So full their eyes are of that glorious sight,
And senses fraught with such satietie,
That in nought else on earth they can delight,
But in th'aspect of that felicitie,
Which they have written in their inward ey;　*285*
On which they feed, and in their fastened mynd
All happie joy and full contentment fynd.

Ah then my hungry soule, which long hast fed
On idle fancies of thy foolish thought,
And with false beauties flattring bait misled,　*290*
Hast after vaine deceiptfull shadowes sought,
Which all are fled, and now have left thee nought,
But late repentance through thy follies prief;
Ah ceasse to gaze on matter of thy grief.

And looke at last up to that soveraine light,　*295*
From whose pure beams al perfect beauty springs,
That kindleth love in every godly spright,
Even the love of God, which loathing brings
Of this vile world, and these gay seeming things;
With whose sweete pleasures being so possest,　*300*
Thy straying thoughts henceforth for ever rest.

274. **faire lampe:** i.e., earthly beauty; **useth to enflame:** customarily inflames.
278. **and so much:** and which they so much.
282. **fraught:** charged.
284. **th'aspect:** the sight.
286. **fastened:** steadfast.

293. **late:** belated; **through thy . . . prief:** for the results of your folly.
294. **on matter . . . grief:** on what has only brought you grief.
299. **seeming things:** appearances.

Bibliography

Ariosto, Ludovico. *Orlando Furioso* (selections from the translation of Sir John Harington). Edited by Rudolf Gottfried. Bloomington: Indiana University Press, 1963.

Bestiary, The. Edited and translated by T. H. White. New York: Putnam's Sons (Capricorn Books), 1960.

Castiglione, Baldassare. *The Book of the Courtier.* Translated by George Bull. Harmondsworth: Penguin Books, 1967.

Ellrodt, Robert. *Neoplatonism in the Poetry of Spenser.* Geneva: Librairie E. Droz, 1960.

Ficino, Marsilio. *Commentary on Plato's "Symposium".* Edited and translated by Sears R. Jayne. Columbia: University of Missouri Press, 1944.

Form and Convention in the Poetry of Edmund Spenser (selected papers from the English Institute). Edited by William Nelson. New York: Columbia University Press, 1961.

Greenlaw, Edwin. *Studies in Spenser's Historical Allegory.* Baltimore: Johns Hopkins Press, 1932.

Hamilton, A. C. *The Structure of Allegory in "The Faerie Queene".* Oxford: Clarendon Press, 1961.

Hieatt, A. Kent. *Short Time's Endless Monument.* New York: Columbia University Press, 1960.

Homer. *Iliad.* Translated by E. V. Rieu. Harmondsworth: Penguin Books, 1963.

————. *Odyssey.* Translated by E. V. Rieu. Harmondsworth: Penguin Books, 1960.

Hough, Graham. *A Preface to "The Faerie Queene".* New York: W. W. Norton, 1963.

Jones, H. S. V. *A Spenser Handbook.* London: Crofts & Co., 1930.

Kristeller, Paul O. *Renaissance Thought.* New York: Harper Torchbooks, 1961.

Lewis, C. S. *The Allegory of Love.* London: Oxford University Press (A Galaxy Book), 1965.

————. *English Literature in the Sixteenth Century (excluding Drama).* Oxford: Clarendon Press, 1954.

————. *Spenser's Images of Life.* Edited by Alastair Fowler. Cambridge University Press, 1967.

Lotspeich, Henry G. *Classical Mythology in the Poetry of Edmund Spenser.* Princeton: Princeton University Press, 1932.

McNeir, Waldo F., and Provost, Foster. *Annotated Bibliography of Edmund Spenser, 1937–1960.* Pittsburgh: Duquesne University Press, 1962.

Macpherson, Jay. *Four Ages of Man.* Toronto: Macmillan, 1962.

Mattingly, Garrett. *The Armada.* Boston: Houghton Mifflin (Sentry Edition), 1962.

Neale, John E. *Queen Elizabeth.* London: Jonathan Cape, 1934.

Nelson, William. *The Poetry of Edmund Spenser.* New York: Columbia University Press (A Columbia Paperback), 1965.

Ovid. *Metamorphoses.* Translated by Rolfe Humphries. Bloomington: Indiana University Press, 1955.

Panofsky, Erwin. *Studies in Iconology.* New York: Harper Torchbooks, 1962.

Plato. *Phaedrus.* Jowett's translation, selected and edited by Irwin Edman. New York: Modern Library, 1928.

————. *The Symposium.* Translated by W. Hamilton. Harmondsworth: Penguin Books, 1966.

————. *Timaeus.* Translated by H. D. P. Lee. Harmondsworth: Penguin Books, 1965.

Rix, H. D. *Rhetoric in Spenser's Poetry.* University Park: Pennsylvania State College (Studies, no. 7), 1940.

Sidney, Philip. *The Apology for Poetry.* Edited by Geoffrey Shepherd. London: Nelson & Sons, 1965.

Smith, G. Gregory. *Elizabethan Critical Essays.* 2 vols. Oxford: Clarendon Press, 1904.

Smith, Hallett. *Elizabethan Poetry: A Study in Conventions,*

Meaning, and Expression. Cambridge, Mass.: Harvard University Press, 1952.

Spenser, Edmund. *The Works of Edmund Spenser: A Variorum Edition.* Edited by E. Greenlaw, C. G. Osgood, *et al.* 10 vols. Baltimore: Johns Hopkins Press, 1932–49.

———. *The Poetical Works of Edmund Spenser.* Edited by J. C. Smith and E. de Selincourt. London: Oxford University Press, 1912.

Tasso, Torquato. *Jerusalem Delivered.* Translated by Edward Fairfax. New York: Putnam's Sons (Capricorn Books), 1963.

That Soueraine Light. Edited by William R. Mueller and Don Cameron Allen. Baltimore: Johns Hopkins Press, 1952.

Virgil. *Aeneid.* Translated by W. F. Jackson Knight. Harmondsworth: Penguin Books, 1958.

Williams, Kathleen. *Spenser's "Faerie Queene": The World of Glass.* London: Routledge & Kegan Paul, 1966.

Wind, Edgar. *Pagan Mysteries of the Renaissance.* New Haven, Conn.: Yale University Press, 1958.